# THE NAZI IMPACT
## ON A
# GERMAN VILLAGE

# THE NAZI IMPACT ON A GERMAN VILLAGE

Walter Rinderle

and

Bernard Norling

THE UNIVERSITY PRESS OF KENTUCKY

Publication of this book is made possible in part by support from the Institute for Scholarship in the Liberal Arts, College of Arts and Letters, University of Notre Dame, and by a grant from the Vincennes University Foundation.

Scholarly publisher for the Commonwealth,
serving Bellarmine College, Berea College, Centre
College of Kentucky, Eastern Kentucky University,
The Filson Club, Georgetown College, Kentucky
Historical Society, Kentucky State University,
Morehead State University, Murray State University,
Northern Kentucky University, Transylvania University,
University of Kentucky, University of Louisville,
and Western Kentucky University.

*Editorial and Sales Offices:* Lexington, Kentucky 40508-4008

**Library of Congress Cataloging-in-Publication Data**

Rinderle, Walter, 1940-
    The Nazi impact on a German village / Walter Rinderle and Bernard
Norling.
        p.    cm.
    Includes bibliographical references (p.    ) and index.
    ISBN 0-8131-1794-1 (acid-free)
    1. Oberschopfheim (Germany)—History.   2. National socialism-
-Germany—Oberschopfheim.   I. Norling, Bernard, 1924-
II. Title.
DD901.O2397R56   1992
943'.4626—dc20                                                    92-10030

∞

# CONTENTS

Acknowledgments vii

Introduction 1

1. The Legacy of Centuries 7

2. The People of Oberschopfheim 23

3. Management of the Village 44

4. World War I and Its Aftermath 58

5. The Great Depression 71

6. The Rise of the Nazis 88

7. The Nazi Era in Peacetime 106

8. Offering the Nazi Carrot 138

9. The Strength of Tradition 154

10. World War II and Its Aftermath 165

11. The Breakdown of the Old Order 190

12. A New Age Emerges 205

Ruminations 225

Notes 229

Bibliography 260

Index 273

# ACKNOWLEDGMENTS

We two writers are indebted to many for information and advice. We would especially like to thank the present and former mayors of Oberschopfheim, Friesenheim, Kuerzell, and Lahr as well as several members of the Baehr and Messerer families, who helped us in many ways. We are particularly grateful to an old friend and excellent critic, Professor Charles R. Poinsatte of St. Mary's College, who read the manuscript and offered a multitude of suggestions for improvement.

# INTRODUCTION

THIS STUDY CENTERS on Oberschopfheim, a village in south-western Germany. In it we seek to indicate some quite different yet interrelated things. First and foremost, we strive to assess the impact of the Nazi era (1933-1945) on the village and its people, as similar studies have attempted to do for other German communities. Because the people of Oberschopfheim remained relatively unmoved by the blandishments of the Nazis, we devote much attention to the causes of their relative indifference; to the structure of their village and to their traits, habits, attitudes, and expectations; to the ballast that kept their community on a relatively even keel in a tumultuous era. Finally, we seek to determine which of the many tempests of the revolutionary twentieth century *did* shake the village and its people most profoundly.

Oberschopfheim was chosen for several reasons: some general; some quite specific, even personal. One general reason was that the dramatic upheavals of the modern age have been especially marked there. In 1900 it was still essentially a medieval community of about fifteen hundred people. It was inhabited exclusively by full-time or part-time farmers and dominated by its pastor and village officials, with its religious and social life centered about the village church. Most of its people had only an elementary formal education, limited intellectual horizons, and few contacts with the world beyond their own community. They idealized, though they did not attain, economic self-sufficiency. Most of them had little interest in changing their mode of life and little belief that such change was possible. Many still believed in ghosts and feared the few wolves and wild boars that lived in nearby forests.

By 1988 Oberschopfheim had grown to twenty-five hundred people, a high proportion of whom worked in nearby cities and merely lived and slept in the village. Most families had radios, television sets, and automobiles. Their children rode in buses to consolidated city schools, and many of them aspired to attend universities. Everyone except the aged shared most of the interests, plans, hopes, and habits common to hundreds of millions of people throughout the Western world. Who or what was responsible for this metamorphosis?

Why choose a German village? A major reason is that Germany did more than any other nation to keep the world in turmoil from 1870 to 1945. This was especially true during the Nazi era. Germany also has been racked more thoroughly by the upheavals of the twentieth century than other major European nations save Poland and Russia. Between 1914 and 1990 Germans experienced two world wars; four changes of political regime; two extended periods of foreign occupation, one of which has still not ended at this writing; two currency inflations that proceeded to total repudiation; the Great Depression of the 1930s, which hit Germany harder than any other country; domination by the Nazis, the most bizarre and reckless political adventurers of modern times; division and reunification; and the "economic miracle" that followed World War II.

We selected a village because large and middle-size cities have attracted the attention of far more historians and sociologists than have villages and rural areas, even though the vast majority of human beings were farmers in all societies at all times before the industrial age. Before World War II some 35 percent of the population of Germany, representing 94 percent of all the communities in the Third Reich, still lived in villages of fewer than two thousand people.[1] Finally, the village chosen was 99 percent Catholic, whereas most previous studies of this sort have been of Protestant or mixed communities.

The selection of Oberschopfheim also owed much to the personal consideration that Walter Rinderle, one of the writers of this book, happened to be well acquainted with the place. His father, Herman Joseph Rinderle, was born in the neighboring village of Kuerzell in 1902. Numerous relatives still live in Lahr and in the nearby villages of Friesenheim, Schuttern, and Ottenheim. Some of them are well known in these communities and in the past have held local public offices. Thus they were ideally situated to provide information to the writer and to allow him access to county, village, and parish records. The importance of these fortuitous circumstances can hardly be overrated, for in many German villages the inhabitants distrust inquisitive strangers seeking information about some of the bitterest controversies of modern times. Finally, Oberschopfheim was chosen because its records were more extensive than those of other communities in Lahr county. In several of them many records were destroyed in World War II, either by Allied bombers or by local citizens anxious to cover their tracks. Nevertheless most of the generalizations offered about Oberschopfheim in this study are largely applicable to the other villages in Lahr county.

The personal interest of Walter Rinderle was awakened when he lived intermittently in Kuerzell and Oberschopfheim from 1962 to 1967, while he was pursuing graduate study in Innsbruck. He lived there again in 1970 and went back once more for six months in 1973 to do research. Both writers spent additional time in the village in 1988 and have corresponded extensively with people there since. Most of the source material for this study came from village archives. These contained copies of correspondence sent and received and detailed information about such matters as agriculture, local government, the manifold endeavors and concerns of the church, the distribution of welfare, community discord, and the activities of the police. The pastor, village officials, and ordinary citizens alike were generously cooperative. They provided such materials as church records, personal and club diaries, and a draft copy of Oberschopfheim's early history. County officials and the editors of the county newspapers, *Lahrer Anzeiger* and *Lahrer Zeitung,* were also gracious and helpful.

The files of the Berlin Document Center might have provided much useful material but officials in Bonn assured us that documents pertaining to Karlsruhe and Freiburg, the two cities closest to Oberschopfheim, were destroyed in the Second World War. Likewise, one might suppose that the Baden State Archives in Karlsruhe would be valuable. Staff people there did show us many boxes of materials about Oberschopfheim and environs, but almost all of it concerned archaeological finds, artifacts from Roman times, and other miscellany from centuries past. Extremely little concerned Lahr county in the twentieth century. In Freiburg both the university and city libraries had only printed books that related to our subject. Of course uncounted tons of records of many Nazi agencies were destroyed by Allied bombing in World War II. The Nazis themselves got rid of much more in an effort to cover their tracks. Whether any significant quantity of pertinent material relating to Lahr county remains and, if so, in whose hands it now resides can only be guessed at.

Written sources were supplemented by extensive personal interviews. Many local citizens, too numerous to mention individually, helped by answering questions about documents, clearing up apparent inconsistencies, and performing such seemingly minor but actually invaluable services as differentiating between persons with identical names. By the 1970s the great majority of residents (though not all) were willing to speak freely about many matters, usually pertaining to the Nazi era, about which prudence, and even safety, had long counseled silence.

Personal interviewing as a technique of historical research has deficiencies that are well known. If it takes place long after the event at least some people who could have imparted important information will have died. Moreover, everyone's memory is fallible, and this increases with the passage of time. These drawbacks were as apparent when interviewing people in Oberschopfheim as they are anywhere else. All that can be said about it, ultimately, is that consultation of records frequently corrected errant memories and that the information imparted and the opinions expressed by people in personal interviews frequently facilitated understanding of bare records. On balance, we do not believe we were seriously misled by either.

Throughout this study comparisons are offered between what was thought, said, done, feared, and hoped for by the people of Oberschopfheim and those of other cities, towns, and villages, either in Lahr county or in other parts of Germany. Comparisons are especially numerous with "Thalburg," a small city in Westphalia that was the subject of a book by William S. Allen (*The Nazi Seizure of Power,* 1965). That book attracted much attention and inspired a number of similar studies. A second edition of it, in 1986, revealed that "Thalburg" was the town of Northeim. By that time, however, "Thalburg" had become firmly fixed in the minds of thousands, including those of the writers of this book, who had read the first edition. Thus we decided to retain the familiar "Thalburg" in our own book, though there is no compelling reason to shun Northeim.

Some comparisons are also offered with rural conditions and practices in other countries. In all cases the purpose is to place deeds and developments in Oberschopfheim in perspective: to indicate when and in what ways they were unique, when they varied in some particular from those elsewhere, and when they were merely typical of the whole German nation, villages anywhere, or the entire Western world.

Something should be said about terminology too. Because the administrative unit whose capital was Lahr city was called at various times *Bezirk* Lahr and at other times *Kreis* Lahr, it is referred to in this book merely by its American equivalent, Lahr "county." The governing body of several counties is called by the generic name "district."

A more daunting issue is whether countrymen should be called farmers or peasants; and if "peasants," whether "peasant society" is a more accurate term than "folk society" or if "half-society" is superior to both; whether the best definition of "peasant" is "structural and rational" rather than "occupational"; whether "semipeasants" and "postpeasants" can be meaningfully distinguished from ordinary garden variety peasants; whether "peasant" is a permanent sociological category or merely a transitional designation; whether a "true peasant society can exist without a Great Tradition"; and much more.[2] One's thoughts turn irresistibly to medieval theologians striving to define the precise relationships among the Persons of the Blessed Trinity. The Nazis muddied these waters still further by distinguishing sharply between farmers and peasants. They referred deprecatingly to the former as people interested only in making money from agriculture and lauded "peasants" as persons who possessed superior qualities of race and character and whose attachment to the land had a spiritual dimension. To the Nazis, "peasants" fed the nation, defended it against enemies, maintained it demographically, and personally typified most Germanic virtues. We, less enamored of terminological niceties than many anthropologists and decidedly less romantic than the Nazis, have used "farmer" and "peasant" interchangeably to indicate anyone who made his living primarily by tilling the soil.[3]

There are many reasons why German politics, industry, and urban problems have been studied more extensively than German agriculture or local history. Perhaps the most fundamental is that the state has played a larger role in national life in Prussia and Germany than in most other countries and that in Germany, as in Russia, reform and innovation have so often come from the top down rather than from the bottom up. As one scholar puts it, it was only after the Nazi era that historians ceased to view everything through the eyes of rulers and "at last discovered the German people."[4]

Another reason for the lack of study derives from the predilections of historians. Most historians in the Western world were born and raised in cities and are the intellectual and spiritual children of the Enlightenment. The philosophes of the eighteenth century regarded peasants as mindless dolts, hardly better than animals, altogether incapable of sharing the splendid visions of superior persons like themselves. To later liberal historians, German peasants appeared to be enemies of progress. Sunk in medieval superstitions that enlightened souls had abandoned, subservient to authoritarian Junkers who were themselves enemies of democracy and modernism (not to speak of being advocates of high tariffs), peasants and Junkers alike were "backward" elements whose malign influence in Germany had much to do with the coming of the Nazis.[5]

Most obtuse of all are the Marxist historians. It is not merely that latter-day Marxists share their master's famous prejudice against "the idiocy of rural life." Boundless faith in philosophical materialism, state planning, and "economic laws" renders one uniquely unsuited to understand farming—as the prevalence of agricultural difficulties in twentieth-century communist states has repeatedly demonstrated. To a devout Marxist, a peasant can only be a medieval anachronism destined to be swept shortly into that tirelessly invoked "dustbin of history."[6] As late as 1966 such a figure as Theodor Adorno would express his disdain for rural provincialism and conservatism by asserting that a top educational priority of Germany should be the "de-barbarization" of the land.[7] Nevertheless the biases of leftists, like those of others, do erode. Social historians of Germany have gradually become increasingly interested in peasants and less supercilious toward them. "The idiocy of rural life now (1984) seems less idiotic than it once did."[8]

If peasants have been patronized by liberals and scorned by Marxists it is also true that they have often been ludicrously romanticized by nationalist and racist writers. In the pages of these lyricists, peasants emerge as paragons of all the conservative virtues: they are humble, wise, pious, simple, good, industrious, loyal, patriotic, and respectful of tradition.[9]

Real, live German peasants seldom fit any of the varied stereotypes bequeathed to them by intellectuals. For one thing, they showed great diversity in customs and outlook from one region to another—much more so than urbanized proletarians, for instance. Generally, they have been and are more intelligent than other classes assume. A small stock of ideas or an abbreviated formal education is not the same thing as stupidity—inability to learn. Like other classes and other occupational groups, peasants tended to be knowledgeable about what was of immediate concern to themselves. They knew a great deal about crops, soil, animals, weather, trees, and insects. They were resourceful in coping with overlords, from feudal nobles to powerful abbots. They knew how to fend off the avaricious and the importunate, whether these were tax officials, army recruiters, itinerant peddlers, or sly gypsies; and they knew how to live tolerably with their neighbors. They learned about as well as people of other classes in times past how to deal with plagues and epidemics, floods and famines, wars and depressions, individual illnesses and personal sorrows that have been the lot of humanity through the ages. Likewise, peasants were as susceptible to appeals to their generosity and idealism as were other Germans, but they were also just as concerned as others about defending their possessions and were just as ingenious in doing so. In short, like everyone else in Germany and the rest of the world, peasants were touched both by the sublime and by what theologians used to call Original Sin.

# 1

# THE LEGACY OF CENTURIES

BEFORE THE UNIFICATION of Germany in 1871 Baden was an independent grand duchy in southwest Germany. Its name derives from the many sulfur-bearing hot springs that exist in the area and from the fertile plowlands thereabout. Baden province is shaped somewhat like a human leg wearing a fifteenth-century Burgundian shoe. It is bounded on the west and south by the Rhine river and on the north by the Main. Eastward it extends irregularly into the Black Forest, to Hesse and Wuerttemberg. Baden is 138 miles from north to south, about sixty miles from east to west at its southern extremity, and from fifteen to thirty miles wide farther north.

The mountains of the Black Forest cover most of Baden, but the richest area is a strip of land five to fifteen miles wide along the east bank of the Rhine facing France. This "Garden of Germany" has long seemed particularly favored by nature. It has the most fertile soil in Germany and a climate that, though capricious, is so mild that finches stay over the winter there. Nearby streams running out of the hills provide abundant water for people and animals and make it possible to grow a variety of grains, vegetables, and fruits—even grapes. The hills themselves provide ample wood for fuel and sandstone for building. A large marsh supplies great quantities of reeds and "sea grass," materials useful for making baskets, stuffing mattresses, and other household purposes. Looking down from the hills into this valley in springtime one can see lush green meadows and countless blossoming fruit trees. Most of the population of Baden has lived and continues to live within this area.

Midway up this valley lies Gau Ortenau, in which Lahr county is situated. Originally established by the Franks, Gau Ortenau formerly looked a few miles northwestward across the Rhine to Strasbourg as its commercial, cultural, and religious center. Lahr county contained forty-three communities, one of which is Oberschopfheim, a farm village situated in a "kettle" between hillsides seven miles east of the Rhine at the base of the foothills of the Black Forest. In 1929 the property boundaries of Oberschopfheim stretched from the Schutter river in the valley to the

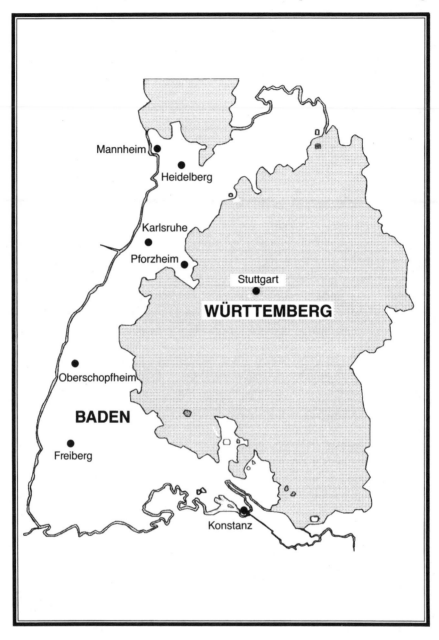

mountains three miles eastward. It comprised 2,562 acres, with the village in the center.

Little is known of the pre-Roman history of Lahr county. The Romans reached the area in the first century A.D. They brought with them grapevines and fruit trees of good quality that have been a source of livelihood to the present day. About 100 A.D. the emperor Trajan built a major highway from Basel northward to Mainz. For centuries thereafter it was the main artery of north-south transportation along the upper Rhine. Unfortunately, it was also an easy, obvious route for invaders of this rich, low, level valley. For the next eighteen centuries this locale was one of the most fought-over and pillaged sectors of Europe.

Throughout the Middle Ages churchmen and nobles attempted to increase their control over peasants, the latter to resist and reverse this process. From the late sixteenth century to the early nineteenth century fortune favored the peasants. All over southwest Germany compulsory labor and feudal dues were gradually transformed into simple rent payments. Nonetheless, the history of Oberschopfheim was hardly a cheery chronicle of the "good old days." Quite the contrary: most of the time it was a saga of unremitting toil, punctuated by poverty, misery, and grief. Specifically, life was normally short because it was a constant struggle with three of the Four Horsemen of the Apocalypse: starvation, pestilence, and war.

The worst of these was war. Records of this and neighboring villages show that in 903 A.D. kinsmen of the Magyars ravaged the whole area and sacked the monastery of Schuttern two and a half miles from Oberschopfheim; that many starved during the bad harvests of 1338-1339; that mortality was ghastly during the Black Death of 1348-1351; that Oberschopfheim and other villages were destroyed during wars between local nobles in 1443; that more such wars, 1482-1486 and again in 1502, occasioned widespread pillage and suffering; that the destruction was repeated during the Peasants Revolt of 1525 and yet again by troops of William of Orange and local noblemen in 1569. From the thirteenth century to the eighteenth century scores of villages in southwestern Germany vanished under the relentless hammer of these recurring wars, most of which also brought pestilence in their train.

Perhaps the most interesting of these innumerable conflicts was the Peasants War of 1525. Though Marxist writers have managed to depict the revolt of that year as a forerunner to the Communist uprisings of the twentieth century, in fact it was precisely the opposite—a "reactionary" struggle against the growing power and pretensions of lay and clerical overlords. In the specific case of Lahr county, peasants from Lahr and Friesenheim made it clear in April and May 1525 that they had no quarrel with Holy Roman Emperor Charles V or with the city of Strasbourg but that they were determined to compel the abbot of Schuttern monastery to restore meadow rights taken from them in 1510. Accordingly, they demolished the walls around the monastery, plundered it thoroughly for four days, dug up the boundary stones in the fields, and forced the abbot to flee to Ettenheim and then to Freiburg. Alas for them! Their victory was short. In June 1525 they were defeated, forced to return their plunder, fined the huge sum of 6,000 gulden, and saw their leaders severely punished.[1]

The worst strife and the most material damage was done during the Thirty Years War (1618-1648). The whole area was ravaged by successive waves of Neapolitans, Burgundians, Swedes, Croats, Austrians, French, and a dozen others. They tortured the men, raped the women, commandeered the farm animals, ate and drank what they could find, stole everything that could be carried off—even to the bells in the churches—and burned what little remained. When one detachment of troops left Friesenheim, three miles away from Oberschopfheim, only the Lutheran church and a few houses were still standing.[2]

Despite the horror of these depredations, the ensuing drastic population decline was due less to hapless civilians being murdered by soldiers than to the plagues and starvation that almost invariably accompanied military operations in times past. Those peasants in and around Oberschopfheim who managed to survive both battles and pestilence struggled to subsist on potatoes, which had been introduced during the war and which marauding soldiers were usually too lazy to dig up. Potatoes were supplemented by rats, mice, snakes—even by leaves, grass, twigs, and roots. By 1630 the population had dwindled to about 600 in Oberschopfheim, by 1648 to perhaps 150.

Other collateral effects of the war were comparably grim. By 1648 little of either stored grain or seed grain was left. Almost all the farm animals were dead or gone, leaving peasants without plow beasts, meat, or fertilizer. Many fields lay uncultivated. The people, shorn of all their movable possessions, were scattered, and squabbles abounded among villages, families, and individuals as the dispossessed sought to recover what they had lost. If lands were regained, only small portions of them were farmed because the depopulation of towns had reduced the demand for food and had caused a fall in grain prices. Recovery was slowed further by governments that raised taxes for what was perceived to be the vital necessity of strengthening defenses.[3] Popular superstition and fanaticism added the final dimension of suffering. In the nearby town of Offenburg some sixty persons were burned as witches from 1568 to 1630.

Such a succession of Dantesque experiences surely would have killed most twentieth-century urban people. Peasants, however, had learned from many centuries of grim experience that much of one's fate was always in the hands of nature, the upper classes, or outside enemies and that little could be done about this. Consequently, everywhere in Europe they developed an incongruous mixture of resignation and indomitable pertinacity that often served them better than any purely rational response to their fate.[4] One example here will suffice. In each of two villages in the neighborhood one old horse had managed to survive the murderous campaigns. The two hapless beasts were hitched together and the peasants began to plow once more.[5]

The respite was short. In Louis XIV's war against the Dutch a bare generation later the Sun King's Imperial opponents quartered their armies a mile away from the remnants of Oberschopfheim in 1675 and again in 1678. Sometimes they extorted "contributions" in money, horses, hay, wine, grain, or bread under the threat of burning the village if its inhabitants did not comply with their demands. Sometimes they did not trouble themselves thus but simply stole whatever they wanted from anyone who could be found—or caught. Not to be outdone in villainy, French troops tore up the walls and floors of Schuttern monastery in their search for presumed treasure. The Imperial troops of Montecuccoli riposted by sacking the village of Sasbach in 1675. Years afterward their successors degenerated into mere bands of robbers who pillaged the countryside indiscriminately.[6] Little wonder that a new pastor, sent to Oberschopfheim in October 1676, began his baptismal book thus: "Dear reader: Do not be astounded that most names at the beginning of these records are not here; for the largest part of the parish wanted to get away from the money-hungry and looting soldiers and saw themselves forced to seek shelter far from their homes. At the same time the church books which my predecessor kept have been lost . . . In war there is nothing good, therefore we all implore peace."[7] But peace did not come to Oberschopfheim. Time after time during the next sixty years French troops destroyed local castles, sacked eighty of the ninety houses in Oberschopfheim, plundered much of the city of Lahr and its environs, and subjected the whole county to forced contributions.[8]

The aftereffects of war were sometimes nearly as bad as the conflicts themselves. In 1725 the abbot of Schuttern monastery brought suit in a civil court to compel the peasants of Friesenheim, Oberweier, Heiligenzell, and Oberschopfheim to pay him back taxes that had gone uncollected during the many wars provoked by Louis XIV. The villagers protested that they should not be required to pay because the French armies had either taken their crops or had prevented them from planting in the first place. Their appeal to equity was fruitless. The abbot won his case, though the peasants had to pay somewhat less in money, free labor, and farm produce than they did in normal times.[9]

Four years later residues from the same conflicts almost provoked an intramural "war" between Friesenheim and Schuttern. The people of Schuttern, pressed hard to pay off debts incurred during the French wars, decided to drain a meadow they had long shared with Friesenheim as pasture land. They planned to farm their half to get cash crops with which to pay their debts. Since there had long been much rivalry among the farm villages of Lahr county, it was no surprise that Friesenheim was unwilling to cooperate. So the peasants of Schuttern, backed by their abbot, simply went ahead alone. They dug a ditch to drain the meadow and fenced off their half. The Friesenheimers bided their time until the abbot was called away. Then, armed with agricultural tools, three hundred of them descended on the area, filled in the ditch, tore down the fence, drove their animals in to graze in the newly planted field, and defied Schuttern to do anything about it. Luckily, no blood was shed, and the whole dispute eventually evaporated in a long and inconclusive lawsuit.[10]

During the French revolutionary and Napoleonic era, the French were back in Lahr county once more. From 1796 to 1807 they intermittently extorted the usual money, food, and supplies and drove the villagers deeply into debt to buy straw from neighboring hamlets to supply the invaders' animals. To add the proverbial insult to injury, these new pillagers were dogmatically antireligious and so confiscated lands belonging to the Oberschopfheim parish and to two monasteries. As usual, too, invading armies brought not merely violence and rapine but disease as well, in this case a typhus epidemic (1793-1794).[11]

Ordinarily, there is almost no way unarmed people can defend themselves against professional soldiers. In this instance, however, there lived in the neighboring village of Kuerzell, a scant three miles distant, a remarkable man named George Pfaff, a *Gasthaus* (tavern) keeper who managed to keep the French at bay for almost half a year (1796-1797). The feat was attributable about equally to amazing courage and to phenomenal luck.

As a reward for his exploits Pfaff was variously praised at Mass by the pastor of Kuerzell, was given an Austrian Lancer's uniform by the abbot of Schuttern, and was awarded a gold medal by the Austrian general Merveldt.[12] Pfaff's deeds and his willingness to wear the Austrian uniform and medal presented to him indicated clearly enough that he recognized the emperor of Austria as his sovereign. Also, he obviously respected the abbot who bought him the uniform and the priest who praised him for his heroism. Yet soon after, when he was a tavernkeeper again, he served everyone impartially. Plainly, his paramount interests were local and personal, not national or ideological. It would be the same with Oberschopfheimers in both world wars, 125 to 150 years later. It was also the same with most of the inhabitants of Baden at the turn of the nineteenth century.

Those men mustered into the army dutifully followed their prince wherever he led during the wars. Several thousand of them were captured by the French and pressed into service in Spain in 1808 and in Austria in 1809. By 1811, twelve thousand Baden men were being trained to support the catastrophic Napoleonic invasion of Russia that would follow in 1812. After Bonaparte's defeat, a Czarist host rolled westward and replaced the French as an army of occupation along the Rhine. At once there began a new round of atrocities and new demands for contributions. During these occupations many Oberschopfheimers, who had somehow managed to survive the previous twenty-three years of the war, now fled to the mountains as their ancestors had done, leaving their unplanted fields to wolves and foxes.[13]

Those who stayed behind fared but little better. Everywhere food was scarce because all the potatoes had been taken by the armies of occupation. As an emergency measure soup kitchens were set up in Lahr city. Government agents went from house to house collecting bones for the indigent, and bread was sold below cost to the poor. In Lahr county about 22,000 gulden was spent for poor relief in 1816 and 1817. The whole dismal situation was summed up aptly on one side of a medallion struck in Nuremberg in 1817. It bore the inscription, "O give me bread! I am hungry."[14]

Gradually, some nine hundred stolid, bruised, and exploited peasants straggled back to Oberschopfheim. They had suffered far more during the wars unleashed by Bonaparte than their remote descendants would endure in Hitler's war (1939-1945). Tenacious as ever, they began once more to rebuild their community and their lives. This time they were assailed for decades by a coalition of all the elements. Immediately, the weather was so wet that crops rotted in the fields and starvation became rampant. This was followed intermittently over the next half century by floods from both untamed mountain streams and the Rhine river, which between them inundated large stretches of Lahr county. In 1831 there was a strong earthquake. Then between 1840 and 1847 more abnormally wet weather ruined most of the crops. To make matters worse, it flooded the low-lying wetlands and produced a population explosion among snakes. The whole dolorous litany was capped by a series of exceptionally cold winters that forced villagers to purchase expensive firewood. As in 1816-1817, soup kitchens were set up to provide at least a noonday meal for those inhabitants facing starvation.[15] Inevitably, thievery flourished.

The catalyst in the crisis was failure of the potato crop. Potatoes produce more calories per acre than any grain crop, even rice. Thus in many parts of southwest Germany, where farms were tiny already and where peasants often married early and had large families, the population had grown rapidly even though there was as yet (1840) no major outlet in industry or crafts for the surplus people. This condition could endure only as long as potatoes remained plentiful and cheap. When crops failed, the result was less catastrophic than in the Irish potato famine a few years later, but it was grave nonetheless. Thousands of peasants poured into towns where they turned to peddling, or they tried to enter trades that were already overcrowded.[16] It is clear that the real problem was not absolute overpopulation but population that could not be readily absorbed, since cries of "overpopulation" were loudest in areas where absolute population growth was slowest.[17] It is equally clear that the plethora of "dwarf" farms was a contributory rather than a decisive factor in the problem, for Wuerttemberg had far fewer such tiny farms than Baden or Hesse yet experienced the same crop failure and subsequent emigration overseas.[18] Nonetheless, both village authorities and those in the state of Baden were convinced that the whole area was overpopulated and so offered financial aid to anyone willing to emigrate to America.

A general rush to take advantage of such government subsidies followed. Many sold their lands cheaply. Overall, more people emigrated from Lahr county in the 1840s than at any time before or since.[19] The alacrity with which peasants in and around Oberschopfheim sold their land testifies irrefutably to the depths of their despair. It is sometimes maintained that the wholesale transference of farm strips and the flight of farmers to the cities in twentieth-century Germany shows that the attachment of peasants to the soil has been exaggerated,[20] but if one converses with older farmers rather than merely examines courthouse records, he can hardly fail to be impressed by their reluctance to sell or trade ancestral lands.

Of course there were other considerations apart from sheer desperation that had already induced many southwestern German peasants to take their chances in America. Stories about the New World emphasized its abundance of land, food, and firewood, all of which were expensive and in short supply in Germany. There was also free hunting and fishing in the New World, neither of which was available to ordinary Germans even in time of starvation. Once in America, the new immigrants, especially Wuerttembergers, were often esteemed as able farmers and as industrious, capable artisans.[21]

In the case of Oberschopfheim's emigrants, dozens of families went to America between 1840 and 1930, but only one returned to Germany to live. The father of the family was the great-grandfather of Bernhard Messerer, a prominent citizen of Oberschopfheim in the late twentieth century. The elder Messerer was wounded in the American Civil War (1898) and so received a veteran's disability pension, which was paid in American dollars. The latter proved a priceless boon during the catastrophic inflation of 1923 when anyone with access to foreign currency could purchase property and other valuables for a pittance. The crippled veteran, then well into middle age, had to walk the fifteen miles to Strasbourg each month to collect his pension, but it was well worth the effort, for his U.S. money enabled him to lay the foundation for his family's subsequent prosperity.

Around Oberschopfheim the threat of starvation abated only slowly. From 1850 to 1854 more wet summers ruined most crops, even hay, so that livestock could not be fed and had to be slaughtered. Alternating wet and dry periods diminished harvests once more after 1854, while field mice suddenly proliferated and ate much of the produce in 1861 and 1862.[22]

As if bad harvests and famine were insufficient, the ravages of man returned in 1848-1849. In that famous year of revolt all over Europe, the towns of Baden were virtually in constant turmoil. By contrast, the peasants of Oberschopfheim, Kuerzell, and other rural villages were largely ignorant of contemporary intellectual currents. Few ever thought of political revolution as a solution to their various problems, and even their thin ranks had been depleted when the most restless of them had emigrated to America. To those who remained behind, the momentous year 1848 was memorable primarily because Prussian troops were sent into Lahr county to repress those who sympathized with the uprisings. Like their French, Imperial, and Russian predecessors, these new invaders compelled the villagers to support them. In particular, they demanded the best food and drink, especially *Kirschwasser* (cherry whiskey). Local people who failed to cooperate to the satisfaction of the Prussians were subjected to public whippings.[23]

Despite this seemingly unrelieved saga of disasters and calamities, the century of 1815 to 1914 was one of general progress in Lahr county just as it was in most of the rest of the Western world. In Oberschopfheim the most obvious part of it consisted of building: a new Catholic church and rectory, a new courthouse, a firewagon, three successive new grade schools, dozens of new houses, several stone bridges, and many roadside statues,[24] all of which together gave Oberschopfheim the external appearance it bore in the 1930s.

Less tangible improvements were no less real. In 1833 tithing of one's produce was abolished and replaced by a system whereby a percentage of one's wages was collected by the state, which then paid salaries to pastors of all faiths.

In 1845 a railway was built from Offenburg to Freiburg. Though it passed outside Oberschopfheim and soon became the most heavily traveled railroad in Europe, it never had the decisive impact on Oberschopfheim that nineteenth-century railroads so often had on American towns and villages. One reason was that Lahr county villages had few commodities to ship elsewhere. At any time before 1914 the small surplus they did produce was marketed almost entirely locally. Hence no depot was built in Oberschopfheim and the trains did not stop. Farmers with wine or tobacco—or briefly, chicory—to sell loaded it in a wagon and used horses or cows to haul it to Friesenheim or Niederschopfheim, only a couple of miles away. Not until 1950 did Oberschopfheim get a station of its own, and then it was abandoned within a decade. What the railroad meant in 1845 was that a handful of local men secured good jobs as railway workers, and if villagers made their way a few miles to the depots in Lahr city or Offenburg a new and much improved mode of travel became available to them.

In 1892 a vastly improved system of water distribution was built. Instead of the old practice of storing water in ponds, it was now piped from the mountains to village fountains connected to watering troughs, simultaneously providing a more satisfactory way to water animals, to collect water for home use, and to fight fires. An even more momentous victory in the realm of hydrology had been gained some twenty years earlier. Farmers not only in Oberschopfheim but throughout a good deal of Lahr county had always had to contend with the unpredictability of local streams. Apart from periodic torrents emanating from the mountains, floods from the Rhine river and its numerous tributaries frequently cut channels though rich farmland, leaving behind devastated crops and villages, drowned cattle, unusable islands, piles of sand and gravel, and new breeding grounds for mosquitoes. The latter were ubiquitous in any case because of the extensive marshland (Ried) that lay along the Rhine. Their multiplication added malaria to the other crosses carried by the villagers.

In 1817 the governments of Baden and France began to build permanent stone walls and earthen dams along the Rhine from Basel, where the river abruptly bends northward, to Mannheim. Meanwhile, floods inundated the area in 1824, 1845, and 1851, ruining most of the crops and many houses.[25] In the 1860s the government attacked the problem in earnest and completed the work in 1872, the year of still another flood.[26] Then, four years later, a dam broke. Farmers in the fields heard a roaring noise and saw great numbers of wild animals dash out of the woods. In short order muddy water a meter deep inundated the higher land while that nearer the Rhine was three or four meters under water. All the crops in the valley were ruined, dead animals floated everywhere, and storage basements were filled with water and mud. The only saving feature of the whole disaster was that as the water receded farmers were able to catch many edible fish—no small matter in a time of general devastation. After 1876 many deep holes remained as ponds, but except for 1896 floods became less severe. The dikes, meanwhile, stabilized the Alsace-Baden border, added 10,000 hectares of new farm land on the Baden side, and deepened the river channel sufficiently that ships could now travel up-stream to Switzerland.[27]

Within the village of Oberschopfheim inhabitants faced the additional—and perennial—problem of heavy rainfall. The forest-clad mountains trapped low storm clouds over the village, producing periodic cloudbursts that washed away vineyards in the hills. In addition, two creeks flowed to the village center where they met to form a single stream. During heavy rainstorms this combined stream often rose over its banks and destroyed houses. Of the two calamities, damage to the vineyards was worse, for the people then had to load the displaced soil into baskets, laboriously lug it back up the hills, carefully restore ravaged nature, replant the vines, and hope for better luck in the future.

During the fall and winter the Ried, a maze of creeks and underground streams meandering through a marsh to the Rhine, produced a thick fog that spread inexorably over all the villages in the valley. It turned Oberschopfheim into something like a musty cavern for months at a time.

Perhaps the most important element that shaped the history and character of Oberschopfheim was the dedication of its people to the Catholic church. No other factor, shared hardship, or even economic interdependence, was more important in binding the villagers together and providing them with a feeling of unity in the face of a flinty external world that often seemed to regard them with sheer malevolence. For centuries loyalty to the church remained strong, even though quarrels between ecclesiastics and lay people were neither infrequent, trivial, nor always nonviolent. For instance, peasants and the monks of Schuttern monastery persistently disagreed about who should take how much and what kinds of wood from a forest where both had "rights" and where both interpreted past agreements in their own favor. In 1743 village peasants became so incensed over monastic claims that they raided the monastery and stole much meat and other food. The abbot retaliated by sending out squadrons of his retainers to search village houses. The peasants responded by taking up axes and driving the searchers off. The abbot then appealed to authorities in Freiburg for military aid. Police were sent first, eventually followed by a hundred soldiers. As might have been predicted, the soldiers plundered the whole neighborhood, including the monastery, and took some prisoners before the dispute petered out. A century later the farmers rebelled again, this time mostly against the abbot's claim to all the oak trees in the forest.[28]

Sometimes the monks appeared to be simultaneously exploiters and victims. Such a case occurred in 1770 when Marie Antoinette, daughter of the Austrian empress Maria Theresa, visited Schuttern monastery on her way to France to wed the future ill-fated Louis XVI. Despite having been burned, sacked, and rebuilt many times in the past, in 1770 the monastery was imposing and opulent. Its main building contained eighty-four rooms, four kitchens, three halls, and a wine cellar. It was surrounded by a number of smaller side buildings, a fishpond, and about ten acres of vegetable and flower gardens. Since the monks received notice of the coming of their royal guest long in advance they were able to spend a full year making suitable preparations. Several of the existing monastic buildings were renovated, and a completely new one of fifteen rooms was erected. New furniture, plate, and bedding was purchased, not to speak of damask cloth to grace the royal bedchamber. Seventy-three people were engaged to work in the monastic kitchen on the sublime occasion. At length Marie Antoinette arrived at 2:00 P.M. on May 6, accompanied by 256 retainers, 57 wagons, and 450 horses. Cannons were fired and bells were rung, presumably to indicate the joy of the hosts. The Great Lady (then fourteen years old) presented the abbot with a specially printed greeting and a valuable monstrance. He reciprocated with a fireworks display, accompanied by an orchestra. Suitably greeted, entertained, and fed, Marie Antoinette arose early next morning, heard Mass, and departed amid another orgy of bell ringing and cannon fire. The expense of the extravaganza was so great that the monks had to sell a tract of land in Herbolzheim to retire their debt, even after exacting extensive "contributions" from Oberschopfheim and all the other villages in the area.[29]

The Reformation came to this portion of southwest Germany in 1523. Squabbling between denominations was endemic thereafter, as it was in so much of sixteenth- and seventeenth-century Europe. The turmoil was exacerbated by frequent changes of religion on the part of ruling families. The subjects of the Margrave of Baden-Baden, for instance, were compelled to change their confessional allegiance no less than seven times within a century. After several such compulsory transformations Oberschopfheim became Catholic in 1629.[30]

Ironically, it is from these tumultuous times that we have our first specific, detailed information about local communities. Paul Volz, a sixteenth-century abbot of Schuttern, began to write the *Annals of Kloster Schuttern*, the first such local records that survive. The oldest regular church records in Oberschopfheim date from 1660.[31]

In the course of the next three centuries Lahr county as a whole became about 60 percent Catholic, 39 percent Protestant, and 1 percent Jewish, roughly the average for the whole state of Baden. Individual communities within the county were usually Catholic or Lutheran, depending on their location, and have remained largely so to the present day. Near the foothills of the Black Forest and in the south Catholics were more than a two-thirds majority in twenty-five villages. Near the city of Lahr, itself 59 percent Lutheran, and in the Ried, ten villages were very heavily Lutheran. On the borders of these areas the two major religions were about equally mixed in seven villages.[32] In the early twentieth century Oberschopfheim harbored only seventeen Lutherans, about 1 percent of its population.

In many parts of Europe, particularly in Mediterranean lands, popular religion often seems sharply at variance with official Christian doctrines. A South Italian peasant once remarked to an American academician that, locally, the church supplied the pageantry of life, but the real religion was fatalism.[33] In the mountain villages of southern Spain, where many people are anarchists at heart, most men regard politics and government as their domain, church and religion as the business of women.[34] Greek villagers seemed to one American anthropologist to believe that life is an intense Darwinian struggle, the main purpose of which is to outwit and outshine others. To them, priests, icons, and ecclesiastical ministrations are merely window dressing, as the Italian peasant (above) viewed them.[35] This was decidedly not the case in Oberschopfheim. For its inhabitants, Catholicism was not "the opium of the people" but the mainstay of existence. It was their principal psychological support in the aftermath of hardships and disasters. From it they drew the strength and courage to rise and struggle again.

For centuries the parish church was the center of village activities. In the 1920s nearly all Oberschopfheimers still took their religion seriously and attended Sunday Mass faithfully.[36] Catholic customs and celebrations were for many, perhaps most, the brightest and most joyous part of village life. No fewer than seventeen church holidays were still celebrated. The showiest and most important was the feast of St. Leodegar, the patron saint of the village. In the morning all the village clubs, arrayed in their distinctive costumes and carrying their flags, met in the church for Mass. Afterward they paraded through the village. This was followed by an afternoon of music, soccer, and dancing. Though less elaborate, the Palm Sunday procession caused more excitement among the young—and anger among the foresters. On that occasion Oberschopfheimers would not be content to embellish the procession with the customary pine branches. Instead, they would try to outdo one another by cutting and decorating entire trees, which they would then strive to maneuver through church doors.[37] During Lent all the villagers joined in the frequent processions to stone crosses in the fields and to the *Leutkirche*, a pilgrimage church first built on the outskirts of the village in the eighth century and many times restored. At Easter nearly all adults displayed holy cards as proof of taking the sacraments.

Perhaps the most convincing evidence of villagers' faithfulness to Catholicism was financial. Despite centuries of poverty, hardship, and misfortune, despite being habitually and conspicuously frugal,[38] Oberschopfheimers always managed somehow to find the money, time, and energy to erect statues and stone crosses and to rebuild churches and shrines, all to seek Divine protection from famines, wars, and diseases and to give thanks for at least partial past deliverance from these scourges. By the twentieth century most local contributions went to foreign missions, the diocesan poor, seminaries, a parish library fund, and for upkeep of the graves of those who had died in the Great War. "Poor" families gave as freely as the rest when the sacristan passed the *Klingelbeutel* (bell-ringing basket) to the men's and women's sides of the church. The *Gemeinde* (village government) set the pace by contributing a thousand marks in annual salaries and gifts to the pastor, organist, and parish, considerably more than a local church tax would have produced. After 1933 the Nazis tried to cut off such support. Significantly, they failed.[39]

Of course Oberschopfheim's Catholicism was not monolithic or without flaws. As in most "Christian" lands, there were more than a few whose orthodox reverence was inextricably mixed with remnants of pre-Christian preoccupation with spirits, devils, fairies, witches, spells, and curses. Many Oberschopfheimers still believed in ghosts; others were quite as confident as their medieval ancestors that holy water was a magical cure for anything from personal illness to bad crops. Inevitably, too, there were a few scoffers who questioned customary religious usages, though no one left the church or opposed it openly, as some did in cities.

As in most communities, attitudes toward the Christian moral code tended to be selective. Much emphasis was laid on such sins as larceny and laziness. Citizens were conspicuously less zealous at loving their relatives if an inheritance was at stake, or neighbors if a property line was in dispute. Premarital chastity among girls was admired and advised on moral grounds, yet pregnancy before marriage indubitably demonstrated female fertility and thus the ability to carry on the family line, a matter of high importance to any prospective groom and his parents. Consequently, lapses from grace in this sector were officially disapproved but, in practice, not taken with undue seriousness. The worst that could happen to a girl clearly guilty of a sexual transgression of the ordinary sort was to be made the object of a prank with embarrassing overtones. Young men who aspired to become village humorists would sometimes do such things as tie a baby buggy to the chimney of a house where an unmarried pregnant girl lived, pile manure in front of such a house, or make a sawdust trail between the houses of known paramours.[40] If a child was born out of wedlock people accepted both it and the mother without shaming her, though the matter would be discussed with sufficient enthusiasm and thoroughness that no one could forget it. Such a flexible scale of values could not be changed much even by the pastor, and most pastors did not try.

Unlike many of their rural clerical brethren in France, Oberschopf-heim's priests regarded the *Gasthaeuser* (village taverns) with equanimity.[41] The places did not have a bad reputation. They were the headquarters of the various village clubs and the local priest often went to them for an evening beer.

By most ways of reckoning the pastor was the most influential person in the village. Once pastors had truly dominated German Catholic villages. They had conducted censuses, listed recruits for the army, managed and inspected schools, registered births, deaths, marriages, orphans, and bastards, and recorded the blind, deaf, dumb, maimed, and homeless. Often they had chosen local chiefs of police, with whom they then administered poor relief and other public services. In Oberschopfheim, by the twentieth century most of these duties had been taken over by the *Gemeinde* (village government), though the pastor still enjoyed virtually complete control over the hiring of teachers in the public school and taught in that school himself.[42] He also possessed much influence over the selection of local candidates for political office and "guided" the votes of his flock in state and national elections. Even the aged and ailing Pfarrer Isele in the early 1930s organized most local cultural activities, such as parish evenings of music and drama. He also moderated the numerous parish clubs, to one or more of which most of his flock belonged. In addition, he helped plan the periodic "outings" of such groups as the Mothers' Club or Young Men's Club to monasteries or shrines within a fifty mile radius. Above all, he was the principal arbiter of village feuds, both religious and secular.

The most significant feature of the pastor's position was intangible: the feeling his parishioners had for him. In most of the Catholic portions of Germany, as in the Catholic regions of Belgium and Switzerland (but not in most of France), the priest was not seen as the representative of a privileged old order that the common man should want to overthrow. Rather, he was looked upon as the father and leader of his community and its champion against a privileged *new order* whose members most villagers disliked and whom they viewed as a threat to their properties. "Emancipated" German secularists had little success convincing Catholic peasants that their church and clergy were parasites and exploiters. To the peasants it was the urban secular liberals and socialists *themselves*—journalists, speculators, officials, atheist professors—who were the parasites.[43] The pastor, by contrast, seemed a part-time peasant himself. Though others had to plow for him since he had no farm animals, he raised much of his food in his own garden and lived as quietly and simply as most of his people.

Although there was a parish council to advise the pastor, in practice its members let him do as he wished. Children were even more deferential. They never dared to disobey the priest's orders, to miss his religion classes, to ask him questions, or to misbehave in his presence.[44] As late as 1960 they genuflected promptly when encountering him and greeted him formally with the words, "Praised be Jesus Christ." The decline in the prestige of the village pastor has been one of the most marked changes in late twentieth-century Oberschopfheim.

# 2

# THE PEOPLE OF OBERSCHOPFHEIM

FROM A LOW of about 150 during the worst stages of the Thirty Years War, the population of Oberschopfheim rose sporadically to around 950 by the end of the Napoleonic wars and to 1,324 in 1854.[1] Growth would have been faster had not scores of citizens, mainly young men, left because of insufficient farmland and overcrowded trades. Thus Oberschopfheim numbered more women than men and more people less than twenty-one years old and over fifty-five years old than the German national average. Still, unlike many villages all over the Western world, its population continued to increase. In 1939 36 percent of all inhabitants were married, 57 percent (mainly children) were single, and 7 percent were widowed.[2]

Physically, the village was overcrowded. Its houses were irregularly shaped to conform to the streets and alleys that had come into existence haphazardly through the centuries and packed close together to use as little as possible of the valuable farmland. Each house ordinarily held two or three generations of one family—depending on how long the "old folks" lived. At any time before the twentieth century this was usually not long. In the sixteenth and seventeenth centuries natural deaths generally occurred at around fifty-five or sixty years of age. Since the usual age at marriage then was about twenty-five for women and over thirty for men, most of the time three generations resided under one roof for only a few years, if at all. When people *were* compelled to endure such a living pattern, nobody welcomed it. A local saying summed up the general feeling: "To sit at the children's bench is for the old folks a difficult seat."[3] Only in the early twentieth century when average life expectancy rose did it become common for three generations to live together for many years.

In ages past Oberschopfheim's houses had been made of wood, but in the nineteenth century most were rebuilt on sandstone foundations that extended four feet or more above ground to resist flooding. Most had cellars with dirt floors for vegetable storage. Many consisted of a kitchen, a dining room, and one bedroom on the main floor, with another upstairs or attic bedroom for all the children. Generally, the only really warm room was the kitchen since it held the cookstove. The rest of the living quarters were usually cold, dark, and damp, with the result that arthritis and rheumatism were common among their dwellers.

Before World War II by far the most important activity in the village was agriculture, and most villagers thought of themselves as farmers. Vestiges of feudalism lasted long in Germany, and modernization of agriculture was slow. The population of seventeenth century Europe had remained roughly static, but in the eighteenth century it began to grow—especially toward the end of that century. Higher agricultural productivity became increasingly imperative. Better plows were invented and better methods of plowing devised. New crops, most notably potatoes and turnips, were introduced or cultivated more widely to replace or supplement grains. The old manorial system of rotating crops among three fields to preserve the fertility of the soil gradually passed away, rendered unnecessary by the introduction of clover, which enriched the soil by fixing nitrogen in it. It also provided more nutritious feed for cows than did open pasture. Larger yields and correspondingly greater incomes for peasant families followed apace. This, in turn, quickened agitation for legal and social changes that would provide additional incentives for peasant producers. In Baden peasants were personally freed from serfdom in 1783, and the drive to establish unconditional property rights accelerated to completion by 1830. Even so, victory was not total. Many of the regulatory functions that had been the province of old feudal lords were merely transferred to the new *Gemeinde* (village government).[4]

Overall, in 1900, the peasants of Oberschopfheim still farmed in a fashion little different from that of their medieval ancestors.[5] The average family had about three acres of land that was divided into perhaps fifteen long, narrow strips to accommodate the work psychology of cattle who dislike frequent turning when plowing.[6] As in the old manorial system, these strips were scattered all over the village domain.

This state of affairs has always looked to city dwellers, Marxian economic analysts, and sons of the Enlightenment as proof of the ignorance, backwardness, and irrationality of peasants. Such urbanites tend to think of agriculture as merely rural industry and to assume that a combination of better tools and better techniques should raise food production just as they raise industrial production. Rational analysis by "experts," followed by the "education" of peasants, should show the way.

Unfortunately, this approach to farming seldom works. The main reason is that agriculture is not a rational activity in the sense that industry is, and the psychology of peasants is unlike that of either industrial entrepreneurs or proletarian laborers. No two plots of land or two animals are exactly alike. Farming techniques related to a certain crop will vary with the weather from one season to another, with the latitude, and with the soil type. Soil types often vary greatly within small areas so that a tool or technique may be practical for one peasant and impractical for his neighbor only a couple of hundred yards away. Thus "factory farming" of a single crop over a large area with machinery may be eminently sensible in some circumstances and foolish in others.

Moreover, farming has always been a risky business. Throughout history in most parts of the world peasants have lived close to the brink of survival. Thus their first concern has always been to "play it safe," to make sure that they and their families survived. This has often meant that each peasant family in a typical village needed a bit of the best village land to grow vegetables, a larger portion of somewhat less good land to grow grain, at least some land that was either watered naturally or could be irrigated during a drought so the peasant was sure of having seed grain for the next year, some land that would produce hay to maintain his animals during the winter, and rights to a common pasture where his animals could graze during the rest of the year. Soil suitable for each of these purposes (and often others as well) was usually scattered about over the countryside and so the shares of it accruing to individual peasant families had to be scattered too.

Peasant villages in many parts of the world resemble Oberschopfheim in that they seem to have much surplus labor. Yet at certain times of the year, when fruit or grain is harvested, when trees must be pruned, when dams must be built or irrigation ditches dug, all the available labor is needed—and it is needed at once. Harvesting in particular cannot wait. This makes every peasant dependent to a considerable degree on the goodwill and cooperativeness of his neighbors if he is to reap his crops. If he fails to cooperate himself, if he ridicules the customs and opinions of others, he will make himself unpopular and thereby endanger the very survival of himself and his family. Hence many peasant families who spend with seeming brainlessness on weddings, christenings, birthday parties, and the like are not necessarily being profligate. They are displaying their generosity by giving everyone in the village a day off—with entertainment, food, and drink to embellish it. They are buying the goodwill of their neighbors and indispensable helpers.

Often it is close to impossible to say whether a given action by a peasant is rational or not. A small farmer who goes in debt to buy a tractor may seem foolish and improvident if he can use it only for short periods during the year. Yet the tractor enables him to do a *better* job than before and to do it more quickly and easily. Thus he feels better about his whole existence. Furthermore, possession of a tractor elevates him somewhat in the eyes of his neighbors and may make it possible for him to arrange a more advantageous marriage for his daughter. So, even if he has trouble paying for his tractor or perhaps cannot pay for it, is he obviously unwise to buy it?[7]

Much seeming peasant obtuseness, too, has always existed because peasants have different objectives from those of "experts" who seek to "help" them and because they mistrust such "experts." Peasants have generally sought to preserve their way of life and to minimize their dependence on outsiders. They find it satisfying to grow good crops and raise fine animals, to divide their time among several tasks instead of concentrating on one, to live close to nature, and to manage their own affairs. If government officials or urban agricultural experts try to persuade a peasant to grow some new crop, adopt a new method of tillage, or consolidate scattered lands, if they assure the peasant that such action will promote his prosperity, the first thing the peasant is apt to think is that these new "friends" have never been interested in his prosperity before and probably are so now only because they want to tax him more heavily. After all, they come from the same urban, official classes that have always mustered people like himself into armies and burdened them with rules, regulations, laws, and taxes. Often the peasant sees quite accurately that adoption of some recommended innovation will eventually change his whole mode of life: it will deprive him of his pasture rights and therefore his animals, as English peasants were despoiled by the eighteenth-century enclosures; it will compel him to invest heavily in expensive seeds, fertilizers, and machinery that he does not now need and does not particularly want; it will make him increasingly dependent on the mistrusted outside experts; or it will soon require him to read books and journals and attend agricultural meetings, all of which are of more interest to his son than himself and so will gradually result in increasing the influence of his son at the expense of himself in their joint enterprises.[8]

In reality peasants were not always slow, backward, and unwilling to accept any innovation. Often they would do such things as exchange sickles for scythes to facilitate grain harvest, plant more acres of a certain crop if its price rose, or bring suit in the proper court if they believed their rights were being infringed. They were willing enough to innovate if *they thought it would be to their advantage,* and on such occasions they knew what the advantage was, what it was worth, and how to go about its pursuit. They were not stupid at all; just unwilling to change something merely because such action seemed "reasonable" to an outsider while gain for themselves appeared problematical.[9]

The farmers of Oberschopfheim clung to their small, scattered plots for many of the same reasons that peasants did in most other parts of

Europe. Yields and prices of crops like grain, fruit, wine, or tobacco varied with weather, insects, and the unfathomable vagaries of urban markets, but strategically located plots of good soil would always grow food to keep a family from starving. To be sure, time and energy were wasted while people and animals traipsed from one strip to another. Worse, virtually everyone had to cross the strips of several of his neighbors, a situation guaranteed to promote acrimony.

In summary: in agriculture everything depends on all sorts of circumstances. Economies of scale indubitably exist in procurement, processing, marketing, and credit, but farm work of the sort that involves much close hand labor or experimentation is usually done better on small family farms. Also, "efficiency" means different things at different levels. If a society has a large labor surplus overall, it may be better for the whole nation to keep most of the underemployed or "unemployables" attached to rural pursuits than to pack them into large cities. Some European governments long sought to keep many people on the land because they believed rural men made better soldiers than those from cities. Finally, the whole subject has been muddied by ideologues, whether Marxists, Catholics, social conservatives, or others, who want either a preponderance of small family farms or of large industrial farms for social, political, or religious reasons that have little to do with agricultural efficiency per se.[10]

Given the circumstances that characterized agriculture in Oberschopfheim, much forbearance and even more cooperation was essential for economic survival. Village families exchanged work, shared tools and work animals, traded an excess of some commodity to neighbors who had an excess of something else, and helped each other through hard times and bad luck. Few sought indefinite expansion of their enterprises or profits. Rather, as in the Middle Ages, they strove to produce or acquire enough to maintain their status and their normal mode of life. All sorts of local customs and regulations existed to promote those objectives.

Like people the world over who have lived all their lives close to the subsistence level, Oberschopfheimers wasted nothing. All the productive land within the municipality was cultivated assiduously. Even the edges of the road were plowed. If a cow needed to eat fresh alfalfa or clover to boost her milk production, she was not turned out to pasture at her own pleasure. Instead, her owner cut the desired amount of fresh feed each day and carried it to the beast. This insured that no fodder would be wasted by the animal walking or defecating on it. Besides, a closely enclosed cow could not damage a neighbor's crop and thereby cause the owner to be fined. Even more important, stall feeding made it possible to collect animal manure systematically and thus fertilize the land evenly.[11] This practice, which probably began around 1800 with the introduction of clover, was one of those carried out much more satisfactorily by the owner of a small farm than by hired labor on a large estate or a state farm.

As such practices indicate, Oberschopfheimers had to work very hard. Traditionally, peasants have valued physical strength and energy, the capacity and willingness to work hard, above other human qualities. It has been mostly since the advent of the machine age, primarily in the twentieth century, that farmers have devoted increasing attention to employing machinery to spare themselves physical hardships. German farmers have long had a global reputation for industry or at least for a special attitude toward it. Where a Frenchman or Italian might appreciate the unavoidable necessity of hard toil in order to live in a desired way, Germans often seemed to be compulsive workers, to regard any sort of toil, but especially heavy physical labor, as a positive good in itself.[12]

Within Germany this reputation was preeminent among the people of Baden and Wuerttemberg, and among *them* the inhabitants of Lahr county were regarded as the most industrious. Yet even among such zealots of labor as these, Oberschopfheimers stood out. Perhaps the explanation is sheer poverty combined with a shortage of land and a plentiful labor supply. In a village like Oberschopfheim many unskilled and semi-skilled workers (women, half grown children, the partially disabled, landless men, natural dullards, and such) were always sorely needed at harvest time, but, save for the women, they had much less to do at most other times of the year. If they could be put to work in these relatively slack seasons raising some sort of cash crop that required much close attention, their labor might not be cost effective in an accountant's sense, but they would be employed rather than idle, and their efforts would add appreciably to a family's income.[13] A part-time job often served the same purpose. Certainly it was the need for supplementary income that, by the 1920s, caused virtually every adult in the village to have two jobs: farming, but also as a worker in a cigar factory, as a petty merchant, on a railroad in a nearby town, as an artisan of some sort, or for the village government.[14]

But perhaps the reason Oberschopfheimers worked so hard was mostly psychological. Those in neighboring communities believed that Oberschopfheim was more favored than their villages, and thus implied that its greater prosperity was mainly because of luck. Oberschopfheim owned a good forest; most other villages had only some scrub trees. It had a sandstone quarry in the mountains; only a few others did. It had long possessed several cigar factories that gave much employment and paid wages in cash, thus generating more purchasing power than existed in most other villages. Even so, neighbors granted grudgingly that village traditions seemed different too—that Oberschopfheimers were simply more ambitious and energetic than themselves. For instance, few people left any of the communities in Lahr county to pursue higher education or to try to make their way upward in the world, but more did so from Oberschopfheim than from other villages.

Whatever the case, Oberschopfheimers were looked upon by their neighbors somewhat as other Americans view Texans: as extremists in everything. Villagers often seemed to derive a certain sneaking enjoyment from listening to others talk about what hard workers they were. It increased one's prestige and seemed to demonstrate one's hardihood. It also implied that one had other laudable qualities as well. Perhaps a subtler point was missed by the object of the adulation: that he who bestowed the praise thereby advertised his own generosity, fairness, and broad-mindedness.[15] Apparently no one in Oberschopfheim had heard the jaundiced American observation that to say one is a "good worker" is an excellent compliment to pay a horse but not a man.

Whatever its origin, profound or trivial, the industriousness of Oberschopfheimers was legendary and jokes about it were plentiful. One was that villagers slept in their work clothes so they could begin their jobs more quickly in the morning. Another was that they did not go to bed at night at all: they just roosted like the chickens so they could go to work at the first rays of dawn. Villagers even joked about themselves: that they went to bed with the chickens and got up with the roosters. Local proverbs had it that "Work makes life sweet," while "Laziness makes limbs stiff."

Truth was, if anything, grimmer than either jest or proverbs. Though in some parts of Germany, as in England, much agriculture gradually became mechanized in the nineteenth century and most farmers began to purchase tools and clothing that they had once made for themselves, such changes came slowly to Oberschopfheim. For instance, until the Second World War most farmers still plowed with cows rather than horses because the cows ate less and could also be milked.[16]

When it was time to do field work whole families customarily went out together. Infants were carried out and set on the ground where they could be watched by their fathers and mothers. The parents, joined by their older children both before and after school, then pursued their common task with hoes, shovels, plows, and rakes.

When hay was mowed farmers got up at 2:00 A.M. in order to take advantage of the dew, which made cutting with a scythe much easier. During the planting season they were more fortunate: they could "sleep in" until 4:00 A.M. before they put homemade harnesses on their cows and trudged barefoot behind them into the fields. After breakfast they went to whatever their "regular" jobs might be, then back to farming again from six to eight in the evening, with time out along the way to milk the cows a couple of times. Cows had to be milked every single day—Sundays, holidays, whatever—no matter what the owner might wish or how he might feel. Not for nothing have dairy farmers made mordant jokes about the resemblance of dairying to slaveholding: that the cow is on one end of the chain and her owner on the other.[17]

Overall, women worked even harder than men. On the huge collective farms in Soviet Russia men operated the machines while women did nonmechanical stoop labor.[18] On American farms, also usually large, it was the opposite. Women occasionally ran the machines but almost never did hard physical hand labor. In the Ortenau, by contrast with both, there was no specialization by age or gender. Worse for women, male work tended to fall into a set schedule while women were expected to adjust their tasks to seasonal needs and to monopolize "odd jobs." Not only did they sweat in the fields, they gathered firewood, made and mended clothing, did the family washing, cooked, canned food, tended the garden, carried water, shared the cow milking, brewed medical remedies, nursed the sick, and looked after the children. Not surprisingly, they also aged rapidly and died young. When a wife did die the husband usually married again without delay. Hence half brothers and half sisters were common in Oberschopf-heim.

As for children, sometimes they were allotted some specific task of their own such as herding cows; sometimes they merely worked alongside their elders as well as they could. Normally, Oberschopfheim's kids were neither petted nor indulged. They regarded their fathers with some trepidation, especially before 1914. Back talk to elders was not allowed, and they might get an occasional whipping for some misdeed. Even so, it was rare for children to be treated brutally by their parents,[19] and there is no indication that the youngsters themselves thought of their existence as mere drudgery. Their regular household and field chores were just part of their lives, like going to school four or five hours a day, six days a week. If, along the way, they managed to find some time to play or merely to daydream nobody cared—but nobody thought it important either. Play-time for children did not become a "concept" until the second half of the twentieth century. It was the same with an allowance. None was given; none was expected. A child, of whatever age, remained under the author-ity of his parents until he established a family of his own or left home.

Generally speaking, the worst fate that could befall a child was loss of a parent, especially the mother. A common practice in the Ortenau was for various relatives to gather on the very day of a funeral and divide the surviving children. There were no legal adoption procedures, and the personal wishes of the children were ignored. They were then kept by their new guardians until they had finished grade school. If they worked, and nearly all did by the time they were twelve, whatever they earned passed without question to the relative-guardian just as it would have to the father in an ordinary family. Of course most relatives treated such youngsters kindly, or at least in a civilized manner, but there were always some who did not and the unlucky child in such a case had little recourse save to bear his burden or run away. Most villagers had heard of some unfortunate child who had once been chained to a bed by a malicious cousin, who had been exploited heartlessly by an uncle, or who had committed suicide in despair.

Courtship and marriage customs in Oberschopfheim clearly reflected the importance that capacity for work assumed among the villagers. Marriages did not result from handsome, sleek young people swooning over one another in the moonlight, as in Hollywood movies. Matrimony was primarily an economic relationship. As an old German proverb had it, "It's not man that marries maid, but field marries field, vineyard marries vineyard, cattle marry cattle."[20] The parents of the participants, who normally presided over the negotiations that preceded matrimony, often did such unsentimental things as inspect each other's property and draw up a legal document specifying what was to be included in the bride's dowry. In some countries, notably Greece, where peasants attached great importance to "rising in the world" and being thought "modern," it sometimes seemed that the major purpose of everyone's activity was to provide a splendid dowry for the daughters of a family in the hope that they would then be able to marry educated or "city" husbands. Such unions would shed luster on the bride's entire family and perhaps make it possible for her brothers or nephews to exploit contacts with the new in-laws and elevate the status of the whole family even further.[21]

Few people in Oberschopfheim were so enthralled by the remote prospect of dramatic social elevation that they paid much attention to the establishment of munificent dowries. What did stimulate their imaginations was the prospect of marriage to a distant relative, to a member of a family to which they had been previously allied, or of a marriage of two members of the family to two members of another family. All such cases raised the scintillating prospect of merging adjoining properties, of rejoining lands that had previously been divided, or in some similar way adding to or simplifying landholdings. Such preoccupation did not reflect mere acquisitiveness. How much land one owned, its value, and its location frequently determined whether one could live in the village, had to live in a nearby town, had to work outside the village, or had to leave the locality altogether.[22] People who had to work outside Oberschopfheim, for instance, were regarded as unlucky since they often had to get up at 4:00 A.M. to get to work on time.

Given these circumstances and attitudes, whether the bride was "lovely" was incidental. What was crucial was that she be acceptable to her mother-in-law, for she would have to live under the latter's tutelage and that she be healthy and strong, able to bear children and work alongside her husband, since he could not do all the farm work alone and ordinarily would not have enough money to hire a regular helper.

Down through the centuries no subject has seemed more important to the inhabitants of rural Europe than the inheritance and transfer of property. Though laws, regulations, and customs relating to inheritance have been almost infinitely varied from country to country and even within individual states, the peasant's main concern has always been to gain ownership of his land, to get rid of feudal dues, to pay off loans and mortgages, to work for himself rather than others, and to grow enough to feed his family and pay his taxes. Only then could he feel reasonably sure that his family would survive. This assured, his next concern was to pass his lands on to his heirs—ideally undivided, otherwise fragmented as little was possible. National governments, grand seigneurs, lesser landlords, and churches have generally liked inheritance systems and customs like primogeniture and entails that tend to keep estates together and to bar inheritance by stepchildren and bastards, for such arrangements make administration easier and provide more escheats for governments and churches. Sons of the Enlightenment and admirers of the American and French revolutions, though, are partisans of legal equality and so have usually preferred partible inheritance—equal or comparable division of family assets among all children. In nations or districts where partible inheritance is established by law, those with land to bequeath have devised every imaginable subterfuge to evade its intent and pass on their properties undivided. In practice, inheritance customs vary whether it is land, animals, or personal property being transferred; whether nobles or commoners are involved; whether the donor is a landowner, a sharecropper, or a tenant; whether the bequest is arable land or pastureland; whether or not compensation has to be paid by the heir to siblings and if so, what sort of compensation; and so on. All family planning has been heavily influenced by such considerations.[23]

German inheritance customs varied widely from one locality to another. Regional surveys and the compilation of law codes relating to inheritance usually tend to systematize whatever has previously been the custom in a given locality. Since such systematic surveys were not undertaken in Germany until the late nineteenth century, local customs before that time can only be conjectured, albeit with a high probability of general accuracy. The surveys indicated that, nationwide, primogeniture was more common in northeastern Germany and partible inheritance in the southwest and that the extremely numerous tiny holdings in states like Baden imply strongly that this condition had existed for a long time. Nonetheless, the innumerable local exceptions to these generalizations indicate that everywhere law and official arrangements had been bent to suit local exigencies and desires.[24]

Inheritance customs in and around Oberschopfheim were diverse. It was quite common there for an adult to marry the brother or sister of a dead spouse to avoid loss of property. When the man of the family died, his property ordinarily went to his children rather than to his widow. She usually received the right to use a room or two in the family house but little else. In some German villages one child was always wanted so parents might have someone to look after them in old age, but more than three children were regarded as undesirable because of equal inheritance laws or because of fear that a large family might need public assistance.[25] In early twentieth-century Oberschopfheim large families were common, partly because the village was Catholic, partly because many children died, and partly because many young people left the village. Inheritance customs varied even from one family to another, but whatever they were they affected every child in that family. Perhaps the commonest rule was primogeniture, though the other children were usually compensated in money by the new heir or, sometimes, had their education financed in lieu of an inheritance. Sometimes the heir was a younger child, even the youngest. Usually, whoever stayed on the farm and looked after the parents in their old age eventually got the farm, though he or she was always expected to compensate brothers and sisters appropriately—but not necessarily equally.

Just *when* property was transferred was a comparably complex—and perplexing—matter; doubly so in Oberschopfheim since land there was not plentiful, was high priced, and was nearly always inherited rather than purchased. If the land was to go to the youngest son, the parents were apt to be old by the time he was ready to marry and begin farming the family property, so transfer might take place easily. If the eldest son was to be the heir matters were more difficult. Centuries of hard experience had taught aging heads of households not to surrender their property lightly, for once their land was gone their prestige fell sharply in the eyes of all, and they were left at the mercy of heirs who often proved ungrateful. Consequently, a father tried to hang onto his property as long as he could. Yet he was apt to be no more than middle-aged when his eldest son was ready to marry and begin a new family. The son needed land, and his parents needed someone responsible to work the family farm competently if it was to support both their son's family and themselves in their latter years. This virtually compelled the father to make the transfer years earlier than he would have preferred. He usually did the best he could in the circumstances and had a legal document drawn up specifying precisely what he and his wife would retain for the rest of their days. Ordinarily, this included the right to a certain part of the house, milk from the best cow, and stated quantities of such commodities as wool, fruit, wheat, oats, and butter.

Inheritance became almost preternaturally complicated if one or both parents had been married more than once, especially if they had children from more than one marriage. Laws pertaining to the subject were legion all over Europe, and conflicts were endless. Many times heirs tried to cut Gordian knots by buying out brothers and sisters.[26] At other times or in other locales prospective heirs tried to persuade siblings to remain celibate and thereby prevent fragmentation of an estate.[27] Elders everywhere were inordinately concerned with "arranging" the marriages of younger people or widows, ostensibly to protect their morals but really to avoid alienation of family property and, if possible, to add to ancestral holdings.[28] All over old Europe most of the "better classes" thought of peasants as mean, stingy, avaricious people whose thoughts and plans revolved almost exclusively around the acquisition of land and money, particularly gold.[29] They seem never to have considered what had made so many peasants thus. It had been lifelong poverty and centuries of observing that the possession of land was the road to respect and security, compounded by many generations of hard dealing with relatives, neighbors, and especially with their supercilious "betters."

Winter provided only a slight respite from toil for families. Long winter evenings were often spent carving wood or spinning yarn for cloth, since the purchase of factory-made cloth did not become common before the 1870s. The necessary light was not provided by candles, for they were too expensive, but by wooden sticks or chicory sticks dipped in resin and lighted. Oil lamps eventually became available in the 1860s and electric lights about the time of the First World War. Perhaps most surprising to twentieth-century urban Americans, the villagers did not appear to mind their grinding regimen, though it is noteworthy that their late twentieth-century descendants have abandoned it when they have become able to do so.

In any case, toil was not wholly unrelieved. Sunday, after all, came once a week, and Sundays were supplemented by funerals, weddings, baptisms, and numerous feast days in honor of various saints. The last were usually combined with traditional festivals associated with planting, harvesting, and slaughtering animals. On most of these occasions there would be family gatherings or visits by relatives from neighboring villages followed by much feasting and drinking, in sharp contrast to the simple meals eaten during the rest of the year. The drinking was particularly enthusiastic. If someone had too much in a friend's house or in another village, little was thought of it. If the imbiber had a horse, it would know the way home. If he didn't, someone would help him.

To American teetotalers, or apostles of "moderation," early twentieth-century Oberschopfheim would have seemed like an outpost of Alcoholics Unanimous, for most of the population, even children, drank intermittently all day long. A common local saying was "water is for horses," and there were old people in the village who hardly knew the taste of water. Still, appearance was decidedly worse than reality. Most of what was consumed was beer and light wine, and most of it was soon "worked off" through manual labor. Drinking was simply an ingrained habit, by now centuries old. Most likely it originated from realization that drinking water often produced diseases. Alcohol also helped laboring peasants feel less wet and cold or reduced the pains of aching teeth and arthritis in a community that lacked serious medical facilities.[30]

By the nineteenth century, farmers were ordinarily able to grow most of the food they needed, to sell some, and to earn enough in some subsidiary occupation to support their families. In fact, oftentimes the "subsidiary" occupation became the primary source of support for a family and the cultivation of some labor-intensive crop merely a supplement. Until approximately 1800, the principal cash crop to be cultivated extensively for this purpose was grapes, which were made into wine. Then for about twenty years wine was superseded by chicory. Because the latter was difficult to grow, wash, and prepare for sale, however, as early as 1820 it was being displaced by tobacco. The popular reputation of tobacco, like that of coffee before it, varied erratically.[31]

When it was first introduced, suspicious villagers, like many other Europeans, maintained apprehensively that anyone exhaling smoke surely must be on fire, quite possibly possessed by the Devil as well. Some smokers were doused with water, others thrown in jail. Then public sentiment swung around abruptly, and the new plant acquired a reputation as a medical panacea. Ground and mixed with urine it became a matchless ointment to put on wounds. In liquid form it cured headaches, stomachaches, and toothaches. Chewed, sniffed, or smoked, it calmed the nerves. The smoke itself was alleged to ward off earaches; indubitably it warded off mosquitoes. Then, quite as abruptly, tobacco once more became a menace to public health when citizens who were addicted to nicotine but not to fastidiousness began to pick butts from open sewers and smoke them.[32]

As is so often the case when substantive or aesthetic judgments are divided, what carries the day is money. After 1860 small tobacco shops appeared in villages throughout Lahr county, though decades later most local tobacco was sold to outside wholesalers. By 1870 it had become clear to all that tobacco cultivation and work in cigar factories provided people an opportunity to earn cash with which to raise themselves from laborers and renters to landowners. One such was August Rinderle, the grandfather of one of these writers. He was made overseer of a cigar factory in 1890 and thereby became the first member of his family to advance economically and socially. It soon became equally evident to modern governments that taxes on tobacco were a painless and reliable source of considerable revenue.

Harvesting tobacco in Baden required much more labor than in the United States, where farmers merely cut the entire tobacco plant and hang it up to dry. German farmers harvested the leaves in three stages as they ripened. First came the lower leaves, the least valuable. They were used to make cigars that would be smoked locally. Then the middle leaves were harvested and finally the upper ones. At night families sewed individual leaves together according to category and hung them up to dry in barns. In 1867 eighty acres of tobacco were raised in Oberschopfheim, a figure that gradually fell to fifty acres in the twentieth century as other villages introduced tobacco and started cigar factories. Imposition of state and county production quotas followed. In the 1920s Oberschopfheim received 2 percent of the quota for Lahr county. The county, in turn, raised 25 percent of Baden's tobacco crop and 15 percent of the Reich's total.[33] From the 1890s cigarmaking was so much the leading industry in Oberschopfheim that the community was sometimes called "cigar village." By 1910 small "factories" employed 370 persons, 76 percent of whom were women. They comprised 60 percent of the total work force of the community. These "factories" were misnamed. None of them possessed any power machinery. Most were merely rooms in the owners' houses where employees were assembled to do handwork. The employers themselves were somewhat more prosperous than the average citizen of the village, but they were by no means tycoons. None lived in palatial homes or kept servants.

During the late nineteenth and twentieth centuries wine, mostly white wine, which had been used as a medium of exchange since Roman times, became an increasingly important cash crop once more. Superficially, it seemed the perfect crop for a region of tiny farms since a family could make a living from five to eight acres of good land planted to wine grapes, where several times that acreage was essential if it was planted to grain. Moreover, grapes did not require expensive machinery of any kind or even a horse. A hoe, a spade, and shears sufficed if supplemented by much careful hand labor the year round. Most of this could be supplied by a farmer's family.[34] By 1929 Oberschopfheim was the second largest producer of wine in Lahr county. Although the vineyard *acreage* had grown from 115 to about 150 since 1816, total production increased several times because of the growing use of fertilizers and insect sprays. Even so, grape growing remained far from an ideal pursuit. Farmers were perennially troubled by grape lice, soil erosion, and, in wet weather, mildew.

Like wine, fruit was another major crop dating from Roman times. In 1913 the village had 8,500 fruit trees, mostly apple, plum, and cherry. The entire county had over half a million trees, and Baden 11,500,000, by far the most of any state in Germany. Individual families ordinarily sold their best fruit and kept the rest, often disfigured by worms or other imperfections. The inferior fruit was canned or made into hard cider.

Other important crops in modern times were potatoes, barley, and rye. Taken together, they constituted the basic diet of most of the people. Since women had little time to cook, meals often consisted of one large pot of barley soup or boiled potatoes. This was served until the container was empty, several meals—or days—later. Families usually baked their own rye bread, making enough loaves to last about two weeks. The hard bread was dunked in hot milk for breakfast. The cultivation of rape (for oil), hemp, and wheat declined steadily, replaced by corn (maize) and sugar beets. The last two products provide more food value per acre for animals than does wheat.

Cattle raising gradually assumed some importance in Oberschopfheim, although it never rivaled conventional grain, fruit, or vegetable farming. The main reason appears to have been rooted in a quirk of rural psychology: the widespread belief that each village should emphasize one main activity. In the case of Oberschopfheim, village authorities in generations past had wanted their community to retain a pristine "farm" character and so had discouraged the raising of animals. An ordinance of 1766, for instance, had limited each farmer to two cows, one calf, two hogs, two sheep, and four geese. A day laborer was allowed even fewer animals. As time passed the rules became less restrictive. This led to a rise in the number of cows, calves, goats, hogs, and chickens and a rapid decline in geese and ducks. Horses were never numerous for the reason noted earlier: when only small plots of land were plowed, cows served as well as horses, ate less, and gave milk in the bargain.

Economic determinists would maintain that this explanation given for the effort to preserve Oberschopfheim's "farm character" is inadequate, that it must have been shortage of fodder or some other tangible condition that accounted for the attitude described. Of course that is possible, and fodder *was* generally in short supply before the nineteenth century, but it is also true that peasants often remain tenaciously attached to old ways when there is no longer a sufficient "reason" to remain so. Perhaps it merely raises once more the old question of whether all significant phenomena are shaped ultimately by economic factors or whether it is "ideas that rule the world" and eventually persuade us to alter our economic, political, and other practices.[35]

Oberschopfheimers also raised pigs and expended more labor on their charges than do American farmers. Like many other Europeans, villagers not only kept pigs in stalls next to the house from birth until death but cooked their food (chiefly potatoes) for them as well and in winter heated water for them to drink. This personal attention, which might seem grotesque to the uninitiated, had a sound purpose. Pigs treated so royally ate better, gained weight faster, and stayed healthier without medicine than if they were turned into an open field with only a makeshift shelter. When a new litter was due, solicitous families took turns camping in the stall all night to rescue each newborn piglet so it would not be mashed or eaten by its mother. A proverbial visitor from Mars, viewing the attention Oberschopfheimers lavished on their hogs and the patience with which they cut clover and carried it to their cows, might easily have concluded that on earth people existed to serve animals.

Families usually raised one or two pigs for their own meat. All over Germany and Austria, when the pampered porkers were ultimately slaughtered, parcels of fresh meat were commonly given away. Relatives and friends got some, portions were given to persons who might be helpful in the future, and a poor family might receive a share. Later, when those recipients who also raised hogs did their own slaughtering, they were expected to give back the same kind and amount of meat they had received. Sheer generosity had nothing to do with the matter since all the pertinent details in the exchanges were carefully noted on paper. It was, rather, something akin to long-term life insurance. Before the age of refrigeration it avoided loss of meat through spoilage, and it insured that everyone could have fresh pork at different times of the year.[36]

Besides farmers and cigar workers, some twenty different sorts of skilled laborers lived in Oberschopfheim. They were mainly holdovers from a bygone age. Before the onset of rapid industrialization about 1870 a higher proportion of Germans were trained artisans than was true of any other European people.[37] In the last third of the century whole categories of them (dyers, spinners, bleachers, and weavers, in particular)[38] simply disappeared or retreated to isolated backwaters like Oberschopfheim. Quite a few had no settled abode. They wandered about the countryside seeking work, along the way bringing much news to illiterate and semi-literate peasants. Not the least valuable of their services was to circulate information about suitable marriage partners among young people in other villages. By 1900 about fifty such craftsmen lived permanently in Ober-schopfheim, where they were controlled by local officials and served the needs of the community. Many such artisans were the fathers, grand-fathers, or great grandfathers of the factory workers of mid- and late-twentieth-century Germany.

Undoubtedly the most forlorn among such men had been poverty-stricken weavers. Before the twentieth century, bad times had been accepted as a normal part of existence, to which the individual was expected to make whatever adjustment he could. If one was poor he was supposed to seek help from relatives and not look to the community to support him. There were laws that forbade begging and others that required a man to support himself and his family or possibly face prison as an alternative. Municipal officials often refused to allow a man to marry unless he could demonstrate that he could support a wife and children.[39]

Such policies doubtless kept down the overall birthrate by delaying marriages, but in Baden and Bavaria it appears to have also stimulated illegitimacy.[40] Occasionally, in Oberschopfheim anyway, an indigent man who wished to marry would evade the economic roadblock by impregnat-ing his compliant fiancée. Much more commonly, a man would delay marriage until he had accumulated a little money, usually between the ages of twenty-five and forty. Then he would marry a woman who was perhaps a decade younger than himself. Many a weaver never escaped this dilemma at all and never became sufficiently affluent to marry.

All artisans had to join the Handworkers Association in Freiburg and Lahr and pay dues. They were also required to open and close their shops at specified times during the week and, except for the town barber, to close on Sundays and holidays.[41] The latter functionary was one of the most interesting figures in Oberschopfheim, for he was the last local representative of the medieval profession of barber-surgeon. His official duties were not confined to cutting hair and shaving the faces of his customers. He also treated wounds and, until 1915, pulled teeth.[42]

Small businessmen were also a sizable category of citizens. None of them could be called industrialists. One operator was a man from Ober-weier who married a woman from Oberschopfheim in 1901. Soon after, he started a sawmill, which is still operating nearly a century later. The rest were merely the keepers of some twenty little shops in the village, all locally owned. In addition there were five family inns (*Gasthaeuser*), two breweries, and one bank, also locally owned. Like everyone else in Ober-schopfheim, proprietors of these establishments were regimented. They had to join and pay dues to their associations and abide by state and local rules. Most of them made only a poor living, even in good times, for there were few commodities that could be sold to inhabitants who had a psychology of "doing without" and who had little money in any case. Even in prosperous times few families could afford such prices as 125 marks (nearly a month's wages) for a bicycle or 30 marks for a suit.

People who live all their lives packed close together in small rural villages inevitably develop many village bonds, tangible and intangible. Among the most important of these are common problems, worries, and suffering. In Old Europe, other bonds were induced by rulers—local, regional, or national.[43] Many others were the product of bad weather, insects, disease, or unhealthful conditions of life and employment.

In the cities of the world's "advanced" nations people seldom recall that from time immemorial not only the poor but often merely the rural inhabitants of the earth rarely had regular access to anything approximating professional medical treatment. Only occasionally did a doctor from Lahr or Offenburg visit an ailing school child or some dying person. Such "medical care" as villagers ordinarily received was whatever they were able to give each other, supervised in a general way by two nuns and a midwife.[44] Certain village women commanded special respect because they possessed unusual expertise in doctoring either people or animals. Oftentimes they had begun their quasi-medical careers as dairymaids. Here long and close association with cows had gradually sharpened their awareness of changes in the health and moods of their charges. One useful corollary of such knowledge was that the women often developed exceptional skill in handling cows in the field. Another was that they sometimes acquired a heightened sensitivity to human ills as well.

Generally speaking, though, association with farm animals did not promote human health. For European peasants to keep their domestic beasts adjacent to the family house with only a thin wall separating the two, unquestionably encouraged sociability but was hardly a boon to sanitation. Worse, farmers piled animal manure only a few feet from their front doors. While a village ordinance in Oberschopfheim required all families to clean the streets in front of their houses twice a week, the smelly heaps of offal produced a steady seepage of dirt and liquid manure into village streets and streams and attracted swarms of disease-bearing flies and mosquitoes.

Other circumstances of village life also produced ill health. Cirrhosis of the liver was common because of the high consumption of alcohol. Arthritis was endemic because of the everlasting dampness. Typhus epidemics broke out periodically because no one understood the connections among filth, germs, and disease. Undiagnosed food poisoning was common, just as it was everywhere in Europe before the modern age. Nobody knew anything about the body's need for iodine, hence many suffered from goiter. Many children had bad teeth or bad tonsils or both, and a few suffered from the effects of rheumatic fever. Many of all ages caught communicable diseases of various sorts merely from wearing the clothing of deceased sufferers. Such maladies as cancer, diabetes, and gall bladder troubles were common.

The tobacco industry produced much ill health apart from the effects of smoking. Workers stayed hunched over their benches from seven o'clock in the morning until six o'clock in the evening, breathing tobacco dust in small, unventilated rooms that at night served as bedrooms for the proprietor's family. As might be expected, many acquired tuberculosis, though according to official reports few died from it.[45] The malady did spread quickly, however, not only because it is quite contagious but because families lived in cramped quarters. It was not uncommon for several people, adults and children alike, to sleep in the same bed, a situation guaranteed to spread any communicable disease and a contributing factor to the high mortality among young children. Tuberculosis is also one of those diseases that afflicts humans and animals impartially, thus making it easy for each to infect the other. Since it was common among the livestock of peasants until the 1930s, many of Oberschopfheim's children must have acquired it from drinking the milk of tubercular cows.

Cigarmaking required considerable skill and a great deal of continuous hand labor that frequently produced chronic skin irritation. Cigarmakers rolled the cut tobacco and leaves with their fingers and palms, licked the leaves to keep their products from unraveling, and bit off the ends of the unfinished cigars. At times their hands and mouths became so swollen that they could not work.[46] After 1933 the Nazis cited the high incidence of tuberculosis, skin irritation, and other ailments in Oberschopfheim as a pretext to condemn the nuns who served as nurses, though their real motive was to replace the nuns with their own party equivalent, the "Brown Sisters" (NSV).

Overall, how lethal were all these maladies? One can only guess, for there are no statistics worthy of the name. Until late in the twentieth century there was no doctor in the village, so cause of death was set down only in general terms by some village official and no autopsies were performed. Because villagers had access to water from the streams that came out of the mountains, one might expect that they would have had fewer waterborne diseases than most Europeans—save that few of them drank much water anyway. On the average they were less pessimistic than South Italian peasants, but the gloom of the latter doubtless derived as much from bad government and a meager life generally as from high death rates. Infant mortality rates were certainly high but probably comparable to those in eighteenth- and nineteenth-century French villages, which were, in turn, comparable to those in twentieth-century India and Pakistan.[47] Old Oberschopfheimers say that deaths in the village from "fevers" were common before 1930. Beyond such vague indicators one cannot venture.

The relative prevalence of mental illnesses is similarly uncertain. Since there has never been an agreed-upon definition of what constitutes mental disorder and since statistics on the subject were not kept in times past, nobody can say for sure that mental aberrations were more or less common in Oberschopfheim than in other European communities, large or small. For the same reasons, nobody knows whether they used to be more prevalent than they are in the late twentieth century when increased knowledge and changed nomenclature have transformed many former "mental" disorders into physical diseases or "emotional" upsets. What is quite clear from village folklore and from ordinary observation in our century is that Oberschopfheim and nearby villages were plentifully endowed with "odd" (as distinguished from "nonconformist") human beings.

The condition is hardly surprising. The intermarriage of close relatives had been common for centuries. Until very recent times, too, pregnant women had routinely consumed alcoholic beverages, a practice now known to retard intelligence and to be physically harmful to fetuses. The wholesale use of arsenic sprays in the vineyards for decades probably had a similar malign effect on the users. Some men and women must have broken psychologically under nothing more complex than the strain of lifelong hard work. Fear of dying in childbirth undoubtedly destroyed some women psychologically at any time before World War II. Some people, especially women, were driven past the brink of sanity by being forced into marriages of misery from which there was no escape save by fleeing the village. How many? No one knows.

Until very recently Oberschopfheim had no treatment for mental disorders. Even if psychiatric services had been available in such a country village, most people could not have afforded them. Moreover, a strong stigma accompanied mental aberrations. They were commonly regarded as something one was "driven to" by other members of the household or something into which one had descended because of some secret sin or vice or punishment for violating the commonsense principles of seniority and reciprocity that prevailed in properly adjusted households.[48] Either way, it would have been an affront to a husband or relatives to suggest that a family member should be treated openly for mental illness.

Senility was not thought to be a physical disease but a social one—an indication of the habitual bad temper or persistent unsociability of the one afflicted.[49] Village idiots, commonly regarded as nature's mistakes, were often teased and mocked, though no one would admit this. Nonetheless, whether in Oberschopfheim or other villages, they were ordinarily looked after locally rather than dispatched to asylums.[50]

# 3

# MANAGEMENT OF THE VILLAGE

THOUGH GERMAN NATIONALISM seemed especially menacing to foreigners from 1864 to 1945, regionalism and particularism have been as evident in Germany as in other major countries. Germans from small towns and villages, like their counterparts elsewhere, have usually thought of their communities as "natural societies" and the state as a distant and artificial structure. In domestic matters ordinary Germans at all times have been governed more by state, county, and local officials than by national dignitaries in Berlin.[1] These local functionaries have generally considered their most important concerns to be keeping taxes down and defending village interests against all threats from outside.[2]

In Oberschopfheim official supervision of local life was detailed and minute.[3] Local governmental bodies *(Gemeinden)* ordinarily owned much farm and forest land, enjoyed subsoil rights, and usually provided for or supervised power and lighting systems, waterworks, education, building, local libraries, social assistance, and an array of cultural activities. Not for nothing was pre-1914 Germany called the world's most socialized nation. In Oberschopfheim the *Gemeinde* was overwhelmingly the largest village landowner. It owned all the forest in the mountains, half the wet meadows, all the village land that lay unused or was in roads, several municipal businesses, and some rental houses. It also regulated the use of all private property, whether the 157.5 acres of grapes in the foothills, the 1,207.5 acres of grain and tobacco in the valley, or the 120 acres of hay in the *Ried*,[4] and it regularly employed some fifty to sixty persons.

Not surprisingly, the *municipality* of Oberschopfheim was usually prosperous. Though there had been a decline since 1912, in 1929 it still had a net worth of almost a million marks. The *Gemeinde* had several sources of revenue. The largest came from the sale of timber for lumber and firewood, less from the sale of such commodities as fruit from the trees along the road, sandstone from a mountain quarry, village water and electricity, and even manure from the village barn. This was supplemented by the rental of hunting and fishing rights on all village lands and the collection of breeding fees for bulls and boars. The *Gemeinde* also owned a kindergarten daycare center, a grade school, a shed for the firewagon, and the bell tower of the church. Finally, it managed a county-owned factory that made soap from animal carcasses.

Besides ownership of these resources and control over these sources of income, the *Gemeinde* exerted a degree of control over the lives of its citizens that, in America, would have produced calls for revolution. Politically, it specified who could run for office and who could vote in local elections. In nonpolitical matters it directed associations and cooperatives for all general farm needs: the growing of tobacco, grapes, and fruit and the threshing of grain. Executive committees determined what crops each farmer could plant on his private lands and in what quantities, the dates for planting and harvest, where the resulting produce might be sold and often even the price of the products, as well as the work each person had to perform to keep up roads, forest trails, and village ditches. While every citizen had the right to take wood from the village forest, it was the forester who decided who got how much wood of a certain kind and quality and at what time.

Building regulations in the village were numerous, detailed, and strict. Nobody was allowed to build or alter a house merely because he wished to do so. He had first to hire architects or engineers to make detailed plans showing that the new or refurbished structure would be built correctly, in other words, that it would be the proper height and color and would otherwise harmonize with neighboring houses. Then he had to consult with local and county authorities, resolve any problems to their satisfaction, and secure the required permissions to build. The whole procedure usually required months, not infrequently a year or two.

Everything relating to the management of animals, even to the disposal of the corpses of dead ones, was specified with equally punctilious nicety. Owners had to obtain and keep up-to-date registration papers specifying the lineage and productivity of each cow and pig. They also had to report animal illnesses to the mayor, call the meat inspector before and after slaughtering any animal, follow regulations on the sale of milk, and pay a yearly water fee of two marks per cow. Though all these regulations and decisions were made not in Berlin but locally, usually by friends and neighbors, it is still obvious that such a longstanding tradition of governmental direction was ready-made for any collectivist political movement.

Obviously, too, in all these ways the *Gemeinde* had merely replaced the old medieval lord of the manor. Yet villagers accepted the system without demur. They were accustomed to it, and everyone understood that the regulations existed to even out sudden shifts in the quantity of needed commodities, to prevent price gouging, and to keep a few entrepreneurs from exploiting their fellows. Moreover, the village government was more democratic in reality than in appearance. It did not act arbitrarily, and it was ordinarily benevolent, at least in spirit. For instance, the most powerful governmental organ in the village was the *Gemeinderat* (inner council), whose members were elected. This body of five to eight citizens *looked* dictatorial since it issued ordinances, managed village finances, and made appointments to public jobs. Nonetheless, its members were restrained in their actions because they had to live and work beside those whom they ruled. As in most small, closely knit communities anywhere, the power of public opinion and the fear of local censure were more important constraints on unjust or unreasonable actions than anything written in law books.

The council members worked with the mayor. Together they appointed such officials as recorder, treasurer, policeman, two foresters, and half a dozen teachers, most of whom remained in office for many years, often until retirement. Though the pastor was not officially part of the political structure, he met with the *Gemeinderat* and other officials and enjoyed much influence in shaping their deliberations and decisions.

Second to the *Gemeinderat* in political power was the part-time mayor, who was elected independently for a nine-year term. Most mayors were farmers, though a cigar manufacturer named Beiser was mayor from 1918 to 1927. Mayoral elections were often hotly contested. That of 1927 was especially so. During the six weeks prior to the election the two candidates passed out free beer, tore down each other's posters, and otherwise inflamed the tempers of the villagers. The winner by a narrow margin was Wilhelm Einsele, who had been a farmer and tailor until he lost a thumb in World War I. Afterward he became a clerk in the village bank. After the heated campaign of 1927 many inhabitants said that local elections had grown too volatile to be held again safely, a view embraced by the Nazis in 1933 as a pretext to appoint their own mayor.[5]

No local mayor ever had an easy job. Einsele tried to maintain good relations with the *Gemeinderat* and to keep peace between Oberschopfheim and neighboring communities. He also tried to persuade his constituents to routinely accept decisions made by various village commissions. Of course any executive likes to see administration run smoothly. Newly elected officials also sometimes "feel their oats" and so dislike any opposition. In much of Europe, too, there has long been a general feeling among local notables that ordinary ignorant peasants should not question the judgment and decisions of their "natural betters."[6] Whatever Einsele's motivation, it did not impress his constituents. They usually blamed him for the misdeeds, or merely the unpopularity, of any village official. Moreover, since Oberschopfheimers were a litigious lot, at any given time it was a good bet that there would be court cases pending against the mayor, the village government, or some nearby community.[7]

Next in political power after the mayor were the leaders of commissions and cooperatives. The former had jurisdiction over rents, building permits, taxes, aid to the poor, and state insurance for buildings and cattle. Farm cooperatives specified certain days for farmers to clear ditches, prune fruit trees and grape vines, even to bring potato bugs to the courthouse as proof that they were controlling insects on their land. Nothing was too minute to escape the scrutiny of village Big Brothers, yet anyone who was dissatisfied could appeal their decisions.

The village court also exercised considerable authority in Oberschopfheim. Since major crimes were rare in German villages, municipal courts either in Oberschopfheim or elsewhere spent most of their time settling personal squabbles, trying to make reasonable adjustments in cases of property offenses, punishing minor misconduct of various sorts, imposing fines on those who disobeyed the orders of commission and cooperative leaders, and otherwise upholding local ordinances. In a typical year the village court fined twenty to fifty persons between one and fifteen marks each for such offenses as breaking night curfew, damaging a neighbor's crop by driving over his land, failing to come to Fire Fighter's practice, or merely making too much noise at night. Ordinary citizens served as juries.

The lowest tier in Oberschopfheim's political pyramid was the outer council, a group of forty-three elected members who ratified the decisions proposed by the inner council, especially those pertaining to the budget. This body was little more than an Acclamation Society—a miniature German version of the Supreme Soviet of the USSR.

Most of the routine chores of village life were managed by twelve to fifteen municipally appointed and paid officeholders. They were supplemented by some forty to fifty petty functionaries, most of them part-time, such as coroner, postman, midwife, village crier, gravedigger, chimney inspector, electric meter reader, and animal keeper. Perhaps the most interesting, though hardly the most essential, of these public servants were the two paid night watchmen, aided by four or more unpaid citizens, who were supposed to make the rounds of the village between 10:00 P.M. and 4:00 A.M. Village watchmen do not appear to have been truly satisfactory anywhere. Drunkenness on the job was a common fault among them in some communities,[8] and they seem to have been quite generally unable to prevent theft, particularly from the fields. Those in Oberschopfheim did not drink unduly but most of them disliked their duties. Moreover, all of them had already worked all day at other tasks. Consequently, when beset by the impulse to sleep on the job they seldom resisted. As a deterrent to thievery they were farcical.

Many historians have viewed the social and political structure of nineteenth- and twentieth-century Germany as highly authoritarian and class-ridden. While this was true of northern and eastern Germany and of

Bavaria, areas where primogeniture was common, it was much less evident in the southwest where generations of division of lands had markedly reduced differences among landowners and between small landowners and mere agricultural laborers.[9] In Oberschopfheim and other villages in Lahr county, "class" did not mean much. Some farmers were indubitably more prosperous than others either because they owned five acres when most of their neighbors had only three or simply because they were more accomplished husbandmen. Even so, this was not apparent to outsiders since village houses looked much alike. Moreover, everyone grew the same crops and so were affected in the same ways and to about the same degree by changes in commodity prices, the prices of seed or agricultural implements, or the interest rates on mortgages. They were closely linked by kinship, went to the same church, joined the same clubs, and shared the same experiences.[10] Some "side" occupations enjoyed greater prestige than others, but all occupational groups tended to be complementary rather than competitive. The only "large" landowner in the village was a Roederer. Though he was hardly a gargantuan land baron since he was the master of a mere eight acres, his worldly grandeur was amplified somewhat by the consideration that his son became the village recorder.[11]

In societies where ordinary people make it a central objective of life to outshine those who would otherwise be their equals, such matters as dressing more splendidly than peers or striving to be ostentatiously "modern" assume great importance.[12] Most Oberschopfheimers did not share this outlook. Before about 1960 most of them had one "good" suit or dress that was reserved for all public occasions. By and large, they believed they were quite as good as any of their fellows, and they refused to accord anyone, save the pastor, special rights or privileges. If anyone tried to "put on airs" there were unwritten and unspoken ways to put him in his proper place. Ordinarily, these were some combination of gossip and personal isolation. Since women did as much physical work in the fields and cigar factories (really craft shops) as men and since their labor was quite as essential for the family welfare as that of their husbands, within the family they were treated as equal partners, although the man was "boss" of the family publicly.[13]

Nevertheless, short of Heaven, equalitarianism has its limits. Minor differences existed, deriving from land ownership, job prestige, political authority, material possessions, or claims to ancient family lineage. As one might expect, the most respected persons in the village, after the pastor, were officials and businessmen in approximately the following order: *Gemeinderat* (members of the inner council), mayor, chairmen of the farm cooperatives, school principal, "factory" owners, recorder, treasurer, policemen, teachers, and foresters. These were also the highest paying positions in the village and were normally reserved for men.

In some communities, seats on the village council became virtually hereditary in "leading" families. In Kiebingen 87 percent of all village councillors between 1820 and 1940 were sons or sons-in-law of previous councillors. Of a total of seventy-two individuals who served on the municipal council in these four generations, only two were day laborers, factory workers, construction workers, or weavers, even though these "lower class" men and their families comprised two-thirds of the population. Until the 1860s "elite" families in Kiebingen married only among themselves.[14] Not so in Oberschopfheim. There, where economic differences were not great and where intermarriage among all inhabitants had been common for generations, most families had had a councillor or two among their ancestors at some time in the past.

Those who possessed lesser but still discernable prestige were members of the cooperative boards and leaders of the numerous village clubs. Those with the least were ordinary citizens and holders of low paying, unskilled jobs.[15]

In the Middle Ages, before modern nation-worship had dawned, the loyalties of most Europeans were local. They thought of themselves not as Germans, Frenchmen, or Italians but as Bavarians, Gascons, or Venetians, inhabitants of a particular province or town. As late as World War I this psychology was still marked. Russian peasant soldiers then thought of themselves as natives of Penza or Tambov who were also subjects of the czar.[16] Attitudes in Germany generally, and Oberschopfheim in particular, were similar. The sharpest social differentiation Oberschopfheimers made was between those who were citizens (*Buerger*) of the village and those who were not. Where Oberschopfheimers differed from many communities, near and far,[17] was that no effort was made to discourage applications for citizenship. An aspirant simply petitioned the *Gemeinde* and awaited developments. Applications were seldom rejected since the village needed the money that sale of citizenship brought. Once accepted, the new citizen could become a candidate for local office, vote in local elections, receive free firewood, use parts of common lands, and acquire eligibility for welfare if he needed it.

In 1929 resident male Oberschopfheimers over twenty-five years of age paid a one-time fee of six marks for village citizenship. An outsider, by contrast, even if a citizen of another community, had to pay over two hundred marks (about fifty days of common labor) if he wanted to become a citizen of Oberschopfheim. Because of the economic and political advantages involved, village citizenship was more important to inhabitants than was citizenship in the Reich. Despite the severe hardships occasioned by the Great Depression, nearly all native men purchased village citizenship. By contrast, only one newcomer did, agreeing in 1930 to pay no less than 330 marks on an installment basis. By 1933 Oberschopfheim listed almost three hundred men as citizens.[18]

Family name was occasionally invoked as a pretext for differentiating inhabitants. Roederer was the most prestigious. Roederers were descendants of a Freiherr whose mansion still stands two miles away. Back in 1648 the mayor, three out of six village judges, the town crier, the forester, and the sacristan had all been Roederers. This really did not count for much in the twentieth century though, since centuries of intermarriage had long since caused nearly everyone to become related to nearly everyone else. Thus anyone could allege, with some plausibility, almost any lineage he fancied. More important anyway was the prestige accruing to sheer longevity—the heavy hand of tradition. Anyone from the outer world who had become an Oberschopfheimer by marrying a resident of the village or who had moved in from elsewhere within the previous fifty to a hundred years was still considered an outsider.[19] Much more important than any of these picayune social differences was the essential solidarity of Oberschopfheimers: the pride all families took in their community *(Gemeinschaft)*.

In many German villages, clubs and interest groups were a source of discord for they were often linked to certain classes, causes, and ideological commitments. Thus one's own standing in the community or his philosophical orientation was often expressed by his membership, or lack of it, in some particular civic or recreational group.[20] This was not the case in Oberschopfheim, where social differences were small, nearly everyone was Catholic, and the vast majority of inhabitants faithfully supported one political party, the Center. Clubs were usually, though not always, a source of village unity.

Of these various groups *(Musikverein*, Military Club, Sport and Gym Club, *Gesangverein* or song club, and others) by far the most important was the ninety Free Fire Fighters, for they alone offered not recreation but security. Whenever a fire occurred it usually burned an appreciable part of the village because houses and hay barns were adjoining units, each of which provided fuel for a blaze starting in the other. All men over eighteen had to belong to the "Free" Fire Fighters, while middle-aged men helped as inactive members. When the church bell sounded, everyone from mayor to factory owners to children rushed to their preassigned jobs to protect the village. "Inactives" carried water in buckets from the village streams while "actives" pushed the fire wagon from the courthouse shed to the water reservoir nearest the fire. In these crises mutual dependence was crucial and total. Outside help was never a part of the plan of the village government since it would have to be paid. Besides, in an emergency it would be too far away to be effective. In addition to combating fires and practicing regularly, the fire fighters had a yearly outing of their own and showed up in uniform for other village festivals.

The Military Club was composed of veterans from previous wars. In the 1920s and 1930s four members were veterans of the Austro-Prussian War of 1866, thirty-four of the Franco-Prussian War of 1870, and about 350 of World War I. In 1890 at the village "Y" where the streams met, the club erected a war monument, which was enlarged in 1929 to include the names of the forty-five men who had died in the Great War. Every year on Memorial Day members joined other organizations with their flags at Mass. Whenever a member died the club fired a salute at the cemetery with the eight 1870 rifles they were allowed to possess. Unlike such clubs in many parts of Germany,[21] this one was not militaristic; it was, rather, a *Kameradschaft*, a group of men with a common experience and friendship who remembered the dead of the village.[22] Even the Nazis had little success in trying to make German nationalists out of these veterans.

Informal activities and customs also strengthened the bonds of unity in Oberschopfheim. While villagers would visit a *Gasthaus* in another village or in Lahr only rarely, the five *Gasthaeuser* in their own village were especially important as meeting places. In them each club had a special room with its flags, trophies, and pictures. Village commissions also met there. Not least, ordinary persons came there to talk business, to play cards, to visit, or to settle some personal disagreement over a glass of beer. *Gasthaeuser* were most patronized for dances, weddings, and Sunday morning *Fruehschoppen*, a drinking session after Mass, when the men discussed the sermon, the weather, and the crops.

Homes, on the other hand, were normally not open for social visits except to relatives from other villages. Families customarily visited each other only on New Year's Day to drink a toast to each other's health, at *Fasching* (Mardi Gras) to show off their homemade costumes, and in November to sample each other's new wine with *Zwiebelkuchen*, a dough resembling that of pizza with onions on top. Outside of these occasions, home visits were not appreciated—not even during a wake when families might come ostensibly to view the body but, according to some wives, really to inspect the cleanliness of the house. Nor were they welcomed at *Poltarabend*, the evening before a wedding, when the groom's friends would throw stacks of old plates on the steps of the groom's parents' house and demand free food and drink.[23]

Community solidarity was cemented somewhat by the local dialect, which was used in conversation. Each village had many words, expressions, songs, and axioms that differed from those of even nearby communities. When children first went to school they had difficulty learning a new language, *Hochdeutsch*, since they had never heard it before. Adults could always spot a stranger by his speech and felt more at ease speaking the local dialect with their neighbors than *Hochdeutsch* with outsiders. If an outsider spoke or acted unlike local people, this was accepted, but if a former resident came back for a visit, he was expected to speak in dialect. If he did not, he was criticized for being "snobbish." [24]

Peasants and manual laborers anywhere tend to have an ambivalent yet intensely "practical" attitude toward education. Generally, they prize physical strength above knowledge, yet they value education if they can see some immediate, tangible advantage accruing from it: a better job, a higher income, or a "better" marriage that will bring prestige to the family. [25] On this score Oberschopfheimers did not differ from their fellows in other lands or in other parts of Germany. [26] They also had an ideological reason to be suspicious of schools. Bismarck's *Kulturkampf* was still fresh in the memories of Catholic Germans before World War I. Thus, when secular authorities talked about educational reform, Catholic peasants raised their antennae immediately. The new proposal must surely be an attack on their traditional way of life, the forerunner of nondenominational schools, a threat to their use of their children for farm labor, or a malign scheme to raise the expectations of children unduly. [27] Thus Oberschopfheim's parents and officials might express pride in the existence of local schools, but they did little to encourage learning, and the council was always niggardly about appropriating money for education. Both parents and council had a far more liberal attitude toward support of a nursery-daycare center, since it freed more adults for manual labor. In 1929 Oberschopfheimers took pride in completing a new two-story nursery and residence for the local nuns who staffed it. [28]

In the nineteenth century the oldest children had gone to school from 6:00 A.M. to 8:00 A.M., younger ones from 8:00 A.M. to 10:00 A.M., and the smallest from 10:00 A.M. to noon. By the 1920s this had been extended somewhat. Then some 250 grade school children met daily from 8:00 A.M. until noon in an old building without lights or enough books or benches, while older children learned trades in separate rooms without much equipment. All village children attended basic grade school for four years. Then they proceeded to the "trade school" portion of the building to attempt to master some craft or occupation. Nobody received any further education unless he left the village. Yet some *did* leave to attend the *Gymnasium* (high school) or even a university so they could pursue careers elsewhere. In 1929 eleven such expatriates had become teachers, seven were priests, seven civil servants, four businessmen, and many others artisans. Several had obtained doctor's degrees. One had become president of the senate in Karlsruhe. When such emigré sons *did* make names for themselves elsewhere, they were invariably spoken of with pride by their kinsmen and neighbors back home.[29]

Early in the twentieth century, most of Oberschopfheim's adults still read little, though opportunities were available. In the late 1920s the pastor gave every family the diocesan newspaper and established a small library of about one hundred volumes. Unlike their mainly Lutheran counterparts in the much larger town of Thalburg,[30] Oberschopfheimers paid little attention to county newspapers. Some families subscribed to the Catholic newspaper, *Lahrer Anzeiger.* It included the pastor's periodic column about Oberschopfheim; news of the county, state, and world; serial novels; and a weekly section for farmers. The *Anzeiger* also defended all the activities of the Center party in Baden and the Reich and even showed readers how to mark their ballots. A few Lutheran families read the *Lahrer Zeitung*, which claimed to be politically independent but supported the German Nationalists. Most families could not afford a county newspaper, though they would sometimes read a copy in a *Gasthaus*. Likewise, few people had radios or the time to listen to them. Consequently, at any time before 1930 most villagers had only a limited and confused knowledge of the outside world. In contrast, many French peasants had become sufficiently aware of the larger external world by the 1870s that they had begun to evaluate politics and politicians ideologically.[31]

In this respect they differed little from their fellows elsewhere in rural Germany—or in rural areas in other lands, for that matter. In the late nineteenth century, there were many German farmers who, like their medieval ancestors, had never strayed more than a few miles from their birthplaces. Many rural women had never *seen* a town in their entire lives.[32]

Since the people of Oberschopfheim lived in such close proximity, secrets could hardly endure and gossip was endemic. People eagerly discussed the latest domestic or intramural quarrel, recent pregnancies, and news that the crier had proclaimed in the streets. Adults also awaited the mayor's announcements immediately following Sunday Mass. Here he explained governmental decisions that related to the village, announced punishments to be visited on troublemakers, and directed talebearers to apologize publicly for starting rumors.[33] The mayor's actions symbolized how the village had come to stand indeterminately between the Middle Ages and the modern world. In medieval times the announcements would have been made at the same time and place but by the priest.

In spite of its people sharing a commonality of heritage, religion, customs, outlook, even illnesses, Oberschopfheim was the scene of numberless petty conflicts and feuds, though, as in so much else, it is impossi-

ble to say whether these exceeded the norm among other Germans, other
Europeans, the poor of any nationality, or the whole Western world. What
is clear is that, apart from the habitual contentiousness of humanity,
circumstances contributed much to the frequency of village squabbling.
Frequent and detailed decisions by the village government, though ordinarily made with care and with a regard for equity, necessarily affected
the wealth, status, and freedom of virtually every person and so provoked
endless jealousy and acrimony. Perhaps even more fundamentally, everyone lived and worked so close to everyone else that personal friction never
had a chance to abate. As for specific causes of specific quarrels, more
involved property rights than anything else. One neighbor would accuse
another of such a misdemeanor as moving a property marker in a field,
driving over another's land, or moving a gate too close to someone else's
property line. Squabbles also developed over such momentous matters as
stealing firewood, rolling cigars too slowly, or even calling someone's wife
an "old bag." Injured parties often seemed to positively relish taking of-
fending neighbors to the village court *(Ortsgericht)*. One reason was merely
that it cost them nothing. Another may have been that if derogatory gossip
about someone persisted without the injured party demanding redress in
court, most people would assume that the victim must be guilty.[34] During
1929 alone, in a population of only sixteen hundred, more than fifty such
cases came to the local court for judgment.[35]

Club life was marked by conflict too. For instance, from its foundation
in 1927, the Young Men's Club was divided between those who wanted it to
be strictly a soccer club and others, including the pastor, who wanted the
club also to present religious plays, to hold monthly communions, and to
keep a statue of St. Bernhard in their *Gasthaus* room. The quarrel was so
violent that the club eventually disbanded. Two years passed before the
majority agreed to reestablish it with two separate leaders and programs.[36]

Like their fellows all over rural Europe, Oberschopfheimers were
mistrustful of the outside world. Some of this reflected mere peasant
ignorance, but most was the fruit of centuries of hard experience. Mistrust
was most extreme in the lands around the Mediterranean where economic
and social isolation from the urban world has been most pronounced until
well into the twentieth century. Mid-century Greek shepherds, for instance, looked only to their kinsmen for sympathy and support. The rest
of humanity they regarded as opponents of various sorts, self-seekers of
every type who would act only to benefit *their own* families and so were
never to be trusted.[37] Oberschopfheimers would concur to a degree: they
would trust relatives before anyone else but would also regard their fellow
villagers with general warmth and respect. Andalusian mountaineers so
valued the esteem of their neighbors that they would go to neighboring

villages to commit crimes and would attribute all sorts of character defects and bad conduct to those in the next town rather than to those in their own.[38] Oberschopfheimers would sometimes display this mind-set to the extent that they would go to a nearby village to get drunk, but they did not pretend even to themselves that vices existed only elsewhere. Isolated Sicilian and South Italian peasants often evinced an attitude that one scholar calls "campanilismo," an unarticulated but habitual and pronounced disinterest in anything that occurred beyond the sound of the village church bell (around 25,000 acres).[39] Oberschopfheimers were not *this* insular. They had been marketing their chicory, tobacco, wine, and lesser products for several generations, after all, and so had acquired at least a limited knowledge of the ways of the outside world and some interest in it.

The agents of governments raised the hackles of most Oberschopfheimers faster than did any other outsiders, but even here they never positively hated governments as did so many Russian peasants who had been victims of centuries of relentless despotism.[40] Rather, they disliked governments for the same reasons peasants had always done so nearly everywhere. Governments cared for common farmers only to load them with unjust or burdensome taxes, to take their crops, to interfere with their religious practices, and to conscript their men into armies—often in the middle of the summer when they were most needed for harvesting.[41] Nearly as bad, distant governments were always avid to punish somebody for violating some sweeping, impersonal ordinance. Most peasants valued custom above law in the first place and in particular cases usually wanted to consider circumstances, to repair damages to interpersonal relationships, and to restore community harmony rather than to vindicate some general ordinance and call it "justice."[42] Of their village leaders, those they prized most were those who were most vigilant and successful in defending local interests against outside meddlers.[43]

In normal times the attitude of Oberschopfheimers was not unlike that of Russian peasants during the early Bolshevik years: they wanted not domination by old czarist landlords, not domination by new Red zealots, but simply to be left alone. A typical "oldtimer" from early twentieth-century Oberschopfheim might have added, "All I want from the rest of the world is a market for my excess produce." To be sure, during crises this attitude moderated markedly. At such times Oberschopfheimers did look to the county, state, and national governments for aid and protection, which they regarded as due them for years of obedience and taxpaying. Since rulers seldom had the same table of priorities as their rural subjects, Oberschopfheimers were habitually discontented with their secular superiors and periodically involved in verbal and legal battles with officials in

Lahr and Karlsruhe. During state and national election campaigns they indicated their mixture of resentment and disdain by rarely attending political meetings in other communities or inviting speakers into their village.

Outside politics, there was usually some half-plausible reason to dislike or mistrust certain categories of humanity. Beggars were held in low regard because villagers believed each man had a duty to provide for himself and his family. Gypsies were detested everywhere as thieving liars.[44] Socialists were disapproved because of their official atheism and feared because they talked about nationalizing the land. Army officers were not exactly disliked but were looked at askance because they maneuvered troops nearby. The troops were almost invariably accompanied by many horses, who were believed to spread hoof-and-mouth disease. Veterinary surgeons wore top hats and kid gloves, mouthed Latin phrases, and charged high prices. Representatives of agricultural associations also were addicted to Latin words and chemical formulae. They held tiresome meetings that never seemed to have any relevance to what real farmers did or needed. The whole lot of them, along with arrogant officials, landlords' agents, tax collectors, grain dealers, traveling salesmen, distant financial manipulators, and Jewish peddlers preyed on productive peasants while scorning their way of life. They were all pernicious "outsiders," representatives of the evil side of cities and governments, the personification of that amalgam of financial unscrupulousness, administrative caprice, and condescension that the country man is so quick to detect—or imagine—in the urban man.[45]

The Jews were a special case. They had dwelt throughout Baden for centuries. Beginning in 1807 and continuing at irregular intervals for more than a century, the medieval restrictions that had been laid on them were gradually lifted. They were finally made equal to other citizens by the Weimar constitution of 1919. In 1900 Jews constituted 1.4 percent of the population of Baden, though this number fell off somewhat by 1930. They were concentrated in the cities of Karlsruhe, Mannheim, and Freiburg. In Lahr county there were communities of Jews in Friesenheim and other villages near Oberschopfheim, though none in Oberschopfheim itself. Most of them earned their livelihood as petty merchants, traders, and animal sellers, though some Jewish communities produced impressive numbers of lawyers, doctors, dentists, and teachers.[46]

Oberschopfheimers generally disliked Jews *not primarily because they were Jews* but because there were set prices for most commodities in stores throughout Germany and peasants hated to spend hours haggling with some wandering peddler over the price of a cow or a milk can, especially when the adversary was a more experienced and skilled bargainer. The last was significant. Oberschopfheimers found many categories of people repugnant, yet their animosities were all qualified. Nobody in the village ever urged that Jews, socialists, gypsies, or any other unloved aggregation of humanity be exterminated. The very ignorance and insularity of Oberschopfheimers at least immunized them against some of the ideological poisons of modern times and made them unpromising human material for Nazi purveyors of militarism and anti-Semitism.

Since 1914 it has frequently been charged both by historians and by polemicists that Germany has been the premier "outlaw state" of modern times—persistently militaristic, aggressive, harsh, and domineering.[47] While this thesis has undeniable plausibility for certain sectors of German society, many middle and upper class Germans, many major figures in the world of intellect and the arts, have never shown much interest in politics.[48] The charge is equally wide of the mark if directed toward the insular, tradition-bound peasants and laborers of Oberschopfheim and a thousand other German rural villages. If queried about some international issue before 1914 an Oberschopfheimer would have been likely to shrug his shoulders and remark, "Die grosse Politik ist dumm," a belief that became fixed during the postwar turmoil and economic catastrophes of the early 1920s. Villagers thought little about the German people or the nation and much about themselves, their families, relatives, neighbors, lands, and animals. If such unconcern for "big issues" constitutes lack of political wisdom, by itself not beyond debate, it is well to recall that comparable folly has been repeatedly demonstrated by Frenchmen, Englishmen, Italians, Russians, Americans, Japanese, and virtually any other people who have an extended national history.[49]

To summarize: centuries of contending with floods, famine, pestilence, war, governmental exploitation, and religious rivalry had led the villagers to develop a set of economic, social, and political structures and a defensive mentality that changed little. Religiously homogenous and inhabited by people who were intensely self-centered and suspicious of the outside world, at the turn of the twentieth century Oberschopfheim was still essentially a medieval village. The storms of our savage and revolutionary age were to shake it to its foundations.

# 4

# WORLD WAR I
# AND ITS AFTERMATH

IN 1914 the last European war that had gone on for years had been the series of protracted conflicts of the French revolutionary and Napoleonic era, 1792-1815. Newspaper pictures and film clips from the great cities of all the major European powers in late July and early August 1914 show cheering, flag-waving crowds of civilians surrounding masses of smiling soldiers marching off to war. A mixture of expansive patriotism, thirst for adventure, and relief from the monotony of ordinary existence had produced an atmosphere reminiscent of that at the proclamation of the First Crusade in 1095.

This mass emotional debauch, though real, was misleading since it was far more evident in cities than in the countryside. So lacking in both interest in and knowledge of the outer world were so many European peasants in ages past that, for instance, even though the whole French people were supposed to be burning to reverse the verdict of the Franco-Prussian War of 1870-1871 and regain the "lost provinces" of Alsace and Lorraine, six out of ten recruits in a French cavalry squadron in 1901 had never heard of the Franco-Prussian War.[1]

Martial zeal was comparably tepid throughout rural Lahr county. It was not that ordinary love of one's country and deference to one's rulers did not exist there. Nor did reluctance to go to war, on the part of Oberschopf-heimers anyway, spring from the dislike of Catholic South Germans for the militarism, brusque ways, and high taxes of Protestant Prussia, whose troops had occupied the area in 1848. Rather it sprang from historical memories whose roots were far deeper than the political events of the nineteenth century or the nationalist passions that engulfed Europeans in that era. Peasants have always been the anvils on which marauding armies have pounded. The villagers had long been fearful of war, and when it came in 1914 they accepted it with the same dour fatalism their ancestors had displayed during comparable calamities in ages past. Few of them knew anything worth mentioning about German national objectives in the war or the strategy that would, or should, be pursued to attain them. They merely trusted higher authorities and followed orders, comforting themselves with the thought—according to taste—that their leaders knew best or that it was all God's Will.

In the first days of the war numerous reservists from Oberschopfheim and neighboring villages were called up for duty. The drafting of 403 able-bodied men followed soon after. At no time in Oberschopfheim were there any demonstrations or protests against the war or against service in it, not even during 1917-1918 when the socialists in German cities belatedly remembered the antiwar principles they had so lightly cast aside in the intoxicating days of August 1914. Most villagers went into the infantry where they fought alongside their relatives, friends, and neighbors, as their fathers and grandfathers had done before them in 1866 and 1870. Nearly all served on the Western rather than the Eastern Front. As soldiers they were, overall, routinely loyal and routinely competent. No one from Oberschopfheim or nearby villages rose to high rank or was celebrated as a war hero, but none deserted either. When the war was over people back home treated veterans with respect and, as elsewhere in Germany, went to considerable expense to erect a monument to the forty-five of their fathers, brothers, sons, and husbands who had died. Seven of the dead were buried in Oberschopfheim. Of the other thirty-eight, most were interred in cemeteries in France. In a few cases, bodies were never found. A fighter pilot from a village some thirty miles away was held in high esteem as a war hero, though the main reason for this was not the brilliance of his personal exploits but the mere fact that he was a *pilot*. In 1914-1918 airplanes had been in existence for only a decade and were still regarded popularly with considerable wonder.

There is no indication that the populace feared invasion in 1914. Women and small children stayed in the village throughout the war, whereas in World War II they were moved deep into the Black Forest from fear of Allied bombing or invasion. No place in Lahr county was bombed in 1914-1918, and no fighting took place there. At various times during the war villagers could hear cannon fire from the Western Front and see airplanes and dirigibles overhead, all of which was quite exciting, especially to the young. Now, in the closing decades of the twentieth century, when the only people alive in Oberschopfheim who remember the Great War are a few graybeards who were children in 1914, they say that the airships and artillery fire are their main memories of the conflict. All deny ever hearing their elders tell stories about the horrors of service on the Western Front.

Psychologically, the heaviest burden Oberschopfheimers bore during the conflict was its uncertainty. Local newspapers printed little about military operations beyond conventional government claims of "successes" and "progress." Berlin did not even tell the public who was still alive and who had been killed. Letters sometimes came from men at the front but they were heavily censored. About all civilians could do was pray that someday their menfolk would return. They prayed a lot and kept fresh flowers at the feet of village statues. As for the men themselves, most came home on furloughs two or three times, but since all were common soldiers none knew much about how the war was going outside his immediate sector. Some, including the grandfather of one of these writers, August Rinderle, were captured and put to cutting stone or doing similar work in French prisoner of war camps. An occasional postcard would come from such a prisoner, embellished with a preprinted message to the effect that the sender was in good health and good spirits but with no indication of when he had been captured or how long he would be held. Some were not released until two years after the Armistice. When the fighting stopped those soldiers from Oberschopfheim and elsewhere who were still alive and able to walk and who were not inmates of some Allied prison camp simply formed groups and walked home, which was, after all, not a vast distance from the Western Front. Whenever they passed through a town or village along the way people rushed out to see if someone from their own locale was in the troop or to ask if anyone knew whether such-and-such a man was still alive.

Materially, the heaviest burden of the war for those who stayed behind in Oberschopfheim was the wholesale disruption of the rhythm of village life by the departure of the men and the imposition of government economic controls. The years before 1914 had been the best times ever for local farmers before the 1950s.[2] Most families had come to own their own land and were not in debt. Few needed to hire laborers to supplement family workers. The main cash crop of most families was tobacco, supplemented by the sale of small amounts of fruit and wine. Enough grain, mostly wheat and rye, was grown to feed a family and its animals. Few attempted to raise grain for sale.

The outbreak of war, however, immediately created dilemmas from which there was no escape. Some of them existed merely in the nature of things, but many sprang from the failure of the prewar German government to carefully think out some system to ensure an equitable division of scarce necessities among consumers while assuring fair rewards to producers. The reason for this was that Kaiser Wilhelm II's military and civilian experts were, like almost all those in the other belligerent nations, convinced that modern weapons would bring military decisions so quickly that such economic and social planning would be pointless.[3] When it became clear that the war would last much longer than had been anticipated, Berlin's efforts to devise nationwide economic controls were hasty, haphazard, sometimes unreasonable, and easily evaded. A generation later, in World War II, the blunders of 1914-1918 were heeded sufficiently that the Third Reich was able to manage its food problem more efficiently.

In 1914, Berlin, understandably, wanted to increase national grain production, but all its actions necessarily militated against attainment of this objective. To start with, most of the young and middle-aged men, the most productive workers, were taken into the army. Then young boys from twelve to sixteen were called up to do a great variety of war work, most notably running trains and loading their cargoes. This left only women, a few old men, small children, and a few semi-invalids to do all the agricultural work previously done by entire families. Of course considerable farm work has always been done by women in virtually every part of the world. Children and the elderly have customarily helped too. One thinks immediately of simple sewing, cooking, and housecleaning, feeding chickens and farm animals, cleaning barns, caring for vegetable gardens, picking fruit, certain tasks in the tobacco business, even light field labor. Even so, the limitations involved are obvious.

Efforts were made to keep up food production by such expedients as deferring some farmers, persuading men home on leave to work on their own farms or those of neighbors, importing foreign workers, impressing prisoners of war, and assigning unemployed young people to farm work. Most of the farmers thought the urban young people were either so weak or so lacking in incentive that they were hardly worth having[4] and that the prisoners were little better.

Loss of work animals was, if anything, more grievous than the general absence of men. When the war began, one of the army's most pressing needs was for horses, so the government seized the best ones everywhere. Compensation was paid to the owners, of course, but the act itself deprived many peasants of their best draft animals. Worse, if anything, was the intangible aspect of the matter. Farmers who feed and work their animals, even talk to them, virtually every day, usually become closely attached to them as individuals. To know that in the army a beloved family horse would be worked mercilessly, probably fed badly, and then, if it was injured or ailing, simply shot, was heartbreaking to many a peasant family.

This particular blow was lighter in Oberschopfheim than in most agricultural parts of Germany because most villagers plowed with cows. Nevertheless some of the more prosperous peasant families had purchased horses, and there were about fifty of them in the village in 1913. In 1919 only ten remained.[5] Losing the horses meant that on many a peasant plot, in Oberschopfheim and elsewhere, one often saw several women pulling a plow guided by another woman. Inevitably, production plummeted and many families shifted from raising grain to growing hay or simply using the land for pasture, both of which were less labor intensive.

As soon as the war was well underway Berlin realized the need to keep up food production, to forestall hoarding, and to make sure city people were fed. This practical necessity collided head-on with a permanent fact of rural life: the peasant never lived who truly believed that government regulation of his activities was designed to benefit him rather than rulers, bureaucrats, or urban parasites.

A whole series of government edicts followed. They set maximum prices for farm products at levels below those of the free market of 1913 and required farmers to surrender fixed quantities of eggs, milk, meat, and grain at those prices. This meant that farmers would now be deprived of much of the food they had previously raised to feed their own families and their livestock. Naturally, they were resentful; doubly so because the regulations had been imposed piecemeal, according to no overall plan, obviously in mere response to urban clamor for more food at lower prices. The farmers' response was utterly predictable: wholesale evasion.

To point this out is not to cast special opprobrium on farmers. Every adult in the Western world with any knowledge of public affairs is well aware that people of a hundred professions and occupations, scattered all over the globe, wallow in political corruption, tax evasion, commercial chicanery, legal obfuscation, and general abuse of the public interest for their own benefit. If the sharp practices of farmers are emphasized in this book it is because the book is primarily about farmers and not about business corporations, labor unions, government officials, lawyers—or academicians for that matter. Indeed many such groups frequently connive *together.*

In wartime Germany, Berlin replied to rural evasion of government edicts with more directives forbidding the feeding of grain or potatoes to animals. Of course the grain was needed for human food, but animals that are worked must have some grain to supplement the rest of their diet, or they toil poorly and often grow sick. Pork was the principal meat consumed by most Germans, especially peasants. Just what pigs were supposed to thrive on if denied both grain and potatoes was never made clear. The Gordian knot was cut in 1915 by slaughtering about two-thirds of the pigs in Germany, thereby irrevocably reducing the supply of much-needed fats for everyone.

The proverbial salt was poured in this wound when it was soon discovered that stores of potatoes existed in sufficient quantity to have fed both pigs and people for a considerable period.[6] Peasants were left for the remainder of the war in a state of mingled wonder and outrage: unable to secure feed for their remaining pigs but ordered not to kill any more without permission, then tarred with charges of lacking patriotism if they tried to give up pig-raising altogether.

Equally understandable, and equally quixotic, was another government regulation requiring farmers who took grain to be milled to pay the miller in cash. Formerly, farmers had paid the miller by giving him a percentage of the milled grain, in return for which he gave back to them the hulls from all the grain for pig feed. Now, forbidden to pay the millers with a share of the grain, usually unable to pay them in cash and often so short of grain to start with that their wives were driven to mix potatoes with it to make bread for their families, farmers seemed hopelessly trapped. Not so. Matters grew worse! As the war lengthened the grain shortage grew so acute that even grain *hulls* were added to the breadstuff, thereby depriving pigs of still another source of nourishment.

Of course all these problems were circular. Butchering some animals and underfeeding the rest deprived people of needed food and resulted in less animal manure for fertilizer. This reduced crop yields and caused deterioration of the soil, all of which was progressively aggravated by farm machinery wearing out and by the continuing labor shortage.

These intractable farm problems, which were never really solved, would have been sufficiently vexatious had peasants and city people esteemed each other, cooperated willingly, and sacrificed together. But they did not. Most peasants regard country life as innately superior to that in cities, and agriculture as honest, strenuous wrestling with nature in contrast to the basically mercenary character of commerce. City dwellers they view as shallow, superficial people who live by cleverness, trickery, and exploitation of those on whom they depend for food. Urbanites even lack gratitude toward their benefactors, scorning the latter as coarse, stupid, ignorant, spiteful and miserly. Peasants, consequently, have displayed a "reflexive hostility" 7 toward urbanites for "the peasant knows he can never really count on a city man."8

German socialists made the situation worse. As a historical phenomenon, the rise of socialism in the nineteenth century was an urban response to an urban problem: the social and economic dislocations caused by industrialism. Socialists nearly always came from cities. Many of their leaders came from a distinctly urban people, the Jews. Few of them understood agriculture or esteemed rural life. Now they griped bitterly about "greedy rural hoarders" and "black marketeers" who cared nothing for the national welfare and who starved the cities as surely as did the British blockade.

Their complaints were not without substance. Peasants *did* underreport harvest yields, they *did* plant more acres than officially allowed to grow crops that brought high prices, they *did* hide or hold back foodstuffs when they could, and they *did* stretch their imaginations to help themselves rather than strangers in cities. By 1918, 75 percent of the milk produced in Germany disappeared on the black market. In 1917-1918, three hundred thousand cattle and one million hogs disappeared without a trace after being purchased by the official meat distribution agency in the Rhineland.[9] No wonder socialists clamored for the government to force more and more contributions from farmers at artificially low prices to feed the cities! It was equally unsurprising that peasants, who found it easy to sell any kind of food at high prices on the black market, should have concluded that consumers were lying when they pleaded inability to pay higher *legal* prices for rationed food. To the exhausted women of Oberschopfheim, who had to pull plows in the field, run the cigar industry, and spend one day a week merely doing the laundry, all with only old men and children for help, these urban prattlers were merely the same old bureaucrats and busybodies who had vexed working farmers through the ages.

By 1917 government agents were searching farms for contraband. In their zeal they went into every room in the houses, even the bedrooms. This action reaped far more peasant resentment and bitterness than it did additional food. The result, overall, was that the state emerged discredited. Its regulations were flouted everywhere, and it was accused by producers of favoring consumers and by the consumers of kowtowing to producers.[10] Little wonder that antagonism between city and countryside became venomous in Germany during the Great War or that afterward innumerable peasants in small villages like Oberschopfheim would readily believe nationalist claims that the socialists had lost the war and now wanted to nationalize farmers' lands. It was rare to find an informed, convinced socialist in a German village before 1950.

Most history books are written by people born and bred in cities. Those that deal with wartime Germany usually say that farmers did not fare too badly. Perhaps they didn't, compared to their city cousins, especially during the "turnip winter" of 1917-1918 but, withal, it was a time of hardship for them both materially and psychologically. Their attitude toward their relatives in nearby cities like Lahr and Karlsruhe was ambivalent. The latter, who were often hungry and who frequently could not buy either coal or firewood late in the war, would come to a village like Oberschopfheim to beg for food or offer to trade some of their possessions for it. The villagers, who got free firewood and could raise some vegetables for food, were better off and knew it. Sometimes they pitied their hapless kinsmen; sometimes they resented them, especially if the urbanites were the sort who had "lived high" before the war.

Though Oberschopfheimers detested their government's economic regulations during and after the war, there was little public complaint about military decisions made in Berlin. But neither was there any feeling of personal responsibility for whatever resulted from those decisions.

Deferential to authority as ever, they considered it their duty simply to follow orders. Likewise, nobody wept when Wilhelm II fled into exile in 1918, though a few years later, when the Weimar Republic had grown unpopular, it was common to hear middle-aged or elderly villagers speak nostalgically of the departed kaiser and to lament how much better times had been when he had been on the throne. Even the Treaty of Versailles, which evoked so much hatred and bitterness throughout most of Germany, stirred little emotion in Oberschopfheim save to freshen rooted dislike of the French. This was stimulated anew in 1923 when the French moved an army of occupation into the Ruhr in a futile endeavor to compel Germany to pay war reparations. Though no French soldiers were actually stationed in Oberschopfheim, they were in Offenburg, only eight miles away. Since they were the first foreign troops to appear on German soil since the Napoleonic wars their presence called to mind the tales of grandparents and great-grandparents about French and Russian atrocities more than a century earlier.

For Oberschopfheimers who were teenagers or young adults in 1914, the decades from 1914 to 1933 always seemed like lost years, a time of perpetual uncertainty, the end of which no one could foresee. For war veterans the unsettlement and turmoil was moderated a bit, at least on the social level, by the formation of their own organization, which held regular meetings of village veterans or with those of neighboring villages. After World War II such meetings were quite different. Then they drew men from all over the country, reflecting a changed military policy under the Nazis of scattering men from any one locality throughout the armed services rather than keeping them together with their friends and neighbors in single units. For the women, whether those who remained unmarried, the widows who did not remarry, or those who lacked land or money and so often had to defer marriage to their late thirties, it seemed that fate had cheated them, that they were doomed all their days to a regimen of monotony, loneliness, grinding farm work, and declining health. Decades later, in the 1960s, by then long since grown old but still milking cows, slopping hogs, and toiling at the traditional chores that young people would no longer do, these women (and some men) often complained bitterly about the hardness and emptiness of life and the laziness and irresponsibility of modern youth.

The immediate postwar years seemed especially sour. In the last months of 1918 and for several months into 1919 much of the world was scourged by a massive influenza epidemic that certainly took as many lives as had been lost in combat in the most lethal of all humanity's wars up to that time and may have killed as many as 50 million people.[11] In Oberschopfheim and neighboring villages this catastrophe was accompanied by an additional epidemic of diphtheria. The two disasters together killed perhaps twice as many people as had died in combat. So contagious were the maladies that neighbors were often afraid to help the dying.

Some of the bad memories were occasioned by a local depression that followed the annexation of Alsace by France in 1919. On the surface, the loss of Alsace might have seemed positively beneficial since a few industries moved from Strasbourg across the Rhine to towns in Baden, the most notable of which was a peppermint factory that was relocated in Offenburg. The stronger tendency, however, was in the opposite direction. The rupture of fifty-year-old ties with Alsace threw Baden's economy into a tailspin. Over 80 percent of the industries in Lahr county in such areas as leather goods, paper, textiles, metalwork, lumber, and stone were seriously damaged. Most of them lost a quarter to a half of their sales.[12] This slump was accentuated by Allied disarmament of Germany and the consequent closing of the military garrisons at Lahr and Offenburg. Those few Oberschopfheimers who had industrial jobs lost them as nearby city factories closed, operated with mere skeleton crews, or gave jobs only to war veterans.

To peasants, however, the most hotly resented of all their burdens was continuation of the wartime economic controls by the early governments of the Weimar Republic. To be sure, Weimar had its reasons. Foremost was fear of the spread of Bolshevism. Nonetheless, farmers throughout Germany were outraged. They were still being ordered around by urban socialists who kowtowed to workers and consumers and still compelled to deliver quotas of grain and other commodities without consideration for their own costs of production. They wrote letters of protest to national authorities, who merely forwarded the complaints back to local officials. Occasionally they staged brief producers' strikes. Always they sold all they could on the black market and blamed all their troubles on the nation's new government. Socialist and Communist newspapers replied with denunciations of farmers who sought "to starve the cities." Some even longed in print for "the days of Wallenstein" when "greedy peasants" were simply "struck dead if they wouldn't deliver."[13]

Direct controls on the sale and distribution of meat were at last lifted late in 1920, on milk in the spring of 1921, on other foods only during the currency collapse of late 1923. Nonetheless, the crux of the situation had always been psychological. It was the mere existence of the controls that had been most resented.

The terrible inflation of 1922-1923 has been described innumerable times. Superficially, it appeared to benefit farmers since prices for their commodities soared wildly while foreign competitors shied away from the rapidly depreciating mark. Peasants could also pay their debts in increasingly worthless paper money. But the gains were illusory since the prices of whatever farmers purchased rose even more ludicrously than those of what they sold, while the uncontrolled inflation made it difficult to obtain credit. Worst of all was the general psychological malaise engendered.

Historians and economists have long debated the issue of responsibility for the inflation, some blaming Allied postwar policies, others the action of Weimar governments, still others pointing to similar inflations in Austria and Hungary and shrugging off all of them as merely part of the price of losing a war. The farmers of Oberschopfheim had no doubts: it was the French who were to blame.

A casual American reader might assume that such a statement is exaggerated. Not so. A trivial example illustrative of the feeling was related matter-of-factly to these writers by a lady in Oberschopfheim in 1988. She said that when she was a small child in the hard years after World War II she once asked her grandfather why the sun disappeared every night. He had assumed a solemn mien and told her that the French stole it. Of course within a few years she realized that he had merely been teasing her, but she added that she had never been able to entirely shed the animosity toward France that she had felt on that distant occasion.[14]

The character of such animosity should be specified. It was not that every individual in Lahr county hated every Frenchman. Far from it. For instance, there was no hostility toward fellow villagers across the Rhine in Alsace. After all, these people had been legally Germans until 1919. Commercial and social intercourse across the river was commonplace at all times. Indeed after 1871 it was not unusual for individuals from villages in Lahr county to cross the river to work because economic opportunities there often seemed more promising than at home. A few of them married and settled permanently in Alsace. Others drifted back and forth across the Rhine until 1919. Some returned home for good after that date. Decades later, when automobiles became plentiful among ordinary Germans, Oberschopfheimers and others often took Sunday drives over the Rhine to eat, drink, buy Alsatian wines, and sightsee. What Oberschopfheimers disliked and bitterly resented was the French *nation:* the whole people and their government, army, and foreign policy, all of which had been employed, in the German view, to ravage, exploit, oppress, and threaten Germans for centuries.

Of course Germany's ancient foes were not basically responsible for the afflictions borne by Oberschopfheimers, though the French assuredly did their best to make life additionally difficult for their old adversaries. From April 1923 to August 1924 French occupation troops refused to allow German trains from points north to enter Offenburg. Thus cigars made in

Oberschopfheim and elsewhere in Lahr county had to be shipped south and then off eastward across southern Germany on small, single-track railroads and thence into North Germany. Any goods coming from other parts of the country into Lahr county had to follow the same long, slow, circuitous route in reverse. Little wonder that the Weimar government surreptitiously orchestrated the ringing of church bells everywhere in the country when the French occupation troops left in 1930.

Cigarmaking appeared to be the salvation of Oberschopfheim in the early 1920s, but this was only partly true. Throughout Germany in those years the entire industry suffered from increased taxes and ruinous inflation that caused a steep decline in sales. Of the "tobacco villages" in Lahr county, Oberschopfheim suffered the least. It lost only three "factories" and continued to employ about three hundred workers. By 1925 the industry was clearly recovering. In that year 51 percent of the whole village work force, 75 percent of the adult women, 34 percent of the total population, even 4 percent of children under sixteen worked in cigar factories.[15] The number of factories had risen from seven to fourteen, while the number of employees fluctuated between 260 and 500. Since these factories closed during planting and harvesting seasons, the cigar industry harmonized well with farming and caused neighboring villages to envy Oberschopfheimers.

Nonetheless, the "prosperity" of cigar workers was the prosperity of subsistence. Wages were always low compared to those in other industries. Most Oberschopfheimers belonged to the Central Union of Christian Tobacco Workers, but the union could not win pay increases because cigar workers were isolated in separate villages, had no alternative employment, and faced a powerful association of manufacturers. The last became particularly evident in the years immediately after World War I. So depressed was the German economy then that the government ordered women removed from many jobs and the positions saved for men who could thereby, hopefully, support their families. As usual with economic regulations, the first thought of interested parties was how to evade them. Oberschopfheim's women needed their customary jobs as much as ever, and the factory owners still wanted to employ them since they worked for lower wages than men. The solution was a reversion to the old medieval "putting out" system. Women came in the morning to the "factory" bearing baskets. These they filled with tobacco and carried home. There they spent much of the day rolling cigars, which they brought back in the evening, a practice that was also common in other small village enterprises and that lasted into the 1960s. It is hardly surprising that few tobacco workers in Oberschopfheim or elsewhere looked to their unions for help.

Some forty female cigarmakers traveled daily to "factories" in neighboring villages. Fifteen village men worked on the railroad in Lahr and Offenburg, each several miles distant. Men and women alike left for work at five o'clock in the morning, on foot or on bicycles, in fair weather or foul.[16]

Even under these spartan conditions cigar and railroad workers, male and female, were better off than many of the young men of Oberschopfheim. In generations past boys from eleven to sixteen who were not destined for German universities (which in Oberschopfheim meant nearly all of them) were required to learn some trade so they could support themselves. In the 1920s many such newly minted tradesmen could not find employment at home and so wandered long distances to towns in the Ruhr or elsewhere in search of work. Sometimes they found a few days— or even a few weeks—of some sort of employment here and there in their peregrinations. Even with such luck they could earn only a bare subsistence.

An American might wonder what was so remarkable about these travels. After all, it was commonplace in the early twentieth century for small farmers in the western states of America to migrate in large numbers to grain growing regions in late summer and early fall to earn needed money for the winter by helping to "bring in the harvest." In the 1980s whole families of (mostly Mexican) farm workers still roamed from state to state over much of the United States to pick fruit and vegetables in season. In both Czarist and Soviet Russia rural males over seventeen routinely set off in the fall to find work in factories or mines hundreds of miles away in order to earn money during the winter.[17] The difference was that in the cases of both Russians and Americans, those who journeyed knew where they were going, knew jobs were waiting for them, expected to work a certain time at definite tasks, and had homes and farms to come back to by certain dates. The young men who set out from Oberschopfheim and nearby villages in the 1920s had no definite destination, no assurance that they could find any particular kind of work anywhere, and often suffered unusually severe psychological jolts along the way because many of them had never before been ten miles from their birthplaces. Those unable to find permanent jobs usually drifted back to Oberschopfheim where they could at least eat.

What many did, in mingled hope and despair, was write to relatives in the United States and elsewhere for aid and advice and then leave, if they could, for the United States or Canada. Several entire families emigrated from Oberschopfheim (and Lahr county) in those dismal years, as did a larger number of individuals, though overall emigration never reached the one hundred who had departed between 1852 and 1858.[18] Among those who did leave was the father of one of these writers, Herman Joseph

Rinderle, who came to the United States when the German economy hit rock bottom in 1923. An aunt also wanted to emigrate but so spirited was the competition for a limited number of entrance visas that she could not cross the Atlantic until 1926.

When the Depression descended to cap the dreary decade of the 1920s, and Nazi orators loudly promised what German farmers had long wanted—stable prices and guaranteed markets—it is little wonder that farmers everywhere, even the insular Catholic peasants of Oberschopfheim, began to listen. It is difficult to believe that people similarly situated, and with similar experiences, anywhere, would not have.

# 5

# THE GREAT DEPRESSION

FOR THOSE PEOPLE in the Western world who were personally maimed in one of the wars of the twentieth century and for those who lost a father, husband, brother, or son in one of those conflicts, the war in question has ordinarily been the most vivid public event in their memories. For anyone else born before 1925 such has not usually been the case. For them, eclipsing all the wars has been the memory of the Great Depression of the early 1930s. For many, perhaps most, of the farmers in Germany the Great Depression seemed to portend inexorable ruin. Demand for agricultural products fell below even the subnormal level of the 1920s, prices dropped still further, health services were restricted, state unemployment compensation gradually ran out, and the chronically unemployed had to be transferred to makeshift forms of communal aid. For millions, destitution seemed imminent. No other event of modern times (before 1960) touched so many, or imprinted itself so indelibly on their imaginations: not World War I, not World War II, not the French occupation of 1923 nor that of 1945, not even the catastrophic inflation of 1923.

It might be objected that this characterization is overdrawn: that the psychological shock of the Depression was greater in the United States than in Germany because most Americans believed that they lived in a unique "land of opportunity," whereas most Germans did not; that more Americans than Germans committed suicide in the Depression years; that Americans were more chagrined than Germans at having to accept public assistance or to help extended families. Such contentions, while true, seem less than decisive. Tens of millions of American farmers and day laborers were quite as well acquainted with habitual poverty as their German counterparts. American suicides were mostly losers in stock market speculation. Different German attitudes about family aid owed to different historical traditions. Lower sensitivity to receiving welfare reflected mostly the consideration that, by the 1930s, Germans had passed farther down the road toward the welfare state than had Americans. It is hard to resist the general view that Germany was hit harder by the Depression than any other major Western country. Only there, after all, did gang fights, street rioting, and political assassinations become *widespread* between 1930 and 1932: only there did they culminate in the Nazi regime. Of course hatred of the Versailles settlement, fear of communism, and other considerations also contributed significantly to this grim denouement, but the Depression was decisive.

In Oberschopfheim the Depression descended on the village government in two main ways: income plummeted and expenditures for poor relief soared. One major loss of income came from lower timber prices, which in 1930 alone fell from 70 marks per square meter to 48.28 marks. The *Gemeinde* also lost about four thousand marks from delinquent electric and water bills and several thousand more from shrunken fruit and grain prices.[1]

Income from the sale of hunting rights also declined dramatically. Ordinary citizens had never been allowed to hunt or fish at their pleasure. Such privileges were sold by the *Gemeinde,* in the case of Oberschopfheim to two outside businessmen who had agreed to pay nineteen hundred marks per annum from 1 February 1929 to 31 January 1935. The buyers then harvested the game and fish and sold the meat and skins. When prices fell sharply the purchasers demanded that their payment be reduced to twelve hundred marks. When the municipality refused, the businessmen went to court. Not only did they win their case, they won further reductions in succeeding years because of their alleged inability to find healthy deer, rabbits, and other animals.

*Gemeinde* tax collections fell off by fifty-four thousand marks despite an increase in the local property tax. By 1932 total municipal income from both taxes and sales was 40 percent below that projected for 1930. To make matters worse, the state took a larger percentage of the smaller amount collected. Villagers complained bitterly that they were being taxed to support city welfare programs and cited figures to show that cities received four times as much aid per person as did small villages.[2]

Faced with this sharp decline in income, village officials asked inhabitants for suggestions to cut expenses. The response was predictable: reduce officials to the status of "workers" and cut their salaries. The rejoinder of the officials was equally predictable: ignore the unwelcome suggestion and cut expenditures for social welfare and road maintenance. This brought them into immediate conflict with villagers on one side and county officials on the other. Even though in this instance *Gemeinde* members were clearly concerned with saving their own skins it must be acknowledged that, in general, they performed well in difficult circumstances. Somehow, they managed to cut expenses by 124 thousand marks between 1930 and 1933 and to end each fiscal year with a slight surplus—an incredible feat in that era.

Whether the *Gemeinde* was truly "poor" depends on comparisons with other times and places. Oberschopfheim was certainly no stranger to community indebtedness or penny-pinching by the local government. Innumerable times in the past the village government had been compelled to go deeply into debt because invading armies had forcibly requisitioned money, food, horses, hay, liquor, and other commodities. There had been none of this since 1848, to be sure, and in most years early in the twentieth century the *Gemeinde* had balanced the budget. Still, prior to 1930 Oberschopfheim had found it necessary to borrow money for several projects: ditches, canals, and a new kindergarten-daycare center. These debts still existed when the Depression descended. In 1930 the *Gemeinde* began to fall behind in payments to the county and district. The creditors granted delays at a penalty of 5 percent interest. By 1932 Oberschopfheim could not obtain further credit and faced the threat of court action if some of the bills were not paid at once. Officials responded by selling several village businesses. Thus financial disaster was averted but at the cost of reduced *Gemeinde* ownership of municipal properties and a consequent decline in the influence of the *Gemeinde* over village activities.

Throughout the Western world most have assumed that farmers suffered less than other occupational groups during the Great Depression because they were hit less directly by the industrial crisis of that somber era and because they could grow some of their own food. Like many such generalizations, this one is only partly true. In Oberschopfheim all occupational groups save village officials were "poor," no matter how that word is defined. All toiled long hours for meager returns, all dreaded losing whatever employment they had, and all worried about feeding their families.

Even fate seemed to hate Oberschopfheimers during the Depression. In 1928-1929 a fearsome winter killed 40 to 45 percent of the fruit trees in Lahr county. In 1930 persistent heavy rains rotted the grain and tobacco in the fields. In 1931 hail destroyed many crops before harvest time. In 1932 insects ruined most of the fruit and grapes. For four successive years villagers lost money and tightened their belts. The latter was not just metaphorical. In 1932 many of the very poor in the village often had little to eat for supper save bread and some nuts gathered in the forest.

The state government blamed American hybrid grapes for the epidemic of fruit lice and forbade the sale of wine from this variety. Since Oberschopfheimers grew practically no other kind, they were ordered, in effect, to destroy their 150 acres of vineyards and plant new vines, a course bound to cost them three to five years of precious income. It became one more grievance against the interfering bureaucrats from "outside." The state government did soften the blow a bit by paying a small subsidy for new vines, though it did not extend the enraged farmers any other financial aid.

These local disasters symbolized, in microcosm, what was happening to agriculture nationally, even internationally. The last half of the nineteenth century were "champagne years" for European farmers. Output rose rapidly, population grew apace, prices were generally high, and serious overseas competition began only after 1875, so most farmers prospered. Cooperative movements were organized to confront overseas producers. They did not "save" European farmers in the long run, but they did stave off a general agricultural depression until after World War I. Before 1914 farm laborers with steady jobs were regarded by many as better off than factory hands.[4]

The crunch came in the 1920s. Throughout that decade German farmers complained chronically and loudly. So what? one might reply. Was there ever a time or place where farmers did not complain, regardless of circumstances? Such an unsympathetic response would not be without some justification, for some peasants lost their lands or underwent other hardships mainly because of their own shortcomings. Others, like many of their counterparts in America, clamored for state aid to agriculture while at the same time calling for a reduction in government expenditures. Some rural demands indicated mere unvarnished selfishness of the sort common among special interest groups the world over: insistence on concessions that would have to be paid for by others. Many complaints were highly emotional and plainly reflected not so much specific grievances as visceral hostility to the whole "Weimar system" and longstanding resentment that the needs and interests of farmers in Germany always seemed to be considered last and least by governments.[5]

Nevertheless specific grievances did exist. Harvests had been poor in the mid-1920s. Foot-and-mouth disease had ravaged livestock, especially in the pig- and cattle-raising portions of northwest Germany. Taxes were heavy and the whole tax system was unduly complex. The horrible inflation of 1923 had freed many farmers from old debt, but the need to buy seed, fertilizer, horses, and machinery soon plunged them into new debt at higher rates of interest than before. Grumbling was chronic that credit was hard to come by, that interest rates were too high, and that too many high-salaried civil servants were parasitic on agriculture.[6]

Then, in 1928, farm prices declined drastically nearly everywhere and the global agricultural depression began, two years before the general or Great Depression. For German farmers matters were worsened by trade agreements made with Poland, Greece, and other countries to admit their farm commodities free in return for their abandonment of import duties on German manufactures. Irate farmers, unable to pay their debts, de nounced their government for allowing foreign competition to drive them to ruin. The economic malaise descended inexorably and soon spread to other groups dependent on agriculture. Before 1928 many afflicted and outraged peasants had responded by forming pressure groups and supporting various "splinter" political parties. After 1928 they began to gravitate to the Nazis.[7]

Though the farmers of Oberschopfheim were never prosperous or self-confident at any time in the 1920s, before 1928 many of the gloomy generalizations detailed above applied to them only marginally, if at all. For instance, few of them ever joined or voted for any party of the Right trying to make capital out of rural grievances. Instead, they voted for the Center (Catholic) party because their pastor told them they should. Few joined unions or pressure groups save for wine, fruit, and tobacco marketing organizations, all of which were weak. There are no records in the Oberschopfheim courthouse to support the supposition that any great number of villagers were deeply in debt. Indeed it had been bred into their bones that one should never go into debt from mere personal desire to spend but only for pressing reasons of business. Those, now old, who lived through the 1920s speak a good deal about having been *poor* but not about having been in debt. Since most family farms were tiny they had no occasion to purchase expensive machinery. Finally they were less politically aware than many farmers elsewhere since few of them went to the expense of subscribing to newspapers. Nobody in Oberschopfheim attended meetings to discuss agricultural problems until after 1933 when the Nazis compelled it by taking attendance.

All this began to change for the worse after 1928. Hungry urban people from Lahr and elsewhere began to steal half-grown vegetables, even venturing into the fruit cellars of houses during the night. Nationwide food shortages also caused hitherto unknown relatives and forgotten "friends" to come to villages in Lahr county to beg or trade clothes for food, conduct which reinforced Oberschopfheimers' low opinion of outsiders. What truly enraged them during the Depression years, though, was something else: the spectacle of the industrial unemployed openly preferring to live in their towns on paltry doles rather than to take available jobs in agriculture. This confirmed innumerable peasants in their conviction that townspeople were always enemies, were lazy, and did not deserve the social benefits that German governments had showered on them. The opportunities that this belief provided for political parties catering to special interests is obvious.

Even when some farmers managed to save a portion of their crops they received very little money for them. In the fall of 1930, for example, Oberschopfheim's wines sold for prices 57 to 71 percent below 1927 levels. Villagers grumbled that the price of beer in a Lahr *Gasthaus* remained as high as ever while their wine, which had cost them much toil and sweat, brought them next to nothing. Tobacco prices plummeted correspondingly, to which desperate farmers responded by planting additional amounts, even though tax officials threatened to punish an entire municipality if a single farmer was caught exceeding his percentage of the village quota.[8] Altogether, the combination of collapsing prices, natural disasters, rising thievery, and other misfortunes led to substantial losses for farmers throughout Baden. In early 1933 the *Lahrer Anzeiger* concluded that many farmers would lose their lands if the depression continued another three years.[9]

Initially, artisans were as bad off as farmers when the Depression descended. Most of them had inadequate work even before 1930. During the next two years they had even less, despite lowering their wages by 60 percent. Moonlighting also hurt tradesmen. Under the pressure of unemployment many families did their own repairs or helped each other instead of hiring an artisan. Often tradesmen secretly helped farmers without informing the Handworkers Association or paying taxes on their earnings. At times, wandering artisans came into the village and offered to work even below the newly reduced rates. Although the Handworkers Association launched a vigorous campaign against moonlighting, by August 1932 it conceded that "more jobs are completed through moonlighting than legitimate work in Baden."[10] Because of the combination of sporadic work, low wages, and "illegal" competition, five tradesmen left the village between 1929 and 1932. Four younger men, from desperation rather than calculation, quickly took their places.

Nonetheless, unlike farmers, the tradesmen had a stroke of luck. In the summer of 1932 new housing legislation was enacted. It provided loans of up to six hundred marks for each new room added to a dwelling or old room divided, with half the loan then being canceled. The new law also paid 20 percent of house repairs.[11] This immediately stimulated building in Oberschopfheim. Eighteen new homes, three new businesses, several new barns, and room additions to about sixty houses were all undertaken before mid-1933. More than a third of the homes in the village underwent a change of some sort, all to the obvious benefit of previously unemployed artisans.[12]

Retailers received some government aid too, but generally they were less fortunate than artisans. Business never flourished even in normal times because villagers had little money to spend and, in any case, strove for self-sufficiency. When the Depression descended they had even less money, so even mandatory price reductions failed to stimulate sales. Government aid to poor families in the form of food and coal stamps helped but little since only three families received such help for short periods of time. By the end of 1932 two breweries and a bicycle shop had closed, and most other stores feared that they would soon follow.

Village employees fared distinctly better. They at least kept their jobs, although they were never sure how much they would earn or when they would be paid. *Gemeinde* officials, for example, had all received moderate salary increases in 1929, but after Chancellor Bruening's emergency decrees of 16 July 1930, federal, state, and county governments proposed salary cuts ranging from 6 to 10 percent. Oberschopfheim's inner council *(Gemeinderat)* embraced the spirit of austerity and retrenchment enthusiastically. It ignored these modest guidelines and in a quick move to balance its budget slashed salaries from 35 to 75 percent. Outraged, village officials rebelled and took their cases to court. Eventually, on 7 January 1932, they had their salaries restored to within 6 to 10 percent of the 1929-1930 figures.

The *Gemeinderat* was checked but not abashed. Three months later its members singled out the mayor for an additional 25 percent pay cut. Compared to 1929, his salary fell a total of 36 percent. Meanwhile, the salaries of *Gemeinderat* members themselves remained nearly the same throughout the entire period.[13] This inequity, compounded by the earlier attempts of the *Gemeinderat* to slash the salaries of all officials, gave rise to sharp resentments and severely undermined village cohesiveness. It also effectively ended cooperation between village employees and the council, a situation the Nazis would exploit. Nonetheless, despite all the acrimony, local officials and employees still received the highest wages in Oberschopfheim and had the most secure employment in the village.

Those hurt most by the Depression were cigar workers. During 1930 "factories" remained closed until late in the year, when the government suddenly announced the imposition of additional taxes on all cigars manufactured after 1 January 1931. In an effort to produce as many cigars as possible before that date, owners offered jobs to all men, women, and children, provided that they agreed to work ten to fifteen hours each day, six days a week. Families in desperate need of money had no choice but to accept. Many, including the pastor, complained that the protracted work was just as bad as unemployment, that it increased family and village tensions and allowed small children to go unsupervised.[14]

Normally, cigar factories closed for three or four weeks after Christmas, but in early 1931 tobacco sales fell so far that workers had little hope that their employment would be resumed at all. Many could not even collect their December wages. From then until 1933 only a few workers found sporadic employment, and even they had to take 4 to 5 percent pay cuts in April 1931. The lowest wages fell to 21 *Pfennig*, with the average about 26 *Pfennig*. Thus an ordinary cigar worker in Oberschopfheim who enjoyed part-time employment earned about six marks each week. At such wages he would have to save his entire pay for two months to buy a cheap suit.[15]

Pensioners and poor families also suffered grievously from the Depression. In 1930 the village contained forty pensioners, twenty-nine retired war veterans who lived on military pensions, eight widows of veterans, one widow of an official, and two others. Monthly benefits for retired persons increased slightly above 1929 levels, then fell by about 23 percent in 1932 to forty-three marks for a married couple and thirty-one marks for a single person. Single women consistently received less than single men.[16]

Normally, jobless workers anywhere in Germany could rely on the insurance act of 1927, which provided aid for twenty weeks followed by emergency aid for thirty-eight weeks, then welfare help until employment was regained. Those over forty years of age could also apply for an additional thirteen weeks of aid. On the surface this system seemed equitable enough, even generous, but as in most such programs there were conditions, qualifications, exemptions, and exceptions. Moreover, as the number of the unemployed rose into the millions, the government frequently changed the guidelines. Since the insurance act covered workers in large factories only, most Oberschopfheimers were not included in it. Of those few who were eligible and later lost their jobs, most could not register as unemployed and receive aid because of some peripheral consideration: they owned land or some small business, they earned more than a third of their regular salary in some side enterprise, they had not been covered by the program for a year, or they had close relatives who were working. Factors of this sort virtually guaranteed that all women, most men, and anyone under twenty-one years old would be ineligible for such aid. Only forty Oberschopfheimers out of a population of more than sixteen hundred ever received government unemployment benefits, and those did so only for short periods and after waiting many months. The largest number who were aided during any one calendar year (1931) was thirty-one—6 percent of the work force. In Lahr city and its suburban village of Dinglingen, by contrast, a much larger percentage of the work force qualified as unemployed, and of them as many as 62 percent (mostly urban workers) received aid on 15 April 1932.[17] Equally bad, the few Oberschopfheimers who did get aid got smaller sums. Since previous income and the size of one's community bore on payments, Oberschopfheimers who had earned one-third the salary of Lahr workers got about 30 percent less aid: an average of six marks per pay period in 1931 and five and a half marks in 1932.[18]

This disparity naturally intensified ill feeling between the two communities. Since Oberschopfheim's mayor did not want to be blamed for refusing aid to his own people, he sent the local unemployed to Lahr where county officials told them they did not qualify. Villagers of course then blamed these "uncaring outsiders" for not aiding them while the Lahr officials groused about the "stupidity" of village mayors who were too "ignorant" to screen applicants in their own bailiwicks. More important than the mutual vituperation was its long-term influence on voting habits. Most officials belonged to the Center or Social Democratic parties. As villagers fell deeper into the Depression and grew increasingly convinced that they were getting the runaround from officialdom, they began to look to other parties that promised economic help.[19]

Differences between Lahr and Oberschopfheim were equally marked in the allocation of money for public works projects. Most of the five hundred unemployed cigar workers in the village could not find any other employment. Under county pressure, village officials grudgingly hired a few of them to cut timber and rebuild roads in the forest, but the inner council and the mayor managed to end this project within a year on the quite reasonable grounds that money was lacking.[20] By contrast, the city of Lahr received large sums of federal aid for municipal works projects: new water lines, forest roads, a pumping station, renovation of dams in the Schutter river, and private home repairs. The implementation of these programs allowed the city to provide jobs for 60 percent of its workers who were on welfare. This was supplemented by the establishment of a "Free Work Service" in late 1932 and in January 1933 of an "Emergency Work of German Youth." Both were directed to the needs of young people. Together they employed more than 150 persons.[21]

Federal and county welfare aid to the citizens of Oberschopfheim was no more munificent than unemployment compensation or public works expenditures. Since many retired people could not live on their meager pensions and savings, they applied for additional help from the county. To get any they had to "prove" that they would have been able to take care of themselves if World War I and the inflation of 1923 had not occurred. Faced with such a stringent test, it was little wonder that between December 1929 and December 1932 only eleven pensioners qualified. They received an average of eight marks apiece for such commodities as medicine, children's milk, and doctor's care. Some were helped a single time, others for half a year.[22]

Poor families fared little better than pensioners. Between 13 December 1931 and 10 May 1932 three persons received from the county a total of fourteen stamps to buy meat and coal at reduced prices. Annual county aid to needy people in the village did average about four hundred marks, which was spent mostly on clothes. Frequently, however, county and village officials argued over who should give the aid, while poor families, children, and widows waited for many months to receive a pair of shoes.[23] Oberschopfheim's village authorities did make periodic contributions to selected inhabitants for such things as a child's First Communion suit, a dress for a widow, an artificial leg, and food. In 1931 the village helped nine persons at a cost of 133 marks and in 1932 eleven persons at a cost of 434 marks. Officials also gave one apartment free of rent, lowered rents on other houses, gave cheaper electricity to a retired teacher, and performed the mandatory civil marriage free of charge.[24]

Thus the *Gemeinde*, whose own resources, it must not be forgotten, were limited and declining, did make a respectable effort to deal with the plight of at least some of its needy people. For their pains, its members received small thanks for a reason easily understood in human terms. When a "welfare expert," trained in a university, sits in an office in Berlin or some other capital city and contemplates the plight of the poor, he thinks of "cases," numbers, "the underprivileged," and other such abstract categories. When he ponders how to deal with the "problem" they present, his mind turns readily to national legislation. In a small village or rural area, by contrast, officials usually know a good deal about the past life, personal character, and work habits of most of their neighbors and so have decided opinions about who does and who does not "deserve" public aid in time of adversity. Of course everyone who "needs" public aid regards himself as eminently deserving and qualified. Public officials, whose duty it is to decide who is to get aid when there is not enough for all, find themselves in a hopeless situation: whatever course they follow will outrage somebody.

Village officials in Oberschopfheim carefully scrutinized every person they proposed to help. When one family asked for aid to feed their children, the mayor accused them of living extravagantly. He also reminded them that they had paid their debts in the inflated currency of 1923, had stolen potatoes because they were "too lazy" to plant their own, and had foolishly sold two cows instead of two horses. For these reasons and because "ninety-nine per cent of the village" thought they did not deserve aid, they were refused. Instead, the mayor offered the husband a part-time job—but temporarily took away his four children.[25] The feelings of the family toward both their neighbors and the mayor can be imagined.

Little help came from private charity. The *Lahrer Anzeiger* pleaded with urban residents not to throw away their "unfashionable" clothes but to give them to poor families in neighboring villages. Few did so, preferring to trade such garments for food and firewood. Many city organizations raised money for their own people at benefit concerts and dances, then begged food from surrounding villages. The villagers proved more generous: every year they sent several wagonloads of "extra" fruit and vegetables to city people. Generosity to the church also continued. Despite its own annual deficits, the parish gave freely of its collections to Lahr and other places.[26]

Even though most Oberschopfheimers lacked jobs, steady income, and even welfare, families and businessmen still had to pay insurance, the sales tax, and especially local property taxes. Many petitioned the *Gemeinde* for reduction of their property tax, but officials lowered it for only four *Gasthaeuser* and seven small businesses. The best individual families were able to do was to occasionally secure a delay in payment: thirteen did so in 1931 and forty-nine in 1932.[27]

Since many people could not pay their taxes even after delays, their collective debts to the *Gemeinde* increased to 28,202 marks in April 1932, then to a new peak of 30,955 marks (about 80 marks per family) at the end of that fiscal year. To collect these debts officials threatened to take away the privileges of local citizenship, which included voting rights, free firewood, and the use of meadows; to add a 5 percent penalty to unmet obligations; to cut off a backslider's electricity; even to take chronic debtors to court. These were not idle threats. In 1930 village officials did take one man into custody and fined five others for failing to pay dog taxes. In 1931 the *Gemeinde* seized the household goods of three families whose total indebtedness was a mere 355 marks. Despite such threats—and actions— thirteen families still could not pay their debts even by 1934.[28] The fallout from these wrangles over taxes, debts, and aid was more important than the amounts involved. In particular, the attempts of the *Gemeinde* to extract money from families who had neither jobs nor income enraged many residents and led to sharp conflicts with the mayor and *Gemeinderat*.

In some parts of Germany the Great Depression was more psychological than economic. For instance in Thalburg, a small city in Westphalia, the middle class was hardly touched except by the "constant flow of news items stressing the 'misery', which led to fear of losing wealth and position."[29] To be sure, three artisans' shops there went bankrupt in 1930. Six businesses, among which was a cooperative bank, also closed in 1931, and other merchants lost "a small portion" of their businesses. By contrast, artisans outside the building trades had plenty of work, civil servants maintained their relative positions in the city, residents collectively increased their savings, and there was little actual suffering. In Thalburg unemployment was real but not catastrophic: about 8 percent at the most difficult time in April 1932. Some workers suffered pay cuts or shortened work weeks but were often compensated through unemployment benefits, private charities, a work project in the town forest, and stamps for coal at reduced prices.[30]

For the common people of Oberschopfheim the Depression was

real, and ancient memories made it worse. Older people recalled their grandparents' tales of hunger in the nineteenth century. When food grew scarce in 1930-1933, they feared that prices would again reach the legendary levels of 1817 when their ancestors had paid more than 150 days' labor for twenty-seven and one-half pounds of wheat and two days' labor for half a pint of wine. Some said Oberschopfheim would relive the 1840s and 1850s when people had urged their neighbors to go to America in order to save precious food for themselves. Others offered bleak predictions that the village would again open free soup kitchens to feed its starving inhabitants.[31]

Younger people, remembering the years 1914 to 1924, feared that the government would resort to war rationing, that they would face another three to six years of unemployment while their families went hungry, or that they would lose all their savings, as they had in 1923 when 500 billion mark notes had circulated. Families with cash quickly hoarded shoes, canned food, and other goods. One man even walled up several pairs of new shoes in his house. It seemed ominous that owners of shops and factories frequently closed their doors without offering an explanation.

Wild rumors proliferated in Oberschopfheim as German industrial production fell 14 percent from 1929 to 1930, another 18 percent in 1931, and a further 15 percent in 1932. Inhabitants read in the *Anzeiger* that Chancellor Bruening had promised to increase employment and overcome the Depression through the Emergency Decrees of 1 January 1932, but they also read that unemployment throughout Germany had reached a third of the labor force, while many others worked only part-time. Vastly more important, they could see and experience the latter in their own village. By December 1932 net income had dropped 42 percent since 1928 but living costs had fallen only 21 percent. Women in the street and men in the *Gasthaeuser* glumly exchanged the latest gossip about abandoned factories, bankrupt farmers, lost jobs, and starving families. The general tone of their conversation was curious—and ominous. In Oberschopfheim, as in innumerable similar villages inhabited by people with little education and restricted interests, a "communications shorthand" had long since developed. It consisted of an extensive array of local proverbs, pithy observations, and platitudes, nowhere exactly the same in any two villages but serving people in any one community as something of a substitute for both thought and extended conversation. In Oberschopfheim two such hoary axioms were "sometimes one must eat small potatoes," and "sometimes one must bite into sour apples." That people did not now reassure each other with such familiar clichés or resort to such maxims in the spirit of gallows humor, indicates that they feared *die grosse Krise* too much to joke about it, that they thought it a real possibility that their village might be ruined and that all of them might lose their homes and lands.[32]

Superficially, a curious result of the Depression was that the population increased at a rate almost double that of the years 1925-1929. But the anomaly was only apparent. There was no rise in the birthrate: indeed the average size of households declined from 4.9 persons in 1925 to 3.3 in 1933.[33] The cause was more restrictive U.S. immigration laws, initiated in 1921. These indirectly worsened the economic crisis in Europe by plugging a longstanding drain for discontent, though there would have been little incentive to emigrate to the United States anyway since the Depression there was nearly as bad as that in Germany. A further contribution to the general malaise in Europe was that gifts and loans from relatives in America declined sharply in the Depression years.

The various economic crises of the post-World War I years exacerbated class antagonisms in many countries. In Germany this tendency was muted during the relatively prosperous years of 1924 to 1928, but it broke out with renewed intensity when the Depression began. Farmers strove to keep prices up for agricultural products; workers and city people clamored to keep them low to insure that a steady flow of cheap food would always be available to themselves. Sporadic strikes of peasants took place, boycotts were threatened, and the political representatives of warring social and economic groups paralyzed the parliamentary system by refusing to compromise. Hatreds multiplied and grew more intense. Young people especially, often contemptuous of both liberal and conservative ideas and lacking faith in democratic institutions, viewed the Weimar regime as a rotten, dying order. Most of them were not precisely yearning for a violent, bloody revolution, but they were visibly impatient for drastic changes— and soon.[34]

Pale reflections of these general animosities had long existed in Oberschopfheim. The Depression sharpened them abruptly. People warned each other when "thieving" beggars and gypsies were in the area though, unaccountably, village officials continued to allow gypsies to stay one night at a special camp only a mile from the village. Many families spent the substantial sum of thirty marks yearly for the luxury of keeping a watchdog. Occasionally two local field detectives managed to catch a few culprits. The sternness with which these hapless rascals were dealt indicates how testy people had become. It was not merely that outsiders who stole money from the poor box in the *Leutkirche* were duly apprehended and punished. That might have been expected. It was that children who stole rabbits, even grapes, had their names posted in the village, and one or two boys who broke into a house were sent to reform school.[35]

Petty conflict among citizens increased dramatically, raising the number of local court cases by 40 percent. Unlike Thalburg, most of the bickering in Oberschopfheim was not about politics and did not result in violence. Rather, it ran heavily to charges of trespassing on property or defaming someone's character. Some farmers even waited for neighbors to drive over their fields or private lanes in order to sue and collect paltry "damages" of five to fifteen marks.[36]

One such quarrel became so intense that it split the village into angry factions. The case began when Mayor Einsele allowed a common laborer to erect a gate at the edge of his driveway, on the condition that the man's neighbor, Franz Kohler, did not object. After the gate was built the mayor and Kohler, who were brothers-in-law, argued that the final approval had never been given and demanded that the gate be removed. Using village funds, the two men brought the case before the local court and then continued it outside Oberschopfheim until Kohler finally won five hundred marks in damages. The motives of Kohler and the mayor are uncertain. They had no separate social class to preserve against "unwashed" workers, as might have been the case had they all lived in Thalburg. Perhaps they merely wanted to demonstrate their relative power at a time when it was being undermined by the Depression? Whatever the case, during the lengthy proceedings most persons who testified for one side or the other continued their arguments in the streets. Many were offended by the spectacle of prominent men victimizing a common laborer and doing it with village money, while others objected primarily to taking the case outside the community. Though the issue itself was petty, the acrimony engendered over it was fierce.[37]

The mayor and other officials sparked disputes by the stinginess with which they parted with declining tax revenues. When some public expenditure could not be avoided, the *Gemeinde* habitually talked at length about the desirability of both economy and "quality" (that is, "doing the job right"). More often than not they came down on the side of economy, the principal exception in the 1930s being their willingness to spend freely on the upkeep of the church tower. A good example of their more common attitude occurred in early 1930 when they rejected the final bill of 1,065 marks for the kindergarten-daycare center on the grounds that the contractor used too many new stones when old ones were available, that the bill was more than the estimate, and that the basement leaked. After two years of court proceedings the *Gemeinde* finally had to pay a portion of the money and all court costs.[38]

Management of the grade school also became a source of local discord. Officials decided to save money by refusing to buy textbooks for teachers and children, allowing the doctor only one visit per year, and purchasing crushed rock instead of expensive sand for the muddy playground. Angry parents threatened to sue the mayor and *Gemeinderat* every time their children cut or bruised themselves on the sharp stones, while teachers predictably ridiculed "ignorant" officials for "attacking education" at the first sign of an unbalanced budget.[39]

As tax revenues continued to decline, the *Gemeinde* refused to build new water and sewer lines, to pay for the training of the midwife and meat inspector, or to give rebates to businesses for unused electricity for which they had contracted earlier. When economic conditions deteriorated further in 1931 and after, local officials provoked still worse conflicts by curtailing normal services in order to balance the budget.

This penny-pinching by the mayor and *Gemeinderat* soon brought them into damaging conflicts with outsiders. For example, the *Gemeinde* once tried to avoid paying a hospital bill by contending that they had sent a woman "merely for examination" and not for the operation that was performed. As usual, the case went to court. It dragged on for two years before local officials finally had to pay the entire cost. Even then they did not give up. They deducted 4.8 marks from the bill by counting admission and departure as one day, then seized both the woman's and her brother's property to help pay the bill. The latter action provoked howls of outrage and another lawsuit.[40]

The *Gemeinde* also refused to spend money as the county directed. No longer was mud cleared, grass trimmed, or gravel purchased for village roads. The *Gemeinde* even denied that the village used one road, in order to escape paying for its upkeep. When a county commissioner held a meeting to explain that Oberschopfheim had to install a new water system, many council members refused to attend.

Ordinary villagers also fought with outsiders, especially the state insurance company. After a major fire in March 1931 destroyed three factories and a home, the owners refused to accept a settlement. They insisted that their buildings were worth more than the company offered and also claimed a long list of destroyed contents. Since the insurance company was operated by the government of Baden, this imbroglio provided one more pretext to berate the Center and Social Democratic parties then in power in Baden.[41]

All this poisonous contentiousness even undermined club life. During 1930 club life throve. The Catholic Young Men's Club, for instance, played soccer matches with neighboring village teams; presented plays at Christmas, Three Kings' Feast, and the First Mass of a former member; showed films on first aid and the *Graf Zepplin;* sponsored talks on such diverse subjects as witches, Freemasons, Baron vom Stein, and club goals; and held songfests after meetings. On specified occasions members went on retreats, received Communion as a group, and attended Masses for deceased members. In spite of difficult times the club collected 52 marks at one soccer game and 193 marks at a Christmas party and raffle. Obviously Oberschopfheimers, and many neighboring villagers who also attended, still enjoyed these events.[42] During 1931, however, community animosities grew so acute that nearly every club meeting was disrupted by bickering, just as had been the case in 1927. It was ominous that, this time, the squabbling had become political. A clique within the club clearly sympathized with the Nazis, though they were not yet NSDAP members. They wanted to eliminate the club's religious activities and to break the pastor's hold over it. When they elected their candidate as vice-president in April 1933, the Club splintered and the crypto-Nazis left.[43]

Informal activities such as dances and festivals were stricken by the same blight. Even the *Gasthaeuser* gradually lost much of their patronage. Former customers, now short of money and increasingly alienated from each other by local quarrels or larger ideological divisions, preferred to meet their friends on street corners. Common but unequal suffering contributed its bit to the witch's brew. The longer the Depression lasted the more intense became the jealousies among occupational groups, especially between village officials, who had steady jobs, and all others. Officials in turn banded closer together to protect their privileged positions, while individual families grew so obsessed with their own economic survival that they denounced each other over a few *Pfennig*.

Inevitably, this burgeoning malaise eroded the prestige of elected officials, caused a decline in the membership of local clubs, and lessened popular interest in their activities. Then came a stroke of sheer bad luck: the pastor fell terminally ill. Traditionally, he had been a powerful mediator of community disagreements. Now conflicts raged unchecked, community spirit crumbled, and cooperation for any public purpose visibly evaporated.

These somber developments produced among Oberschopfheimers a sharply increased interest in the outside world. No doubt this would have happened anyway, at *some* time, merely because of the scientific and technological innovations of the twentieth century compounded by all its wars and upheavals. That it took place *at a particular time* in Oberschopfheim was because of the unsettlement caused by the Depression and because of the invention of the radio. For people whose scanty education had left them disinclined to read, who had little time to read anyway, and who had become sufficiently estranged from so many neighbors that they no longer wished to socialize, listening to the radio became an increasingly important part of their lives. This development was soon deliberately accentuated by the Nazis who realized the propaganda potential of the new device. Once in power, they had radios manufactured by the millions and sold so cheaply that by 1935 a quarter of villagers owned one. Thus the coming of the radio coincided with a dawning realization among untutored rural people that their fate was bound up with that of the whole nation and that it was imperative to pay attention to national and international events. There is no question that the traditional outlook and mode of life of the citizens of Oberschopfheim was shaken more profoundly in more ways by the Great Depression of the 1930s than by either world war or the rise of Nazism—indeed, by any events prior to a quite different kind of revolution in the 1960s.

# 6

# THE RISE OF THE NAZIS

THE MALAISE of German agriculture in the 1920s and the consequent sense of desperation that gripped German farmers constituted a situation made-to-order for the Nazis. They were slow to grasp their opportunity for several reasons. One was that agriculture was of only peripheral interest to the "artist," Adolf Hitler. More fundamentally, Hitler was determined to build a mass movement that would stand above all mere parties and special interest groups, that would draw its support from many disparate and antagonistic groups in society, and that would represent the whole German nation and people. Moreover, in the years 1924-1928 Hitler was hard at work establishing his absolute personal control over his own Party and building and training its cadres.[1]

A crucial weakness of the effort to stand above all groups was, of course, that any friendliness shown to one set of supporters was bound to antagonize another group whose interests were opposed—or at least different. In the mid-1920s the Nazis had worked hard to try to win industrial workers away from the Socialists and Communists. The effort had been largely unavailing, and it had aroused suspicion among farmers, small businessmen, and other middle-class people who might otherwise have been more readily attracted to the NSDAP. The descent of the agricultural depression in 1928 provoked a reassessment of Nazi tactics, pushed hardest by Hitler himself.[2]

This time the Nazis did not falter. Spurred by Walter Darré, then an obscure NSDAP functionary with a keen interest in agriculture, they quickly posed as bellicose champions of farmers. They attacked the parties in power and their rivals out of power for their real and alleged weakness, corruption, bureaucratic ineffectiveness, and indifference to the welfare of farmers. Lower level Nazi leaders traveled tirelessly from village to village where they held countless meetings. They dilated ceaselessly on the themes that all Germany's troubles had been caused by the "November criminals," the vast sums German taxpayers had had to pay in reparations, and the victimization of peasants and other humble Germans by chain stores, Jewish "money power," and the refusal of banks to provide vital relief from debt in the countryside.[3] Oftentimes they resorted to violence to disrupt auctions of farm properties on which owners had not paid debts or back taxes. This tactic allowed them simultaneously to appear as champions of farmers, to pose as a party that meant action rather than mere talk, and to keep up the morale of the wilder spirits in their own ranks by giving them something to *do*.[4] Always they clamored for unspecified "justice" for the farmer and for aid to the poor. They orated movingly about the *"Volk* community" and promised to set everything right once they gained power. Within two or three years the NSDAP had absorbed much of the following of some forty ineffectual parties on the political Right who professed to be friends of the farmer. Their newfound rural strength would soon snowball.[5]

How was such an amazing transformation possible? In American football there is a cynical adage that "An All-American is a player with weak opposition on the field and a poet in the press box." Not a little of the success of the Nazis derived from weak opposition. Germany had been a geographical expression until 1871. Even after that the new Reich remained divided into numerous hostile political, geographical, and occupational groups that never acquired the habit of compromising their particular interests to serve the national good.[6] Conventional mythology holds that in 1933 beleaguered liberalism waged a heroic battle against the demagogic Right before going down to defeat. That was hardly the case. The Weimar Republic was hamstrung by proportional representation until 1930, and it became an authoritarian system honeycombed with intrigue afterward. It failed in one of the most fundamental requirements of any regime, to gain the acceptance of most of its people. Avant garde intellectuals, filled with self-conscious disdain for the "philistinism" of ordinary persons, have praised the artistic experimentation that went on in Weimar Germany and have viewed as benignly as they deem politic the sexual anarchy that was widespread among what a later generation would call the "beautiful people." Less emancipated persons regarded the first as absurd, the latter as shameful, and both as smacking of Bolshevism. Weimar's admirers did not reflect, either, on what it implied when crowds of ordinary people applauded Nazi promises of a return to order and conventional morality and the restoration of a "healthy" national culture instead of decadence.[7]

None of the major political parties in the Weimar years inspired anyone. Those composed of liberals and moderate conservatives tended to be loose associations of notables, split between "practical" people and "blue sky idealists," lacking in both able leaders and party discipline. They were also pulled in opposite directions by Right- and Left-leaning elements within them. When the Depression descended they veered to the Right and tended to support Chancellor Bruening, who was more concerned with balancing the budget than with expanding welfare legislation for unemployed workers. Thus they looked heartless and uncaring for the plight of the unemployed. Many who in England would have been called "Tory workers" because they disliked the official atheist materialism and avowed socialism of the Social Democrats (SPD) and Communists (KPD), deserted these parties and, having nowhere else to go, gradually became Nazis.[8]

The Center party was also divided and inclined to support any government, regime, or program that seemed civilized and did not interfere with Catholic schools or interests. It is sometimes alleged that supporters of the bourgeois parties and the Center were "bamboozled" by Hitler and the NSDAP. This is only partly true. Millions of Germans in the early 1930s, in the Center party and outside it, agreed with the Center's leader, Msgr. Kaas, that democracy was not always or necessarily superior to authoritarian government and that what Germany sorely needed at the moment was strong leadership, not more parties, more wrangling, and more voting. It is also one of the many ironies of German political life in that era that the Center had long labored under a reputation for being unprincipled and unreliable for the same reason that the Nazis did: it contained so many different interest groups that it had to constantly pretend to be "balancing" them inside the party and to regularly shift alliances with other parties. No less incongruous was the consideration that many in the Center were, like the Nazis, romantics who idealized the past. The Center strove continually to shore up obsolete trades and crafts that had thriven in the Middle Ages. Catholic leaders sought energetically to discover some sort of social harmony that had supposedly existed centuries before, a harmony that was neither capitalist nor exactly socialist and that certainly would not be tainted by the spirit of the Enlightenment. Yet Catholics were generally less enthusiastic about Nazism than any other comparable group in Germany save Jews.[9]

On the Left the SPD and KPD could never unite because they could not be both moderate and revolutionary at the same time. The Communists talked so much about revolution that they frightened the middle and upper classes, yet they were never able to convince many German workers that it was the "historic role" of the latter to lead a revolution. They strove to infiltrate and dominate unions and labored to turn every strike into a revolutionary uprising, but like so many parties in the middle and on the right of the political spectrum, they were divided, ill organized, and ineptly led. The Social Democrats were quite as hopeless, if not in precisely the same ways. For two generations they had talked endlessly about socialization, social justice, a planned economy, and possible revo-

lution, but when in power they had called in *Freikorps* units to repress
Communist-instigated uprisings, suffered a party split over whether or not
to build a battleship, endured the embarrassment of having two of their
leaders (Jews at that) apprehended in a financial scandal, and watched
other leaders resign or take vacations during the lowest depths of the
Depression. To many, the SPD looked more like "Weimar decadents"
than heralds of a nobler and more just society.[10]

As they contemplated their political adversaries, the NSDAP could
charge, with gross distortion to be sure but a certain plausibility nonetheless, that those in the Center and on the Right were mere selfish special
interest groups who either did not understand or did not sympathize with
the plight of the farmers, the workers, and the unemployed. They were
collections of quarrelsome talkers, divided and led by decadent grafters,
who were too lazy or too timid to attempt to *do* anything about Germany's
desperate plight. How could they protect honest Germans from the unpatriotic parties of the Left who cared nothing for German greatness and
who were itching to despoil the nation for the profit of foreign powers and
foreign ideologies? Finally, the Nazis could reflect comfortably that none
of their foes, Right, Left, or Center, had private armies like the SA. After
1928, and especially after 1930, more and more Germans, especially
Protestant farmers and bourgeoisie, began to heed Nazi insistence that
only they and not ineffectual nationalists like Hugenberg could save
Germany from the devilish Jewish Bolsheviks.[11]

But the Nazis did not triumph because of their opponents' deficiencies alone. They consistently displayed much keener appreciation of the
psychology of their countrymen and far greater organizational skill than
did any of their rivals. Contemptuous of truthfulness, Nazi orators depicted every issue as a stark choice of black versus white. Instead of merely
bewailing the descent of Germany into a myriad of warring interest groups
they tried to exploit the divisions, to be all things to all men, to create a
Nazi organization for doctors, lawyers, teachers, war pensioners, civil
servants, farmers, and every other occupational or special interest group.
They then pretended to champion each one, all the while orating incessantly about the leadership principle, the destruction of class barriers,
and the need to launch a national crusade to unite the *Volk* and restore
German greatness. It was all fabulously inconsistent but nonetheless
appealing to any particular group listening to a speech carefully tailored to
fit that audience.[12]

Alone among German political parties, the Nazis established schools
to train Party members as public speakers. Individual Party units enjoyed
greater autonomy than their Center or SPD counterparts, which meant
that fledgling Nazi speakers tried out more themes and techniques than

their rivals. These were studied carefully and their effects on different audiences noted. Speakers were then coached on what themes to stress to which audiences and how to reply to hostile questions. By January 1933, some six thousand Party speakers had been trained and had gained much experience. Each received seven marks per speech, plus board, lodging, and travel expenses. Since most of them were otherwise unemployed in the depths of the Depression, they had every incentive to speak enthusiastically and often, just to make a living. More noteworthy, as they improved in effectiveness they were given more assignments and better pay. The whole endeavor was financed by charging admission, something no other Party attempted. Thus did the Nazis to a considerable degree finance their own propaganda.[13]

Much of Nazi organizational superiority came from the high proportion of war veterans in their ranks. These men had grown accustomed to organization during the Great War, had become disciplined, and had learned the irrelevancy of rank or title at the front when issues of life and death were at stake. They also knew how to gauge the degrees of ruthlessness particular situations required. They had been spat upon by Left mobs when they had come home at the end of the war. They had long since concluded that Weimar was rotten to the core, and they needed no urging to bear down hard on all Left elements in the country.[14] After the disastrous Munich beer hall *Putsch* of 1923, the Nazis developed real expertise in the manipulation of violence. Too little of it, they realized, would be ineffective. Too much would scare off many of their supporters and would bring down upon them the wrath of the national government. The trick was not to attempt the overthrow of the Weimar regime by force but to use violence effectively as propaganda: to impress everyone that they were *serious*, that they were not just a mob of talkers like other parties, that they would stand and fight without regard for bourgeois respectability. At the same time they posed as a party of legality. When they did resort to violence they said they were replying to Communist violence, though their own attacks were more often on Social Democrats. It was all an effort to walk a fine line indeed, but logical or not it paralleled the prejudices of millions of Germans.[15]

Closely akin to Nazi flirtation with force was their use of mass meetings that featured not only impassioned speech-making by Party orators but much marching by uniformed SA units. The latter accentuated the impression of will, strength, unity, discipline, and forcefulness that the NSDAP strove to project, and it intimidated foes in the process. In many rural villages, though not in Oberschopfheim, these displays were good entertainment too, at a time and in places where most people had little of it. Thus were gained many supporters for the movement.[16] By 1932, though, the Nazis had come to believe that it was more effective to concentrate marchers, floats, loudspeakers, and flags in larger towns before bigger audiences and therefore strive to make a more lasting impact on viewers' imaginations.[17]

Nearly all writers on the Nazis, of whatever political persuasion, emphasize their constant, tireless activism and the relentless combativeness that set them off sharply from rival parties.[18] Those Nazi veterans who have written about the early years of the NSDAP have recounted the feeling of excitement and achievement they had when riding homeward in the middle of the night with their comrades after having broken up a meeting of a rival party or stirred up a fight somewhere. Once more, they said, they had felt a sense of purpose in life: once more they had done something for Germany.[19] Where did all this zeal and passion come from?

A lot of it came from the war, from scores of thousands of regular officers, reserve officers, and replacements for those officers who had been killed in combat. These men had been in positions of importance, many for the first time in their lives. In 1919 they did not want to return to humdrum existence under a regime that, in their view, had betrayed the ideals for which they had fought. Many of them had gone into the postwar *Freikorps* to fight the Communists, socialists, pacifists, cowards, and traitors who had "stabbed Germany in the back." After the official dissolution of the *Freikorps* in 1921 many had continued military exercises under the guise of "farm laborers" on East German estates, from which no small number had graduated finally to the Nazis.

By the late 1920s their numbers had been or were being augmented by recruits from other sectors of German society. These were almost all young people. Some of them had lost social status or self-esteem with the onset of the Depression. Some were uprooted young men from the "lost" provinces taken from Germany at Versailles. Most numerous were restless and discontented student idealists. Intensely nationalistic, perhaps in part to compensate for having been too young to serve in the war, convinced that Germany had been both betrayed at home and swindled by the perfidious Allies, resentful that they were graduating into a world that seemed to have no positions for persons of their presumed abilities and training, they yearned to "do something important." The lure of Nazi party jobs, uniforms, and ideology was powerful.[20]

Some scholars maintain that the "rootlessness" of so many early supporters of the Nazis has been overemphasized. They point to the great number of nonpolitical clubs and fraternities that existed in so many German towns, often supported by the local bourgeoisie, precisely to blunt political tensions. Natural activists, "pushers," "booster" types, "opinion makers," the ambitious, and mere congenital busybodies were always prominent in such groups. The Nazis realized this, these writers say, and so deliberately joined such clubs, as well as peasant organizations in the countryside. There they "bored from within," as Communists have long done. Soon they gained much influence in many German towns and villages and were persuading others to spread their message for them.[21]

After 1928, foreclosed farms, falling agricultural prices, and foreign competition began to draw increasing numbers from the countryside into the Nazi fold, from northwestern Germany and Schleswig-Holstein first,[22] then eastern Germany, then gradually from parts of Bavaria. A steadily growing number of them were youths who could not find jobs in cities and who had little prospect of inheriting family lands in the foreseeable future because their elders, frightened by the Depression, clung tenaciously to their farms. Yet economic hardship alone can hardly explain what happened. Voting records then and in succeeding years indicate that the great majority of the new converts to the NSDAP were Protestant even though the economic problems faced by Protestant and Catholic farmers were the same.[23] Richard Hamilton, who made an exhaustive study of German voting patterns in the 1920s and early 1930s, thinks the key differences were that in Catholic areas both the clergy and the press were generally anti-Nazi while the reverse was often the case where there were Protestant majorities; that Nazi militants were more numerous in Protestant than in Catholic communities; that Catholic voters were more faithful to the Center party than their Protestant confreres were to their parties; and that Nazi anti-Semitic propaganda was more effective in Protestant areas because Protestant states had usually removed medieval strictures on Jews earlier than Catholic states. The last had produced a general migration of Jews from Catholic to Protestant communities.[24]

Finally, religion or no, there is no gainsaying a few simple facts. Talent of whatever sort is not the same thing as moral goodness—indeed, it has no connection with it. Much of the success of the Nazis was due to Adolf Hitler personally. Though Hitler was one of history's most malignant scoundrels he was also one of its most charismatic political leaders. He had an unrivaled capacity to inspire and impress those around him, as all his close associates have testified. As a spellbinding orator he has never been surpassed.[25] It is also unpleasantly true that millions of Germans were so desperate at the nadir of the Depression that they cared nothing for the blatant inconsistencies in the Nazi program. If anything, they regarded these as an indication of Nazi frankness and sincerity. Convinced that the Weimar regime was beyond redemption, they merely hoped that those portions of the Nazi menu that looked palatable would be served to them and that what they disliked had been included only to attract others.[26]

The pattern of Nazi progress in Baden was much like that elsewhere in Germany. The Party was outlawed there in 1922. It continued to organize and meet clandestinely for several years, but it never gained much support and few took it seriously. Hitler's speeches attracted little notice, and not until 1929 did the local Nazi paper pay for itself. In Baden, as in Schleswig-Holstein, it was the agricultural depression of 1928 followed shortly by the Great Depression that sent Nazi stock soaring—to 7 percent of the vote in 1928, 19 percent in 1930, 37 percent in 1932.[27]

For years in the 1920s the NSDAP went unrepresented in Oberschopfheim. Few there voted for the Nazis even at the end of the decade, and the Party grew later than in most other parts of Baden. Superficially, this might appear odd. Party leaders, after all, might have expected villagers to be sympathetic to the call of German nationalism. Had not Oberschopfheimers served in the Great War, shared the burden of reparations after it, lost all their paper money in 1923, and observed nearby French occupation from 1923 to 1930? When the French troops left at last didn't the church bells in Oberschopfheim ring just as they did throughout the rest of Germany in celebration of the end of twelve years of foreign occupation? All true, but the villagers nonetheless remained parochial in outlook and lacking in the fervent patriotism and militarism of the inhabitants of Thalburg and Marburg.

The Hessian Marburgers did respond like Oberschopfheimers to Nazi efforts to deal with Germany's economic problems: that is, they cheered successes and grumbled about failures. To NSDAP debasement of democratic processes both communities were largely indifferent. What really stirred the souls of Marburgers and Thalburgers alike came later: rearmament, the resurgence of German nationalism, and Hitler's triumphs in foreign affairs, especially the seizure of the Sudetenland in 1938.[28] This side of Nazism simply had little appeal to Oberschopfheimers. Though the Depression had exacerbated their ancient village squabbles and created a lot of new ones, they were not sharply divided between workers and *petit bourgeoisie*, each with their own subculture, clubs, and political and economic organizations. Thus, unlike Thalburgers, they did not harbor venomous, principled bitterness for the Nazis to exploit.[29]

The ingrained political responses of Oberschopfheimers likewise offered little to comfort the Nazis. In many German villages, both Catholic and Protestant, clerical influence on the voting habits of church members was so effective that it was sometimes positively embarrassing, producing results that approached in predictability those in post-1945 Communist states.[30] In most elections in the 1920s only about half of the eligible voters in Oberschopfheim had bothered to go to the polls. Of those more than 80 percent routinely obeyed the pastor and voted for the Center (Catholic) party, thereby earning for themselves the sobriquet, "black nest of the Center."[31] That the NSDAP had "socialist" in its title certainly made farmers, especially Catholic farmers, wary since it conjured up visions of Marxism and land confiscation. Moreover, the vision of Hitler as the potential savior of Germany from Marxism was much weaker in Oberschopfheim than in the country at large. After all, there were only two people in Oberschopfheim who voted for the Communists (KPD) and twelve for Social Democrats (SPD). Everyone knew who they were, they had never harmed anyone, and no one bore them any personal animosity. Feelings about the SPD as a party were mixed. For years the SPD and the Center had been coalition partners in Baden and in the nation. There they mistrusted one another, one symptom of which was *Anzeiger* editorials that were increasingly critical of SPD opposition to a proposed concordat with Rome. Though the Nazis exploited this and eventually split the SPD-Center coalition in Baden, Oberschopfheim's Catholics did not reflexively abominate Social Democrats as "November criminals."

As for this most recent variant of "socialism," the NSDAP did not seem to pose a real threat to private ownership. Had not Hitler taken pains to explain that the Nazis did not advocate confiscation of family farms but only of lands secured by "speculation"? Likewise, when the Nazis espoused tariff protectionism, partly from conviction, partly from electoral calculation,[32] villagers cared little. Far more vivid to them was disillusionment with the Weimar Republic, which had always ignored their interests. Hatred being a stronger passion than love, they would have welcomed almost any party that denounced Weimar and promised to protect and defend them. Yet mere Nazi promises to introduce a controlled economy did not exactly fire their hearts because many villagers feared that it would mean more pestiferous outside interference.

Altogether, then, the Nazi program seemed a mixed bag to Oberschopfheimers. The NSDAP first began to gain serious sympathy among them when it promised to end unemployment, to raise the prices farmers obtained for their produce, and to limit competition among retailers. It also gained favor by attacking the government for its alleged economic blunders, especially destruction of the vineyards and higher taxes on tobacco. This array of motives for smiling on the NSDAP was reflected in the varied occupations of Oberschopfheim's earliest Party members. Though the popular Pastor Hirt of the 1930s and 1940s would record that business people avid for profit and comparatively well-off farmers were prominent among them,[33] a list of the thirty-four members of the Nazi party at the end of 1933 indicates a cross section of the community: four farmers, six small businessmen, three teachers, three self-employed men, three municipal officials, three salaried workers, and twelve manual workers.[34]

At least as important, the Nazis attracted followers for the same reasons that fascist movements did anywhere between the wars: they appeared aggressive, serious, and determined to act at a time when most of the "well behaved" democratic parties looked timid, torpid, corrupt, unimaginative, even senile.[35] Less important but still discernible reasons to regard the Nazis with favor were lingering resentment of seeing French occupation troops around for a decade and disgust at the spectacle of French culture displacing German culture across the Rhine in Alsace.[36]

A few young people in Oberschopfheim were attracted to the Nazis for some of the same reasons that impelled youths to flock to the swastika all over Germany: its slogans of "community" and "common weal before private gain," its call for loyalty and sacrifice, and its vigorous attacks on many unpopular institutions. Moreover, even though people of all ages belonged to the NSDAP it *looked* like a party of youth because the real activists, the Party members whom everybody saw most often, were mostly young people. This impression was accentuated by the Nazi practice of appointing young people to positions of power and influence— in marked contrast to the Social Democrats, who were dominated by aging bureaucrats.[37] Neither these youthful enthusiasts nor other villagers, however, really understood Hitler's goals. Most thought his party would form another coalition, one that they hoped would finally do something to end the economic malaise. While this attitude seems surprisingly naive more than half a century later, it must be remembered that few people anywhere carefully examine the programs of the parties they support, much less try to probe the characters of their leaders or guess what a given party might actually *do* in power years in the future. None of the ill-educated farmers in Oberschopfheim had ever read *Mein Kampf.* Even if they had, political sham is ordinarily detected more easily by foreigners than by people who wish to believe their own national leaders. More damning by far is the consideration that many *intellectuals*, both German and foreign, believed in 1929-1930 either that the Nazis would never amount to anything, that their violent talk was just political blather designed to win votes, or that if they gained power they would soon be sobered by the responsibilities of office, or that in power they would bring real benefits to Germany.[38]

Most uncomprehending of all were the Communists and Social Democrats. They excused their inaction by invoking the sacred texts of Marxist scripture to the effect that a Nazi triumph would be merely an "inevitable" stage in historical development that would have the effect of cementing the loyalty of a miraculously reunited working class to themselves. Following this, presumably, the terrestrial heaven envisioned by the Marxist prophets would be realized at last.

Villagers got most of their news about the Nazi party from the pages of the Catholic *Anzeiger,* which poked fun at Lahr's Nazi newspaper, *Gruesselhorn,* and carried on a running debate with it, thereby inadvertently giving the Nazis much publicity. Those Oberschopfheimers who had access to radios also learned from that medium of Nazi activities and speeches in nearby villages. However, despite some growth in knowledge of and sympathy for the NSDAP, in early 1930 this was still so limited and tepid that the Lahr county NSDAP organization was unable to establish a local unit or to hold parades and rallies in Oberschopfheim.

The main resistance to Nazism in Lahr county, and in Baden gener-ally, came not from the Socialists (SPD), as in Thalburg, but from the Catholic clergy.[39] Priests told their people from the pulpit, at meetings, and on the streets that they must vote for the Center party, for if the Nazis were elected they would attack both the Church and individual freedom. Opposition from this quarter weakened in 1930 and 1931 in Oberschopf-heim when Pfarrer Isele fell so ill that he retired to the rectory and had to call for an assistant. This new, young priest was no less vigilant to condemn the Nazis and warn the villagers not to vote for them, but he was less influential because he was an unproved newcomer and so lacked the old pastor's moral authority.

The *Anzeiger* was also a bulwark against Nazism but a flawed one. Oberschopfheimers read in its pages that most of the hierarchy con-demned the Party for its "un-Christian blind hatred of the Jews" and for its addiction to violence. Like so many, however, the *Anzeiger* failed to take the Nazis with sufficient seriousness. Instead, it called the NSDAP "pranksters" *(Lausbuben),* ridiculed them for tearing down posters and breaking up opponents' meetings in Lahr, and made fun of their leaders.[40] Thus opposition to the NSDAP anywhere in Lahr county was only half-hearted.

The big break in the fortunes of the Nazis, both nationally and in Oberschopfheim, came in the general election that followed the dissolu-tion of the *Reichstag* in 1930. At the time, the *Anzeiger* blamed political opponents of the Center party for subjecting the nation to the expense of new elections and for the violence that accompanied the campaign. As usual, it urged Catholics to do their duty by voting for the Center and printed a letter from the bishop of Freiburg in support of this.[41] In Oberschopfheim political activity was minimal. Nazis from Lahr held only one meeting, at which they spoke carefully of the desirability of uniting all Germans and returning a "new, dynamic *Reichstag.*" Center party lead-ers held a mere three short meetings. In dramatic contrast, some parts of Baden experienced so much violence that the government forbade all open air assemblies, including loudspeakers on cars, while in Thalburg, up in Westphalia, the NSDAP mounted a strenuous campaign of meetings and parades that often flared into violence. All over Germany Nazi orators hammered away at the claim that all the middle parties were hopelessly ineffectual and that the only real choice before the voters was themselves or the Bolsheviks.[42]

In excellent weather on Sunday, 14 September 1930, German voters went to the polls to choose a new *Reichstag*. Not the customary 50 percent or so of Oberschopfheimers turned out but a record 76 percent, though this pales before the 94 percent of Thalburg's voters who went to vote. The result was astounding, both nationwide and locally. The total Nazi vote soared from 600,000 in 1928 to 6,500,000. In Oberschopfheim support for the Nazis rocketed from less than 1 percent of the electorate in 1928 to over 28 percent. In percentages this was roughly the same meteoric rise that the NSDAP showed throughout Lahr county and in Thalburg, and well beyond the 18 percent they secured in the whole nation. Abruptly the Nazis had sprung from nowhere to become the second largest party not merely in Oberschopfheim but in all Germany.

These amazing election returns and the equally amazing ones from the elections of 1932 have been subjected to innumerable analyses. Some scholars have tried to account for the Nazi successes, at least in part, by emphasizing that some three million elderly voters had died since 1928. The implication has always been that these people would have been anti-Nazi. In the 1980s this assumption was called into question, especially by Richard Hamilton, who emphasizes that considerable Nazi *voting strength* came from retired people, particularly aged pensioners.[43] It has been more common to stress that some six and a half million new voters had come of age after 1928 and to assume that these young people, disillusioned with the old parties, yearning for action, and heavily over-represented on Nazi party membership lists, had swelled NSDAP totals.[44] Other scholars have noted that many people who had hitherto not bothered to vote (like many of the villagers in Oberschopfheim), began to do so during the Depression. They think most such new voters supported the Nazis. Others emphasize impressive Nazi gains among country people, especially Protestants.[45] Many consider that the Nazis gained more electoral support from people disillusioned with other parties than from any other source. In Oberschopfheim such erosion came primarily from the Center.[46]

In the early 1980s Richard Hamilton undertook what proved to be an exceptionally thorough study of German voting patterns in the years immediately preceding the Nazi advent to power. One of his major conclusions was that the common assumption that the Nazis' main support came from the lower middle class is not necessarily false but remains unproved, unsupported by serious evidence, merely taken for granted.

How did this come about? From Marxist theology and the predilections of intellectuals, he says. Marxists, and most intellectuals of the non-Marxist Left as well, analyze most serious problems according to "class," whether this fits or not. Moreover, like so many intellectuals of all sorts at all times, they like to explain important developments in terms of the clash of great ideas or impersonal forces because this seems more profound than to attribute them to the mere foibles of individuals. Those of the Left believe that economic considerations, especially tensions, outweigh every other consideration as shapers of human history, that economic and social structures develop independently of the human will, that in advanced capitalist societies these develop steadily in ways inimical to the position of the lower middle class, and that this social group then turns to extremist parties or movements in an effort to regain its former position. Lower middle class people are especially vulnerable to demagogic appeals because in modern times they have been deprived of their traditional ties and beliefs. Hence they *must* have been the main support for the Nazis. Finally, this is a conclusion particularly congenial to intellectuals. All self-conscious groups need someone to disdain and deprecate. Among Western intellectuals it is unacceptable to sneer at other races or nationalities but acceptable to scorn "lower middle class philistines" who lack respect for intellectuals and are either hostile or indifferent to the interests and values of the self-anointed elite.[47]

Hamilton's criticism of the "lower middle class thesis" is detailed and convincing. He points out that innumerable writers use the term "lower middle class" without ever trying to define just whom they mean. Yet the designation encompasses all sorts of quite diverse people, urban and rural, most of whom lived intermingled with people of other "classes." He stresses that in his own research one of his most vexing problems was trying to determine just what *was* a "middle class" or "working class" district. In German cities around 1930 many people who had minor white collar jobs continued to live with families, friends, neighbors, and former classmates in the same "workers" communities where they had grown up, often in the same houses. Many voting areas in Berlin were the dwelling places of people ranging from major executives to file clerks, all of whom happened to work for the same company. Apartment houses often contained all sorts of people from the affluent to the relatively poor, the former living in expensive, spacious quarters with a fine view, the latter in smaller rooms in the back of the building. Yet they all voted in the same district. Servants of the wealthy often lived in the same houses as their employers. All voted. But which voted for the Nazis? The bosses? The cooks and the maids? No one can say for certain.[48]

Some of Hamilton's most telling criticisms of the "lower middle class thesis" arise from mere common sense. The whole thesis interprets everything in terms of class, occupation, and ideology. In the real world most people, especially the young, from working class families, or those of the "lower middle class" for that matter, take whatever jobs happen to be available when they need work. If they continue to live at home they continue to associate with the same family members, friends, former schoolmates, and neighbors they have always known. Most of them are not likely to change their whole ideological outlook merely because they happen to have acquired a job of a certain type. Many join a particular union not because they prefer it to all others but because it happens to be the only one where they work or its insurance program is better than some other one or its recruiters are more persuasive than those of rival unions. Most people in most societies are not passionately interested in politics on a daily basis. Thus they pick their jobs, their personal friends, and their places of residence for all kinds of reasons having little to do with "class" or ideology. Like the "Tory workers" in England, they often vote for certain parties or against others for religious reasons or because their family has always supported a particular party or for some other consideration having no connection with economic interest.[49] In the cases of some "lower middle class" supporters of the Nazis they were such not *because* they were lower middle class. Rather, they had been pushed down into that class because they had spent so much time on Nazi political activity that they had neglected their jobs and had been passed over for promotion, demoted, or fired.[50]

Hamilton's positive conclusions about the sources of Nazi voting strength are at least as interesting as his criticisms of other scholars. He found that the strongest support for the Nazis came from the upper class and the upper middle class,[51] though the notion that the Nazis were mere creatures or protégés of big business is not supported by any convincing evidence—as distinguished from mere assertions.[52] The Nazis undoubtedly benefited from favorable treatment in many newspapers, especially those of the great press lord, Hugenberg. These publications emphasized the Marxist menace and thus made the stridently anti-Marxist Nazis seem important and respectable, yet Right newspapers supported *all* the conservative parties, and it is hard to believe that Hugenberg wanted to exalt the Nazis at the expense of *his own* following. Moreover, journalism is a *business,* and most papers, even conservative ones, did not want to alienate advertisers who favored other parties over the NSDAP. Thus support of the Nazis was often muted. Finally, the Nazis got much attention in the press for a nonideological reason. They were the most indefatigable activists of their day. They were always *doing* something. Thus they would have attracted much attention no matter what their political complexion.[53]

As for other occupational classes, Hamilton concludes that many manual laborers who had previously voted for middle class parties shifted to the Nazis by 1932 but that, overall, workers' support for the Nazis was lower than that of any other social group, that the support the NSDAP received from mixed lower and lower middle-class areas has often been overrated, and that lower middle-class support alone, insofar as it can be distinguished, was about average for the whole country.[54]

Hamilton's researches have seriously undermined some other common claims about Nazi support too. If "lower middle class" includes farmers, then to say that it supported the Nazis is untrue because it was mostly Protestant farmers who extended such support. Likewise, to say that "peasants" supported the Nazis is inaccurate for the same reason: most of the Catholic peasants didn't. Generally, rural areas voted more heavily for the NSDAP than did cities, especially big cities, but NSDAP strength in the whole nation from 1930 to 1932 is easily overrated because a higher proportion of Protestants and the religiously uncommitted voted than did Catholics. Thus even though some of the heaviest support for the NSDAP came from the Protestant countryside, this was far from the whole nation embracing the Nazis.[55] It also undermines the notion that totalitarian movements thrive on support from the "uprooted masses" in huge modern cities. Lumpenproletarian districts in cities usually gave the Nazis less electoral support than any others. By contrast, the Protestant countryside and the upper and upper middle classes, in all of which most people were surely well-rooted, supported them above the national average.[56]

Electoral results in Lahr county in 1930 support Hamilton's analysis overall. In spite of strong support for the Nazis everywhere there and without minimizing widespread hope that once in power the Nazis would alleviate everyone's economic plight, it is clear that religion was still the most important shaper of the voting preferences of local villagers. The NSDAP was preferred by two-thirds of all Lutheran villages, the Center party by all Catholic villages save one and by all villages of mixed religion except one. In Oberschopfheim, though the Nazis got 28 percent of the votes, the Center party received more than twice as many (61 percent) and this with the influential pastor *hors de combat*. Still, the psychological impact of the Nazi rise was immense: greater than mere numbers would indicate. Because of the many parties that had an appreciable following in the towns of Lahr and Dinglingen and because Communists had polled impressively there, the Nazis actually emerged as the largest party in the county seat. Clearly, whether regarded locally or nationally, the NSDAP was now a threat to the traditional ruling parties. Most newspapers expressed astonishment at what had happened. Some attributed it to the alleged lack of wisdom of new voters; some blamed it on distrust of the old parties.

A month later elections for county and district offices took place in a less intense atmosphere. Voter turnout dropped off generally, greatly to the disadvantage of the Nazis, and the Center, Socialist, and State parties hurriedly formed post-election coalitions to keep Nazis out of top positions on district and county boards.[57] In Lahr city, by contrast, the Nazis gained 35 percent of the votes. There they secured six of the fourteen seats on the municipal inner council and twenty-five seats on the outer council. At once they began to plan to elect their own mayor and to exert pressure on rural villages.

In the fifteen months between the end of 1930 and the presidential elections of 1932 the Nazis ceaselessly provoked trouble throughout Germany. They staged mass meetings, parades, and demonstrations, started street fights, and defamed the Center and Social Democratic parties. The old parties, they charged interminably, were corrupt. They had imposed unjust taxes, even deliberately caused the Depression. In Lahr city the Nazis on the council kept that body in constant turmoil by emulating the Irish Nationalists in the late nineteenth-century British Parliament: deliberately fomenting trouble so as to render impossible the orderly conduct of regular business. In this particular case they proposed countless ordinances dealing with such "issues" as preventing Jews from operating butcher shops. Baden's *Landtag*, like that of Prussia, responded to what was really low-level guerrilla warfare by short-term prohibitions of parades, open meetings and the wearing of party uniforms and by ordering the surrender of all weapons such as swords and butcher knives. All to no avail. Street fighting between rival gangs of toughs from various parties accelerated, as did what Moscow journalists would later call "hooliganism."

Despite all the violence and turmoil, which is commonly alleged to alienate persons of intelligence and refinement, increasing numbers of such people began to join the Nazi party. Some were intellectuals who admired Hitler's Social Darwinism, for it provided a means to distance themselves from the democratic masses and the vulgarity of modernism. Some were high-ranking civil servants, convinced that Weimar democracy had failed and was dying. Quite a few were teachers. Some were not really intellectual types but troubled members of the SPD who had lost faith in the party of their past. Not a few were mere opportunists or hitherto uncommitted people who now judged that the Nazis were destined to come to power soon.[58]

In Lahr city local NSDAP speakers and the Nazi paper, *Gruesselhorn*, tried to win Catholics to the party by claiming that the bishop of Freiburg attended Nazi meetings and allowed church burial for Party members.

The *Anzeiger* found itself repeatedly denying Nazi statements and explaining that church burial of Nazi party members did not mean acceptance of Nazi ideas. The *Gruesselhorn* riposted that as soon as the NSDAP controlled Lahr it would silence the *Anzeiger*. The peasants of Oberschopfheim, mercifully spared the turmoil and physical violence engulfing the rest of Germany, listened to the din of controversy and were unsure what to believe.[59]

Since a stable parliamentary majority in the *Reichstag* did not exist after early 1930, Chancellor Bruening used Article 48 of the Weimar constitution to rule by decree and, in effect, to end parliamentary democracy. He was thus able to avoid national elections until early 1932 and thereby deny the Nazis a chance to demonstrate new gains. This respite ended with the presidential election of 13 March 1932 and the runoff a month later.

During the campaigning from February to April, posters, meetings, and newspapers raised tensions in Oberschopfheim, though this was insignificant compared to the wild charges, character assassination, incessant parading, street fights, and general atmosphere of violence that prevailed in Lahr, Thalburg, and many other German towns.[60] The choice before the electorate was essentially between the aged, senile Field Marshal von Hindenburg, who had the support of the Center, State, Peoples, Socialist, and splinter parties, and Hitler, who was backed by the Nazis and the Nationalists.

In the first election of 13 March and the runoff of 10 April, 70 percent of Oberschopfheim's voters went to the polls. Although almost two-thirds chose Hindenburg, the Nazis made significant gains over the 1930 elections, receiving 35 percent of Oberschopfheim's vote in March and 37 percent in April. This was close to the national figure, a bit below Lahr county's support for Hitler and significantly below that of largely Lutheran Thalburg (51 percent and 56 percent).[61] Hitler did so well in both Lahr county and Oberschopfheim because he had convinced a growing number of farmers, shopkeepers, and others that if elected he would at once end the Depression by a massive distribution of economic aid.[62]

Catholic and Lutheran villages again divided along religious lines. Even though the Lutheran church officially supported Hindenburg, all Protestant villages voted overwhelmingly for Hitler. Most Catholic villages chose Hindenburg overwhelmingly in both elections, and most mixed villages voted narrowly for the old Marshal. The urban areas of Lahr county gave Hitler almost as many votes as Hindenburg.[63]

Throughout Germany voters went to the polls in record numbers. The Nazis lost the election but made impressive gains, and political tensions intensified since the *Reichstag* elections were scheduled for July. In Thalburg, political violence became a way of life.[64] In Lahr county the *Anzeiger* warned that frequent elections would allow radical parties to take over the government. It followed up with renewed attacks on the Nazis, pointing out that they routinely employed violence against all their opponents, even to the assassination of churchmen. They told their readers that if they would only examine "the cat in the sack" they would see that the Nazis were not the right people to govern Germany and that Hitler would lead the country into a European war. Even if the Nazis changed in essentials, the editor predicted, the Catholic church would never countenance their party.[65] Despite all these admonitions in the newspapers and turbulence in the cities, Oberschopfheim remained quiet. Inhabitants grumbled not about the political issues at stake but that the cost of frequent elections added to the village debt.[66]

In the July election, Oberschopfheim briefly fell behind the nation in its support for the Nazis, giving the NSDAP 30 percent of its votes against 37.3 percent throughout the Reich. In November, however, the situation was reversed: support for the Nazis fell about 5 percent in the Reich as a whole but increased 5 percent in Oberschopfheim. Perhaps the change was because of the waning influence of the dying pastor and the example of two villagers who joined the Nazi party before the November election.[67]

Whichever, villagers' support for the NSDAP in the *Reichstag* elections was still below that given to Hitler in the second presidential election seven months before, indicating that Der Fueuhrer was more popular than his Party. Voter participation also dropped sharply in both *Reichstag* elections because inhabitants blamed all parties for fighting among themselves instead of attacking the economic crisis.

Once more religion dominated voting in Lahr county, though a steady drift toward Nazism was quite perceptible. All the Lutheran villages went Nazi, as before, but this time over half of the mixed villages did so too, and even a fifth of the Catholic villages.[68] Both Lahr county and Thalburg supported the Nazis more enthusiastically than did the nation at large and more so than did Oberschopfheim. Ironically, in the same months fierce intramural struggles within the NSDAP in Lahr and Dinglingen reduced the local Nazi party organization to shambles. Though the earlier warnings of the *Anzeiger* about the malign nature and proclivities of the Nazis were to be vindicated by events, its writers now succumbed to wishful thinking and predicted that the Nazi threat would subside. Many readers agreed.[69]

# 7

# THE NAZI ERA
# IN PEACETIME

ONE OF Adolf Hitler's favorite ploys was to take others by surprise. Many of his successes, both at home and abroad, owed much to shrewd employment of this tactic. In an action that would become all too typical, after his unexpected appointment as chancellor on 30 January 1933, the Nazis immediately refused to work with other parties in the *Reichstag*. Everyone was shocked.

In Lahr county the *Anzeiger* received the news with apprehension and changed its editorial policy. It stopped all anti-Nazi articles for fear of losing official advertisements and intensified its attacks on the Social Democrats, primarily because the latter had opposed a concordat between Baden and the Papacy. For good measure, the *Anzeiger* blamed the SPD for persistent lack of cooperation in the *Reichstag* throughout the Weimar era, though it expressed skepticism about Nazi charges that the Socialists had burned down the *Reichstag* building.[1]

Oberschopfheimers were much less alarmed than editors of the *Anzeiger*. When Hitler scheduled new *Reichstag* elections for March, the main response of frugal villagers was to complain once more about how much elections cost and the social conflict they engendered. Perhaps luckily, an influenza epidemic spared the village the fiery oratory and campaign violence that afflicted most communities in Germany, including Lahr and Thalburg.

This is not to say that Nazi electioneering did not exist in Oberschopfheim, or that it was not effective. For many weeks NSDAP radio propaganda reminded voters incessantly that Hitler had never held a public office. It depicted him as an honest, sincere man who liked children and dogs; one who freely foreswore his salary and refused to enrich himself "like Weimar politicians." Promises were endless that he would conquer the Depression if only a Nazi majority was returned to the *Reichstag*. Many Oberschopfheimers were impressed by this litany of real and alleged virtues combined with promises of ardently desired wonders to come. A record 82 percent of eligible voters from the village went to the polls on 5 March 1933, and 48 percent voted for the Nazis. Though villagers still gave the Center party a few more votes than the NSDAP, Oberschopfheim had clearly lost its old reputation as a "black nest of the Center Party." [2] The winds of change continued to blow throughout Lahr county too. This time the Nazis carried 49 percent of the whole county: all the Protestant villages, all but one of the mixed communities, and more than a quarter of the Catholic villages.

Many accounts of Germany's nazification give the impression that Hitler and the NSDAP possessed almost supernatural powers. In the first six months of 1933, one reads, political opposition melted away without much of a fight. Nazi leaders simply coordinated and assumed all offices in the government, police, and judiciary, and the NSDAP established "totalitarian controls" over individuals, churches, the media, and the armed forces. The truth was more prosaic. There is no question that the Nazis *wished* to attain all these objectives and *tried* to attain them and that had they won the Second World War they would have carried through to completion all these fundamental changes and more;[3] yet much time is required to effect sweeping changes in any society. It is easily forgotten that the whole Nazi era lasted only twelve years, six of which were spent at war.

Although the "Nazi Revolution" began in Berlin it had to be carried out by the rank and file members of local NSDAP organizations. These varied widely in size, unity, fervor, and quality of leadership. Local party organizations also chose diverse methods and timing in pursuit of their objectives. Some communities were farther removed geographically from central authorities than others. Insularity and suspicion of outsiders was by no means uniform. Some localities prized their churches and local institutions more than others. Many workers, farmers, and other special interest groups accepted the new regime externally but never became enthusiastic, unreserved Nazis.[4]

Understanding the onset and ultimate pervasiveness of Nazism is also muddied by longstanding disputes among scholars about what should properly be called "totalitarian";[5] when, if ever, Germany became a true totalitarian state;[6] from which groups in society the Nazis derived their chief support,[7] whether or not distinctions between Party members and nonmembers are meaningful,[8] whether there was ever any effective "resistance" to the Nazi regime,[9] and whether open resistance to a twentieth-century dictatorship is even possible.[10]

In spite of their impressive victory in the March elections, the NSDAP was not strong enough to immediately seize control of all levels of government in Germany. Throughout most of the country nazification came gradually, in three stages: (1)"coordination" (*Gleichschaltung*) of all opposition parties and newspapers immediately following the March elections; (2) "concentration of power" (*Konzentration der Macht*) over local organizations and their members after the Roehm purge of 1934; and (3) establishment of a "Party State" (*Parteistaat*) that achieved outward control over citizens in 1935. During each phase most large Nazi party organizations in cities resorted, in varying degrees, to violence, bloodshed, and imprisonment of their more obdurate opponents.[11]

In Thalburg, Nazi victories in city elections in mid-March 1933 were quickly followed by the arrest of non-Nazi councillors and officials. Since the town's local group leader was also deputy mayor, he, with the backing of the Nazi county leader (Kreisleiter), needed only three months to reduce the mayor and town council to insignificance and assume full powers himself. A month later the county leader had similarly reduced the county council to a mere ceremonial body.[12] In the Hessian university town of Marburg, by contrast, the Nazis did not so much seize control of local government as destroy it. It met far less frequently than before and its actions were no longer publicized.[13]

In Baden and Lahr county, now renamed Gau Baden and Gau Ortenau, the new regime proceeded much as in Thalburg. Immediately after the March elections State Nazi Leader (Gauleiter) Robert Wagner began to "coordinate" state and local government by arresting the minister president and reorganizing the *Landtag* according to the election results— but with the Communists left out. In April he helped Lahr restructure both city councils with Nazi majorities. The next month he reorganized Lahr's district and county councils to favor the NSDAP. In July he appointed a Nazi Kreisleiter for Lahr county with power to organize the Party in every village.[14]

It might appear that Nazi domination of Lahr county was less speedy and complete than that gained in Thalburg, since not many local Nazis were qualified civil servants. Gauleiter Wagner solved the problem nicely by simply keeping on most of the old bureaucrats and "salting" them with a few Nazis in key positions. The incumbents worked just as efficiently for the Nazis as they had for previous governments and as they would for the French occupation forces after 1945. One of them, the Lahr county executive (*Landrat*), actually served the Nazis so well that within two years he was promoted to Baden's ministry of the interior.

Wagner supplemented his domination of state and local government by securing control over the local press and disbanding opposition political parties. The numerically strong Center party succumbed to the pressure 5 July 1933, after being offered a concordat between Baden and the Papacy that guaranteed religious liberty to Catholics. Many of its supporters in both Oberschopfheim and Lahr county verbally denounced this act as a betrayal, but they did nothing save comfort themselves with the rationalization that their leaders knew best.[15]

For the Nazis, the newspapers were no more troublesome than the rival parties had been. As in Thalburg and other German cities, scores of small newspapers throughout Baden fell silent in March and April 1933. An exception was the Center's *Anzeiger* in Lahr, which remained untouched until September, following which it survived only after a sharp warning. Since the Nazi *Gruesselhorn* was a third-rate paper with few readers, the Nazis did not expand it as they did their Party organ in Thalburg, but merely made the Nationalist *Zeitung* the official NSDAP organ for Lahr county.[16]

If the rapid nazification of Lahr and Thalburg might be likened to an earthquake, what took place in Oberschopfheim was more like a weak aftershock. Though nearly half of the villagers had voted for the Nazis in the election of March 1933, few had any clear idea about what political changes, if any, would follow from an NSDAP victory. This is hardly surprising. In modern societies many public questions, especially those related to government finance, defense policy, agriculture, and welfare, are so complex that few people, educated or not, ever really understand them. Most despair of trying. Thus, in practice, even in the most advanced nations the majority of voters are ill-informed, illogical, emotional, lazy, and prone to believe what they want to believe. The democratic article of faith that they will be calm, rational, wise, and humane when they go to the polls is as far removed from reality as was the cult of the Noble Savage in the eighteenth century.[17] Even in democratic states successful politicians habitually make conflicting promises to different constituencies. On this score, Hitler was merely more extreme than most. In Oberschopfheim some expected Hitler and followers to "throw the rascals out" in Berlin, Karlsruhe, and Lahr but (somehow) to leave Oberschopfheim alone. Others hoped that Nazi supporters would be rewarded with jobs in the courthouse or on the railroad.

It was not long before the near fifty-fifty split between the Center party and the NSDAP in the March election was reflected in village daily life. When people realized the extent of Nazi control, when they read that their bishop had condoned friendship with the Nazis, when they heard that the NSDAP promised jobs and money, many Oberschopfheimers urged the mayor and council to cooperate with Germany's new rulers. Mayor Einsele and others, however, steadfastly refused. Soon the village was divided into two hostile groups, with most of the unemployed advocating collaboration while others warned that Nazi fanatics would try to bully local citizens. Deprived of the decisive voice of the pastor who had died

and had not yet been replaced, tempers flared and the village was paralyzed.[18]

Mayor Wilhelm Einsele did not openly defy the Nazis. Instead, he
temporized. When Nazi directives called for a smaller council he interpreted them in such a way as to eliminate his opponents. Once obtained,
however, the smaller council did not by itself end the conflict. In October
1933 the *Gemeinderat* accused an employee of embezzling village funds.
Two of its members immediately complained that the mayor had been
remiss in supervision, and demanded that the Nazi Kreisleiter punish and
replace him. Welcoming this call for intervention from a divided village,
the county leader in October 1933 decided to appoint new officials who
would swear to follow Nazi orders. Even so, he had to proceed cautiously
since the village was solidly Catholic and, a year earlier, had contained a
mere two Party members, Karl Butz, a self-employed artisan, and Andreas
Mueller, an unskilled worker. Consequently, he contented himself with
appointing deputy mayor Franz Roederer as mayor and placing two village
Party leaders on the council. No other officials or village employees were
touched. Thus Nazi intervention in the government of Oberschopfheim
was only partial, and it began months later than in Thalburg or in most
other German cities.

The Kreisleiter also handled former mayor Einsele with care. When
the vindictive new council sued Einsele for mismanagement, terminated
his pension, and refused to reimburse him for village purchases, the
Kreisleiter let the conflict drag on for a year and a half, then pressured the
council to drop the action for lack of evidence. Nonetheless, the rancor
engendered was only submerged: it burst forth again after 1945 when
Einsele once more became mayor.[19] Despite their vigorous hostility to
Einsele, the new mayor and council did not on that account surrender
control of the village to the Nazi Kreisleiter. Instead, they cooperated just
enough to receive favorable treatment for jobs and federal funds. Bavarian
villages were, if anything, even more ingenious in devising ways to thwart
Nazi designs on their ancient customs and ways of life.[20] After Hitler
assumed power, most Nazi organizations throughout Germany tripled in
size within three months. In Thalburg new members flooded the Party
rolls at a rate far above the national average.[21] But not in rural areas. In the
Bavarian villages of Laimering and Warmesried, both heavily Catholic,
few joined the Party either before 1933 or afterward. In other villages
people joined, if urged by the pastor, so they could influence the organization. Some even hoped to control it.[22] In Oberschopfheim the county
leader established a local unit by decree in October 1933 and used threats
to persuade thirty-four people to join it. Membership crept upward to
forty-two in 1936. Then, under more serious pressure from the county

leader and a new local group leader, it rose more rapidly to 135 by 1944. Fourteen of these were women, mostly wives of male Party members. Twelve of the men joined neighboring SA units and two joined SS units.[23]

Although Oberschopfheimers joined the NSDAP reluctantly and later than the average in either Baden or the Reich as a whole, eventually the percentage of Nazis among inhabitants and voters was only slightly below the state and national average. As in the nation at large, Party members were a good cross section of village society. Ideologues and Allied wartime propaganda have always insisted that the Nazis were the "scum" of German society, and of course the Nazis did have their quota of brutes, thugs, and monomaniacs, particularly among the leaders and in the SS. Nonetheless, the history of many other countries in the twentieth century (Turkey, Russia, China, Nicaragua, Indonesia, Argentina, Salvador, Chile, Pakistan, Iran, Iraq, Spain, South Africa, Ethiopia, Cambodia, Nigeria, Uganda, Syria, Korea, and Japan, to cite only some of the more egregious cases) has demonstrated that "Nazi types" in the contemporary world are by no means confined to Germany. A vastly greater number of Germans, both inside and outside the NSDAP, showed a distressing inclination to simply obey any orders that came from superiors. But even this was and is hardly a uniquely German phenomenon. People anywhere find it difficult to resist any regime or ideology on principle unless they strongly cherish some counterideology. Not many Germans were as strongly supportive of other parties as the Nazis were of the NSDAP. Finally, those who happen to live in one of the world's mild Western democracies easily forget how lucky they are and how open opposition to any of the harsh authoritarian governments so common elsewhere usually gets an ordinary person into serious trouble.[24]

Whatever their occupation or social standing in the village, most of Oberschopfheim's Nazis justified their membership in the NSDAP in economic terms. Like Germans elsewhere, if they were unemployed or worked only part-time, they expected membership to guarantee steady jobs. A few even believed that they would become mayors. Officials and village employees hoped that joining the Party would enable them to keep their positions. Some store owners anticipated exclusive rights to redeem government coupons for food, clothing, and furniture. Farmers expected loans and high prices for their crops. Self-employed persons were attracted by Nazi promises of economic protection for the "small man." Debtors hoped that the Nazis would cancel their obligations.[25] If asked to justify their actions, villagers would often reply, "Whose bread I eat, his song I sing." Since their ancestors had for centuries invoked this proverb during wars and invasions, many inhabitants believed that they were merely acting traditionally. In Oberschopfheim most people hoped—and perhaps most believed—that they could secure benefits without giving the Nazis much in return. Those few people who gave up their jobs rather than join the NSDAP were sometimes reviled by others for their "stupidity."

Aside from economic considerations, most officials and influential citizens joined the Party in hope of keeping some control over their own destiny. Convinced that it was futile to resist the Nazis openly, they hoped they could protect their village from radical change merely by ignoring certain Nazi orders that they considered unacceptable. Attitudes like these usually appear unworthy to intellectuals, whose stock in trade is ideas. They seem evidence of low intelligence, deficient education or moral inadequacy. But to ordinary people, it must be repeated, politics is not the mother's milk of existence. Most people think of their spouses, families, friends, jobs, career prospects, hobbies, and local communities much more than they do the ideologies that mean so much to those who write books, teach in universities, perform in the communications industries, or dream of a nobler future for humanity. Whether in Nazi Germany, Soviet Russia, or scores of other societies, authoritarian or democratic, spartan or lax, many people become party members not from enthusiasm for "doctrines" of any kind but merely to get a job, to keep a job, or to gain power and privilege.[26] Many others join parties merely to "drift with the current," to be part of the majority, to avoid real or seeming risks. If queried about such action they are apt to shrug their shoulders and reply something like, "What can you do?"

This is not to say that Nazi ideals had no appeal at all to Oberschopfheimers. One of the most potent talking points of the Nazis was that they had ended the incessant, sterile warfare of political parties. They constantly invoked such slogans as "People's Community" *(Volksgemeinschaft)* and "Common Good before Personal Good" *(Gemeinnutz vor Eigennutz)* in an effort to persuade Germans that they should feel and act as one rather than remain split into contentious factions.[27] As in the rest of Germany, many in Oberschopfheim found such injunctions heartening. Several teachers joined the NSDAP and a few young people became members of the Hitler Youth because they wanted to dedicate themselves to a cause.[28]

Levels of commitment among villagers were as varied as their motives. According to Party records, "active" members, which included anyone who attended meetings regularly or who took part in organizing Party events, slightly outnumbered nonactive or mere dues-paying members. This was reputedly true of the whole country too, though the proportion of officially "active" members in Oberschopfheim lagged behind that of either Baden or all Germany. The true difference between "active" and "inactive" members was often hard to ascertain because "active" bore a vastly different implication in some cities than it did in others or than it ordinarily did in villages. In Thalburg "active" members really were such. They frequently staged parades, marches, speeches, and book burnings, and they did not scruple to terrorize their opponents. In Marburg, by contrast, only five NSDAP functionaries devoted any considerable time to such activities, and even they were notably less zealous than their counterparts in Thalburg. In most of the villages of Lahr county, as in most Bavarian villages, "active" members were merely those who collected money for Nazi causes or attended infrequent Party meetings.[29]

Oberschopfheim's "active" members included seven officials, six self-employed persons (including farmers), three salaried men, and six workers. The most important of them were Local Group Leader (Ortsgruppenleiter) Karl Merkert, who rivaled Mayor Franz Roederer and the council for power and influence, and Local Farm Leader (Ortsbauernfuehrer) Franz K. Roederer II. The latter was a close relative of the mayor. Before 1933 he had shown no interest in politics, but when he realized that the Nazis might gain power he openly expressed sympathy for them. As a "wealthy" farmer (one with more than three acres), he managed to have himself appointed Nazi leader of agriculture, which allowed him to distribute farm aid in the village. That his motives were probably personal and pecuniary is suggested by the consideration that during the entire Nazi era he attended only a few Party lectures and read little propaganda.[30]

Group Leader Merkert's actions and motivation were comparably ambiguous. The retired rector of a Lahr school, Merkert gained his position because of his capacity for leadership and his sympathy for some Nazi goals. Though he organized the local Hitler Youth and lectured to Party members, nobody regarded him as a fanatic. He did crave power, however, and so struggled to become the dominant political leader of the village, an endeavor opposed by the mayor and strongly opposed by the pastor, neither of whom wanted any changes in the traditional political structure of Oberschopfheim.

Helping the former rector were three obedient teachers: Eugen Kern, Franz Lebfromm, and Lehrer Wenz. Like teachers elsewhere in Germany, those in the village were more politically "reliable" than the general run of the population,[31] perhaps because, as outsiders, they were more interested in their own advancement than in protecting the village from change. Even so, they did only what they were required to do—which was little. Other "active" members included persons officially in charge of such matters as Party "cells," neighborhood "blocks," propaganda, finances, welfare, labor, and the German Girls' League. They were mainly bearers of empty titles. Although one might expect "active" Nazis to be antireligious, this was not the case in Oberschopfheim or other villages in

Lahr county. Members continued to attend Sunday Mass, though a few did follow the Kreisleiter's orders and refused to join church processions that were considered a firm demonstration of support for Catholicism.

"Inactive" members merely paid dues and attended as few meetings as they could. Though it accords ill with either Nazi propaganda or with American stereotypes of Nazi enthusiasts cheering *en masse* for malign NSDAP principles, this widespread indifference to Nazi meetings ought not to surprise anyone since it is extremely common among rank-and-file members of all sorts of mass organizations everywhere. The German Social Democrats, for instance, had always had a hard time keeping the minds of their ordinary members fixed on ideology and long-term Party objectives. Many older working men came home at the end of the day tired from toil. Such leisure as they had they often spent sleeping off their exhaustion, drinking, or growling at their wives and children. They paid their Party dues so they wouldn't lose their jobs, but they had little interest in attending dreary Party meetings that were invariably dominated by the leaders. Younger workers were often attracted to the Party by its sporting and social clubs. Many Nazi party members differed little from the Social Democrats in these respects.[32] So it was too with the farmers of Oberschopfheim and neighboring villages. They looked forward to planting and harvesting seasons when meetings and other political events were canceled and they were left alone.[33] Like their ancestors, the main thing they wanted from the external world was a market for their excess produce.

By late 1934 most active and nonactive members alike had grown accustomed to being ruled by the Nazis. They thought little of outward acceptance of Party demands and had become genuinely enthusiastic about the highly visible economic improvements that were taking place. It was an attitude common throughout Lahr county and the whole nation.

Besides coercing some villagers to join the NSDAP in October 1933 and thereafter, the county leader tried to control the votes of others. In November 1933, for example, he told voters to approve both an all-Nazi *Reichstag* and German withdrawal from the League of Nations. All over Germany balloting was preceded by days of meetings, parades, and impassioned speechmaking. In Oberschopfheim the atmosphere was more subdued. Some families among whom enthusiasm for the new regime was strong turned their radios on full volume so everyone would hear Nazi propaganda. Zealous teachers questioned students about how their parents would vote. The group leader pressured some families to fly the Nazi flag but otherwise contented himself with making a couple of speeches.

Election day itself proceeded in a fashion dismally familiar among the dictatorships and "guided democracies" of our century. Voter participation was extremely high all over the country. Party members watched how everyone voted, and the NSDAP counted the ballots. Voila! The Party scored an overwhelming victory everywhere. Whether in Oberschopfheim, the state of Baden, or Germany overall, more than 95 percent voted for withdrawal from the League of Nations, Oberschopfheimers leading the way with 98.6 percent. Everywhere over 90 percent approved an all-Nazi *Reichstag*.

Of course the Lahr county leader took credit for controlling the votes of his flock but the truth was somewhat different. Many times in the 1930s foreign observers who had no personal sympathy for National Socialism wondered why Hitler bothered to claim 98 or 99 percent approval of whatever the government happened to put before the public in some plebiscite when, seemingly, he could have secured 80 to 85 percent approval in a completely fair, open election.[34] In this particular election industrious Oberschopfheimers warmly approved Hitler's insistence that all people, including beggars and gypsies, do a full day's work. Their attitude supports the contention of those who have argued that a major source of Hitler's popular appeal throughout Germany did not derive from Nazi ideology per se but from general affection for Hitler the *man* and widespread confidence in him. Comparatively few German hearts were fired by the pen of Alfred Rosenberg or the oratory of Josef Goebbels conjuring up visions of racial purity and Aryan supermen ruling tens of millions of *Untermenschen* in the heartland of Eurasia. Far more were inspired by another creation of Nazi propaganda: Adolf Hitler, champion of the German people, defender of traditional values, and relentless foe of Weimar rottenness.[35] Most important of all in Oberschopfheim, by October 1933 people were becoming increasingly convinced that the Nazis were "miraculously" overcoming the Depression and would soon give more aid to small villages like theirs. Finally, local newspapers were supportive. The Catholic *Anzeiger* encouraged readers to vote "yes" in the plebiscite and quoted the bishop in support of the action, while the *Zeitung* told its Lutheran readers that the election was an opportunity to regain international equality for Germany, end the Marxist revolutionary menace, and overcome the Depression.[36] Small wonder that voters dutifully responded with so many "*Ja*'s."

The importance of ecclesiastical guidance in elections seemed as evident as ever nine months later when voters returned to the polls to choose a Reich president to succeed the deceased Hindenburg. The *Anzeiger* again told its readers to vote for Hitler, who "is of our faith," surely one of the most grotesque assessments of a public figure in modern times.[37] Throughout the Reich nearly all voters went to the polls once more. Nearly 96 percent of them did their duty and voted for Hitler. In Oberschopfheim, though, where the new pastor, Dr. Hirt, strongly opposed the Fuehrer, voter participation fell off noticeably from that of November 1933: "only" 82.7 percent voted for Hitler.[38] Of course any politician or party in a true democracy would have rejoiced at such an overwhelming endorsement, but the zealots who espouse the various forms of twentieth-century secular messianism are notoriously insatiable. The county leader drew the conclusion that Pastor Hirt was dangerously uncontrolled.

Hitler's destruction of six million Jews has been the subject of so many thousands of speeches, articles, books, conferences, movies, and television programs that the world has largely forgotten that this ghastly atrocity was only *part* of the NSDAP program of biological engineering. The Nazis also planned to exterminate dissident intellectuals, the political leaders of enemy countries, socialists, communists, gypsies, the mentally ill and retarded, some categories of the sick and deformed, various "undesirable" religious sects, the clergy of the major Christian churches, and a hundred million East European Slavs. They had in fact made a start on some of these categories of humanity before World War II and began to murder others during the war.[39]

Early in 1933 the Nazi party and the major Christian churches viewed one another uneasily. At bottom Nazi doctrines were totally incompatible with Christianity of any sort, but Nazis, Catholics, and Lutherans all had reasons to downplay their differences and seek accommodation. Lutherans had some common ground with Nazis in that their church had long been nationalist and conservative. Both Catholics and Nazis disdained Weimar, disliked democracy, and hated and feared the Bolsheviks. Many individuals in both churches were anti-Semitic. Both churches feared loss of state support, and the clergy and people of both disagreed a good deal among themselves. Thus it was easy to make distinctions between the things of God and the things of Caesar and to search for common ground. Hitler, one of history's most accomplished and convincing liars, began by persuading the Center party to accept the Enabling Act (23 March 1933) in return for praise of the Christian churches and promises of respect for law and administrative regularity in the future.[40] Negotiations with the Vatican for a concordat followed. Later in the year the agreement was signed. One of its provisions forbade priests to participate in politics. The concordat was a victory for Hitler because it gave an aura of respectability to his regime abroad and neutralized much potential opposition to it at home. For the Catholic Church it was anything but a triumph. It wrecked the remnants of the Center party[41] and proved to be the first of many unsuccessful foreign attempts to appease Hitler. For the rest of the 1930s Catholics struggled to assert the privileges granted them in the concordat while the Nazis tried to curtail them.

For Catholics Hitler presented the same problem Napoleon had presented for Pope Pius VII after the concordat of 1801: he immediately set about to violate, wholesale, what he had just signed.[42] Soon the Nazis were confiscating monastic properties, instituting criminal action against troublesome priests, endeavoring to suppress Catholic youth organizations, attempting to oust both Catholic and Protestant clerics who taught religion classes in public schools, trying to take kindergartens away from religious teachers, forcing nuns out of the nursing profession, and striving to gain for themselves the primary loyalty of youth. They had some success in co-opting Protestant clerics but little with their Catholic counterparts. The latter resisted with obstruction and delay as they grew increasingly convinced that the Nazi world view was incompatible with their own. They denounced such Nazi publications as Julius Streicher's *Der Stuermer* for its pornography, regarded the circulation of Alfred Rosenberg's *The Myth of the Twentieth Century* as proof of the necessity of maintaining Catholic education, grew suspicious of the Hitler Youth on moral grounds, and opposed all efforts to displace Catholic teachers and nurses.[43]

Sometimes the Nazis responded with intensified repression of troublemakers. After *Anschluss* in 1938 they undertook special efforts to win Austrians from Catholicism to Nazism. Mass executions of Polish priests began after the conquest of Poland in 1939. During World War II Martin Bormann, Reinhard Heydrich, and various Nazi Gauleiter attempted to intensify the struggle against Catholicism, especially after Cardinal von Galen of Munster publicly condemned the Nazi practice of euthanasia in the summer of 1941. Several Catholics were prominent among the plotters against Hitler in 1944 because they had discovered that the Gestapo was already collecting "evidence" of unpatriotic activities by priests that would be used to promote a general proscription of Christianity after the war.[44]

One might wonder why the Nazis so often pulled back and temporized in the face of growing and obvious Catholic disapproval, why they did not simply smash these pesty malcontents. The main reason was tactical. Hitler feared to alienate great numbers of faithful churchgoers while World War II was in progress. The Reich still needed churches to celebrate victories and keep people quiet. There would be time enough to settle with them and their obstreperous clergy when the war was won. Perhaps another reason was rooted in Nazi psychology. Unlike the Bolsheviks, who always wanted to liquidate any enemy, the Nazis cared little about the opposition of individuals as long as it remained ineffective. Perhaps because of Hitler's contempt for the masses and his belief in the "leadership" principle, he was content to destroy opposition *organizations* and to kill or jail their leaders.[45] What took place in Oberschopfheim from 1933 to 1939 illustrates the strategy of the NSDAP and its response to opposition.

Unlike the Lutheran clergy in Thalburg, former Pastor Isele strongly opposed the NSDAP. Since he also influenced the selection of the mayor and village schoolteachers, and often determined important political matters, he would be an obvious target for any revolutionary party. Immediately after the elections of March 1933, Lahr Nazis tried to discredit him by charging that he opposed their Party because he feared the loss of his income. This tactic failed completely. When the ailing pastor died on 26 June 1933 all the villagers dressed in their best black clothes, joined the elaborate funeral Mass and procession, and watched while Mayor Einsele placed flowers on the grave. The village council then approved an expensive stone cross and tombstone for the deceased priest.[46] The whole episode highlighted a significant difference between Germans on the one hand and Englishmen and Americans on the other. Ordinary religious Germans were much more concerned to defend against the Nazis what they saw as the rights of their religion and church than they were to stand up for what Anglo-Saxons regard as political "freedom."

In the absence of a pastor during the summer of 1933 county Nazis won enough sympathizers to establish a local party unit and plan changes in Oberschopfheim's government. In late August Bishop Groeber of Freiburg, an ardent nationalist who believed he could deal with the Nazis,[47] was prodded by state officials to exile Dr. Hermann Hirt to the pastorate of Oberschopfheim. Hirt, then the thirty-nine-year-old editor of *Der Donaubote*, was already a notorious anti-Nazi writer and activist. He arrived under strict orders not to interfere in politics. Dutifully, he did nothing to block Nazi activities in Oberschopfheim during October 1933. In fact he seemed unexpectedly conciliatory, even accompanying the local group leader and village students to a Nazi celebration in Lahr. Privately, however, he spent much time visiting parishioners to win their confidence before reentering the political arena.[48]

Dr. Hirt is still remembered as the most beloved and respected pastor in the history of Oberschopfheim. Once he became acquainted with his parishioners he became the unquestioned leader of the village and single-handedly brought about a considerable religious revival. Father Hirt possessed unusual theatrical talent too, and was a moving and effective speaker. He introduced new German songs into his services, and he wrote and staged numerous plays that incorporated local legends and traditions. The latter were so popular that neighboring villagers flocked to Oberschopfheim at their presentation. Inspired by their new pastor, villagers soon made their Patron Saint's Day, "Christ the King" Sunday, and other religious feasts the most elaborate celebrations in Lahr county. Perhaps the most impressive of Dr. Hirt's productions was presented in April 1934, when, with the help of the mayor and the group leader, he arranged a "First Mass" celebration for one of Oberschopfheim's sons. At the mayor's urging, county leaders allowed the villagers to cut evergreen branches from the forest and erect triumphal arches throughout the village. The celebration lasted two days and included a reception at the village entrance, music, parades, and speeches from Mayor Roederer, Group Leader Merkert, and Pastor Hirt.[49] Many from all over Lahr county attended, while others read about it in the newspapers.

In spite of Oberschopfheimers' reputation for being tight-fisted, villagers were decidedly not stingy when their hearts or minds were touched. The same village councillors who were reluctant to spend money on anything not deemed absolutely essential contributed as much as two thousand marks annually to the church to compensate for shortfalls in weekly collections and, as noted before, honored the popular Pastor Isele with a handsome monument. The ordinary people of Oberschopfheim were comparably generous once Dr. Hirt had won their confidence. Despite the Depression, they refurnished the church with two Persian rugs, three silver candle holders, four altar crosses, new vestments, a tabernacle for a side altar, and a regilded tabernacle for the main altar. More noteworthy, in 1937 the parish council began to make plans for a new church building. As early as 1941 they had already collected the necessary money. To be confronted by a man capable of eliciting this response from his flock and who was a well-known anti-Nazi clearly posed some problems for local Nazi functionaries.

When Pastor Hirt saw that he had won most of the villagers, he chose St. Sylvester's Day (31 December 1933) to denounce Alfred Rosenberg's racist writings as contrary to Catholic doctrine months before Bishop Galen of Muenster and the Fulda Bishop's Conference did so. The sermon immediately precipitated a village crisis. Mayor Roederer angrily resigned as church trustee. Several Party members, including the group leader, vowed never to attend Mass again. Although Dr. Hirt later mollified the mayor and NSDAP members somewhat, this sermon marked the beginning of his open attacks on Nazism from the pulpit in Oberschopfheim.

During all of 1934 Hirt spoke repeatedly on the errors of Nazism and tried to keep his people away from Nazi organizations. He did this by arranging youth days, plays, and processions, not only for Oberschopfheim but for all of Lahr county. Since outsiders regularly attended these events, the county leader publicly forbade two youth conferences and ordered a neighboring SA troop to expel the crowds by force if the conferences took place. Hirt met this with a change of tactics. Knowing that the county leader could not prevent church services, which were guaranteed by the concordat, he rebaptized his youth conferences as "liturgical celebrations" and transferred them to the safety of the church building.[50]

Angered by this trick, the county leader arranged for Local Leader

Merkert to hold a compulsory meeting on Easter Sunday in order to keep people from attending Mass. Although the pastor countered by twice changing the time of the Easter service, Merkert responded by rescheduling his meeting to conflict with it. Finally Dr. Hirt confronted the group leader. He threatened to cancel all church services and then to publicly blame Merkert for the disruption.

Conflicts of this sort between pastors and NSDAP functionaries were not uncommon in Germany, particularly when some party to a dispute was also a teacher. Teachers were state employees and were sometimes sent by state officials into villages without any prior consultation with village officials or people. The villagers usually resented such treatment; doubly so because the teachers generally enjoyed better salaries, pensions, and medical benefits than did ordinary villagers. Merkert was such a teacher in the Oberschopfheim school. He knew that if the pastor publicly blamed him for preventing people from attending Mass on Easter, villagers would soon make life miserable for him and his family, so he quietly forgot about his "important" meeting.

On the feast of *Corpus Christi*, which featured the most important church procession in Oberschopfheim, Merkert prompted several Hitler Youth members to paint anti-Catholic messages and slogans on the streets during the preceding night. His object was to disrupt the procession. He and the county leader also tried to keep the pastor from teaching religion in the school since this interfered with their own efforts to inculcate Nazism. Far from curbing the pastor, such measures caused most villagers, including those who were Party members, to side with Hirt against the local group leader. By the end of 1934 Oberschopfheim's pastor had become not only the most significant anti-Nazi in Lahr county but one who had consistently evaded Party control with impunity. Exasperated county leaders wanted him silenced.

At about the same time the NSDAP launched a general attack on the Catholic church throughout Germany. It was reminiscent in some ways of Bismarck's *Kulturkampf* of the 1870s. Despite guarantees in the concordat Reichsinnenminister Frick demanded the abolition of church clubs. Baden's Gauleiter forbade Party members to attend traditional Christmas celebrations. Lahr officials prohibited the sale of "confessional-political" newspapers such as the Catholic *Junge Front*. Other officials forbade public collections or processions without permission. To avoid confrontation with the regime, Bishop Groeber ordered all churches to give up their flags, uniforms, and clubs.[51]

The indefatigable Dr. Hirt remained undeterred. He continued to attack the NSDAP every Sunday in his sermons, even though he knew that two local Party members, Stefan Jaeger and Josef Schwendemann, took notes that they delivered to Local Leader Merkert, who promptly forwarded them to his superiors in Lahr.[52] Often the pastor denounced persecutions of Jews, Christians, and ordinary citizens. One Sunday he was especially bold and dramatic. After he read the Gospel story of Jesus sleeping in a boat during a violent storm while the Apostles feared for their lives, Hirt declared that a comparable event was taking place in their own time. The mounting waves and driving winds that had threatened the lives of the Apostles were actually the violence of the NSDAP menacing Germany. The Lord, he said, was testing their faith, as He had tested that of the Apostles before smiting the storm. Hirt ended by crying out to the Lord to save Germany, as He had saved the Apostles. On the Feast of Christ the King, Hirt chose to contrast a king and a president with a Fuehrer. The first two, he said, were limited in power and could not continue in office if they broke the law. A Fuehrer, however, was "one who usurped full power and unjustly imposed his will without allowing people any choice."[53]

Besides such direct attacks on Nazism and Hitler, which had counterparts elsewhere, the pastor encouraged his Young Men's Club to protect defenseless people from haughty Hitler Youth. On several occasions the Catholic young men physically broke up Nazi assaults and contemptuously called their adversaries (mostly from other villages) "Swine Youth" to their faces.

After receiving reports of such events, outraged Nazi leaders in Karlsruhe decided that they had had enough. Without warning, twelve SS men and six policemen from Lahr arrested the leaders of the club at 4:00 A.M. on Friday, 3 May 1935, and took the men to a Lahr prison. There Nazi leaders tried to make them sign statements against Hirt and his club.

Villagers reacted with disbelief, then anger. To calm the turmoil Nazi Group 169 from Lahr paraded through the village that evening. Its commander announced that the head regional commander (Obergebietsfuehrer) from Karlsruhe would explain everything at the war memorial. Soon the commander justified Nazi actions by displaying a telegram from Mayor Roederer that accused the pastor of creating chaos and called for his immediate removal. The Nazis followed up by searching all the houses in the village for club flags, emblems, and insignia. They were nothing if not thorough, taking a whole week to complete their investigation. Nearly forty years afterward an old villager, Wilhelm Mussler, who had been recorder of the Catholic Young Men's Club in 1935, proudly showed one of these writers the club flag and official book he had managed to hide so securely in his attic that they had gone undiscovered. Meanwhile, *Gestapo* chief Bender from Offenburg confronted Dr. Hirt at the rectory and ordered immediate dissolution of all Catholic clubs even though their existence was guaranteed by the concordat. Thus Oberschopfheim's Young Men's Club disbanded two years later than its counterpart in Thalburg but four years earlier than such clubs in many German cities and villages.[54]

When the Nazi outsiders finally left Oberschopfheim, hostile villagers confronted Mayor Roederer, who promised a full explanation next day. After the usual Sunday Mass and announcements, he said that the Nazi chief had forged the telegram and that village officials had no advance knowledge of the affair. The accuracy of this "explanation" was problematical. In any case, spies soon reported the mayor's words to the county leader, who promptly replaced Roederer with a Nazi council member, Adolf Holzenthaler. Club members were kept in the Lahr jail from twelve to eighteen days, with a menacing German shepherd dog as a cellmate. After payment of a fine they were released. They still refused to sign a condemnation of Dr. Hirt, even when threatened with transfer to the Kisslau concentration camp.[55]

Several months after this fiasco the head regional commander again came to Oberschopfheim, this time to address the Hitler Youth from four villages. He admitted that "the tactics in May might have been a mistake" because they had aroused the ire and resistance of villagers, but he quickly added that "political Catholics" like Pastor Hirt would soon be silenced.[56]

While the NSDAP was attacking churches throughout Germany, rumors reached Karlsruhe that Bishop Groeber would appoint Dr. Hirt permanent pastor of Oberschopfheim or editor of the diocesan newspaper. The minister of the interior immediately forbade the bishop to do either. Although Groeber was generally accommodating to the Nazis, this time he ignored the order and quietly did both.

Several weeks later, on the anniversary of the Munich *Putsch* of 1923, the county leader commanded all villagers to fly the Nazi flag. Dr. Hirt promptly flew the Weimar flag to show his contempt for the Nazi "Holy Day." New mayor Holzenthaler quickly removed it, forbade Hirt to raise any flags henceforth, and tried to keep the scandal quiet. No luck! Lahr Nazis heard of the incident and decided to get rid of Hirt, even if they had to murder him. Three obstacles stood in their way: the villagers, the mayor, and, improbably, Oberschopfheim's ghosts.[57]

Should we be surprised that many people in Lahr county, even some Nazis, still believed in ghosts in the 1930s? Hardly, if one reflects that gypsy women and others were then and still are believed by some Mediterranean peasants to be capable of casting an "evil eye" or that in the 1960s Spanish villagers were confident that "wise women" (sabias) possessed supernatural powers of healing that derived from the goodness of their personal characters[58] or when innumerable newspapers in Western countries still print horoscope columns and when the wife of an American president publicly acknowledged regular consultation with an astrologer on important occasions. The same general tradition has had deep roots and a long life in Germany too. Belief in witches there lasted until quite recent times. Only a few generations ago if a family was given a loaf of bread by a neighbor it was commonplace for the recipients to feed crumbs to the chickens before giving it to the family. As late as 1796 the inhabitants of the Wuerttemberg village of Beutelsbach sought to combat a local epidemic of the hoof and mouth disease by burying a bull alive.[59]

In Lahr county each village still had its "devil's pond" and its "ghost house." Oberschopfheim had the added distinction of possessing a ghost-infested rectory. A century earlier a pastor there had killed himself after fathering a child by his Alsatian housekeeper. Ever since that time local inhabitants and outsiders alike had sworn they had heard strange noises coming from the rectory, had seen vestments fly downstairs, and had seen a girl appear in Alsatian costume. More immediately important, Dr. Hirt claimed to have befriended the ghosts, who then gave him their constant protection. By 1935 it was commonly believed that anyone who harmed the pastor would be driven violently insane by his spectral bodyguards.[60]

Meanwhile, outside Nazis, either ignorant of village legends or unmoved by them, were engaged to kill Hirt. First they tried poison, then knives. Both efforts failed. The pastor claimed that on the first occasion ghosts warned him that the apples he received were poisoned and that on the second, when he was walking back to Oberschopfheim at night, a ghost appeared as a fierce dog and kept four SA men from killing him.[61] When Dr. Hirt told such stories from the pulpit and ordinary people repeated them in the streets of Oberschopfheim and neighboring villages, frustrated county Nazis feared to renew attacks on the pastor. Villagers themselves believed the tales and were convinced (and still are) that Hirt did not concoct them.

The pastor also benefited from the more tangible protection of the mayor and villagers. Although the circumstances of Mayor Holzenthaler's appointment made him look like a Nazi pawn, he did not act like one. Many times he studiously neglected to carry out Party orders against Hirt and, like mayors in Bavarian villages, he warned "imported" speakers not to denounce the pastor or the Catholic Church. Villagers, even including some Party members, also acted like their brethren in Bavaria, boasting that anyone who tried to take away their pastor would not leave the village alive.[62]

Unable to destroy Dr. Hirt because of his supporters, both celestial and terrestrial, disgruntled county Nazis tried again to curtail his activities. In December 1935, they sent to Oberschopfheim Dr. Walter Albiker, a "missionary" Nazi and fanatical anti-Catholic, to be both new group leader and principal of the school. A chess game with pastor and villagers commenced immediately. As group leader, Albiker began by forbidding Hirt to sell Catholic newspapers, to take servers on Communion calls, or to hold processions. The pastor riposted by giving away the newspapers to each Catholic household and holding processions inside the church building. As school principal, Albiker interfered with the pastor's religion classes and attempted to stop him from holding song practice in church after school. Albiker reminded parents that song practice was not a school requirement, adding that the extra session deprived children of badly needed exercise. He also warned that those who attended this after school function would not be excused from school when they were needed for farm work. Parents remained unmoved. Worse, the few members of the local Hitler Youth and German Girls' League sometimes used their unsupervised class time to secretly attend Communion classes. Consequently, much of the time the group leader lived in a state of barely suppressed rage. Once in the school he yelled at the other teachers in disgust, "What state and law demand has little importance to them (parents), but what a priest merely asks or wishes is for them a command." [63]

Other citizens were hardly more compliant than pastor, school children, or parents. An order forbidding employers to give holiday pay to those who joined church processions was ignored. Efforts to persuade Party members to discontinue attending Mass were unavailing, in contrast to much of the rest of the diocese.

Cooperation was quite as wanting on the part of the mayor and the *Gemeinde*. Backed by state and county leaders, Albiker ordered the *Gemeinde* to stop making large gifts to the parish church. As a substitute, the Party introduced the traditional church tax, which gave the parish less money. The mayor and council responded by allowing parish groups to take up frequent street collections—which thereby left less money for Party collections. They also claimed that the church tower and clock belonged to the village rather than the church and promptly made lavish provision for their upkeep. When reproached by the county NSDAP for allegedly failing to enforce official policy, Mayor Holzenthaler feigned ignorance or forgetfulness or promised that he would end violations "as soon as possible." [64]

All in all, the NSDAP never achieved its goal of winning the loyalty of Oberschopfheimers away from either their church or their village. The nearest the Party came to "success" was to deny citizens permission to build the new church they had planned and for which they had collected the necessary money.

Should we be surprised that the "totalitarian" Nazi regime would swallow so much insolence from an unimportant farm village? Not really.

Those with an avid interest in public affairs and those who write history are sometimes too easily impressed by slogans and speeches, by charts and programs, by avowed objectives and proclaimed ideals. No human society ever operates on a day-to-day basis in the way its leaders like to represent it. The Third Reich was no exception.

The Nazis wanted foreigners to believe that their state was monolithic and totalitarian, free from the political, economic, and social conflicts that vexed democratic states. The fundamental falsity of this pose was always apparent to some degree. It grew even clearer years after World War II when Albert Speer began to talk and write at length about his experiences near the top of the Reich government. By now the myth has been thoroughly exploded by the research and publications of Karl Bracher, Martin Broszat, Hans Mommsen, and many others. The Nazi movement was in fact incoherent from its inception. It could not have been otherwise because it claimed to be a national movement, above mere parties. This meant that every diverse group, interest, and movement in the country was supposed to be assimilated into and represented by its own organization in the NSDAP. The result was both unstable and ludicrous. Every occupational group considered itself the best interpreter of National Socialism and struggled to extend its influence over the whole movement. To make matters worse, Nazi ideology was not worked out in much detail before 1933 because the Party had been engrossed primarily in trying to appeal to as many voters as possible and gain power.[65]

Coherence was doubly difficult to attain because the movement was primarily negative. Nazism was woven from a broad array of hatreds, frustrations, and passions buried in the past history of Germany, all muddled together with lust for power and a desire to smite enemies. Nazi leaders were quite clearheaded, single-minded and consistent about what they hated and intended to destroy—Marxism, Jews, pacifism, and Weimar "rottenness"—but much less clear about their positive aims. Some were real socialists; many subscribed to varying portions of pan-German preoccupation with race, anti-Semitism, agrarianism, neo-pagan religion, eugenics, and hyper-nationalism; many others sought merely jobs and wealth. Hitler himself believed passionately in the dominance of the strong and the "necessity" of the destruction of the Jews but not much else. A genius at demagoguery, he appreciated the practical necessity of at least pretending to champion the interests of farmers and proletarians, but he cared nothing for consistency or truth themselves and so espoused and abandoned causes, invented and discarded slogans, to serve the tactical needs of the moment. Overall, the Nazis were much more avid to rule, give orders, and attack enemies—and much more adept at it—than they were to develop any consistent, reasoned, positive program.[66]

Another source of endless uncertainty was the consideration that the

Third Reich never had a constitution. Thus there was no recognized, orderly way to draw lines of demarcation in the government and settle jurisdictional or other disputes. Hitler's own power was not based on either hereditary right like a king's or on control of the apparatus of state like Stalin's but on his personal prestige and charisma as "Fuehrer." He never tried to govern the nation in any consistent, predictable way but merely intervened from time to time to jolt either the state or Party apparatus into some desired action. This suited him perfectly since he cared little for law of any kind and wanted to remove legal and constitutional obstacles so he could do as he pleased. He was always willing to insist that such vague concepts as "healthy popular feeling," "the welfare of the national community," or "the will of the Fuehrer" should shape the application of formal law. When the law was interpreted by judges trained to take cognizance of such concepts, it became whatever Nazi leaders wished it to be, encompassing such practices as protective custody for political offenses, concentration camps for "anti-social elements," and the transformation of ordinary criminal offenses into political crimes on the grounds that they undermined the national community while it was struggling to survive in wartime.[67]

As a Social Darwinist Hitler believed that when many different individuals or organizations competed freely the most able tended to win out. He liked and encouraged any NSDAP member who displayed initiative and ability, who "got things done" without any special concern for law, tradition, precedent, or administrative regularity. Thus he let the SS under Himmler absorb the police functions of the regular state administration and appointed Goering minister of economics where he was free to undertake anything private industry was unable or unwilling to do. The result of years of such practices was that by the end of World War II there was a regular government of civil servants and a separate government composed of Nazi party personnel or merely representatives of the Fuehrer, with the latter predominating. This situation pleased Hitler for another reason: like many a ruler before and since he understood that parallel authorities could be played off against each other and so be more easily dominated by the man at the top. It was also one of his techniques of ruling to retain his personal popularity by refusing to take sides in disputes among factions inside the Party and government. He would often order ministers to iron out differences among themselves before presenting proposals to him or, if some personal decree of his aroused opposition or encountered difficulties, he would order ministers to redraft the edict and would then forbid any further public discussion of the matter. Such practices often cut red tape ruthlessly but just as often multiplied it needlessly. They always made administration haphazard and unpredictable.[68]

Finally, Hitler was simply a disorderly man. He worked regularly in his office as long as Hindenburg was alive but once he became president as well as Fuehrer he soon reverted to the bohemian habits of his youth, sleeping until noon, associating mostly with chauffeurs, bodyguards, would-be artists, and Party cronies, and staying for weeks at a time at his mountain retreat at Berchtesgaden while day-to-day administration was all but ignored. It was not that Hitler was uninterested in the techniques of *ruling*. These in fact preoccupied him far more than ideology, as is indicated by the consideration that he seldom read the works of NSDAP "intellectuals" like Rosenberg and rarely gave them any important office in the Reich. It was, rather, that he regarded ruling as manipulation of the masses rather than orderly legislation and administration.[69] In the latter realm he would habitually restrict information to those who "needed to know," thereby greatly reducing the number of people in the government who had overall knowledge or were capable of forming overall views. Especially during the war he would then exacerbate the resulting confusion by issuing vaguely phrased secret decrees, sometimes filled out by subsequent oral instructions, about such matters as murdering Jews or Russians or settling Germans in "cleared" areas in conquered Poland.[70]

One way to illustrate the fundamental incoherence that suffused the Third Reich is to pose the question: after 1933 what purpose did the Nazi party serve? To act as one-third of a trinity of state, people, and party? To encompass the whole nation? To oust all rivals for power and impose the Nazi program on the whole society, as Party ideologues insisted? To be a permanent elite guiding and inspiring everyone? To select and indoctrinate future leaders? Or, as scores of thousands of essentially nonideological Party members obviously thought, mostly to provide state jobs for people like themselves?[71] As with so many questions, Hitler never finally made up his mind. He kept NSDAP headquarters in Munich but left the apparatus of state centered in Berlin, giving the explanation that the nation could be seen better through two pairs of eyes. For years he contemplated schemes to integrate the Party into the state government but never really attempted to do it. Meantime, from the first, Party organs interfered with the regular machinery of state while ideologues, conservatives, technocrats, spokesmen for different factions inside the NSDAP, and mere careerists waged incessant intramural struggles for Hitler's favor, or at least for his attention.[72] If some petty Fuehrer out in the hinterlands disliked a particular directive from Berlin, he could often appeal to some top Nazi who was a rival of its author and get it countermanded. In such a political wilderness, reminiscent in some ways of the old Holy Roman Empire or of Europe in the tenth century, both ministers in Berlin and thousands of local officials paid formal obeisance to either national policy or Nazi ideology and quietly did much as they pleased most of the time.[73]

Contradictions between desire and necessity were legion. The official ideology of the Nazi movement was anti-capitalist and anti-industrial. It envisioned a vastly expanded, classless, and largely rural Germany. Yet it was impossible to acquire the necessary "living space" without war. Successful war in modern times requires extensive armament and *that* requires extensive expansion of the scientific, industrial, and urban sectors at the expense of agriculture and the stimulation of big business at the expense of small. Hitler wanted to aid peasants but he was always afraid to raise farm prices lest this set off inflation and, as ever, alienate the urban millions who would have to pay more for their food. Moreover, again as ever, it would alienate big industrialists. They wanted imports of cheap food to keep down clamor by their employees for wage increases and to provide income for foreign food producers who might thereby be induced to become customers for German industrial exports.[74] Party ideologues pushed hard to establish the *Erbhof* farm system, while pragmatists predicted that it would reduce peasants to state serfs and create mass rural discontent without raising agricultural output.[75] Some Nazi farm experts were concerned mainly with preserving small farms, others with protecting the interests of Junker grain growers on East Elbian estates. Some supported the establishment of rural cooperatives; others sought to undermine them because their success would doom rural private entrepreneurs. In Baden Nazi race enthusiasts closed Jewish department stores only to have their superiors temporarily reopen them because closure had thrown many people out of work. Small shopkeepers clamored to have *all* chain stores closed and expected Nazi support since NSDAP orators had denounced them for years as veritable works of Satan. In power, however, the more intelligent Nazis understood that to deliberately destroy more modern and rational ways of doing business to aid the inefficient and the obsolete was absurd, especially in a depression, and that the principal result of such an idiotic policy would be to raise prices, to worsen unemployment, and to undermine both the companies that ran the stores and the banks that stood behind them. The result was a series of ludicrous compromises. The stores would be closed if the small shops would agree to employ all the chain store employees who would be laid off.[76] Then special taxes were laid on large concerns (1935), and they were ordered to close various of their departments. This produced some reduction in their sales, but only for a short time.[77]

One NSDAP faction called for women to withdraw from the labor market, another advocated the opposite and even urged military training for women.[78] Hjalmar Schacht and Karl Goerdeler, both economic liberals, opposed guaranteed government prices for farm products on the grounds that it protected inefficiency, but Walter Darré, who wanted the Reich of the future to be, above all, an Aryan agrarian society, thought preserving and fostering racist objectives should take precedence over mere economic calculation.[79] Not least of the many ironies associated with the Nazis was that they, who had come to power as champions of some of the most socially and economically backward-looking elements in Germany, ended their brief tour by modernizing the nation more and faster than any of their predecessors.

Below the level of policymaking similar conditions prevailed. It is easily forgotten that even such remorseless absolutists as Hitler and Stalin required immense bureaucracies to implement their plans and orders. Bureaucrats do not automatically become more honest, industrious, intelligent, resourceful, and wise because they happen to serve some authoritarian regime rather than a democracy. Nor do they think less of their salaries, promotions, vacations, and perquisites of office. Only a few, anywhere, are pristine idealists. For years the NSDAP had to tolerate innumerable non-Nazis in the administration, schools, judiciary, and elsewhere, while trying both to indoctrinate and to train hordes of indifferently qualified Nazi replacements. To have immediately swept out all the old functionaries in favor of the new and frequently bewildered Party faithful would have plunged Germany into administrative chaos at a time when millions were unemployed and Hitler's dearly sought foreign triumphs still lay in the future. Thus, at the moment, attainment and preservation of national unity to facilitate pursuit of major long-term objectives seemed much more important than insistence on ideological purity.[80]

Into this jungle of conflicting policies, administrative overlap, and bureaucratic confusion, the only ray of light that penetrated was the Fuehrer's will. If the administration became hopelessly clogged, if passive opposition or obstruction grew too egregious to be tolerated, if some question was too important to permit delay, in the Nazi state there was always the *Gestapo*, torture, the concentration camp, or, ultimately, some decisive, barbarous act like the Night of the Long Knives, 30 June 1934. Hitler's chieftainship in this wondrous realm resembled an exaggerated and intensified variant of the rule of Louis XIV in seventeenth-century France. Enormous energy could pour forth from the throne periodically, but it never resulted in lasting harmony, stability, or regularity. Most of the time Nazi domestic policy, like Topsy, "just growed."[81]

It was much the same with propaganda. Nazi propaganda was effective generally, but it had its limitations, especially in peacetime. Many, probably most, people only skim lead articles and editorials in their newspapers and do most of their reading in the crime, sports, sex, scandal, and other "recreational" sectors. Nazis made radios both cheap and easily available. Rural people did listen to them and were indubitably influenced by what they heard, but on the average they listened less than urbanites, either from lack of time or from lack of interest in the programs.[82] Nazi movie-makers were energetic and productive, but peasants seldom went to the movies.

Finally, attainment of a monolithic society without flaw was impossible in Nazi Germany for the same reason it always proved evanescent in the Soviet Union: it foundered on the hard rock of human corruption. Thus, while it was always *possible* for state and county officials to utterly crush obstructionists in Oberschopfheim, they could not do so without resorting to measures that never seemed worth the effort. Berlin, after all, was primarily engrossed in plans for a sweeping political and racial reorganization of all Europe. In that context, Oberschopfheim was merely an obscure backwater where occasional obstreperousness could be dealt with appropriately at some less pressing time.

As for Pastor Hirt, his studious noncooperation and "selective resistance" was more effective than open, organized opposition. The latter could not have been ignored and would have brought about Hirt's immediate imprisonment or death. Unquestionably, too, the exceptional devotion of his parishioners made possible a degree of success that could not have been gained by most urban pastors even had they made equivalent efforts.

Like Dr. Hirt, other Catholic opponents of the Nazis had to feel their way. Sometimes they judged their relative positions and strengths accurately, sometimes not.[83] In 1937 Nazi authorities ordered all job applicants to fill in the lines on application forms indicating the applicant's religion. Well aware of Nazi hostility to Christianity, many Catholics had heretofore left the line blank. Now the Archbishop of Freiburg, conciliatory as usual, directed his people to comply. Journalistic adversaries in Baden fared less well. In Lahr county the sixty-eight-year-old *Anzeiger,* formerly the foremost opponent of Nazism in the county, was finally silenced 31 December 1935, though the county leader allowed its book publication and retail store to continue. The diocesan newspaper, *Konradsblatt,* suffered stricter censorship and several prohibitions before finally ceasing publication.

Nazi efforts to master Oberschopfheim's governmental structure were only superficially more successful than their endeavor to muzzle Dr. Hirt. Throughout 1935 the Lahr county leader used the new Uniform Code, which embodied the "Leadership Principle," to disband the elected assemblies of the district, the county, Lahr city and most villages and to consolidate power in local puppet mayors. Oberschopfheim was an exception. Here he let the council continue in order to control Mayor Holzen-thaler and to reward the Party faithful.[84] Thus power remained divided among the mayor, the council, and the group leader, with the pastor exerting much informal influence. Of them, only the group leader tried to make the village a Nazi enclave. From the viewpoint of the county leader, Oberschopfheim's group leader was by far the most reliable local Nazi and therefore the obvious candidate for mayor, but he dared not appoint him lest Oberschopfheimers, like Bavarian villagers, drive the unwanted man from the village. Instead, Lahr county's chief Nazi confirmed Holzenthaler as mayor for a six-year term.[85]

Though village conflicts continued as they had before 1933, new mayor Holzenthaler rarely took sides in them and discouraged families from undertaking legal action against each other. When pressed for a decision about some private squabble he would answer in a slow, monotonous voice, "It. . . doesn't. . . concern . . . me." Although Holzenthaler had joined the NSDAP in October 1933, he often "mislaid" or "forgot" orders and protected village liberties when he could. Hence he was always "well liked," in contrast to group leaders Merkert and Albiker and Farm Leader Franz K. Roederer II. Ironically, at the end of World War II the French arrested Holzenthaler as just another "Nazi mayor" and treated him far worse than any other local Party member.[86]

Council members and courthouse officials had almost as difficult a time as did the mayor, for they too received orders from the county leader yet wanted to preserve village independence. Compared to pre-Nazi times, officials now had to send slightly more information to Lahr and Karlsruhe and to donate to more causes. In addition they had to organize air raid shelters, process young men for the armed forces, and collect all produce from farmers under the state monopoly. Mistakes were liable to be punished more severely than previously too. With these added burdens, a job in the courthouse or on the village council no longer made the holder an object of envy.

Meanwhile, the new group leader, Herr Albiker, tried to compensate for the flaccid enthusiasm of village officials. He compelled Party members to attend weekly lectures, to collect money for "Winterhelp" and World War I "victims," and to bring to him their Party membership books, duly signed by superiors, attesting that the bearers had done appropriate work for the NSDAP. He forced everyone to give the "Heil Hitler" salute and greeting—at least to himself and a few other "Fanatiker." He also ordered the removal of all crucifixes from public buildings and all symbols of Weimar Germany from homes. He was equally forthright in the classroom. He kicked and slapped young boys in an effort to compel them to join the Hitler Youth, tried to force children to report on the political reliability of their parents, and made all kids say "Heil Hitler" at the beginning and the end of each school day.

By mid-1936 Albiker had brought about outward conformity to Nazi regulations and destroyed what remained of mutual trust among villagers. Though this did not compare with the achievement of the group leader in Thalburg, who had used terror, raids, and arrests to enforce total control, it was much more than group leaders had accomplished in many Bavarian Catholic villages.[87] Nonetheless the victory was pyrrhic. Oberschopf- heimers, whether pastor, Party members, or ordinary people, disliked Herr Albiker so intensely and made his stay so unpleasant that he left the village within two years. The county leader swallowed the failure, bowed to local pressure, and appointed Mayor Holzenthaler as local group leader. After 1938 Holzenthaler ran the village by himself, using his authority to relax NSDAP controls and moderate the process of nazification.

The whole Albiker-Holzenthaler controversy illustrates a recurring problem in the Third Reich, one for which the Nazis never discovered a satisfactory solution. A local government law of 30 January 1935 prescribed that mayors should exercise absolute authority in their towns. This was an ideal situation if the mayor was also the local Nazi party leader and if he was a Nazi zealot. If the mayor was only a nominal Nazi, the decree strength- ened his hand against real Nazis on his town council. To avoid this poten- tially ruinous situation NSDAP officials often objected to this decree of their own national government. If the mayor was not a Nazi or only pretended to be one, he usually had trouble with either the local or district Party leader, as Holzenthaler did with Albiker. In the latter case Nazi officials usually concluded, as they had with Pastor Hirt, that Oberschopf- heim was not a sufficiently important place to undertake a fight to the finish with some unsatisfactory but popular local notable.[88]

Although Oberschopfheimers disliked Albiker and the county leader, they held Adolf Hitler in as high esteem as did most Germans elsewhere. This might seem incredible, since Hitler inflicted more bloodshed and suffering on more human beings than any man in history, with the possible exceptions of Josef Stalin and Mao Tse Tung. But if propaganda is filtered out, appearances are changed. Many in the 1930s who depicted Nazi Germany as a land undergoing grave economic hardship and whose people had been terrorized into supporting a monstrous regime, were themselves admirers of the USSR, whose society *did* fit that description. In Germany the Nazis did terrorize their enemies, to be sure, but the NSDAP regime did not seem oppressive to the politically passive majority beyond requir- ing them to attend meetings and participate in occasional public political functions. They sometimes heard stories about grim events in other parts of the Reich but most people paid little attention to what happened elsewhere or to persons they did not know. In any case, the *wholesale* crimes of the Nazis were committed during World War II, in as much secrecy as the regime could manage. By then the whole system had long since become fixed on the German people and it had grown too late for effective resistance. Most notably, people live on hope, and Hitler in the 1930s gave hope to the hopeless and provided illusions at a time and place when these were desperately needed and were not apt to be examined critically.[89]

Like Germans elsewhere, some Oberschopfheimers saw little difference between Bismarck's domination of the Second Reich and Hitler's preeminence in the Third or between Bruening ruling by decree after 1930 and Hitler doing so after 1933. More important, they saw Hitler as the first national leader to actually do something for their village: to build them a water pumping station and a new highway and, it cannot be repeated too often, to give jobs to some of them. Germans who received jobs between 1933 and 1936 venerated Hitler just as Americans with WPA jobs esteemed Franklin Roosevelt.[90] Moreover, anyone could *see* that the country was much more peaceful domestically than during the years of political turmoil and uncertainty from 1930 to 1933. Prior to World War II foreigners traveled about freely in the Third Reich and Germans traveled abroad if they chose. Far from being terrorized, most ordinary Germans had more pride, hope, and confidence than at any time since 1914.

Again, the parallel between Hitler and Franklin Roosevelt is pertinent. In the 1930s many Americans who had regarded previous presidents with indifference or tepid admiration were enthusiastic supporters of the "second Roosevelt." Ancestors of Oberschopfheimers had viewed various of their grand dukes, kings, and emperors with the mixture of respect and deference common among European peasants in ages past, but Adolf Hitler was the first ruler, indeed the first noteworthy "outsider" in the history of the village, to arouse real affection and enthusiasm there. As among Germans elsewhere, if some NSDAP program was crowned with success villagers gave Hitler the credit; if it failed they denounced the Party bureaucracy. As with peasants of old, the king could do no wrong; all injustices and foul-ups were the fault of the king's men. Even after 1945 some refused to believe that Hitler was responsible for the war, Germany's defeat, or the "supposed" mass murders.

Contemporary Anglo-Saxon, especially American, writers frequently distort the history of people who live under any authoritarian regime because they assume that democracy is the natural, normal form of government anywhere, that the mass of "normal" people everywhere admire and desire it, and that any deviation from it is some sort of civic disease or "problem" requiring diagnosis. If one begins merely by noting the historical record—that some form of absolutism has been the usual mode of government at most times and places and that democratic experiments have generally been short-lived historically—then fascism does not appear to be a social sickness but only another variant of authoritarianism. At once, all sorts of human conduct in Nazi Germany and elsewhere becomes demystified. By focusing relentlessly on the most bizarre features of Nazi ideology and the most base cruelties of Nazi practice it is easy to forget that for the ordinary nonpolitical person day-to-day life in some authoritarian society does not differ markedly from that in a democracy. One must be wary of exchanging political opinions with others, to be sure, and a prudent individual should not attract attention to himself. One should also be careful to obey the law, since authoritarian regimes are usually less lenient to transgressors than are democracies. But these are not especially onerous restrictions to most conventional, nonideological persons. Even under the most strident despotisms more of the time of judges and courts is spent dealing with taxes, licenses, applications, civil lawsuits, thievery, public drunkenness, brawling, and marital discord than with the persecution or enslavement of political dissidents.[91]

In the case of the Germans Nazism seemed to many just an extreme version of what they had always believed in or taken for granted. It was nationalistic, respectful of the armed forces, socially conservative, disdainful of laziness, hostile to eccentric or incomprehensible ideas that came from cities, disapproving of homosexuals and other unconventional human types, and avid to achieve "greatness" for Germany. They welcomed parts of the Nazi political and social smorgasbord and told themselves that the rest was less important or was not meant seriously anyway. After 1933 they were cut off from their old party organizations and allegiances, and they heard little but the Nazi version of what went on in the world. Some entertained misgivings periodically; some beamed in public while criticizing in private; many were indifferent to politics or tired of it and simply quit thinking about it.[92]

Public response to Nazi anti-Semitism was more ambiguous. Many Germans were attracted to Nazism because of its hostility to the Jews,[93] yet others found this repugnant, and many clergymen denounced it. Some Germans risked their lives, even gave their lives, to hide Jews or smuggle them out of the Reich.[94] Yet if one judges from the actions of a majority, this attitude was not typical. Many Germans bore no particular hostility toward those Jews whom they happened to know personally, indeed often liked them, but they cared little about what happened to *Jews in general*, to those disembodied, devilish Jews of Nazi propaganda.[95] Often they were affronted more by the principle of property being vandalized with impunity than by the consideration that it was Jews who were being despoiled.[96]

Once more, should we be surprised? Ashamed, certainly; surprised, hardly. Most people are always more concerned with what affects them personally than with the fate of others. Many rumors circulated in the 1930s about the persecution of Jews, but few knew if there was any truth in them. Even among Jews themselves the very idea that the government of a major "civilized" twentieth-century nation might seriously undertake the destruction of a whole people seemed madly unthinkable. Thus it was easy for Jews and gentiles alike to recall that most of the atrocity tales of World War I had turned out to be false. Now the Nazis warned against "rumormongers," and fear of the *Gestapo* was widespread and well-founded. Of course heroes would have spoken out or attempted some action anyway, but most people, in most places, most of the time, are not heroes. It simply seemed more prudent to still one's forebodings, mind one's own business, and not seek knowledge that would certainly be profitless and might easily prove dangerous. [97]

In 1933 there were 374 Jews in Lahr county: 1.1 percent of the population. [98] Perhaps because of their numerical insignificance, when the Nazi *Zeitung* continually attacked Jews as the foremost criminals in Germany (worse even than Christians) and tried to persuade people to ostracize and boycott Jews, this was less successful than were similar Party assaults in Thalburg. [99] Until 1938 Jewish families in Lahr county believed themselves to be well-integrated into their communities. In Lahr city they received permission to form an NSDAP "Party of Jewish Youth" in 1935, and in Offenburg Jews founded their own group of patriotic War Veterans. Only later during "Crystal Night" in 1938 did Jews suffer physically at the hands of raging Hitler Youth, who demolished all the synagogues and damaged stores, houses, and cemeteries throughout the county. Finally, in 1940, about a hundred Jews who had not fled or been arrested were transported to Gurs in southern France. [100]

Strictly speaking, there was no "Jewish problem" in Oberschopfheim because no Jews lived there. To be sure, whether in Oberschopfheim, Bavaria, or elsewhere in Germany, many peasants, whether Catholic or Protestant, regarded Jews with some disdain. Educated Catholics might dislike them for having been prominent supporters of the *Kulturkampf* in the 1870s, but the relatively uneducated villagers of Oberschopfheim distrusted them as "exploiters" of peasants and representatives of the distasteful, hostile, external world of cities, atheism, and moral laxity. [101] Anti-Semitism of the wilder, more flamboyant type that flowed so readily from the lips and pens of professional anti-Jewish writers and spellbinding Nazi orators was a different matter entirely. Assertions in the writings of Houston Stewart Chamberlain that the Jews had always been a negative factor in Western civilization meant nothing to people who had never read a line from Chamberlain or anyone like him. "Discoveries" that such varied individuals as Theodore Roosevelt, Leopold von Ranke, the boxing champion Jack Johnson, eight popes, and dozens of cardinals had been Jews[102] did not impress peasants who had never heard of any of them. Neither did ancient Christian religious prejudices that associated Jews with natural calamities of various sorts. Had not the popular pastor, Dr. Hirt, strongly condemned anti-Semitism on religious grounds?

The handful of Jewish farmers who resided in communities around Oberschopfheim lived and acted much like other farmers and so attracted little attention. Jewish peddlers and merchants one encountered occasionally. While they were not cultivated as personal friends, they were undeniably useful as commercial intermediaries. They paid higher prices for livestock than did their Aryan competitors, and they paid in cash. Sometimes they could be depended upon for a needed loan. Thus to many villagers attacks on Jews seemed gratuitous and in poor taste, not to speak of religiously repugnant as well.

Yet Oberschopfheimers did nothing to protect Jews in neighboring villages. The reasons were twofold: unconcern about events outside their own community and fear that aid to Jews might produce persecution of Catholics. Actually, what they did or did not do mattered little for they had no means of protecting Jews in neighboring villages or in Lahr, where the SS and the rest of the Nazi apparatus was more powerful than in Oberschopfheim. What would they have done had Jews lived in Oberschopfheim itself? Obviously, nobody knows.

Everything considered, the Nazi "seizure of power" in Oberschopfheim was small potatoes. The county leader and his various underlings and agents changed mayors at their pleasure, made the village council appointive rather than elective, required everyone to fly the Nazi flag, badgered the troublesome pastor, forced an unwanted principal on the village school, and imported outside NSDAP functionaries to push nazification. But the recalcitrant pastor remained so; and the "Nazi" mayor, "Nazi" officials, and local "Nazi" party members defended the pastor and village liberties rather than National Socialism's vision of the future. Oberschopfheim eventually got a local unit of the Nazi party comparable to units elsewhere in numbers, occupational grouping, social standing, and percentage of officially "active" members, but pressure had to be exerted to swell membership lists, only two or three members became real zealots, even the "active" members had no serious duties, and the rest of the members showed little interest in any NSDAP function that took them away from manual labor. If more people voted for Nazis in elections, this owed considerably to the Catholic *Anzeiger* and to Bishop Groeber, who told them to. Altogether, what was established in Oberschopfheim was hardly a "merciless Nazi police state."[103]

What *was* remarkable was that for the first time in their history villagers transferred their loyalty to an outsider, Adolf Hitler. Had Der Fuehrer died as early as the autumn of 1936 or as late as the summer of 1940 most Oberschopfheimers (not to speak of most other Germans and innumerable foreigners) might well have proclaimed him the greatest ruler in German history.[104] Even so, their adulation had limits. As the years passed and Hitler moved swiftly from one triumph to the next, extending Germany's frontiers farther and faster than even Frederick the Great and Bismarck had, some Germans began to regard him as a superman, endowed with magical, even semi-divine powers. Even his generals largely gave up objecting to his increasingly daring adventures in foreign affairs. Not so Oberschopfheimers. They admired the Fuehrer, to be sure, but never supposed that he bore any sort of mandate from heaven. Swallowing Nazi ideology was even farther beyond them. Like the people in many Bavarian villages, Oberschopfheimers remained "too homogenous, too suspicious of any outside world, too loyal to . . . [their] faith" to have their community turned into a miniature Reich.[105]

# 8

# OFFERING THE NAZI CARROT

ALTHOUGH NAZI political activities interfered sporadically with village liberties, Oberschopfheimers were much more concerned with economic problems. The village had reached an apex of prosperity in 1914, had suffered conventional "hard times" from 1917 to 1929, and then had been scourged by widespread unemployment, low farm prices, and bad weather until 1933.

Before the election of March 1933, Hitler campaigned on the promise of immediate solutions to the nation's economic ills. His actual program, insofar as anyone could fathom it, consisted mostly of slogans like "Common Good Before Private Gain" and the injunction to have faith in Der Fuehrer. Marxists never understood the appeal or effectiveness of this, indeed never understood the rise of Nazism at all, because they regarded the "economic base" as the leitmotif of everything and denied that nationalist passion could still be the prime concern of advanced peoples in the industrial age. That a "race state" could be established and could thrive among the very people who, before 1914, constituted the heart of the international Marxist movement was quite beyond their blinkered imaginations.

It was also beyond the imaginations of German liberals and Social Democrats, not to speak of innumerable foreigners, both leftists and capitalists. That the ruler of one of the world's foremost nations could boast that he had no economic theory at all was undeniably odd. That he planned only sporadically was hard to account for when he headed a party that called itself socialist. That Hitler then turned about and periodically dictated to his capitalists just as he did to all other Germans, instead of being their "pawn," as Marxist metaphysicians insisted he must be, fit no known political or economic formula.[1]

The popularity of the Nazis would have been a good deal more comprehensible if observers had thought less about logical harmony and more about the concerns of ordinary people. Educated minds crave ideologies that are coherent, consistent, and intellectually satisfying, but, as party platforms and political propaganda reveal every day all over the world, ordinary men want full employment, leaders to follow, and a sense of direction and certainty in an uncertain world. In Germany the Nazis promised all this and provided most of it.[2]

Aside from political mythology, Nazi treatment of Germany's economic plight was not revolutionary and not even new. Like anti-Depression measures in the United States and elsewhere, it consisted chiefly of deficit spending, economic controls, and inspirational oratory. The propaganda element bulked larger in Germany than in other countries because Adolf Hitler was exceptionally skilled in this sphere. In most of Germany the NSDAP quickly surmounted the psychological depression and made impressive inroads into the actual one, while amassing political power for themselves. Some scholars have argued that in many cases all the Nazis did was take money that had formerly gone for doles, pump it into public works projects that provided employment, and then claim they were economic wizards.[3] Others have contended that Nazi economic successes were illusory or that they were secured by exploiting the workers[4] or that only World War II truly brought the Reich out of the Depression. Such claims contain some truth, but they are as irrelevant as to point out that after four years of the New Deal American unemployment in 1937 was nearly as high as in 1933 or that in the United States it also required World War II to finally overcome the Depression. In both cases what was important was not sterile statistics but what tens of millions of people *thought* about the matter. In each country the foremost achievement of the ruler was to reverse public attitudes, to replace fear and pessimism with hope.[5]

In this sphere, Hitler's May Day speech of 1933 was especially impressive. Presenting himself as a common man who had risen to become chief of state, he called on all Germans to abandon rigid class distinctions, to foreswear hatred for one another, and to work in unity to build a new Reich. As an example of this recommended spirit of cooperation, the accompanying parade included all classes of people marching together in ostensible friendship. At the nationwide celebration of the "Battle of Work" on 21 March 1934, Oberschopfheimers, like innumerable Germans elsewhere, were moved by the impassioned pleas of Nazi orators to spend, hire, borrow, consume, and thereby turn the wheels of the economy,[6] even though, ironically, they had been taught for centuries to *save* money, which was always scarce, and, where possible, to do without rather than to buy. The *Anzeiger* and *Zeitung* enthusiastically publicized all such Nazi entreaties and printed voluminous statistics on work projects, collections, employment, and production, indicating that the Nazi government was leading the nation out of the crisis. Many Oberschopfheimers, though personally unhelped, became convinced that never before had any government done so much for ordinary people.

To be sure, some tangible aid did accompany the psychological uplift. It consisted mostly of public works projects supplemented by welfare assistance to the needy. It was implemented primarily by the *Arbeitsdienst* (labor service), an organization that combined existing youth service programs in order to "unite the youth of the nation into a real community, irrespective of class distinctions."[7] Like the Civilian Conservation Corps in the United States, the *Arbeitsdienst* was quasi-military, quasi-conservationist, and widely regarded as a great success. It provided employment for thousands by draining and bringing under cultivation some 300,000 acres of new land. In Thalburg, road building provided much employment, while the labor service gave jobs to great numbers of young people and seasonal workers by erecting an open air theater, beautifying the town, and initiating conservation projects. Finally, a military garrison markedly stimulated local business.[8]

In Lahr county generally, and in Oberschopfheim in particular, Nazi economic "miracles," while real, were markedly less spectacular than in other parts of Germany. One reason was that the area consisted mostly of small farm communities. A more important one was that the whole district lay adjacent to an undefended border with France. Hitler was always reluctant to improve anything, especially communications systems, that might one day be useful to a French invading army.

The most important enterprise undertaken in Lahr county was flood control. As with numerous comparable projects elsewhere, the Nazis began the undertaking with a public ceremony in order to instill confidence in their leadership. Baden's minister president, Herr Kohler, came to the groundbreaking to recite the Nazi creed: "With faith in our Leader, Adolf Hitler, I dig the first shovel full of dirt." At once the labor service went to work. It contained a few young people from Oberschopfheim and neighboring villages, supplemented by unemployed adults, a few of whom also came from Oberschopfheim. These workers began to dig a new seven-kilometer canal from the Schutter to the Rhine river, to clean waterways, and to build dams, bridges, and waterlocks. The plan called for 140,000 workdays, with two-thirds of the cost to be paid by the national government and one-third by local communities. Oberschopfheim welcomed the project, obviously, but local officials, frugal as ever, paid their assessment of twenty-four hundred marks reluctantly.[9] By 1936 the project had accomplished more for Lahr county and Oberschopfheim than the combined work of several previous decades. It had brought new fields under cultivation, controlled much flooding, and eliminated many breeding grounds of disease-carrying mosquitoes. Moreover, the camp that had housed the laborers had brought considerable business to Lahr merchants. Yet, considered strictly as a measure to combat the Depression, the whole effort had given work to fewer than a dozen Oberschopfheimers.

Road building provided even less employment for villagers than flood control. In his May Day speech of 1933 Hitler promised that road construction would not only provide thousands of meaningful jobs but would help unite Germans and aid in the transportation of everyone's goods. Work on the *Autobahn*, which had been planned since 1924, began four months after Hitler's speech. It commenced with the usual public ceremony featuring hundreds of "singing workers" carrying shovels and, on this occasion, with Der Fuehrer himself turning the first spadeful of dirt.

Since Hitler promised that Germany would build 6,900 kilometers of *Autobahn* and 6,000 or more kilometers of other roads, Oberschopfheimers waited anxiously for construction to begin on the Karlsruhe-Basel *Autobahn* that would bypass their village. To their intense disappointment Berlin canceled this section, which would lie only seven miles from the border, giving the familiar excuse that it would facilitate a French invasion. Nonetheless the government did rebuild a state highway that passed the village. At first many local people found employment on the project, but soon the county labor department allocated their jobs to communities with higher percentages of registered unemployed. As a result, the Reich road building projects provided only brief employment for Oberschopfheimers. True to form, the inhabitants did not blame Reich officials or the NSDAP but instead loudly cursed their ancient antagonists, county officials and the French, for keeping them unemployed.[10] Other work projects on railroads, rivers, and post offices provided neither employment nor business for anyone in Oberschopfheim.

Nor did rearmament. After the remilitarization of the Rhineland in March 1936 Lahr city benefited economically from the presence of soldiers and from the construction of forts and barracks. In May 1938 construction of the West Wall began, ostensibly to provide Germany with defense against France should the French screw up sufficient courage to attack Germany in the west while the Fuehrer was implementing his anticipated campaign against Poland in the east. During the following year most of the villages in Lahr county made considerable money from the two to three thousand workers from elsewhere who were brought into the area. *Gasthaus* keepers did well, providing food and sleeping quarters for the workers. Many private families also rented out sleeping rooms or hastily converted attics into such rooms for rental. Less welcome were other needs and appetites of the workers, notably for liquor and prostitutes. The former assumed such dimensions that local sale of schnapps and other bottled alcohol was prohibited for a time.[11] Alas! for Oberschopfheim. It was touched but little by any aspect of the brief prosperity, licit or illicit. Though it was not true of Germany as a whole, government loans and subsidies were more important to Oberschopfheim's economy than were either public works projects or rearmament—and even then performance fell short of promises.

The Nazis were indefatigable in devising programs for the alleged benefit of farmers. Their motives were mixed. In the short run Hitler wanted to win rural support. Over a period of years he wanted peasants to make the Reich agriculturally self-sufficient and thus capable of successfully waging a major war. As Walter Darré put it succinctly in February 1935, "it must be made clear to the peasant that we have not created special laws for him for the sake of his bonny blue eyes (schoene Augen) but because he has a job to do for Germany." [12]

The strong strain of antimodernism in late nineteenth- and early twentieth-century German thought figured too. Such turn of the century academicians as Karl Oldenberg, Max Sering, and Adolf Wagner were prominent among many who claimed that rural life in its contemporary form must be preserved in Germany by state policy regardless of narrow economic considerations. Rural people were morally superior to urbanites, they claimed, as well as more patriotic. They made better soldiers than their city cousins, and they were a bulwark against the revolutionary currents in the modern world. They typified the finest German virtues and so it was in the national interest to afford them privileged treatment. [13]

Nazi race doctrine amplified this thesis to an extreme degree. Liberals and socialists might make peasants the butt of common jokes, but NSDAP race theorists and practical politicians alike preferred to praise them as ideal parents of Nordic children who would replenish the demographically depleted cities. Party propagandists lauded their "pure blood," elevated them to the dignity of *Landesvolk* in the "New Agrarian State," heaped honors and awards on them to publicize the service of agriculture to the nation, and, as a supreme distinction, frequently referred to Hitler as "the peasant Chancellor." Of course Oberschopfheimers were pleased to be officially esteemed so highly. One of the most important reasons for their general dislike of the Weimar Republic, after all, had been that it had, in their view, taxed them unduly to support city riffraff and had put the interests of the latter above their own. Of all forms of aid that rulers can bestow on their subjects flattery is the cheapest.

This is not to deny that much aid was tangible and not mere racist bombast. Nazi farm programs provided subsidies for the purchase of fertilizers, insect sprays, fruit seedlings, grapevines, and chickens. They also expanded the existing system of crop insurance and extended loans to build barns. In addition, farmers with more than three acres might receive free labor from young people for a year or more under the *Landhilfe* program. Five families in Oberschopfheim employed these youths, and others used young men from the labor service during harvest season. One persistent difficulty in the program was that the amount of aid any one farmer received depended on the will of Local Farm Leader Roederer. At times he withheld fertilizer or chicken feed from families for no reason that seemed sufficient to them. At other times, villagers believed, he kept some of the aid for himself and his friends.[14]

In Germany there had long existed free government lectures and courses on such subjects as animal slaughter, the care of fruit trees and grapevines, and the best methods of raising various crops. These the Nazis expanded. At the insistence of the district and local farm leaders, Oberschopfheimers regularly attended such conferences and, for the first time, sent several of their sons to agricultural schools. More important, the Reich subsidized the consolidation of medieval land allotments. Tiny plots of a third of an acre or less, dating from centuries past, were now to be exchanged to form larger, more compact units. This would save both farmers and their draft animals time and energy formerly wasted plodding from one minuscule plot to another, and it would eliminate countless disputes over borders. Yet so ingrained was rural conservatism that, lacking outside pressure, the peasants themselves would never have agreed to trade these tiny parcels (many of which even had names) that had been in their families for generations.

Because the Nazis paid more attention to local farmers than had previous governments and gave them more aid in the form of tax reductions and suspension of interest on their debts, the Party gained its foremost objective: increased political support.

Other gains were ambiguous or problematical. Nazi efforts to reclaim lands, use more fertilizer, increase the mechanization of agriculture, and teach better farming techniques increased productivity by about 7 percent in 1933-1936 and improved the quality of many farm products in the bargain.[15] German consumption of food rose perceptibly,[16] and the farmer's share of the national income increased slightly at the expense of food consumers.[17] Yet despite much more government prodding and regulation of agriculture than of industry, increases in farm production lagged well behind those in other sectors of the economy. There were several reasons for this. The most fundamental was that it is intrinsically more difficult to expand food production than industrial production. Other obstacles were faults in the program, peasant stubbornness, and persistent bad weather. In Oberschopfheim the weather was the worst. From 1933 to 1936 alternating wet and dry summers ruined most crops. Farmers toiled from sunup to sundown yet had so little produce to sell that they netted less than unemployed city workers on welfare. Grape yield declined and the quality of local wine was so poor that it brought only a quarter of its 1928 price.

Thus the subsidized fertilizers and sprays proved useless. The loan program, too, was flawed in that it did not sufficiently encourage farmers to buy new machinery and modernize their operations, though to be sure the small size of village farms tended to keep alive such practices as sowing crops by hand and using homemade tools. Finally, the eminently sensible consolidation of bits of land was not pushed hard enough. Even after reform some five thousand minuscule parcels still remained in the village area.

The farmers themselves did little to further the success of Nazi programs. Only halfhearted Nazis at best, they clung to old traditions, resented the antireligious flavor of the new Reich, disliked attending political meetings, were patently wearied by incessant Nazi celebrations, and contributed only grudgingly to Party "welfare" collections. They welcomed price supports that gave them security from market fluctuations but distrusted the agricultural advice thrust on them and had little confidence that the government would stand firm against urban demands for cheap food at their expense. Generally, they were more avid for additional benefits than grateful for past favors. What they disliked especially was Nazi replacement of private sale and barter of farm commodities with extensive government direction: licenses to grow certain crops, limitations on the acreage of other crops, and required sale of all vegetable oil, milk, and butter to the government at low prices.

Here both government and farmers faced dilemmas that were insoluble. Berlin considered that food prices had to be kept low at any cost to insure support for the regime, or at least tolerance of it, in the cities. Yet farmers could not be other than alienated when they were legally required to make food deliveries at set prices, after which the state sold their produce at considerably higher prices to city dwellers. Worse, if anything, farmers had to compete for labor with urban industry where wages were less rigidly controlled. Hence available labor tended to move off farms into cities, not the reverse. Mechanization of agriculture was hampered by lack of investment capital, but banks were reluctant to lend to farmers whose lands were entailed under the *Erbhof* system. In any case, agricultural machinery was chronically in short supply because of the pressing need for every sort of metal for the rearmament program.[18]

One main result of these interlocking dilemmas was that all over the Reich farmers took advantage of their relative geographical isolation to cooperate halfheartedly, to procrastinate, and to evade,[19] even at the risk of incurring fines of one hundred thousand marks and long jail terms. From 1933 to 1936 courthouse officials in Oberschopfheim recorded 105 violations of tobacco allotments alone. Perhaps there were so many because offenders never felt the full force of the law but habitually got off with token fines plus the loss of a portion of their crops. Farmers who sold products on the black market or who kept some of their milk, butter, and vegetable oil were seldom caught. Often they sold their commodities above fixed prices quite openly or got around regulations by some transparent subterfuge like including the sale of an unwanted hat at an exorbitant price or of a pet dog who would promptly return to its master. Even though Farm Leader Roederer knew what was happening and occasionally demanded that offenders confess their misdeeds to him, no action ever followed. At other times nobody would admit his guilt, least of all the farm leader himself.[20]

The Nazis tried to aid agriculture by spending a third more in three years from 1933 to 1936 than Weimar governments had spent in seven years from 1926 to 1933 to help farmers clear up their debts. But the well-meant endeavor was useless to the inhabitants of Oberschopfheim since nearly all the money went to those who owned middle-sized or large farms.[21]

It was the same with the Erbhof system. The Nazis enacted a hereditary farm law (*Erbhofgesetz*) that protected farms over seventeen acres from division or foreclosure. Designed to perpetuate a numerous German peasantry, it was eventually extended to 44 percent of all arable land in Germany. The merits and drawbacks of this scheme have been debated for years by historians of agriculture, but to the inhabitants of Baden it meant little because only 16.6 percent of farms there were large enough to qualify.[22] In Oberschopfheim none were.

Thus, despite much effort expended financially, manually, and oratorically in Berlin and in Oberschopfheim, the practice of agriculture and the material condition of village farmers was only marginally better in 1936 than in 1933. So it was for the rest of the nation as well. In 1938-1939 Germany still imported about as much food as in 1934, plus 45 percent of its fats and 30 percent of its fodder. The Nazi Back to the Soil movement amounted to little for another reason, too: highly industrialized modern societies are necessarily highly urbanized, especially when engaged in extensive rearmament programs. Thus the Nazi farm program was like so many of their other ventures: irregular, opportunist, and incoherent, longest on oratory and aspiration. Even so, it did attain its primary political objective, to get rearmament underway without a rural rebellion.[23]

Throughout Germany government loans and subsidies for construction had a more dramatic effect on the economy than did agricultural aid. Anxious to get conspicuous "results," the Nazis everywhere eliminated or reduced the red tape that had long impeded construction. Thus unfettered, artisans built 250,000 new homes and repaired many times that number from 1933 to 1935. By 1936 the construction boom in Thalburg was so flourishing that workers had to be imported.[24] By 1937 the number of craft apprentices in the Reich had soared 47 percent.

In Oberschopfheim gains and benefits were real but more modest.

During the three years after 1933 villagers completed nine new homes, refurbished rooms in seventy-five other homes, built four *Gasthaeuser* and three cigar factories, and finished thirty small projects costing upward of two hundred marks each. Building tradesmen enjoyed steady employment throughout, and the number of artisans grew by 25 percent.[25] But, as was so often the case with Nazi economic programs, benefits were transitory. After the government ended the housing program in March 1936, many artisans lost both their jobs and their shops.[26]

Oberschopfheim's businessmen and workers reaped even fewer benefits from the loans and subsidies than did artisans and farmers. Store owners redeemed a few marriage loan and welfare certificates. Three factory owners who belonged to the DAF *(Deutsche Arbeitsfront)* received small business loans.[27] Neither was sufficient to stimulate the local economy or to increase employment. Although workers were offered subsidized vacation trips, Oberschopfheimers lacked the time to take advantage of the opportunity and had never been in the habit of taking vacations anyway. All that can be said for such meager aid was that it kept up the local credit of the Nazis and stimulated hope that more substantial help might be forthcoming later.

The Reich also offered subsidies and loans to local communities so they could hire the unemployed. Oberschopfheim's *Gemeinde* praised this action and hoped to obtain grants to repair public buildings, to construct new forest roads, and to replace its 1893 water system, which went dry every summer. This euphoria evaporated when the mayor and council discovered that the money thus acquired would have to be repaid with interest. Then they refused to apply. Finally they bowed to county pressure and agreed to employ thirty-two persons in the village forest, but paid them from the regular budget.[28]

In late 1935 the *Gemeinde* finally agreed to build a new water system by borrowing a third of the money from the government and raising the rest from timber sales and private loans. At first villagers applauded this decision and waited impatiently for hiring to begin. Then they heard rumors that the jobs were promised to outsiders. They promptly marched on the courthouse where local officials prevented a riot by threatening severe punishment for such "unfounded" talk. Alas! The talk was not unfounded. County officials again demanded that preference be given to communities with the highest percentage of registered unemployed and to workers who were members of the DAF. Much to the outrage of villagers, only a few local men got jobs on their own village project.[29]

Borrowing for the new water system actually undermined village finances, since Oberschopfheim already had overdue mortgages and debts. Left to solve its own economic problems, the *Gemeinde* sold 84,600 marks worth of electric lines, farm machinery, and businesses. With this money, supplemented by tax increases, local officials managed to repay all the *old* village debts by July 1935. But it was merely the old case of Peter being robbed to pay Paul. Increased welfare expenses, new borrowing for the water system, and the inability of many inhabitants to pay the increased taxes, left the village poorer than it had been in 1913 or 1928 and with its unemployment problem still unsolved.

Other communities such as Lahr and Thalburg, already burdened with massive welfare payments and debts, readily applied for and received government loans. Lahr got money for a new city auditorium, an enlarged park, new asphalt streets, a sewage system, a remodeled courthouse, and a tourist bureau. Thalburg embellished its parks, repaired roads and public buildings, and encouraged the tourist trade. City authorities in Marburg, by contrast, emulated their brethren in Oberschopfheim. In 1935 the mayor, an avid devotee of creative bookkeeping, cited figures showing that he was paying off the municipal debt. He neglected to add that he was also borrowing anew. When possible, Marburg's county government cut expenses and raised both taxes and "contributions" to improve its fiscal image; when not possible, authorities simply declined to publish inconvenient statistics.[30] The lesson, of course, is that deficit financing to promote extensive public works will reduce unemployment promptly, if temporarily, whether in Nazi Germany, New Deal America, or anywhere else. In the case of most German cities the sting in the scorpion's tail was that it added to the burden of municipal debt that was in most cases already unmanageable.

The NSDAP also employed extensive economic controls to combat the Depression. Just as many New Deal programs in the United States were anticipated in the Hoover Administration (1929-1932), many Nazi economic regulations were little more than extensions of the system of modified state socialism that had developed in Germany since the late nineteenth century.[31] The Reich had long owned key industries, set prices, and effectively controlled banks, transportation, and many businesses. Further, economic activity was organized into self-governing chambers *(Kammern)* by occupations and by territorial states. Local municipalities exercised additional economic controls. As noted earlier, the *Gemeinde* of Oberschopfheim owned half the village land and numerous local businesses and regulated in detail much village life.

Many of Hitler's ideas were widely shared and were workable. Of course, since 1940 anyone striving for intellectual respectability in the Anglo-Saxon world can hardly admit this since in our favored part of the globe the faith of the Enlightenment is still strong that knowledge is virtue or the path to it. Therefore, evil men must also be stupid men; therefore, everything that Hitler believed must be pernicious and everything he attempted must be unworkable. Be that as it may, one of Der Fuehrer's convictions that experience bore out to a degree that amazed the more conventional economic thinker, Dr. Hjalmar Schacht, was that a government can temporarily improve the economy by sheer willpower and force. Such action raises public morale and swells the regime's political credit for a time, though it is often damaging in the long run. Like most politicians, however, Hitler was inclined to the comforting view that "in the long run we are all dead" and so was prone to seek immediate "solutions" to onerous problems. For instance, instead of nationalizing more industries or abolishing occupational chambers, Der Fuehrer regimented the "capitalist" economy for political purposes. He extended controls over prices, labor, materials, dividends, and foreign trade. He "unified" owners and workers as "soldiers" in the same army of labor and extended their chambers as organs of the state. He limited competition and private ownership in a fully monopolized and cartelized economy to serve the "general welfare." Yet routine direction of industry was left to private owners, who were not bothered much with regulations until 1937.[32] The resulting "system" bore small relationship to anything in economics textbooks, but it worked for a time.

 Nationally, the Nazis enforced economic regulations much as they did political controls: slowly, in stages, and primarily in urban areas. Many of the regulations, for instance, did not apply to shops employing fewer than ten people. Thus, except for three or four cigar factories, owners of businesses in Oberschopfheim continued to plan, hire, fire, and operate as they had always done. One ruling that did promise to interfere some with their operations was a prohibition against employing persons under fifteen in the tobacco industry, but even this was of minor consequence since family-owned businesses were exempted.

Other economic regulations had even less practical effect in Oberschopfheim. Workers still received the same low wages for two or three days' labor per week. Women, who were paid even less than men, still accounted for 70 percent of all cigar workers, even though the National Socialists had pledged to keep women in the home. One Nazi measure that meant a good deal in most of the Reich was the resurrection of the *Arbeitsbuch* (employment booklet) that workers had been obliged to carry in Wilhelmian Germany. In it was entered all the places the bearer had been employed, embellished with employers' comments about how he had performed his duties. Thus anyone who was an inept worker or who had made trouble or who had a "hostile attitude" could easily be fired, demoted, or prevented from getting desirable employment in the future. Perhaps as bad, if the employer did not want the worker to leave, he could simply keep the latter's book. Burdensome and unfair to working men as this system might seem, it was of no practical consequence in Oberschopfheim. Not a single case was recorded there of anyone either being denied employment or required to remain in an unwanted job. *Gemeinde* employees had to swear obedience to Hitler, to affirm that they were Aryan, and to say "Heil Hitler" around the courthouse, but this produced no noticeable change in their demeanor or the performance of their duties.[33]

Some Nazi regulations were actually welcomed. Store owners applauded fixed prices and the ban on traveling peddlers since this limited competition. Owners of cigar factories appreciated the dissolution of labor unions, which were demanding wage increases. Cigar workers welcomed the law that limited the number of (simple) machines in the factories. Because of the apparent security these controls provided, the village gained three new stores, and the number of part-time cigar workers doubled to four hundred between 1932 and 1935 (though there had been five hundred in 1928). Since the law limiting the use of machines lasted until the 1950s, the legacy of Hitler's concern for cigar workers lasted longer than the Third Reich itself.[34] According to experts on the psychology and needs of the "working class," Oberschopfheimers should have resented the longer hours and meager pay increases that soon were their lot; instead they were thankful that the Nazis had given them more job security than they had known since 1913.[35]

The Nazis justified their extensive interference in the economy by claiming overwhelming success in conquering unemployment, increasing industrial production, and raising living standards. By 1936 they had indeed virtually eliminated joblessness, after only three years' effort, their most impressive single domestic achievement.[36] Though this accomplishment was mostly real it did owe something to imaginative employment of statistics. Since Lahr county had a relatively small percentage of *registered* unemployed, the government was able to formally eliminate joblessness there with a few public works projects, loans, and controls. Yet in the county's rural villages like Oberschopfheim there were many truly unemployed people who were not officially counted because they owned farms or family shops.[37] As late as 1936 most village laborers and cigar workers had jobs only sporadically. During cigar factory closings it was not uncommon for four hundred employees to be idle for months at a time. It was mostly artisans and *Gemeinde* officials who enjoyed steady work. Though some villagers gradually found part-time employment, persistent bad weather and slumping sales kept living standards low for farmers, cigar workers, and small businessmen alike.

Personal financial problems of the sort that can be documented actually increased from 1933 to 1936 in Oberschopfheim. Seven persons defaulted on farming or housing loans, and four cigar makers and two store owners lost their businesses. Of the 423 taxpayers in the village in 1933, thirteen fell behind on payments for taxes and electricity in 1934, and twenty more did so in 1936. In an endeavor to collect taxes due, the *Gemeinde* confiscated tobacco from five families, took seven persons to court in 1935 and three more in 1936, and stopped electricity, free firewood, and the use of meadows for many families.[38]

Nationally, the NSDAP had much more success in elevating living standards than it did in Oberschopfheim. From 1933 to 1934 income for workers rose 21.5 percent and that for most farmers soared comparably. By 1936 most Germans knew they were living better than they had in 1932. Many falsely believed that they had even reached levels above 1928.[39] Industrial production rose sharply. Given 1928 as 100, the volume of production goods rose from 46 in 1932 to 113 in 1936; consumer goods from 78 to 97.5.[40] Nationwide, the Depression had been vanquished. In Oberschopfheim recovery had been only sporadic and peripheral—save in the way people thought about things.

Besides measures to increase employment, the Nazis extended social services to those unable to work. One of the most important of these programs was unemployment compensation. Compared to the whole Reich, few idle Oberschopfheimers, especially women, were counted as unemployed: 10 percent between 1930 and 1933, rising to 15 percent during the first three years of the Nazi era. About half of these unfortunates received benefits, mostly "emergency" aid that ranged from three to six marks twice a month.[41]

Since villagers saw the dramatic increase in aid during 1934, they believed that the Nazi government was providing great sums to combat unemployment. When the aid declined in 1935 and 1936, Oberschopfheimers, true to form, blamed their traditional enemy, Lahr bureaucrats. The latter might have dispelled the misapprehension had they been less inept. Displaying a perverse disdain for peoples' feelings, county officials demanded repayment of aid from several "ineligible" persons, cursed villagers for arriving too early on payday, and compelled the *Gemeinde* to give a job to Andreas Mueller, a man of no distinction, merely because he happened to be the oldest Party member in the village. The main result was to increase tensions between Lahr and Oberschopfheim.[42]

Oberschopfheim's poor, retired, widowed, and disabled also received significantly more help than during the previous three years. In 1933-1934 the number of beneficiaries was three times that of any previous year. Some got small cash payments, about a third of village households received margarine coupons, several families were given coupons for furniture and household goods, and others received them for meat and coal.

Like unemployment compensation, this aid fell sharply in 1935-1936, and some had to be repaid. Once more disgruntled villagers blamed Lahr officials for the decline; but more important, by comparing the striking increase in aid 1933-1934 with the level of 1932, they gave the NSDAP more credit than the Party deserved.[43]

Long before the Nazi era many German political parties had developed private welfare organizations somewhat like the Salvation Army in the English-speaking world. Not to be outdone, the Nazis supplemented regular government welfare programs by creating the NSV (National Socialist *Volkswohlfahrt*) and WHW *(Winterhilfswerk)*. These were specifically Party organizations, designed to collect and distribute "winter aid" and to give free health care to mothers. In much of Germany these new bodies took over the work of private charities and tried to force them out of existence, though in Oberschopfheim *Caritas* collections for the poor and medical services from the local nuns continued undisturbed until much later. (*Caritas* has long been the largest Catholic welfare organization in Germany and Austria.)

Nazi Winter Aid collections had a strong political component. Hitler and Propaganda Minister Josef Goebbels began the first drive in October 1933 with emotional admonitions to all Germans that giving to the poor was not just a momentary indulgence of one's good nature but a strict duty. The message was publicized heavily in the *Anzeiger* and *Zeitung*. It featured such slogans as "Protect the Family"; "No One Is Allowed to Starve and Freeze"; and "The Good Man Thinks of Himself Last," accompanied by a picture of a man rowing to save a drowning person. Such injunctions appealed to the villagers and led them to heap praise on this "humanitarian" Nazi organization.

The rulers of the Reich followed up by sending volunteers into each city and village to collect monthly donations. Since the NSV gave plaques to donors, which the donors then affixed to their houses, neighborhood pressure proved the most effective way to stimulate giving. This does not mean that other methods were neglected. The NSDAP resorted to every expedient human ingenuity could devise to encourage donations. Town and church bells were rung to kick off campaigns. People were induced to pledge to eat "single pot meals" on certain days and to donate the savings to the WHW. Deductions from the pay of civil servants became commonplace. Larger contributions were gouged from private companies and their executives, accompanied by warnings that noncontributors might lose their state contracts. NSDAP functionaries were pressured to meet quotas. Efforts were made to restrict religious contributions so more would be available for the WHW. Streets were even blocked off during contribution drives so nobody could escape the collectors.[44] By such methods monthly collections became quite considerable: in Oberschopfheim several tons of potatoes, fruit, and other foods, some cash, and "voluntary" donations from the *Gemeinde*'s Poor Fund. To sweeten the pill, villagers were allowed to distribute 15 percent of their monthly collections locally.[45] In Baden such aid went to 14 percent of the population in 1935, still to 7 percent in 1938 when economic conditions had improved.[46]

In Lahr the Nazis shrewdly turned the whole "charity" campaign into a countywide contest among villages. As a competitive effort it was managed ideally: it allowed everyone to claim victory. Protestant villages were generally larger than Catholic and so usually gave larger *total* amounts, yet Catholic Oberschopfheim repeatedly won highest honors by giving slightly more per capita than other villages.[47] In fact, most Germans contributed generously to all these welfare programs. The liberality of both Lahr county and Oberschopfheim was especially noteworthy in view of the poverty of the area. The programs themselves were a major coup for the Nazis since they convinced many Germans that never before had citizens been so generous to organized charities.[48]

Though the NSV, WHW, and various offshoots were of genuine benefit to many poor Germans, the real purpose behind them had less to do with welfare than with gaining credit for the NSDAP and advancing the Nazi race program. All the charitable and mutual aid endeavors were managed in such a way that the Nazis could plausibly claim that they constituted preventive aid rather than welfare. The vast sums collected undeniably helped the government to reduce its *official* welfare bill. Finally, the aid went only to those judged eugenically "desirable" and in practice heavily to NSDAP party members. Many have charged, after the event, that the Nazis simply bought public support with pressured charity;[49] that the NSV and the WHW would have been unnecessary if the regime had not depressed wages and reduced state welfare benefits;[50] that much of the money, never accurately accounted for, really went to the armed forces or was squandered by Nazi functionaries;[51] and that the main purpose of all such endeavors was not to dispense charity but to demonstrate that the Reich had become a "national community."[52]

The NSDAP also encouraged local communities to increase special aid to their own people. Oberschopfheim's *Gemeinde* responded with public-spirited generosity mixed with its usual penny-pinching. On the liberal side, property taxes were reduced on vacant or partly empty businesses and on a few private houses. Water and electrical bills were lowered for many citizens, and debt payments were postponed for more than sixty families. Officials also gave jobs to several debt ridden families and increased the total amount of "poor aid" for 1934. Then, as if to defy Nazi pressure, the *Gemeinde* also increased its annual gift to the local

Oberschopfheimers used cattle for farming; they were more practical than horses because they also gave milk.

When villagers look down from the grape area above Oberschopfheim, they see the entire village before them.

Catholic customs and celebrations were for many Oberschopfheimers the brightest and most joyous part of village life. In 1964, the woman on the left dressed in this traditional costume to attend a celebration at church. The woman on the right is wearing everyday clothes. Note the large, rough hands from hard work.

A First Mass was accompanied by more ceremony than ordinary Mass. The whole village turned out in their best to celebrate this one in 1931.

Dr. Herman Hirt, Oberschopfheim's priest from 1933 to 1948, was not intimidated by the Nazis. In fact, villagers were convinced that he was protected by ghosts from the haunted rectory and a stray dog that saved the priest's life when he was attacked by Nazi assassins.

The *Leutkirche*, a pilgrimage church built in the eighth century and restored many times since, stands about half a mile from the center of Oberschopfheim. It narrowly escaped being bombed by the Allies in World War II.

The grandfather of Josef Messerer (shown here) was the only one of Oberschopfheim's early immigrants to America who returned to the village. He made his family prosperous by judicious use of the pension he received as a veteran of the American Civil War.

During World War II, the Nazis confiscated Oberschopfheim's large church bells, claiming the metal was needed for the military industry.

Women in the village did much of the field work, moving from plot to plot between the many other jobs they performed daily. These women are hoeing tobacco, an important source of income in Oberschopfheim.

Tobacco was picked leaf by leaf, graded, sewn together according to quality, and hung up to dry in barns like this one, photographed in 1973.

In the late 1960s a station was built to house new machinery to press grapes (above). By 1973, few villagers pressed their own grapes, as they had done for centuries, but instead brought them to the station and waited their turn.

In 1890, the village Military Club erected this monument, which was enlarged in 1929 to include the names of the forty-five men who had died in the Great War. Members of the Military Club (below) posed for this photograph in the 1960s. They marched in uniform in village celebrations.

Until the 1960s when a renovation boom took place, houses were built to fit the narrow streets, and none of the scarce, rich farmland was wasted on lawns or flower gardens. Since the 1970s, Oberschopfheim has ceased to be primarily a farm village, and people are less concerned with saving and using every bit of land. Streets have been straightened and widened, and many now have lawns, flower beds, and backyard gardens.

church.[53] Familiar attitudes cropped up elsewhere too. Local officials refused to enlarge the cemetery grounds and instead buried the dead in occupied plots. To cut expenses they discouraged girls from attending trade schools; refused aid to many needy families whom they regarded as "spendthrifts"; and made a vigorous attempt to collect certain past debts, which still amounted to 19,500 marks in mid-1935.

Everything considered, for all Germany, the Nazi attack on the Depression was successful, particularly its conquest of unemployment.[54] Nonetheless it was hardly "new," much less "revolutionary," and it benefited Lahr county and Oberschopfheim much less than the national average. Nonetheless, the village was helped *some.* Economic controls accompanied the government aid, but most of them were not onerous and few were enforced severely because county and Party officials did not think probable gains worth the quarrels that would inevitably ensue.

Despite much Nazi fanfare and some action, the economic structure of Oberschopfheim was changed only peripherally after 1933. Farm cooperatives lost their importance as bargaining agents for farmers, since the Nazis required the sale of fixed amounts of produce to the government. The presence of a farm leader with authority to allocate aid and enforce decisions diminished the element of democracy in village life. Tobacco workers lost their union, but since it had been too weak to win them higher wages the "loss" was at least counterbalanced by government concessions. Although the *Gemeinde* sold some businesses to pay off debts, it remained the largest property owner in the village. Local stores and businesses remained in private hands and suffered little interference.

Unquestionably, the greatest value of Nazi programs was the impact they made on the imaginations of most Germans.[55] The NSDAP shrewdly compared all gains in production, employment, and living standards with the low levels of 1932 rather than with figures for 1914 or 1928 or averages for any period. Hence, many Germans became convinced that they were living in an age of unprecedented economic progress in which all problems would soon be solved. So appealing were Adolf Hitler's simple emotion-laden slogans, accompanied by a flood of activity, that even though actual NSDAP programs were of mere marginal value to Oberschopfheim, some elderly people still believe the Hitler regime saved them, and Germany, from economic ruin in the 1930s.

# 9

# THE STRENGTH OF TRADITION

AFTER THE MARCH 1933 elections the NSDAP claimed to have instituted radical social changes throughout Germany. The Party boasted that it had brought social equality and mobility to all Germans, molded the *Volk* into a harmonious *Gemeinschaft* (community), won the primary loyalty of the masses, and saved the family from disintegration. Like most Nazi claims, indeed like the claims of most political regimes anywhere, these were a mixture of truth and puffery.

In a sense the NSDAP tried to *impose* equality on the whole nation by attempting to encompass its entire social life, by establishing Party organizations of all sorts of people for all sorts of purposes thereby getting everybody to work for the Party in some way or to undertake his recreational activity in one of its innumerable satellite organizations. In some ways, too, the Nazis did stimulate upward mobility in German society and accelerate a tendency toward greater social equality. Some of the latter was achieved merely by imposing certain controls on everyone impartially. Some derived from the policy of *Gleichschaltung,* which combined separate groups of workers, shopkeepers, and businessmen into one organization and brought workers and owners together for parades and social outings. The NSDAP also raised thousands of persons to higher positions within business, government, and the Party, even though those promoted did not possess diplomas or impressive family names. Some scholars have estimated that during the first six years of the Nazi era occupational mobility was double that of the last six years of the Weimar era. Perhaps so for Party members or those who became members or who remained politically silent.[1]

Because those who received such promotions often lacked technical training, the NSDAP found it expedient to still depend upon the traditional elites of generals, Junkers, and industrialists to manage and increase Germany's industrial and military power. Yet the newcomers, because they were Party members, often exercised influence much in excess of their titles and so somewhat curtailed the power of particular aristocrats and tycoons. Thus did the Nazis simultaneously promote a society based on equality and one based on established hierarchies.[2]

Confounding the anomaly, the Nazis also superimposed new hierarchies on German society. They divided the country into "accepted Germans" and "outsiders" (Jews, Communists, labor leaders, outspoken opponents of the regime, and lesser undesirables), into rulers and ruled, even into antagonistic and competitive branches of the Party.

These strong and opposing currents that flowed through the Reich at large made scarcely a ripple in Oberschopfheim. Since village society was already homogenous, *Gleichschaltung* led merely to the addition of the word "Nazi" to club names and to occasional encouragement to entertain *Arbeitsdienst* workers and clubs from other communities. Club membership and activities remained basically unchanged. So did social mobility, since the NSDAP merely selected current village leaders to serve as Party functionaries, mayor, and local officials. There were two exceptions. Herr Albiker, as we have seen, was an outsider; and in 1935 the county leader rewarded Oberschopfheim's first Party member, Andreas Mueller, with a seat on the inner council, even though he was an unskilled and unemployed worker. Neither appointment had any lasting significance. Albiker was eventually hounded out of town in August of 1938. The undistinguished Mueller served on the council until 1941 but always in close association with Farm Leader Roederer and Military Club Leader Merkert, former council members appointed by the Party specifically to help the neophyte statesman make "correct" decisions.[3]

Since the Nazi party upheld the "Leadership Principle," which allowed appointees supergovernmental powers over those defined as essentially "irrational" and "inferior," Oberschopfheim's new officials became an instant village elite. They could now remain in power indefinitely and act more independently of village opinion than before—but only to a degree, since they still lived in the same village, cheek-by-jowl with their lifelong neighbors.

Despite these prosaic "facts" many villagers *believed* Nazi claims that they had leveled the nation socially—somewhere else. Though local farmers received only sporadic and peripheral aid from the government, the village was rife with talk about impoverished farmers from some distant place who had gotten important jobs in the agriculture department and poor workers elsewhere who had become factory managers. Thus, while the Nazis "rode off in all directions," simultaneously bolstering elites, inventing elites, and stimulating some leveling, it was the last that caught the imaginations of ordinary people in Oberschopfheim.[4]

It was much the same with NSDAP claims that they had ushered in a People's Community *(Volksgemeinschaft)* of peace and order, in contrast to the turmoil of the 1920s and the early Depression years. Some of the older Oberschopfheimers interviewed by one of these writers in 1973 remarked nostalgically that if Hitler was still in power society's problems would be solved. Welfare recipients and lazy people would work, rebellious young people would be controlled, and terrorist attacks and oil boycotts would cease. Although some of these oldsters actually believed that the Nazis had achieved a *Volksgemeinschaft* with fewer crimes and conflicts, more appeared merely to desire old fashioned "order" and predictability and to dislike a society in which "everything is allowed."

Once more, it is easily overlooked that common people in societies with few democratic traditions do not necessarily crave individual liberty and democratic government in the British and American sense. Many Russians who have emigrated to the United States, Israel, or elsewhere have felt alone and lost in societies without low cost housing, guaranteed employment, free medical care, and a generally "regulated" life. Many more, who stayed home, still admire the bloody tyrant Josef Stalin as a man who kept order, enforced discipline, repressed troublemakers, and made Russia strong. By contrast, they regard Nikita Khrushchev, who downgraded Stalin, as a buffoon. The feelings of the conservative peasants of Oberschopfheim were often similar.

Despite claims that the Nazis reduced conventional crime drastically in Germany and despite the undeniable fact that millions of Germans credited them with this achievement, in Oberschopfheim offenses of the same old kind occurred at about the same old rates. Most "crime" was still such petty thievery as stealing part of a neighbor's crop or filching from the church poor box.[5] Conflicts among inhabitants continued at about the same level as before. Individuals eagerly filed suit against neighbors for supposedly damaging their reputation or property and against the *Gemeinde* for perceived injuries. Even the pastor, Dr. Hirt, was forced to take part in picayune village squabbles that followed such disasters as the mayor's car hitting the rectory and a funeral procession frightening a cow into damaging a farmer's wagon.

At first the county NSDAP tried to mediate local conflicts in Oberschopfheim. For instance, county officials sided with new tobacco planters in a dispute over planting allotments and told the mayor to reallocate the shares in the presence of two Party officials. Old planters, among whom were the mayor and *Gemeinde* officials, responded by urging the state minister for food and agriculture to allow only farmers who could "guarantee quality tobacco" (themselves) to raise it. Then, like a quarreling husband and wife when the police are called, Oberschopfheimers promptly forgot about their intramural tiff and heatedly denounced both the state and county NSDAP for interfering in village affairs.[5] Thereafter Party officials, perhaps from despair, perhaps from disgust, let local squabbles run their course.

Conflicts between Oberschopfheim and other communities continued as in pre-Nazi times. Village leaders, frugal as ever, still resorted to numerous artifices to avoid paying for hospital care, welfare expenses, and a teacher's salary. Village police, who watched especially for outside male-factors, prided themselves on apprehending a "Nazi" mayor from Schut-tern who drove his horse over an Oberschopfheimer's land.[7]

In many parts of Germany the advent of the Nazis seemed not to produce a *Volksgemeinschaft* at all, but the opposite: to stimulate distrust among ordinary people and to increase the incidence of crime. In Thal-burg, where this condition was pronounced, W.S. Allen thinks it was caused by Party raids, harassment of particular individuals by arrogant Hitler Youth, and general Nazi employment of terror. This, he believes, caused some people to leave the community and broke down the morale of others by compelling them to live lives of insincerity.[8] In Lahr, police jailed several communists who publicly denounced the NSDAP as a party of liars and crooks.[9] Hitler Youth also stirred up trouble periodically there, though the level of violence was well below that in Thalburg. In Ober-schopfheim no difference was discernible. On only one occasion did a Party member provoke a fight: he yelled "Heil Hitler" during Con-secration at Sunday Mass. When he left the church, parishioners attacked him and some Party sympathizers. A brawl ensued that the police had to quell.

The village did not suffer from the struggles between Party and political leaders that plagued larger communities. In Oberschopfheim there were only a handful of either, and the two structures were almost identical. Only from 1936 to 1938 did Party Leader Albiker, an outsider and a Fanatiker, provoke turmoil by demanding special privileges for him-self and some Party members. A few Oberschopfheimers even continued to curse the government, as had been their habit for preceding decades, but most people had sufficient prudence to keep quiet. On one occasion in 1935 the mayor warned Herr Messerer, who worked for the *Gemeinde,* that he could not criticize the Party publicly and still keep his job.

Before 1936 the Nazis imposed fewer new social controls on the village than on cities. Many regulations associated with the Nazis in the minds of foreigners had already existed in the Weimar era and were not intensified locally. Travel restrictions for Oberschopfheimers, for example, remained much the same. Individuals who stayed in other communities more than three days still had to register with the police on arrival and departure, and those who went to foreign countries still had to obtain travel permits. How little this amounted to, in practice, is indicated by a few statistics. Between 1933 and 1936 Oberschopfheimers made a grand total of seven visits to other countries, most of them to neighboring Holland on tobacco business. They permitted one foreigner to work in the village and allowed three gypsies to camp outside it. The nightly village curfew continued to be applied impartially. Even the mayor, the farm leader, and lesser officials were fined for continuing a meeting beyond the appointed hour.[10] In Germany at large the Nazis might censor public activities and spy on individuals, but in Oberschopfheim courthouse officials collected information about animals and land rather than people.

The NSDAP did, however, introduce two new social usages: the Hitler salute and the flying of the Nazi flag. In July 1933, Berlin directed its officials and employees to greet each other at work with the raised hand, with or without the words *Heil Hitler,* and promptly extended this to large cities and towns. Use of the greeting was also encouraged on social occasions, a convention later extended to all oral and written communication. As usual, Oberschopfheim lagged behind. Perhaps ten to a dozen enthusiasts dressed in brown, wore boots, and barked "Heil Hitler!" at all and sundry from the first. They were the same persons who played their radios at maximum volume so nobody could escape Nazi oral propaganda. Local officials began to emulate them in 1934 but mostly when greeting outside dignitaries. Ordinary people ignored the greeting until 1936, when it became common in public places. Village response was comparably slow and gradual when Nazi officials changed the national flag to the old imperial colors and made the swastika its equal.

Endeavors of this sort were a further demonstration of how slapdash so much of the Nazi program was. Requiring Hitler salutes, displays of the swastika, and endless contributions to Nazi causes seemed clearly an effort to politicize everyone. Yet the same regime encouraged the mass production of cheap radios that could be paid for on the installment plan. These were supplemented by films, Volkswagens, and other consumer goods or modes of entertainment. Overall, such developments probably weakened rather than strengthened public interest in politics.

In 1934 state officials decreed that the distinctive flags, pictures, and busts of the Weimar era must be removed and in 1935 that citizens must remove from their houses, walls, and gardens all signs that were objectionable to the Party. In Oberschopfheim this meant next to nothing since few persons possessed anything objectionable, and local officials did not check for violations anyway. Later, when state and county leaders called for the removal of crosses and religious statues from public buildings, villagers objected strenuously but unsuccessfully. Nevertheless, they did manage to keep their crosses and shrines in the fields, along roads, and in their homes.[11] Like the common people of Marburg, Oberschopfheimers never thought they were living under tyranny. Only after the war, and from outsiders, did they learn that Nazism was synonymous with mistrust, suspicion, dread, defamation, cruelty, and destruction.[12]

One of the proudest boasts of the Nazis was that they had won the primary loyalty of both adults and young people away from hometown and church to the nation and Hitler. As proof they pointed to the mass support for Hitler shown at rallies and, later, at the dedication of teenage soldiers up to the last days of the war. The claim had some validity in much of the Reich, though it was also true that many German households were divided and suffused with acrimony, usually between sons sympathetic to Nazism and fathers who were not.[13] In Oberschopfheim, however, old loyalties remained mostly unchanged.

After the March 1933 elections the NSDAP made a special effort to gain immediate control of schools and to win the support of youth. Teachers were officially encouraged to pressure boys to join the Hitler Youth. Many did so by giving their charges extra work, keeping them after school, even threatening them with physical violence. In Thalburg and in the Hessian village of Korle, this was a success. The schools became "ideological bastions" of the new regime and school children active instruments of the Party. But not so in Oberschopfheim. Balked, county leaders resorted to extracurricular activities outside the village.[14] The first major effort of this sort was a celebration in September 1933 for all school children in Lahr county. Weeks beforehand, each school received instructions to design its own flag and to learn patriotic and Party songs. Oberschopfheim chose as its flag a copy of the village coat of arms (an evergreen on a silver background) on one side and an 1870 flag used by Baden's military recruits on the other. On the day of the outing, Oberschopfheim's students, teachers, pastor, and several prominent citizens made the two and a half hour hike to an old castle where the celebration took place. In all, three thousand students heard praises of the "New Spirit" of National Socialism, sang songs, had their flags dedicated, and played among the ruins. On the return hike home, Oberschopfheim's teachers obediently flanked the school flag with the Reich and Party flags and sang the *Horst Wessel* song. For the village children the outing was the highlight of the school year.[15]

That autumn Oberschopfheim's teachers were directed to organize "voluntary" units of the Hitler Youth and the German Girls' League. They did so dutifully, but the organizations never became beehives of political activity like their counterparts in Korle and Thalburg. Instead, boys and girls busied themselves learning household and outdoor skills and collecting for the Winter Aid. In 1936 the new group leader and school principal, Herr Albiker, forced all children to join and to attend indoctrination sessions. Again, the dividends proved small. The youngsters did not show much enthusiasm for the "New Reich" or derive any visible benefit from its youth organizations. Unlike the Hitler Youth activists in Korle or Lahr city, they did not stage plays, go to the city of Nuremberg for rallies, or command any notable influence either in the school or in the village streets.[16] Most of them seemed to differ but little from American kids who joined the Boy Scouts or the Campfire Girls. Membership was a chance to wear a uniform, mingle with friends, march with a band, play games, ramble in the countryside, get away from the tutelage of fathers, teachers, clerics, and foremen, and perhaps escape some tedious household tasks.[17] Nationally, the effort to indoctrinate youth was hampered because the most promising youth leaders were usually drafted into military service or some compulsory labor program. In Catholic areas Hitler Youth had to compete with well-organized local confessional youth groups.[18]

Inside the classroom Oberschopfheim's students, like many children throughout Germany, experienced few changes at first. New textbooks were issued in Thalburg in 1933 but not in Oberschopfheim until 1936, since in many areas frugal authorities kept schoolbooks for generations, making only periodic revisions. The sixth to eighth grades in Oberschopf-heim, for example, continued to use the twenty-third edition of the *Badisches Realienbuch*, which contained geography, history, biology, health, and chemistry. The history section had little information about the Weimar era and ended with a prediction of a "dark future" for Germany. Other textbooks were so old that they discussed German history only up to the beginning of the reign of William II (1888-1918).[19]

When Oberschopfheim's children finally got new books, they found surprisingly few revisions or additions. Nazi theorists had developed a lot of half-baked notions in biology and other sciences that could hardly be applied without damaging the scientific and technological expertise essential in German industry and war production, so they had to be soft-pedaled in schools. Mathematics is much the same no matter what the ideological coloration of a regime. The song books merely included a few more selections from the *Heimat* or about national events or soldiers, while songs for church feasts were as numerous as before. Reading books contained only a few additions, such as *Der Fuehrer kommt, Fuer das Winter-hilfswerk*, and *Arbeitslos*.[20] As for history and civics, the Nazis of course emphasized patriotism, militarism, and racism more than is done in any democracy. Even here though, as in many other subjects, a fundamental difficulty was that Nazi ideology was always in such a state of controversy that it was difficult to determine just what constituted the true creed in which the nation's young people should be indoctrinated.

In practice, most of the struggle to win students for the Third Reich fell to the teachers rather than the textbooks. The Party encouraged teachers to join the Nazi Teachers' Organization (NSLB) and directed them to emphasize race studies, national culture, and the glories of German history. In 1937 Herr Albiker made these topics mandatory and urged students to read novels about military history. Response was less than tumultuous. It hardly constitutes news to note that many youngsters anywhere pay only sporadic attention to their lessons. In Oberschopfheim there were many such, partly because they accepted their parents' prejudices, partly because they were often tired from farm work. The zeal of teachers was comparably unremarkable. Many of them, at all levels, had flooded into the Nazi party between 1930 and 1934, whether from lack of sympathy with Weimar educational efforts, resentment of pay cuts, loss of their jobs during the Depression, elitist contempt for democracy, or mere hope that the Nazis would improve their lot. Yet few occupational groups were ultimately as disappointed and disillusioned with the Third Reich as teachers.[21] In Oberschopfheim there was little danger of being visited by a Party inspector, and a teacher who lacked diligence could hardly be demoted to a place smaller, more remote, or less "challenging."

The county NSDAP also tried to win the loyalty of adults by staging Nazi celebrations. In Lahr city festive days were held to commemorate Hitler's birthday, the anniversary of the founding of the Reich, Memorial Day, and the anniversary of the 1923 Nazi *Putsch*. On such occasions plays were presented, and wreaths were laid on symbolic graves of soldiers and Party members. Bands played, slogans were shouted en masse, and newly initiated members of the Hitler Youth swore "lasting loyalty and unconditional obedience" to the Fuehrer.[22] Such activities hardly touched Oberschopfheim. The best Albiker could manage was to bully villagers to hang out their flags on major Nazi holidays and muster them to listen to his speeches.

Attempts to reform villagers personally, whether youths or their elders, were equally fruitless. Though revolutionaries may be thieves, sadists, or libertines themselves, most revolutionary movements and regimes contain a puritanical streak. Nazism was no exception. Party officials forbade smoking by children under sixteen and ordered the names of violators posted publicly, but since most village youths were around cigars all day the edict was unavailing. In the same spirit, the NSDAP dispatched dietary experts to teach villagers how to preserve apple juice in the hope that they could thereby be induced to drink it rather than alcoholic beverages. Results were similarly forlorn.

A favorite Nazi claim in the area of social relations was that they had rescued the German family from disintegration. They boasted of encouraging marriages and births and of persuading women to become full-time mothers instead of competing with men for jobs. As usual with Nazi projects and objectives, the gap between assertion and achievement was considerable.

One of the most successful ways to increase the number of marriages was to offer loans to newlyweds. Each couple could receive up to one thousand marks' worth of household goods, provided certain conditions were met. Both partners had to be "nationally minded" and to pledge unconditional loyalty to the National Socialist state. They also had to be certifiably healthy, both physically and psychologically. Finally, the wife had to quit her job if her husband earned more than 125 marks per month.[23] In Oberschopfheim these conditions were meaningless since marriages to close relatives were overlooked, people's political views were ignored, and incomes were so low that no prospective wife could be compelled to give up her job.

Because of the loan program and general improvement in economic conditions, there was a modest (and brief) rise in the marriage rate all over the Reich. At once the Nazis, like most rulers anywhere, tortured the statistics until a desired political message was elicited. They compared marriage figures in 1934 to those in 1932 when figures were lowest instead of with those of the mid-1920s when they were much higher. No matter. By 1935 and 1936 marriage rates were falling once more because of curtailment of the loan program, the imposition of compulsory military service, and the delayed effect of the low birthrate during the years of World War I.[24]

While encouraging marriage, the Nazis, always concerned with eugenics, strove to limit inbreeding in rural villages by promoting social gatherings at which those from different communities, religions, and backgrounds would mingle. In Oberschopfheim this program proved counterproductive. Although marriages between villagers and inhabitants of nearby communities were becoming more frequent before 1933, this trend was sharply reversed between 1933 and 1936. Marriages between Oberschopfheimers skyrocketed from 36 percent to 75 percent of the total, while those between Catholics rose from 91 percent to 100 percent.[25] The reason for this odd development is uncertain. Perhaps it derived from heightened mistrust of outsiders? Perhaps young villagers were irked by Nazi interference in local affairs, notably the arrest of club leaders? Perhaps it was only coincidental?

The NSDAP had more success raising the birthrate, though again only in the short run. During the previous thirty years Germany's birthrate had declined steadily until 40 percent of all marriages were childless and only 2 percent of all families had more than three children. Family size averaged a mere 3.4 persons in cities of over 100,000 and 4.1 in villages of less than 10,000, for a national average of 3.7 persons per family.[26] In Oberschopfheim, where large families had once been common, both the birthrate and average family size had, by the 1930s, dropped below state and national averages. The parlous state of the local economy since 1913 had certainly contributed to this development. It must also have indicated a silent, as yet unacknowledged, erosion of religious faith as well since the Catholic Church remained as publicly opposed to contraception as ever.[27] Perhaps it also indicated a growing conviction among ordinary people that one could, and should, control his own life to a greater degree than heretofore.

To encourage the birth of more children the NSDAP used propaganda and money incentives, the latter being much more effective in Oberschopfheim. The government offered to cancel one-fourth of a couple's marriage loan for each child they bore and promised both loans and subsidies to families with four or more children under the age of sixteen. With the usual bow to eugenics, both parents and children had to be free of physical and psychological defects. In Oberschopfheim most families with marriage loans canceled some of their debt by having a child or two, and thirty-one families got subsidies or loans. Even so, the lasting effect was small. There were a number of reasons for this, one of which might have been lifted from a comic opera. Generations of intermarriage had resulted in many villagers having identical names, a condition that led to chronic confusion and delay in implementing payments under the programs. Finally, in 1936 the government sharply curtailed the programs themselves.[28]

Incentives less tangible than cash provided a significant stimulus to childbearing in many parts of the Reich, but were of only ephemeral importance in Oberschopfheim. During much of 1935, for example, the "Mother and Child" program provided over two thousand marks' worth of food and clothing to families in Lahr city. It also brought to Lahr some 363 children from other parts of Germany and sent 225 Lahr children and twenty mothers on vacation. The Party also bestowed awards on mothers who bore many children and later sent questionnaires to officials who were single or childless to inquire why this was so and whether any change was forthcoming.[29]

At least in part because of such government prodding, the German birthrate soared 30 percent from 1933 to 1935 and that of Oberschopfheim 40 percent, only to collapse as abruptly as it had risen when aid ended and conscription began.[30] Overall, the village remained unchanged demographically. Women still outnumbered men by 3 percent, and 99 percent of the population remained Catholic. No Jew, foreigner, or outsider moved into the village, save Group Leader Albiker and a few teachers.

Some have claimed that Nazi organizations for women had a generally liberating effect because they introduced women to public life and encouraged them to travel and meet women from other parts of Germany. Perhaps this was true elsewhere in the Reich,[31] but the rise of Nazism had no discernible impact of any kind on Oberschopfheim's women before

World War II. The NSDAP offered them no opportunity to share power in the *Gemeinde*, though there were Party organizations (National Socialist Frauenschaft-NSF and Bund Deutsche Maedchen-BDM) for women. Village wives continued to work in cigar factories as before, to follow their cows and plows in the fields, and to do all the housework. Some of the Nazi failure to inspire women derived from their unique ideas, some merely from traditional attitudes among German men. The latter ordinarily did not want their women to work in industry or far from home.

The conflict of Nazi doctrines and national needs was more complex. Nationally, Nazi programs and exhortations to women to confine themselves to *"Kinder, Kueche, Kirche"* did reduce the number of women workers by 4.6 percent in 1933-1936, although the female population increased in absolute numbers.[32] Then, after 1937, as Hitler began to plan for war in the near future, the Party abandoned its efforts to keep women in the home and encouraged them to work in factories instead. Even so, in World War II, Nazi Germany made less efficient use of its female work force than did democratic England or America, despite the oft-alleged greater efficiency of dictatorships. Yet in German agriculture, which was much less mechanized than American, German women had to relive World War I: to do even more work than usual while their men went off to war. It was primarily urban, middle-class German women whom the NSDAP did not mobilize. As in so many areas, Nazi failure derived basically from trying to ride two (sometimes several) horses at once and so falling between them. In this case, they endeavored to "save the family" and "put women back in the home" from 1933 to 1936; reversed themselves after 1936; then almost fatally undermined the German family in the period from 1939 to 1945.

Overall, many towns and cities in Germany, especially the larger ones, were shaken profoundly in the early Nazi years (1933-1936), but in Oberschopfheim about all that the brownshirt "social revolution" meant was the introduction of "Heil Hitler" and the Nazi flag, a transitory rise in the marriage and birthrates, and the transmutation of village leaders into Nazi officials. Otherwise, farmers and their wives toiled as usual, alternately socialized and bickered with their neighbors, cursed "meddling outside bureaucrats," deferred to their pastor, and remained loyal to their church and their village, much as their ancestors had done for centuries.

# 10

# WORLD WAR II
# AND ITS AFTERMATH

THE CITIZENS of Oberschopfheim greeted the onset of the Second World War with the same resignation displayed by their ancestors in World War I and numberless other conflicts in bygone ages. Three hundred fourteen men from the village were drafted into the German army and dutifully tramped off to war. By 1945 they had been joined by about eighty-five others in some kind of national service. Many of the latter were teenagers called up in the last months of the war.

All of them were regular troops. As in World War I, not one became an officer or a war hero, but none deserted or defected to the enemy either. Every village in Lahr county saw many of its men killed in France, Russia, North Africa, Italy, or some other distant battleground. Their loss was grievous to their villages and to their families; crushing to the latter when several sons were killed or when both father and son died, as was all too often the case. When the Third Reich at last lay in ruins, sixty-eight men from Oberschopfheim were known dead, forty-three were known to be prisoners still, and about 150 were missing.[1] It was an appalling toll for a village of sixteen hundred within a span of six years. In 1991 there were very few old men in any village in Lahr county.

The state of German civilian morale during the war is hard to gauge because the press was controlled, and there were no public opinion polls. Most Germans passively accepted their government's policies, but there was little discernible enthusiasm for a repetition of World War I, particularly if waged against England and France.[2] To be sure, the sweeping successes and low casualties of the early campaigns in 1939-1940 produced widespread elation. To many Germans Nazism seemed to be fulfilling all its promises: battlefield victories, conquest of "living space," political unity at home, full employment, and deportation of the Jews. All the major features of Nazism appeared to have proved their utility in the crucible of combat: the "Fuehrer principle," the single-party state, a controlled economy, subordination of the individual to the state, extensive use of propaganda, and stress on the therapeutic value of struggle. In the town of Marburg, for instance, the populace greeted the news of the fall of France by pouring into the streets, ringing church bells, draping swastikas over any available object, staging a parade, and keeping the beer gardens open all night. Economically, the town prospered. A new explosives factory absorbed all the unemployed, a uniform factory's business expanded, lesser enterprises throve, and many war prisoners became available for farm labor. Even food rationing, an omnipresent reminder of war, was not burdensome in the first year or two of victories.[3] This mood was gradually tempered as Britain remained unconquered, the invasion of Russia stalled, and the United States joined the ranks of the Reich's enemies.

In Oberschopfheim such euphoria did not exist at any time during the war. On the home front the conflict was essentially a repetition of World War I, and, like the first war, it was especially arduous for women. Once more they had to undertake most of the heavy farm work, aided by old men, semi-invalids, and small children. Occasional further help was available from prisoners of war, chiefly Russian, or from displaced persons of various nationalities who were merely looking for work. The labor of such people was of indifferent quality, and it was at least counterbalanced in late 1944 by an influx of sixty-one new and unproductive refugees. Most of the latter were women and children from villages along the Rhine and from such heavily bombed cities as Cologne, Dortmund, Mannheim, and Ludwigshafen. Most stayed only briefly before being moved farther eastward into the Black Forest.

Wartime life in the village was monotonous and dull. Oberschopfheim had had electricity since 1919, but the power was never sufficient for all the normal needs of the village. Even in peacetime it had been regularly shut off for several hours each day. During the war the "off" periods were lengthened, and the Reich was put on "double" daylight saving time to further conserve electricity. Nazi authorities also wanted to keep houses dark so they could not be seen by Allied bombers. Consequently, villagers had a choice of attempting to play cards or engage in some other evening entertainment by the light of a candle placed under a table or merely going to bed when it got dark. Most chose the latter. If there was any relief from tedium it was apt to be of the most dispiriting sort, news of the death of a village serviceman. If the deceased had been married, his overworked and grieving wife now had to go to the courthouse and fill out forms relating such information as the prewar incomes of both her husband and herself and how many children they had. Then she could begin to collect her war widow's pension.

At village schools in Lahr county such essentials as paper and pencils were in chronic short supply, but it often made little difference since the children were periodically evacuated to the Black Forest to protect them from possible Allied bombing. The first such evacuation began on the eve of the invasion of France in May 1940. It lasted six weeks and involved moving not merely children but women and the elderly from the Rhine area to nearby Diersburg and Berghaupten. In 1944 the same groups were evacuated again for a time. When they had a choice between going with their children or remaining in the village most of the women, who really feared to do either, ultimately stayed. Many then walked nightly patrols, on the lookout for enemy planes or soldiers. If they saw any, or thought they had, early in the war, the church bells would be rung. Everyone was then supposed to disperse to refuges prepared in the hills. Most sightings of planes came after 1942, however, by which time four large bells had been sequestered by the Nazis for use as war material, although a small bell remained.

Conscription and military service exposed innumerable young men to cities, travel, new people, new experiences, and new ideas, and thereby profoundly shook their attachment to hoary, static local ways, but for those who lived in Oberschopfheim during the war changes were few and gradual. The population fell off a bit, from around 1,630 people to 1,500. One new business, a quilt and pillow factory, was established in 1944. It flourished to such a degree that by 1953 it employed over two hundred people, some fifty of them from outside the village.

In only one sector was there a marked and permanent change: cigar-making. Several factors bore on it. Women had always greatly outnumbered men in cigar manufacture because everything connected with tobacco production required much handwork and because the pay was low. When they could, men tried to get more remunerative jobs on the railroad or elsewhere. Women, by contrast, often had children to supervise and so wanted jobs that could be done at home or near home. During the war, when they were sorely needed as food producers, the beleaguered women could not also maintain tobacco production at its prewar level. Thus, increasingly, the tobacco fields were allowed to revert to meadow. This was not resisted by Berlin since the need for food was greater than for tobacco. Moreover, while Oberschopfheim's cigars had always been made entirely from local tobacco, cigarettes and other tobacco products had been made from a blend of local and American or Asian tobacco, each of which had a somewhat different flavor from that grown in Oberschopfheim. After 1941 these foreign supplies were no longer available. Public taste was changing too. Ever since 1913 cigar consumption had dropped steadily as cigarettes grew more popular. The upshot was that two of Oberschopfheim's larger cigar factories closed during the war, never to reopen, and the remainder began to depend increasingly on tobacco grown in other villages. In the latter part of 1945 there was a brief revival of cigarmaking in the village and employment shot up to about six hundred, but after 1946 a combination of the factors listed above, the loss of old markets in East Germany, and increased competition, threw tobacco manufacture into a steep decline. The last cigar factory in Oberschopfheim closed in 1954.

Relations between the Nazis and the Catholic church remained strained during the war. Their philosophical conceptions remained as unbridgeable as ever. Insofar as either side dared, no opportunity was missed to score against the other. Because national unity was essential if the war was to be won, the Nazis toned down their antireligious program once fighting began. This afforded Catholics opportunities to circumvent Party restrictions on religious activities by doing such things as organizing volunteer societies under the aegis of the church, resuming religious processions in the streets, burying fallen soldiers according to Catholic rites, giving church burials to deceased Polish Catholics, and even complaining so much about euthanasia in a Wuerttemberg concentration camp that the Nazis shelved the practice there in 1940. Such obduracy enraged Nazi zealots, of course, to such a degree that a few years later, when it became apparent that the war would be lost, some of them began to kill priests.

In Oberschopfheim NSDAP hostility was never violent, but it remained obvious. For instance, during the war all the employees in a tobacco factory once stayed home from work because it was a religious holiday. The Nazis promptly punished them with fines of twenty-seven marks per person, at that time about two weeks wages.[4]

On 1 July 1942, over the vehement protests of the pastor and parishioners, Nazi authorities replaced the Catholic nuns as teachers and nurses with the Nazi "Brown Sisters" (NSV).[5] Plans to build a new, larger church had been completed in 1937, and the necessary money had been collected, but Reich authorities would never give permission so it was not built until 1955. During the war clergymen who dared to criticize the regime could be arrested, even sent to death camps, though if they were from insignificant places like Oberschopfheim they were more often let off with a warning. Even so, the change in atmosphere from peacetime was evident. Back in 1933 the pastor of Schuttern had publicly voiced some anti-Nazi sentiments and suffered nothing worse than a denunciation in the pages of the *Lahrer Zeitung,*[6] but during the war Pfarrer Schleicher of the nearby village of Oberweier, who committed a similar indiscretion, was saved from jail and possible execution only by a stroke of luck. The local Party leader in the village, a Lutheran teacher of exceptional religious sensitivity and concern for his neighbors, interceded on his behalf. This incident, like the prewar attempt to assassinate Dr. Hirt, indicates what would have been in store for recalcitrant churchmen of all denominations had the Nazis won World War II.

It also indicates that the Nazis had their priorities. When dealing with the Reich's farmers, the first priority was not to contest their theological allegiances but to make sure that they produced and delivered enough food to maintain Germany's population for the duration of hostilities. Deeply impressed by the role food shortages had played in Germany's defeat in 1914-1918, the Nazis prepared early to switch from peacetime to wartime agricultural organization. Ration cards were printed in 1937. These were soon followed by the establishment of departments to oversee compulsory deliveries of food, to actually distribute the food to consumers, and to regulate the amounts peasants might save for their own consumption.[7] Though many of the same problems that had vexed the government of Wilhelm II in 1914-1918 cropped up again in 1939-1945, the economy of the Third Reich was managed with much greater efficiency than had been the case in World War I. Most Germans were relatively well fed until 1944, and national morale broke only in the face of actual Allied invasion in 1945.

This achievement was possible only because Germany had long since developed a system of regulation, inspection, and record keeping that exceeded in complexity that of any other Western country. This the NSDAP elaborated and refined until it was incredible in its detail and thoroughness. They also punished noncompliance readily and severely. Records were kept of every farm: its site, soil type, tillage plan, production capacity, numbers and types of livestock, number and condition of farm implements, the members of the family and their ages, and family income from all sources. Farmers were required to make periodic reports on any changes in crops planted, estimated yields, and which of their products were consumed on the farm and which sold.[8] Once the war began inspectors were employed to report on every aspect of agricultural production and delivery. For instance, the Nazis decreed that each cow was to provide six liters of milk per day for delivery to the state. If she did better, her owner was entitled to the surplus. This might seem a trifling matter to dairymen in most Western countries since a good milk cow will produce several times that quantity with ease, but it must be remembered that this was wartime, that most of Lahr county's cows were primarily field workers who were additionally milked, and that they seldom had all they wanted to eat. Hence their milk production was low. Low or not, in Oberschopfheim no less a dignitary than the Party leader would occasionally appear to oversee cow milking and make sure no cheating occurred. Once even the district leader materialized to make such a check. Nazi inspectors sometimes invaded chicken coops in the middle of the night to check on egg production or root cellars to see who might be hoarding vegetables. Pigs could be taken to registry offices and weighed so farmers could not misrepresent their bulk and withhold pork. Quotas for the delivery of specified quantities of grain, milk, eggs, and other foods were established for every producer. Bonuses and decorations were sometimes awarded for excess deliveries and penalties assessed for delinquencies. By 1944 peasants were even required to *exceed* their quotas. Perhaps the ultimate: farmers were threatened with reprisals if they gave more food than the government prescribed to children who dug potatoes for them.[9] Overall, despite much official praise of peasants as *Landesvolk*, after 1938 the Nazi regime reduced them to a state close to serfdom, a condition that did not change until about 1949.

Nazi efforts to increase butter production illustrate their determination to wring the last ounce of food from Germany's modest natural agricultural endowment. Farmers had long been in the habit of selling their excess milk and cream as they chose or churning the cream into butter and selling it thus. To insure an adequate, dependable supply of dairy products of good quality for everyone during the war, the Nazis ordered all milk producers to instead sell their raw milk for a set price to government dairies. Here the milk would be made into butter by the latest and most sanitary technique. The finished product, of uniform quality, would then be rationed and sold to consumers at set prices. Tariffs would protect the whole system from both foreign butter and domestic margarine. To insure compliance, farmers' own butter-making equipment was sealed or otherwise rendered unusable by government inspectors. The entire scheme was designed to raise and standardize quality, stabilize prices, insure availability of the product to all, and modernize the whole industry. Such an endeavor indicates that while the Nazis might have been reactionary romantics in their dreams about future German society, they were undeniably progressive when it came to farm policy here and now. The establishment of rural cooperatives, the requirement of a state permit to breed animals in order to improve stock, and state encouragement to erect new buildings, use more fertilizer, and mechanize agriculture, also breathed the same spirit. Always the NSDAP was concerned with systematizing, modernizing, and increasing production.[10]

No matter how "reasonable" such endeavors were, peasants disliked them. They complained incessantly that government dairymen to whom they had to deliver their milk gave them "short weight"; that they could make more money selling dairy products on their own; that breeding only government approved livestock caused many barren matings; that new fertilizers caused cancer; that all the government controls were burdensome, counter to customary usage, and reminiscent of the Soviet Union; that, as always, everything related to agriculture received the lowest priority; and, increasingly, that this was what could be expected from a regime that held both religion and tradition in contempt and had tried to undermine parental authority through the Hitler Youth.[11]

Peasant griping intensified as many of the same problems began to surface that had vexed the nation's economy in World War I. Agriculture in Baden had always been extremely labor intensive because of the ubiquity of tiny plots of land and a consequent low level of mechanization. Now there was simply too much work for the women, old men, and children. To help them, all sorts of expedients were tried. Hitler Youth members, university students, young people of both sexes from cities, and farm "supervisors" were recruited for farm work. Soldiers home on furlough were urged to do farm work. Nothing worked well. Peasants grumbled that urban young people were lazy and had no interest in farming. Men on furlough wanted to rest, not work, and *their* children, if any, showed little more enthusiasm for agriculture than did city youngsters.

Foreign prisoners of war and laborers, primarily Poles, were often used, but they were never really satisfactory. They were often underfed, and they seldom worked hard. Worse, they talked about Germany losing the war and so undermined home morale. Still worse, they were "racial inferiors," precisely the types the Nazis wanted to push out of Germany permanently.[12] Farm women were particularly hard-pressed. They had to treat the foreign laborers indulgently to get any work out of them. Human nature being what it is, this often led to pregnancies. *That* situation, embarrassing at best, frequently became tragic for there were no doctors in places like Oberschopfheim. Consequently, medical care was haphazard and miscarriages increased markedly among farm women, many of whom were already exhausted from overwork.

Other farm problems were equally vexatious. Pigs and people still ate the same kinds of food, just as in 1914-1918, and if the pigs were put on short rations for the benefit of humans, they grew slowly. This both raised costs to producers and deprived all Germans of needed fats. Reducing the number of pigs and requisitioning horses for the army reduced the amount of natural fertilizer available and lessened the fertility of the soil. Commercial fertilizers could not compensate since the Allies controlled the seas, and most imported nitrates went into munitions production anyway. Even when nitrates were available for agriculture they often arrived too late because of transport difficulties. More and better farm machines were needed to keep up production, but they inevitably wore out at a time when most metals had to be put into munitions and war machines. Badgered farmers switched to more forage crops, which indubitably saved on labor but also produced grain shortages. The problems and contradictions were nobody's *fault* in particular, but they were, withal, endless and, ultimately, insoluble.[13]

Peasant response to this melange of difficulties, grievances, and misfortunes was utterly predictable: evasion, black marketeering, and efforts to cushion anticipated future shock. In Nordlingen markets that had routinely processed hundreds of hogs every spring received only *three* in the spring of 1943. Bavarian peasants who profited from this or some other black market operation hastened to spend their money on improvement of their buildings or equipment or to buy more livestock, from fear that the currency would one day become as worthless as it had been in 1923.[14]

In Oberschopfheim people hid extra chickens. If a cow happened to give birth to twin calves, one would be declared to authorities and the extra hidden or, more often, hurriedly killed and eaten. When an animal was slaughtered an official weighed it. Anything above a certain weight the farmer might keep for himself and his family. If two or more neighbors trusted each other they might all kill their hogs on the same day and then surreptitiously pass around their smallest pig to be weighed by the government inspector. Then all of them would be able to keep more pork for themselves. Ironically, in such cases greater danger came from neighbors than from government inspectors since the former would sometimes threaten to report a violation unless given a portion of the precious embezzled food.[15]

Many villagers unquestionably suffered psychological damage from the war. For some years after 1945 resentments persisted between the few ardent Nazis and the rest of the population. Certain people were avoided entirely. Others were spoken to in a formal manner but otherwise ignored. Still others were addressed briefly and casually but were never visited. Generally, people got along less well in 1945-1950 than they had before the war and thought life had grown harder.[16]

When German defeats began to pile up in the war grumbling became audible. For the first time, it was directed at the leaders and functionaries of the Nazi party. Some Party members even hid their badges, and fewer young people were attracted to the movement.[17] By the last year of the war grousing was skirting the borders of defeatism. Vulgar jokes about the regime circulated, perhaps to cloak unspoken fears of what the Allies might do to avenge the many Jews who had been killed or the innumerable other victims of the SS. Some religious people began to say that God had sent Hitler not to save Germany but to punish the country for its sins.[18]

Ancient animosities based on geography, past history, occupation, and class began to appear once more, particularly in South Germany. Many a Bavarian peasant indicated by word or demeanor that he believed collapse to be not far off.[19] City people grumbled that even though peasants had been "coddled" by the Nazis, they had betrayed the nation once more by failing to deliver enough food to urbanites like themselves.[20] The peasants, who certainly did not feel coddled, observed discreetly to families and trusted neighbors that if wars were won by speeches Germany would surely be victorious or murmured that the whole Nazi era had been an immense disaster for the nation.[21] A Bavarian tobacconist remarked to a Swiss visitor that "the nicest war was, after all, the one when we shot at the Prussians."[22] In late 1944 German troops coming back to Baden from the Western Front were often drunk, undisciplined, and defeatist, while letters from soldiers in Russia were far gloomier than official announcements in Berlin and had a depressing effect on recipients. Too much should not be made of this, of course, for those persons and groups critical of the Nazis were only tepidly so, and few save the actual plotters against Hitler had any alternative regime that they clearly preferred. Nonetheless, that spirits were sinking is unquestioned.

All the troubles the Nazis encountered in wartime agriculture merely highlighted their general failure to transform German society. When the Nazi era was over German cities were bigger than before, and there were fewer people on farms, though the Nazis had persistently preached the desirability of the opposite. The very success of the NSDAP in conquering unemployment had increased the confidence of discontented rural people that they could secure and keep city jobs and so led more of them to leave the countryside. Those who stayed behind tended to be the weaker and the less enterprising, precisely the opposite of what was desired eugenically. Many farm children had been worked too hard and fed too poorly when they were young and so were rejected for physical disabilities when called up for military service, while a larger proportion of their city cousins were in good health and were inducted—just the opposite of what Nazi ideology taught and desired. Nazi leaders wanted eastern lands cleared for mass settlement by German colonists, but few German farmers displayed any enthusiasm for such migration. Hordes of Russian prisoners taken in 1941 might have been compelled to do farm work but Hitler feared that they would pollute Germany racially, so he let 2,800,000 of them die in eight months of starvation and ill treatment at the same time that Germany was trying with small success to recruit foreign workers from much of the rest of Europe. It was a classic example of ideology being allowed to impede prosecution of the war.[23]

Eventually Poles, Russians, and other Slavs had to be induced or commandeered to do essential farm work. Just as had been feared, some of these, along with French, Belgian, and Italian imported workers, impregnated German women. All was in direct contravention of Nazi race principles and policies, and it all ended with a Slavic westward migration in 1945 that undid a thousand years of German *Drang nach Osten* (expansion to the east).

When the Third Reich crashed in ruins, the self-sufficiency long aimed at had never been achieved. Concentration of capital was greater than before, not less. Inequality of income was greater, not less. North and south Germans disliked each other as much as ever, city people still regarded farmers as bumpkins, and the old class patterns were still evident in the universities. Of course the keystone in the whole Nazi ideological edifice was victory in war. Had victory been gained and followed by many years of peace, the rulers of the Reich doubtless would have sorted out the dissonances in German society, crushed their enemies, and redoubled their endeavor to indoctrinate everyone with their ideology. Whether this would have enabled them to turn back the tide of the modern age and keep a high proportion of the German people on the land, nobody can possibly know, but it does not seem likely. All over the world in our century, and especially in the second half of it, in developed and undeveloped countries alike, scores of millions have left the soil and streamed into cities in search of a better livelihood or simply an easier and more interesting life.[24]

Although Nazi economic regulations affected every person in Oberschopfheim throughout the war, the "fighting war" hardly touched the village. On 10 May 1940 when the *Wehrmacht* began pouring into France, Gallic artillery fire over the Rhine was sufficiently intense that the trains from Basel to Karlsruhe stopped running. Whether any particular towns, persons, or objects happened to be hit by the fusillade was a matter of luck. Several villages on the east bank of the Rhine were hit. Oberschopfheim was not.

Likewise, Oberschopfheim was never bombed at any time. Nonetheless, villagers knew that Allied control of the air was absolute, that the enemy *could* bomb them any time he chose and that there was nothing whatever that they could do about it. These were not consoling ruminations. For probably the first time in the history of their village Oberschopfheimers rejoiced to see the everlasting fog roll in, for it hid them from hostile bombers. They also built bunkers back in the hills and forest to provide refuges for themselves when the bombing alarm sounded. These were soon supplemented by other bunkers, built by the *Wehrmacht*, to store military supplies. Though all the bunkers were built hurriedly and so were unstable, and though none of them ever saved a single person from a single British or American bomb, they were pleasantly cool, inviting retreats that were used for some years after the war to store food. In 1944 and early 1945 combined fear of Allied bombing and invasion caused the government to move many women and children out of villages along the Rhine and well back into the Black Forest. In retrospect such precautions appear excessive, but ominous incidents took place often enough to keep everyone on edge. On 16 March 1944 an English bomber crashed near Oberschopfheim, killing everyone on board. Two months later a German plane crashed nearby, though this time the pilot escaped uninjured.

In a larger sense, of course, war is always tragic. Yet wars usually have a certain zany character in that they are punctuated by episodes in which the disjunction between effort and result is so blatant that it seems comic to those who live later and never experienced the fear and danger involved. Whether the British and Americans ever deliberately tried to bomb Oberschopfheim is uncertain. On several occasions Allied bombs fell into the forest east of the village, though none ever hit a bunker, much less the village itself. In March 1944 three bombs landed in the woods. On July 14 a massive raid of sorts took place during which some 250 bombs blasted German trees in every direction. Another bomb fell into the forest in September and still another 7 January 1945. Undiscouraged by these undistinguished performances, Allied airmen tried to destroy the railroad tracks at the edge of the village on 16 September 1944 but nearly hit the *Leutkirche* instead. Two months later they did manage to hit the tracks with two bombs. Perhaps heartened by this success, two days afterward they blasted two cows into that great pastureland in the sky but missed the farmer to whom they belonged, as well as a woman in an adjacent field, who saved herself by falling flat onto the ground.

On 23 November 1944 the war came ominously closer and grew more vivid to Oberschopfheimers when the Allies opened a massive artillery barrage against Strasbourg. All day long villagers could hear the huge cannon and see the shells burst, just as their ancestors had in 1870. Five weeks later when the Allied armies were actually on the point of invading, German authorities in Berlin began to raise a militia. They also directed civilians to build tank traps and barricades and ordered them to resist to the death. To aid in the prescribed resistance, areas along the Rhine were flooded. Little was accomplished by these measures save to hamper both agricultural and arms production in Baden.[25] Moreover, when Allied armies actually came near, each town and village was left largely to its own devices.

The responses of the various communities in Lahr county varied widely. So far in the war, Oberschopfheim had suffered only minor damage to five houses from random artillery fire. Its people wanted, above all, to keep their village from becoming a battleground. It seemed that they might have a good chance, since Mayor Holzenthaler had become group leader and so could act semi-independently of the county leader. People in many other villages were of a similar mind: like their forebears during

scores of earlier wars and invasions, and like many people of other nationalities similarly trapped, their primary thought was to get off as easily as
possible.[26]

As French troops advanced toward Oberschopfheim in April 1945, the
people took what precautions they could. They planted their seed potatoes at night, both to keep the enemy from seizing them and in hope of
having something to eat months later. Some of their pigs they slaughtered
for meat; others they hid in the forest. Still others were secreted in holes or
in the hastily built bunkers. Sometimes these endeavors seemed hardly
worth the trouble; sometimes their results were tragicomic. In 1988, a
former mayor, reminiscing about the war, related that he had once hidden a
pig in a mountain bunker but then had to climb the mountain every night
to feed it, not to speak of undergoing the mental anguish of having a
French search party's dogs smell it. Luckily for the former mayor and the
pig alike, the dogs proved unable to find their quarry. On another occasion, desperate to save a pig from a French search party, he hid the porker
in a bedroom, only to have the dirty beast eat some of the bedding and
defile or tear up the rest.[27]

In the army depots up in the mountains, tanks, gasoline, and other
supplies had been hidden. When they could, villagers now blew them up
in order to avoid giving offense to the conquerors. In their houses they
destroyed or hid all Nazi flags, emblems, and insignia, and all pictures of
anyone in uniform. The tank traps they had been ordered to build were
supposed to consist of wooden stakes stuck in the ground. Though the
efficacy of these was surely problematical in any case, villagers in Oberschopfheim and elsewhere tried to take out some insurance. Heeding
advice from Dr. Hirt, they took care to cut the stakes so short that it would
be obvious to the French that no serious defense had been planned. Like
their sisters in the village of Friedberg in Bavaria,[28] the women of Oberschopfheim tore down the barricades that had been hurriedly raised
against the invaders. Finally, at gunpoint they compelled the Nazi county
officials who were stationed in Oberschopfheim to surrender. Thus
French troops were able to enter the village and its neighbor, Oberweier,
on 16 April 1945 at 4:30 P.M. without firing a shot.[29] All that was left in the
headquarters of what had been a registered NSDAP *Ortsgruppe* of 135
members was sixty marks and an aged, broken typewriter.[30] It was a
forlorn end for this remote outpost of the Thousand Year Reich.

Matters proceeded with far less serenity in many other cities and
towns in Baden. In communities where fervent Nazis were numerous or
remained in control, people resisted, as they had been ordered, and their
villages and towns were destroyed. In Lahr-Dinglingen many factories
had suffered Allied bombing since 1943. Whether from resentment at this

or the zeal of Nazi authorities to fight to the end, Lahr city authorities chose to resist. They paid heavily. The French, employing the church bell tower in Oberweier as a lookout, attacked Lahr for three days while Allied planes bombed it relentlessly. The train station was smashed, seven factories were destroyed or heavily damaged, some 130 buildings containing 500 apartments were demolished, 275 more buildings with 800 apartments were partially damaged, and another 700 structures were slightly damaged. Freiburg, some fifty miles away, was similarly shattered by bombers and French artillery.

Traditionally, victorious armies have been allowed to plunder the vanquished for three days, a convention the French observed punctiliously in 1945. To point this out is not to demean the French. They had, after all, suffered grievously at German hands in 1870, in 1914-1918, and in 1940-1944. As for British and American troops, they "liberated" German civilians and tangible assets alike on a scale that caused wits of the time to observe sardonically that "The Germans fight for Hitler, the Japs for the Emperor, the Russians for communism, and the Americans for souvenirs." Justification or rationalization aside, French troops broke into the houses of Oberschopfheimers, ate and drank whatever they could find, carried off eggs and other commodities that might be eaten tomorrow, stole whatever they fancied from radios to animals, tore apart the household furnishings searching for valuables, ordered civilians to deliver feather bedding and clothing for the use of the invaders, and threw what little remained onto manure piles outside. Everyone was ordered to take to the courthouse any pictures or writings with a Nazi theme, and houses were ransacked to insure compliance.[31] For good measure the "liberators" sawed down the fruit trees in Kuerzell and elsewhere, avenging, both symbolically and in reality, systematic destruction of French and Belgian houses and orchards by retreating German troops in the autumn of 1918. Civilians were often treated roughly. They were forced to step off sidewalks and raise their hats when French soldiers passed. Occasional murders of French servicemen by outraged German civilians were promptly avenged by the taking and shooting of hostages.[32]

For most of the villagers fear of what the invaders *might* do was worse than the reality. During the last year of the war Nazi propaganda had played so heavily on the theme of "hideous" and "bestial" Africans foaming at the mouth in their anxiety to "molest blonde Aryan women" that many German civilians were shaken at the mere thought of their neighborhoods being overrun by French colonial troops. The first such soldiers who appeared in West Germany *were* a strange looking lot. They were Berbers from the Atlas mountains. Often mounted, they served as Algerian infantry and Moroccan Tabors. Black, fierce-visaged men, dressed in black turbans and flowing brown cloaks set off by white gloves and gaiters, they at once recalled to mind stories told endlessly about the "savage" Senegalese whom the French had employed on the Western Front in World War I. There they had pursued such macabre hobbies as making necklaces from the severed ears of those they had killed. The French had used Senegalese again in 1923 to occupy the Ruhr and to "degrade" local German prostitutes. In Oberschopfheim, where hardly anyone had ever *seen* a black person, terrified women and girls hid in cellars, attics, and caves, hoping desperately that the foreign devils would not find them. How many were abused by either European or African conquerors is uncertain. In Kuerzell twelve women went to the courthouse to report that they had been raped. How many others had been victimized but declined to go, nobody knows. There are no figures of any kind for Oberschopfheim. One now-aged woman who lived through those days says she did not know anyone who was raped. Other villagers will say only that it was unsafe for a woman anywhere.[33]

Again, proportion must be maintained. When discipline is slackened during invasions all armies commit some crimes against civilians. The atrocities committed by Russians in the east were incomparably more numerous and savage than anything done by any French, white or black, in the West.[34] Of course Europeans of many nationalities yearned to repay the Germans for the numberless crimes committed by Hitler's legions earlier in the war. As an example of the latter, one of the first deeds of the French near Oberschopfheim was to free the prisoners in a small concentration camp in Haslach, Kinzigtal. Several hundred Europeans of a dozen nationalities had died there during the war, chiefly of typhus and dysentery, while digging out a mountainside for the installation of a German arms plant.[35]

All things considered, French officers restored discipline in their army quickly, and random violence and thievery shrank to normal peacetime dimensions. Ironically, the only civilian deaths Oberschopfheim suffered in the whole war were incurred two months after the fighting was over, when two recently freed Russian prisoners robbed the village grist mill, killing the miller and a farmer in the process.

When the war was over at last, many things in the village had not changed much since 1939. The pastor remained in his place, still loved and respected by his flock, though by 1947 he was already mortally ill with diabetes. His death in 1949 was a great loss to all in Oberschopfheim. Meanwhile, he had less trouble with the French occupation authorities than he had had with prewar Nazi functionaries. The local grade school was operating as usual with about the same number of students (253)[36] as in 1939, and the nuns began to manage the kindergarten once more.

While individual citizens were hard-pressed economically, the *Gemeinde* was positively prosperous, better off financially than it had been for many years. One reason was that during the war women whose husbands were in the army received regular government allotments that they could seldom spend since nearly anything they might wish to buy was either rationed or unavailable. Consequently, many of them used the money to pay off back taxes or other obligations to the village government. Thus, at war's end, the *Gemeinde* had about 90,000 *Reichsmark* in the bank and 8,700 due it in back taxes.[37] There was little unemployment in the village in 1945. The cigar industry was enjoying its last brief spurt of prosperity, and some 158 assorted mechanics, technicians, artisans, and semi-skilled workers were busy.[38] By contrast, nobody was working in heavy industry in nearby towns. Much of it had been shattered by the war, and what remained was currently the subject of Allied negotiation. Anyone else in the village who remained unemployed was likely to be a victim of denazification.

In other respects life had changed a good deal. One interesting development, quite discernable throughout the diocese of Freiburg, in which Oberschopfheim is located, was the return of many fair-weather Catholics to their ancestral church. In Oberschopfheim a small number of enthusiastic Nazis who had ostentatiously refused to take part in religious processions during the Hitler years now quietly resumed these conventional religious observances.

A far more somber and pressing concern in the village in the immediate postwar years was the fate of the soldiers who had not come back from the war. Two years after the fighting had ended some 2,400,000 German men were still "missing." For the next seven years no subject was more persistently in the minds and conversations of villagers than the fate of their absent men. Innumerable prayers were said for them in homes and in the church. Mourning wives and, especially, mothers refused to give up hope. They grasped for any sign or intimation, no matter how remote or evanescent, that their men would return. Over the years, one hundred nine, just over half, did trickle back to the village: thirty-four in 1946, eighteen in 1947, forty-two in 1948, thirteen in 1949, and two in 1950. All but one of these late returnees had been held in the USSR in violation of international law.

Most had worked for many months or years for Russian farmers or in Soviet factories or mines. Like Soviet survivors of the Gulag who have written memoirs, all had vivid recollections of poor and scanty food and intense cold. Many owed their lives to Russian peasants who had given them extra food. Of course the Soviet muzhiks had an ulterior motive: a farm laborer who has starved to death does no work. Still, it was also true that many French and Russian prisoners assigned to German farms during the war were treated humanely too, if they worked well, especially so if they also tried to learn German. It was simply that many, perhaps most, ordinary farmers of European nationalities felt no *personal* responsibility for the war and did not attribute any to those who happened to fall under their control as war prisoners.[39] Doubtless we should rejoice that even in our savage age the essential humanity of many people still outweighs racist arrogance, blood lust, thirst for revenge, and other ignoble passions.

Another jarring experience for Oberschopfheimers was an influx of refugees. Only a stroke of sheer luck prevented it from being far worse than it was. At the end of the war, millions of desperate, penniless people of several nationalities were either uprooted and forcibly expelled from their East Central European homelands by the Russians or fled westward in terror to escape the advancing Soviet army. From the first, French authorities refused to allow these hordes of the destitute and the bewildered to enter the French zone of occupation on the grounds that France had not been invited to the wartime Allied conferences where refugee questions had been discussed. Thus only the British and American zones were inundated with Germans and non-Germans alike. Nonetheless, both during the war and for a short time afterward, German authorities did move many people from the Sudetenland and the prewar eastern provinces of the Third Reich into West German towns and villages in what would become the postwar occupation zones. There they were assigned arbitrarily to certain houses. Some 240 of them were placed in Oberschopfheim. They changed its character permanently.

These "strangers" caused numerous problems. A high proportion of them consisted of women, children, the aged, and the disabled, poor human material for labor or production of any kind. Some possessed skills for which there was no demand in their present location. Thus they had to take unskilled jobs, which they resented, or to refuse to work at all, which was the case with not a few. Most of them belonged to a different culture. Many were city people who did not understand or respect farm life. Others had fled from large estates east of the Elbe. They felt little kinship with the Rhenish peasants of Lahr county. For one thing, the newcomers tended to spend and display freely if they had or were able to get any money and could find anything to buy. To them, the frugal natives were penny-pinching dullards who spoke an odd dialect that the refugees did not want their children to learn and who laboriously cultivated plots so tiny that they seemed more like gardens than farms. All the refugees considered themselves blameless victims of the vicissitudes of war and acted as though they had a natural right to be quartered with Rhenish families. The latter, already overcrowded in many cases, resented the very presence, not to say presumption, of these impudent "guests" who deprived everyone of privacy, lowered hygienic levels, undermined moral standards, and seemed to think the world owed them a living. Many of the newcomers were quarrelsome and most of them had children who got along badly with the hosts' children. Many were Lutherans who had been pushed into Catholic communities, though most of those who were quartered in Oberschopfheim were Catholic. Finally, there was not enough food to go around, and what did exist was of poor quality. Such a situation would have produced acrimony among saints. In some cases the refugees intimidated the host families, stole from them, or turned them in for violations of food regulations, though most of the time each party tolerated the other with as much good grace as could be expected in the difficult circumstances. Even so, nearly half a century later old-timers in Oberschopfheim still spoke casually of these East German immigrants—most of whom stayed permanently—as "outsiders." [40] Of course it could be maintained that the cool reception accorded the refugees proves yet again that German sectionalism outweighs German nationalism, but a more likely explanation would appear to be merely that most people do not like to have crowds of strangers as permanent "guests."

The worst short-term consequence of the war was a severe food shortage. Indeed, those who lived through both as adults usually say that everyday living conditions were worse in 1945-1949 than they had been during the war years. At the time many Americans and some vocal French Leftists blamed this on harsh French exactions of food and the French policy of making the Germans pay the costs of the French occupation. There is no question that Gallic policy was a contributory factor, but the fundamental causes were different. By 1945 many agricultural implements were worn out, the soil had been depleted in many areas, seed quality was poor, fertilizer was in short supply, and several million men had either been killed or disabled in the war or had not yet returned from it. Consequently, the cereal harvest in 1945 was only half that of 1939 and the grape harvest only slightly above that. [41] All this was worsened by the unusually severe winter of 1945-1946.

The Western Allies had envisioned German civilians living on 1,500 calories a day for some time after the war, but by the spring of 1946 the actual figure was down in the range of 1,100 to 1,300 in most of West Germany, even below 1,000 in some areas, though more was available for nursing mothers and those doing heavy labor. [42] Of course those in farm villages like Oberschopfheim could supplement these meager rations somewhat with vegetables from their gardens, augmented by an occasional secretly killed pig, but their gain was minimal since much of their potatoes, root crops, and wheat had to be turned in to French authorities.

By now, of course, the French paid for food rather than merely seizing it, but they paid in old *Reichsmark*. These depreciated daily, leading inhabitants to fear (accurately) that they would eventually be repudiated just as other marks had been in 1923. Meanwhile, little could be bought with them for the simplest of reasons: there was little to buy. This condition owed primarily to military defeat and to the consequent wondrous disorganization that characterized Germany at the end of the war. The nation's transport system was either worn out or had been bombed close to oblivion. Thus underfed people had to spend much of their meager energy walking to work or standing for long periods every day in endless lines, in hope of getting a bit more food. Raw materials might have fed German industry but the former were lacking and the latter had been destroyed by bombing or seized by the victors as reparations. No money existed to pay foreign shippers to bring in raw materials to be processed by a rebuilt industry—if it could be rebuilt. Oil, coal, and gas were all in short supply. Consequently, much timber was cut for fuel, especially during the harsh winter of 1945-1946. Unhappily for them, Germans in the southwest got little of it, either because of the general chaos or because of the French policy of keeping most of the timber for themselves or sending it back to France as reparations.[43] It would have been difficult to attack any of these problems forthrightly, in any case. When the country was divided into four occupation zones and the occupation authorities were perpetually at cross purposes, it was close to impossible. In these dismal circumstances there was small incentive for anyone to work hard to try to save, a condition some observers hold responsible for the decline of the work ethic in late twentieth-century Germany.

By 1946 actual starvation seemed imminent. Food was so scarce that it was often sold by the gram. Beggars were rampant even in July. Farmers had to guard their fields and cellars to ward off hungry thieves. Beech nuts were assiduously gathered from the forest, partly to feed pigs, chickens, and rabbits, partly to make acorn bread for humans, partly, if one could manage to collect twelve pounds, to press them and make a liter of cooking oil.[44] Many meals consisted mostly of watery soup, strengthened by whatever edible substance was in season or could be scrounged. In these dire straits many people in Oberschopfheim and elsewhere in Lahr county were aided immeasurably because they had relatives in the United States to whom they could write to ask for food. They received a good deal from their overseas kinfolk, as well as periodic CARE packages. Whenever a package from either source arrived for someone in the village, within minutes everyone else knew about it and came to ask for a portion.

While semi-starvation is assuredly no joke, this formal and informal CARE program sometimes did have wryly humorous aspects. While many people in and around Oberschopfheim had acquired varying degrees of acquaintance with the English language by the 1980s, forty years earlier nobody there knew any English. Hence when a package arrived containing some strange substance like instant coffee, marshmallows, peanut butter, or Jello, it posed a hopeless dilemma. Nobody wanted to waste anything edible, yet nobody had ever heard of such foreign commodities, and nobody could read the directions on the jars or packages. What to do? The Gordian knot was usually cut by pouring the unidentifiable substance into whatever constituted soup for that day, and hoping for the best. At least once, what resulted was downright grisly. One family in Lahr received a package marked "Grandma's Ashes," a reference to the cremated remains of an aged relative who had died in the United States. Since "Grandma's Ashes" was as unfathomable as "instant coffee," it was assumed that this package, like so many before it, contained some mysterious American food. According to local folklore, "Grandma's Ashes" followed Jello into the soup pot.

In Lahr county, barter and the black market flourished. Once more urbanites flooded the countryside to beg for food or to trade household goods for it. Nobody knows how many cameras, clocks, typewriters, radios, pieces of furniture, blankets, articles of clothing, cars, trucks, motorcycles, even animals, passed from city dwellers to farmers, or from Germans of all sorts to the French, as people eagerly searched for any kind of food. When the brother of the mayor of Oberschopfheim married in 1947, he and his bride managed to secure almost all their clothing and household furnishings in trade for farm produce and schnapps.[45] Rudolf Gissler, who was mayor of Oberschopfheim in the late 1960s and early 1970s, recalled in 1988 that he had gotten a radio in 1947 in what was then the usual way: he had traded food for it.[46] Conditions did improve somewhat in succeeding years. In 1947 the average German in the French zone got about 1,400 calories per day, by 1948 some 1,800 to 1,900;[47] but it still required the formation of the West German Republic and the issuance of a new currency in 1948 to set the country on the road to recovery.

At the end of the war it was official Allied policy that Germany should be denazified and demilitarized but eventually centralized once more politically, economically, and administratively. This was precisely what virtually all Frenchmen opposed, since they were convinced that it would soon lead to a revival of German military power and the freezing of prewar Franco-German boundaries. Hence French occupation authorities regularly followed their own policy of keeping Germany divided and weak. Even though there was general French agreement on this, there was never any agreement among the dozens of ideological, religious, economic, and occupational factions into which France has been fragmented ever since the French Revolution about the *best way to pursue* these objectives.[48] In particular, there were bitter squabbles over whether to merely strip Germany of her resources as an act of revenge or to try to reeducate the Germans and make them democrats.[49] Oftentimes Gallic disagreements resulted in the simultaneous pursuit of contradictory policies. For instance, some French authorities confiscated German machinery to replenish France's own industrial plants and to reduce German industrial potential. They justified this as an act of restitution and reparation. At the same time others tried to develop Germany's economy so she could pay heavier reparations to France.[50] Ultimately, the dismantling of much of West Germany's machinery was beneficial, for the factories were eventually retooled with more modern and efficient machines than those of most of Germany's global competitors. In a matter of lesser consequence, the French dynamited much of the West Wall in the autumn of 1946 and then quarreled bitterly with local villagers over who had the right to salvage the iron from the resulting rubble. Eventually the French won out on this particular point, but forty years later no definitive decision has yet been made about responsibility for clearing away the rest of the rubble.[51]

In other respects French policy was clear and consistent. In the view of nearly all Frenchmen, German adults were irredeemable Nazis who could only be written off. Of course their leaders must be apprehended and punished and their evil influence nullified. Once this was accomplished, France could set to work to reeducate the young. Meanwhile all Germans were to be introduced to, first, French culture, then to overall European culture. This reflected a French conviction that educated Germans would be impressed by cultural achievement, no matter what its source. Only when all this preparatory work had been completed could the gradual political reeducation of Germany begin. Then, after a lengthy period of occupation, the old enemies might at last be fit for democracy.[52]

In pursuit of this objective, Paris allowed its top military people to live in splendor in luxurious hotels at such undamaged spas as Baden-Baden. Lesser occupation authorities followed soon after, accompanied by swarms of wives, children, in-laws, and other dependents. These multitudes staged numberless parades, concerts, lectures, and art exhibits and operated camps for children. One reason for all these profligate displays, embellished by overbearing manners, was merely that the French were sensitive about their poor showing in the war and sought to compensate by being especially arrogant to the losers. The underlying purpose, though, seems to have been something else: to dazzle Germans with the sheer grandeur of it all. Considering the desperate shortages of food and housing that existed on every side, it is hardly to be wondered at that many Germans, especially in rural areas, were more resentful than awestruck.

Many complained bitterly that their old foes were hypocrites who stuffed them with French culture while starving them of food. The stolid farmers of Oberschopfheim, unbeguiled by the blandishments of French "culture," of which they had never been avid devotees anyway, retained their undiluted animosity toward their ancient enemies.

Nonetheless, the French were not entirely misguided in the way they approached their eastern neighbors. Urban Germans had been impressed by French culture ever since the days of Louis XIV, and they were impressed now in varying degrees by these newest "cultural" productions. Gradually, Franco-German student exchanges and the establishment of joint committees to study various "issues" did create personal bonds and areas of understanding among young people who eventually moved upward to influential positions in French and German society.[53] More important was the emergence of two major historical figures, Charles de Gaulle in France and Konrad Adenauer in Germany, who were capable of rising above ancient Gallo-Germanic animosities, developing a real spirit of cooperation between their two countries, and encouraging the United States to provide the investment capital and military protection that made possible the remarkable recovery of Western Europe from World War II.

Of all the postwar policies the Allies attempted to apply to defeated Germany, the least satisfactory was denazification and reeducation of the vanquished. To start with, the Allies were sharply divided among themselves about what the postwar world should be like and so were ill-equipped to undertake the reeducation of anyone. More immediately pressing, somebody had to fill the middle and lower echelons of the German bureaucracy. It was hard to find qualified people who had not been NSDAP members. Inevitably, in all the western zones, denazification was sporadic, superficial, and short.

The French, convinced that teachers and lawyers were the most flagrant carriers of the Nazi virus, took special pains to weed them out. Some 75 percent of the teachers in the French zone were suspended from their jobs in 1945.[54] In Oberschopfheim French occupation authorities followed up by taking 113 books from the school library and 96 from the village library in the courthouse. All were declared to be tainted with Nazism and burned.[55]

Nazi officials were dismissed wholesale, with little regard for whether they had been enthusiastic or reluctant members of the NSDAP. This sometimes produced glaring inequities. One such involved Adolf Holzenthaler, the wartime mayor of Oberschopfheim. Long afterward, nobody in the village had anything unfavorable to say about Holzenthaler. All agreed that he had always been the most tepid of Nazis. Stories abounded about how he had done everything he dared to shelter local people from more violent, dogmatic Nazis. A typical story involved a man who had reported a neighbor for slaughtering a pig secretly. The mayor had promised to investigate the matter and report to the informer in "three or four days," but somehow it slipped his mind and nothing was ever done.[56] Yet the French, who were either unaware of Holzenthaler's real character or simply did not care, threw him into an internment camp, despoiled him of all his possessions, and replaced him with an aged former mayor, Wilhelm Einsele, who had been purged by the Nazis in 1933. Meanwhile, the village recorder, who had been in office continuously since 1929, was allowed to remain. Some thirteen other *Gemeinde* officials and employees were dismissed, along with five leaders of village commissions and cooperatives. Twenty members of the NSDAP were jailed in 1945, though all but one of them were released in 1946. A common additional punishment for such rank-and-file Nazi party members was to seize their animals, though sometimes a former Nazi would manage to save his cows or pigs by effecting their "midnight transfer" to some trusted relative or friend.[57]

All the certified Nazi party members in Oberschopfheim were fined, lost their animals (if any could be found), had their household goods confiscated—even to bed linen and personal clothing—and were barred from voting in the 1947 elections. In addition, fifteen of them were sentenced to pay to the occupation forces anywhere from 10 to 40 percent of their wages for periods of three to twelve years. Six individuals were singled out and fined a total of 4,600 marks, and two others lost half their assets. Before the war a few village officials, *Gasthaus* keepers, and other small proprietors had purchased automobiles, mostly for business reasons. Now some twenty-one of them had their trucks and cars confiscated, along with 390,000 cigars. Persons merely suspected of harboring Nazi sympathies were subjected to protracted questioning, sometimes being sent away as far as Offenburg for the purpose. Finally, the *Gemeinde* was compelled to contribute forty thousand marks to help maintain the occupation forces in Baden.[58] The latter was only a small portion of perhaps a billion marks the French wrung from the small state of Baden between 1945 and 1948 in the form of timber, farm produce, industrial products, confiscated machinery, dismantled factories, commandeered buildings, seized exports, and compulsory lump-sum payments.[59] In recent decades, in Third World countries overwhelmed by domestic problems, grim jokes have circulated to the effect that the best course might be to declare war on the United States, accept the quick, overwhelming defeat that would follow, and then wait for deliverance in the form of American postwar aid programs. Nobody ever made such jests about the French.

The new mayors and lesser county officials installed by the French had almost as difficult a time as the certified Nazis they replaced. Though they usually enjoyed the trust of local people, they were obviously under the direction of the occupiers. Worse, they had little in the way of resources but were given responsibility for finding food, clothing, housing and jobs for their people, maintaining the schools, and leading a general cleanup of all the debris of war.

When it came to collecting food and other farm products for themselves, the French proved quite as vigilant as the Nazis. They counted every pig, every chicken, and every egg each family possessed, and took their quota. Their painstaking searches revealed, among other things, that 110 citizens of Oberschopfheim had stored a total of 15,850 liters of wine. This the occupation sleuths duly "liberated," after the fashion of victorious armies at all times, though they magnanimously allowed the villagers to keep unspecified quantities of homemade applejack that had also been uncovered. Such plundering was always more common and more thorough in the French and Russian occupation zones than in the American or British zones. One reason was that France and Russia had been ravaged by the German army, while Britain and the United States had not, so desire for revenge was greater in the former. Another was that the French and Russian occupation zones comprised the agricultural parts of Germany where it was possible for the occupiers to live off the land to a considerable degree. In the industrial zones, managed by the British and Americans and flooded with millions of refugees, food was so scarce that the occupying powers had to go to great expense just to keep their conquered wards alive.

Like most other Germans, Oberschopfheimers disapproved of nearly everything the Occupying Powers did and, among themselves, complained about it daily. At bottom the reason was resentment of what was regarded as French ingratitude. Villagers felt no personal responsibility for anything that had happened during the war since they had played no part in starting it, and they had fought in it only reluctantly. Then at war's end they had surrendered without resisting and had made no trouble for the occupiers. Had the French appreciated this? No. They had responded only with malevolent oppression. What was resented most bitterly were the food searches and the exactions. Official protests were numerous—and fruitless. Within individual households, domestic rancor proliferated when one member of the family, usually the husband, would advise telling the occupation authorities the truth about family possessions in order to avoid trouble, which might be as serious as loss of the house and land, while another person, more commonly the wife, would want to lie to the hated foreigners in hope of saving more food for the hungry family.[60] Acrimony abounded in the village too, as victims of occupation policies reproached former Nazis for having gotten everyone into such an unhappy fix.

It has often been stressed that immediate postwar Germany was plagued by an increase of depression, despair, and criminality. This was much more the case in big cities, notably Berlin, than in villages or the countryside. What was truly predominant in public affairs everywhere was simple incomprehension. Most foreigners, official or not, did not really understand the physical misery in which many Germans lived. Most Germans did not realize that in France and Britain food was rationed just as it was in Germany. Few Germans had any notion of how numerous and horrible Nazi crimes had been or of how heinous they appeared to foreigners, nor did they feel any sense of personal guilt about the matter. This owed something to the consideration that women and children had been left at home during the war and frequently knew little about what had gone on away from their own communities, while the men who returned at the end of the war or afterward were often unwilling to talk about what they had seen, heard, or done. Moreover, for a considerable time many Germans simply did not believe reports of wartime atrocities, attributing them to Allied propaganda. Finally, in the general postwar scramble for food and shelter there was little disposition to dwell on the disagreeable features of the past. Some observers maintain that the Germans were sunk in such a morass of hunger, confusion, self-pity, and disgust with all politics that they did not even appreciate such foreign relief as CARE packages, acting, instead, as if such aid was owed to them and ought to be greater than it was.[61] Whatever might have been the case in other parts of the country, this was decidedly not true in the rural villages of Lahr county. Any aid received there, whether from relatives overseas or other sources, was welcomed gratefully.

Not the least disheartening aspect of the immediate postwar years was that women still had to bear a disproportionate share of the physical labor. This time it was the hard work of clearing away the rubble of war, restoring bomb damage, and rebuilding. The reason derived from sheer numbers. In the western occupation zones the ratio of women to men was 130 to 100, with some of the men crippled or otherwise discommoded by the war. Perhaps it would have mattered little, though, even had the sex ratio been even. Most survivors of concentration camps thought women were the tougher sex, that they had endured the hellish conditions rather better than men. Others have noted that when France fell so quickly to Germany in 1940 the blow seemed to hit men harder than women. The women displayed more courage and initiative, one observer thought; they made a greater effort to save some property and other assets, to go to work again, and to look after their children. He ascribed it to women being more enmeshed in the small details of life than men and thus less given to brooding on the meaning of the disaster that had befallen them all or the darkness of future prospects.[62] Whatever the explanation, the village women of Lahr county got no respite from toil merely because the war had ended.

# 11

# THE BREAKDOWN OF
# THE OLD ORDER

WHEN ADAM AND EVE were trudging out of the Garden of Eden, Adam allegedly turned to his erring mate and remarked, "We live in changing times." Rudolf Gissler, mayor of Oberschopfheim in the early 1970s, put it a bit differently. In his village, he said, more changes had taken place in his own lifetime than in the preceding thousand years.[1] He did not exaggerate. It was not merely that changes in the physical appearance of Oberschopfheim and in the manner of life of its people had been legion, it was also that the *rate* of such changes had accelerated steadily since the end of World War II, especially since about 1965.

To be sure, the village had already been shaken repeatedly by the two world wars, the great inflation of 1923, the horrific Depression of the early 1930s, and the meteoric passage of the Nazis. Nonetheless the *most drastic changes in the daily regimen* of the ordinary people of the village occurred not because of any of these "historic" events but because of the arrival and rapid acceleration of "modernization" after World War II. Within four decades the political structure of Oberschopfheim was transformed, its occupational composition was altered decisively, "outsiders" of several nationalities became semi-permanent residents, a sizable non-Catholic contingent appeared, confessional allegiances weakened, marriage patterns changed, personal and social mobility increased dramatically, and the world outlook of all save the aged came to be shaped increasingly by outside influences.

For France and most of Germany, the three greatest agencies of change and modernization in the countryside were the school, the army, and railways, and the period of greatest change was from 1870 to 1914.[2] Not so in Oberschopfheim. There the transformation came several decades later, and its main vehicles were school consolidation, the automobile, and television.

All this appeared extremely unlikely at the beginning of 1948. Three years after the end of the war, recovery was barely underway. Though

French seizures, reparations exactions, and purchases at artificially low prices in Baden had done much to revive *French* industry, production in the whole French occupation zone was only 51 percent of what it had been in 1936. Industry in Lahr city had been especially stifled. While the French had improved the transportation system since 1945, both machinery and people remained worn down. Currency inflation like that of the early 1920s had caused everyone to hoard goods and to resort to either barter or the black market when they needed anything. Black market prices were ten times legal prices: twenty marks for a pack of cigarettes, nine marks for a liter of wine. A couple in Oberschopfheim, newly married in 1948, started housekeeping by trading some eggs and tobacco for other food. Then they worked in the fields for some of their neighbors and were paid in wheat, which they took to the mill and traded for flour. Without drastic changes soon, collapse seemed imminent.

Disaster was averted when the drastic changes *did* come. They owed much to strong pressures that developed internationally. As unrest increased steadily in French Algeria and Indochina, Gallic occupation forces were moved out of Germany. Their numbers fell from a million in mid-1945 to fifty-three thousand in May 1948. As the Soviet Union grew steadily more obstreperous in the east, and then suddenly blockaded Berlin in an effort to force out the Western powers, Britain and America pressed France hard to join them in unifying West Germany against what was coming increasingly to look like a new common enemy. In 1948, Marshall Plan aid came at a crucial time for everyone. Denazification was given up. In June 1948, the old worthless currency and all the staggering debts contracted in it were repudiated and new currency was issued. At the same time most controls were lifted from the German economy. As in 1923, angry Oberschopfheimers felt robbed when they saw their hard-earned savings reduced by fiat to worthless paper. Nonetheless, cutting the Gordian knot was precisely what the times called for. As soon as the new *Deutschmark* were issued, the shops miraculously filled up with goods, and the black market vanished. People commenced to work in earnest once more, and the "economic miracle" began to take shape, though neither Lahr county nor Oberschopfheim reached their 1913 levels of prosperity until the late 1950s because of the reluctance of both the German government and private industry to invest so close to the border with France.[3]

The population of Oberschopfheim grew steadily after World War II. From an average of about 1,650 before the war it rose to 1,684 in 1950 and to 1,859 in 1955.[4] The increase did not come from a rising birthrate but from an influx of various "newcomers." For instance, most of the 170 refugees from the prewar eastern provinces of Germany stayed on. Many more people discovered that it was cheaper to live in a small village than in a city and so began to rent apartments in Oberschopfheim and neighboring villages. Since most of them worked in Lahr or Offenburg and merely ate and slept in Oberschopfheim, they had little contact with village natives. The same was true of another group: NATO (mostly Canadian) air force men stationed near Lahr at an air base that had been created in World War I for dirigibles. They lived with their families in nearby villages. Their numbers increased from about thirty in the 1960s to some three hundred in 1988. Finally, there were a number of Mediterranean laborers, primarily Italians, Yugoslavs, and Turks, who lived with their families in the village. Of these "guest workers" the Italians posed the fewest problems. Most simply stayed until they had earned enough money to buy a house in Italy, then they went home. The Turks, Yugoslavs, and lesser groups were frequently not Catholic and had little in common with Oberschopfheimers in any case, so contacts between them and natives were minimal, a condition that had no parallel in the previous history of the village. In the 1970s there were some 2,500,000 such foreign laborers scattered throughout West Germany. They were resented in some quarters for all the reasons foreign workers are disliked anywhere. Their position in Germany was not unlike that of Mexican "wetbacks" and many Puerto Ricans in the United States in that most were poor, were ill educated, filled menial jobs, spoke the dominant language poorly if at all and were isolated socially. Some observers worried that the situation might one day be exploited by a neo-Nazi movement, since many of the foreigners did not want to go home. In the 1980s, though, their numbers dwindled considerably, and the situation eased.

A more intractable problem, which grew steadily worse in the 1980s, was that of political refugees or those who posed as such. These people were, and are, a varied lot. Most, though not all, of them come from countries in eastern Europe. Many are ethnic Germans, descendants of Germans settled in East Prussia, the Baltic states, Transylvania, or along the Volga anywhere from three generations to seven centuries ago. Many others are ethnic Rumanians, Russians, or, especially, Poles. Scores of thousands of them are genuine refugees from various of the world's tyrannies, but other thousands are a motley assortment of foreign workers who have overstayed their visas or work permits, human flotsam and jetsam that communist governments regard as "surplus," and people who merely want to live in any place more affluent than their homelands, all mixed with a smattering of beggars and criminals. For most of these refugees unemployment is not a problem. They can find jobs if they want to, and they usually do, though the perhaps two million unemployed native Germans *regard them* as unwelcome rivals for jobs. Housing is something else: there is too little of it nearly everywhere in West Germany.

Politicians regularly emphasize that the ethnic Germans among the refugees have a right to settle in the Federal Republic and must be accommodated. This is an unimpeachable sentiment, but the sticking point is sheer numbers. Since 1950 some 1,400,000 emigrated to West Germany from eastern Europe. The trend in the 1980s was particularly daunting: about 40,000 in 1986, 86,000 in 1987, perhaps 150,000 in 1988. At the turn of 1990, as the reunification of Germany impended, great numbers of East Germans also began to flow westward. Even more ominous, some 3,500,000 Germans remain scattered through eastern and southeastern Europe. Many of them presumably *want to* emigrate to West Germany. Yet many have lived outside Germany for generations and no longer speak German. More would require considerable acculturation. Fulfilling the "needs" of all these people would be extremely expensive not to speak of the shortage of living quarters.

Refugees who are not ethnic Germans pose the knottiest problems of all. They are not envisioned as eventual citizens; indeed they are not even eligible to be considered for citizenship until after a ten-year waiting period. Yet they have flooded the country. Some have married German women in order to acquire citizenship themselves; some play on the sympathies of religious or humanitarian groups to avoid or at least delay deportation. Many have grown skilled at using the courts for the same purpose, and some simply disappear into the general population. As in other Western democracies, authorities are reluctant to act forcefully against interlopers lest pressure groups or the media accuse them of inhumanity or that handy catchall charge, "racism."[5]

A marked feature of public life in postwar Oberschopfheim was the decline in importance of the village government. This was, fundamentally, caused by a tendency discernible nearly everywhere in modern times: the progressive extension of state power down to the local level. In Baden, administrative consolidation had begun as early as 1935 when the Nazis began to merge small communities into larger ones. Though this action violated NSDAP promises made before 1933 and was unpopular with many of the people concerned, by 1939 some ninety tiny communities had been eliminated.[6] After World War II the Allies granted the various states *(Laender)* in federated Germany broader administrative authority than they had enjoyed in the past, mostly to counterbalance the strong centralist tendencies that had developed in the German government since the time of Bismarck.

Implementation of decentralization was fraught with ironies. To start with, the new state of Baden-Wuerttemberg was created in 1952 not by dividing anything but by *uniting* two old and historically separate domains. In the early 1970s this new entity of nearly 36,000 square kilometers, comprising thirty-five counties, nine cities, and over nine million people, decided to resume the consolidation of county and local government begun by the Nazis decades before. One of its creations was a new, enlarged county with the old medieval name "Ortenau." It was composed of five old counties: Offenburg, Kehl, Lahr, Wolfach, and southern Buhl, and was nearly as large as Luxemburg. The County Reform Law of 22 July 1971, enacted by a CDU-SPD coalition, then pursued the consolidation a step further down the administrative scale by reducing the number of communities in old Lahr county from forty-two to thirteen. As the numbers indicate, anywhere from two to five small villages were to be merged into a larger one for purposes of administration, though individual villages would retain their old mayors as "deputies" to the new overall mayor. The main purpose of the scheme was to promote efficiency in government.

Though the plan was ultimately a striking success, immediately it encountered every sort of opposition. For centuries rivalry had been keen among the villages of Lahr county, even approaching bloodshed in the brief "war" between Schuttern and Friesenheim back in 1743. Few people in 1971-1972 welcomed the prospect of being submerged in some new administrative unit with neighbors whom they had long regarded as rivals. Likewise, each village in a proposed consolidation wanted to be the one that absorbed the others, and no mayor wished to "bend his knee" to one of his fellows. In the case of Oberschopfheim, it lay along the border of old Lahr and old Offenburg counties, and its people were almost evenly divided about whether they should join villages in one county or the other. To complicate matters still further, Oberschopfheim, Niederschopfheim, and Diersburg had once comprised a single community. Many thought this ancient arrangement should be reconstituted instead of Oberschopfheim falling under the aegis of Friesenheim, as the new plan envisioned.

Had the whole question been left strictly to mayors or entirely to a popular vote, it is unlikely that mergers would have occurred anywhere in Germany. In this instance, however, village *Gemeinderaete* agreed to the consolidation in principle and then left it to the citizenry to decide with whom to merge. After long and rancorous discussion 51.5 percent of Oberschopfheimers voted to merge with Friesenheim, Oberweier, Heiligenzell, and Schuttern, while 48.5 percent held out for union with Niederschopfheim, Diersburg, and Hofweier. To bring about this "landslide" endorsement, Friesenheim had to promise Oberschopfheim a "package deal" worth about three million marks. It consisted of a hall for the village sports club, a playground, a new water plant, and a funeral home (though an all-purpose meeting hall was eventually constructed instead). In addition, the victors-to-be undertook to pave paths between strips in the fields, to install a new heating system in the courthouse, and to do extensive work on village streets, sewers, and creeks. All these promises were written down beforehand, signed, sealed, and delivered as promised. The outcome was a ringing triumph for cash rather than democracy. The principle of local representation was saved by retention of the deputy mayors, who continued to look after purely local affairs in their old courthouses. Moreover, each village maintained its own *Gemeinderat* while also sending delegates to the consolidated *Gemeinderat* in Friesenheim.

Though the importance of local government declined after the merger, the *Gemeinde* still handled a good deal of money in the 1970s. It collected several hundred thousand *DM* annually from rents and taxes on land, timber sales, the sale of hunting and fishing rights, the issuance of dog licenses, and the occasional sale of a municipal building. Over 98 percent of this went to support schools, to repair roads and streets, to defray health costs, and to pay the salaries and expenses of village officials. The latter also issued all permits of any sort and handled all the paperwork involved in various municipal activities. In keeping with what seems to be a global law of bureaucratic expansion, these tasks required two full-time assistants to the part-time mayor.

Otherwise, village functionaries had little to do. Criminality was almost ludicrously insignificant, at least by American standards. Occasional cases of vandalism or disorderly conduct, usually traceable to alcohol, received some official attention. If a local celebration got advance publicity there might be a few pickpockets or other thieves to confront. In the 1970s a Feldhueter still patrolled the fields periodically to ward off potential filchers of agricultural produce, but he almost never apprehended anyone since latter-day thieves rob banks for money and stores for television sets rather than fields for potatoes and turnips. By the 1980s the Feldhueter had become so obviously superfluous that the position was abolished. Now and then the "deputy mayor" publicly announced the name of someone caught stealing fruit, but by the 1980s few paid any heed since far more fruit simply went to waste than attracted the attention of apple rustlers. Aside from these Lilliputian concerns, the main business of the mayor was (and is) to manage the fire department, look after the cemetery, take notice of visitors to the village, and perform an occasional marriage.

Despite so much initial opposition and so many misgivings, the merger of villages and consequent withering of local government has been a general success. Old rivalries and feuds between villages have virtually disappeared. The old village mayors, so determined not to submit to one another a generation ago, now get together periodically to talk amiably, to drink wine, and to take trips. In Oberschopfheim a building boom resulted from the merger with Friesenheim, Schuttern, Heiligenzell, and Oberweier. One of its first fruits was a new social center that gave all the village clubs a convenient place to meet and so noticeably increased village sociability, especially among the young. At about the same time (1975) the village got a new pastor, Berthold Schwab, a serious and capable man in his forties who worked hard to renew interest in club life as a means of holding village young people closer to the church. The new social center suited his purpose admirably, and the clubs, which had seemed close to death in 1973, revived notably thereafter.

One unanticipated result of the administrative consolidation was that the value of village citizenship to the ordinary person shrank rapidly. This was only partly because of shrinkage of the scope of local government. As the numbers seriously engaged in farming declined, employment diversified, and personal mobility increased, old prerogatives of citizenship such as access to the common pastureland became meaningless. By the 1980s official "citizens" of Oberschopfheim were chiefly a dwindling band of the elderly, and no new citizenship was being granted.

Perhaps the most fundamental change that took place in Oberschopfheim after 1945 was the alteration of its occupational composition. It was not that everyone abruptly quit farming. The village had, after all, always contained many people who derived their livelihood primarily from trades, small business, or public employment, and for whom agriculture had been only a sideline. Nevertheless a steady drift away from the land was unmistakable. In 1950 about 30 percent of villagers made their living primarily from agriculture. By 1961 this had shrunk to 21 percent; by 1973 to a mere 2 percent. In 1988 over half the people in Oberschopfheim still did *some* farm work—they raised vegetables, fruit, grapes, grain, tobacco, or animals—but for almost all of them it was a peripheral pursuit.

This development was typical of Germany generally. Back in 1850, 85 percent of the population had worked on the land; from 1920 to 1950 about 25 percent; by 1980 a mere 6 percent, and many of them were only part-time farmers. It has become hard to find a village anywhere in Germany where most of the people still work the soil for their livelihood and do not have some outside job.[7]

Some historians of agriculture think that in Western countries so many people have made this transition from rural to urban living that agriculture will soon be thought of and organized in ways quite different from any in times past.[8] One wonders, for innumerable peasants of many nationalities remain attached to traditional folkways and to real or imaginary "lessons" they have learned from experience.[9]

Certainly many older people in Oberschopfheim were so attached. Sometimes there were sound reasons for it, sometimes not. In the 1970s a few old women still plowed with cows, and a few families kept work horses, but most tilling of the soil had come to be done with tractors. Yet there were only about ten tractors in the whole village because it made no sense economically for a family to buy their own tractor to work three to ten acres. It was the same with mechanical blowers to deposit hay in the barns. In some villages they became common,[10] but in Oberschopfheim hay was still pitched in by hand because few farmers had more than a couple of cows and so did not need enough hay to justify the purchase of expensive haymaking machinery. The "logical" solution to such problems as these would have been drastic consolidation of hundreds of small strips of land into a few large farms, but this was done only sporadically. Some consolidation had taken place in the 1930s when a highway had been built through the area, and the village lands devoted to grape cultivation were consolidated in 1964, but nothing further was done *according to any plan*. The result was that some minuscule plots were still worked by hand, some were rented, some were sold, some became building sites, some pasture for animals, and many lay fallow from lack of intrinsic value or the owner's lack of time to work them. Some owners simply let neighbors use the plots free of charge.

The whole situation of course raises once more the question of whether the hard economic facts of life ultimately shape our ideas as well as our conduct or whether the ideas constantly germinating and circulating in human minds ultimately determine economic conduct. In some Catholic countries, notably France and Belgium, some young farmers, inspired primarily by religious conceptions, have tried to adopt modern methods of tillage for traditional, even essentially medieval, ends. To them, it seems obvious that it is their Christian duty to grow as much food as possible in a world where many are hungry. How can there be too many peaches or potatoes when scores of millions are malnourished? How can it be moral for any government to limit production of food to keep up prices when so many need more food to maintain their health? What can be said for farmers who wear out their lands by heavy applications of artificial fertilizers in order to grow the same cash crops year after year in the same fields? This entire approach to agriculture is mad, immoral, an offense against the whole spirit of Christian civilization.[11]

Such views had no supporters in postwar Oberschopfheim. The dwindling band of full-time farmers there were increasingly inclined to regard agriculture not as a mode of life or a vocation but as a business. If some farm practice would exhaust the land but make money, they would simply emulate farmers in other Western countries by trying to renew their soil with chemical fertilizers. Formerly, such conduct would have occasioned surprise, even outrage, among neighbors, but by 1970 or 1980 nobody cared.[12]

The numerical shrinkage of farmers owed quite as much to a mere change of mind as to economic changes, too. More and more young people simply became unwilling to milk cows every day, to shovel manure, and to go into the fields at 4:00 A.M. as their ancestors had done. Ethel Nurge noted that in the 1960s it was already common for young women to leave the small Hessian village of Burkhards because they did not want to become farmers' wives and that in both Burkhards and nearby villages farmers had trouble finding wives.[13] The observation was equally true of Oberschopfheim and any other village in Lahr county.

The advent of tractors had several interesting aspects. Most of the machines were small, and they were something of a status symbol. For a time they were used as much to haul tools, implements, manure, and people quickly from one small plot to another as for plowing. Once transported, the people often carried on actual agricultural operations much as in times past.[14] Before long though part-time farmers were hiring owners of tractors to plow for them and to help with the harvest. This produced numerous disputes about whose land was to be plowed first, whose crop was to be brought in first, and under what conditions. Perhaps worse, access paths to the old strips had been only three feet wide, yet the new tractors and the big wagons they pulled required wider paths. Inevitably drivers trespassed onto the lands of neighbors when moving from one field or strip to another and created quagmires whenever they had to traverse wet ground. The real and alleged injuries sustained thereby became the subject of continuous complaints and arguments that abated only when the *Gemeinde* purchased a few feet from each party on either side and widened the paths.

Mechanization had an interesting sociological side too. When tractors first appeared in Oberschopfheim they were driven only by men because it was assumed that women would be unable to operate anything of such mechanical complexity. But when anyone's labor is needed badly enough he usually becomes a fast learner. Just as their feminine ancestors long before had learned to plow with cows, so by the mid-1970s village women were piloting the mechanized replacements of cows quite as readily as the men.

Tobacco is still grown in Oberschopfheim; indeed for many years after the war it still constituted the principal cash crop of the village. Moreover, it was now insured against hail, so farmers could get their money for it regardless of the caprices of the weather. Even so, its importance dwindled steadily throughout Lahr county. In 1946, 2,878 planters had raised 1,185 acres of tobacco. In 1972 the acreage stood at 1,032, but the number of planters had fallen to 849.[15] By 1988 only eight families in Oberschopf-heim still raised tobacco. Most farmers now planted wheat or American corn instead. As the premier cash crop of the village, tobacco had been displaced by wine.

The latter development owed considerably to expansion and consolidation of grape-growing and winemaking, a process the Nazis had encouraged a generation earlier. In 1964 the top of a hill overlooking the village was leveled with bulldozers to make a single field of about 150 acres. All of it was planted to grapes, with each owner having several rows of his own. A few years later a station was built to house new machinery to press grapes. Soon people no longer crushed their own grapes but brought them to the station. Nonetheless much hand work tending grapes was still required. Most of this remained the lot of women. Perhaps significantly, too, vineyard work remained the last bastion of the traditional barter economy. Where everyone else in Oberschopfheim now worked for cash, those who trimmed and dressed the vines were still paid partly in shares of the wine. Perhaps the difference was symbolic, for greater prestige had come to be attached to winemaking than to other types of agriculture.[16] At the same time efforts were made to improve the quality of the wine. These were sufficiently successful that Oberschopfheim's wine won a gold medal as the best in Baden in 1971; and it has consistently placed well in state competition ever since.

Fruit production has been less successful. Many dwarf fruit trees, mostly apple and cherry, have been planted since 1973, but the total number of trees and total production remain far below levels of decades past.[17] This has not been because of lack of effort on the part of producers but because they have been impaled on the horns of two different dilemmas. One is domestic: as more people have become aware of how many different chemicals and poisons are employed in modern agriculture and how potentially harmful various of them are, consumers have clamored for less spray on fruit. If growers oblige them a smaller percentage of their crop is worm free and thus "first class," and a larger proportion becomes second or third class and so suitable mainly for making cider or jam. At the same time, local fruit growers now have to compete with oranges, lemons, bananas, kiwi fruit, and other imported delicacies that are available from some part of the earth virtually year around.

Crops are considerably more diversified than in the past. Soybeans, peas, and sugar beets are all grown for animal food, and the beets for their sugar as well. Corn and wheat are planted, as ever, though the government has begun to subsidize the planting of sunflowers and rape. Each provides valuable oil. Rape plants also make fodder for animals, and the production of both helps to reduce the national surpluses of corn and wheat.

Changes in livestock production are even more marked than those in fruit and grains. The eight or ten full-time farmers left in Oberschopfheim at the end of the 1980s owned a total of about thirty cows, compared to more than three hundred in the village as late as 1973. As these figures indicate, almost nobody uses cows as beasts of burden anymore. Perhaps the readiest way to indicate how much agriculture has changed in this locale is to describe the situation of a farmer near Friesenheim who was in 1988 the biggest rural operator in the vicinity. A generation before he owned eight or ten hectares of land and a number of cows. He and his family worked the land, aided occasionally by hired men. Everything proceeded with difficulty because the farmer's possessions consisted of many small parcels of land, widely scattered. By 1988 all his old lands had been consolidated and augmented by purchase. They comprised some seventy hectares (175 acres). All were planted with wheat and corn, which was fed to some fifteen hundred pigs who had entirely supplanted the cows. These jet-age porkers also dined on a mixture of barley, fish-meal, and vitamins, all conveyed to them by an automatic feeding appara-tus. It is no exaggeration to characterize them as the prime products of a pork factory.[18]

Whatever the future of German agriculture, it has been much less remarked about than the famed "economic miracle," beginning in the 1950s, which transformed the country. Its most important component, in its early years, was sheer building. Much of this was obviously necessary repair of war damage, but the process acquired a momentum of its own even in places like Oberschopfheim that had not been smashed in the war. Construction of every sort proliferated. Several new power stations were built on both sides of the Rhine in 1958-1959. These were soon followed by a canal parallel to the river and a hydraulic distribution system that carried water into the fields on the German side and kept up the level of the water table there.[19] A new ferry began to cross the Rhine at Otten-heim in 1961. A decade later a new bridge was built over the river, a de-velopment that provided considerable economic stimulus to the whole Lahr area.

In Oberschopfheim the building boom, especially in the 1980s, was the greatest in the history of the village, exceeding even that of the 1930s. In public buildings alone there was a new fire house, a community hall, a sports hall, a house built in the forest where people might have parties or picnics, a new kindergarten, a new station to press grapes, and a new pastor's house.

Such construction did not come easily. Both land prices and labor costs soared in the 1970s and 1980s, while government red tape remained as plentiful and tangled as ever. Moreover, because Oberschopfheim's lands were still divided into minuscule plots, to erect any sizable building required purchasing parcels of land from several different people, who usually wanted several different prices for it. Only the administrative consolidation of 1973 made it possible to penetrate this morass of bureaucratic regulation and personal obduracy, for it allowed the political influence and financial resources of five villages to be focused on a single one at a given time.

Nonetheless, to one familiar with the village a generation before, in 1988 it seemed a new community. No longer did it appear to be sinking slowly into decrepitude. Now it looked prosperous and growing. The streets were wider because the old six-foot wooden fences that had once abutted onto the streets to protect family privacy had been torn down. There were also some new, wider, and straighter streets, laid down when old houses had been razed. Many an old barn, built in the 1930s or earlier, had either been torn down and replaced by a garage or had been extensively altered and modernized to make an apartment or additional rooms for a house. Entrances to the renovated properties were no longer a mixture of gravel and mud but cement blocks or even small granite "bricks" laid down in attractive semi-circular designs. The two village streams that had always flowed openly and served as convenient receptacles for rubbish of every sort were now covered, and the streets above them were kept clean.

Private building has far outstripped public. It began in earnest about 1960, propelled at first by the need of steadily increasing numbers of Canadian servicemen for living quarters. It soon acquired a momentum that persists a generation later. In 1988 perhaps a third of the houses in the village are less than a decade old. Most are built of heavy cement blocks from six inches to a foot thick rather than the familiar sandstone quarried in the hills. This is the case partly because concrete is cheaper, partly because after mid-century there were few artisans left who knew how to cut stone. Thus village structures built before and after 1950 have a different look. Most of the new houses are imposing: large, with interior rooms separated by the same thick, sturdy cement walls, topped by tile roofs. Within, most have all the household appliances and gadgets common in the prosperous sectors of other major Western countries. Many have solid oak doors and a variety of ornate furnishings. A few, belonging to city workers, even have saunas or swimming pools.

Quite as noteworthy, a high proportion of older houses in the village have been so extensively renovated with timber, cement, stucco, paint, and new furnishings that they differ but little from the completely new dwellings. Perhaps two-thirds of the village houses are new or thus refurbished, another 20 to 25 percent have been improved significantly, and a mere 10 percent or so are still essentially in their antebellum condition.[20] It is all a far cry from life as experienced in childhood by a villager who was seventy-two in 1988. His family, he said, had lived in a house built in 1841. It had no chimney; merely a hole in the roof to let the smoke out. In the winter snow sometimes drifted through the hole into the attic and onto him and his five brothers and sisters who slept huddled together for warmth under straw-filled sacks that were stuffed with fresh straw once a year on Good Friday.[21]

Villagers have become quite as concerned with their yards as with the interiors of their houses. Many people still raise vegetable gardens just as their ancestors did and are just as vigilant about purging the weeds in them, but many others plant a great variety of flowers instead. Still others have planted purely ornamental lawns, or trees, or have even landscaped their yards. A generation earlier, such conduct would have been regarded as wastefulness carried to the brink of insanity. Now, perhaps half the householders in Oberschopfheim have undertaken some combination of these motifs, a mixture of vegetables and flowers being the most common.

The whole building boom owed much to television, for once young people saw how the affluent lived they wanted fine houses of their own. Since they were also making more money than at any other time in their lives, they started to build. Even so, an outsider is initially puzzled since many of the new houses, erected on expensive lots, would sell for hundreds of thousands of dollars in some parts of the United States. The apparent gaping gulf between the cost of a house and the income of its dwellers has been bridged in considerable measure by the West German government. Money spent on house building and repair is deductible from one's taxable income and thus actually costs the builder only about half what it appears to. Moreover, if one borrows to make house repairs, he can do so at only half the prevailing rate of interest. Finally, if one starts a savings account for the specific purpose of building, the government will match the interest he earns on it. A common result of rapid movement up the economic scale anywhere is, of course, that former luxuries quickly become "necessities." By 1988, for the first time in the history of Oberschopfheim, there were a few vacant houses, places in which nobody would live because they had not been renovated.

The "economic miracle" did not consist merely of construction. In the decades following World War II industry developed rapidly in what became Ortenau county. Despite the fact that the area has no notable raw materials other than stone, sand, and gravel, most of the population of Ortenau earn their living either from industries employing fewer than a thousand people or from small businesses. Of the industries, the most important are metalwork, the manufacture of street vehicles and other machines, chemicals, papermaking, woodworking, and printing. Altogether they employ about 61 percent of all working people.[22] This pattern of employment is reflected in contemporary Oberschopfheim. An official roster of professionals and artisans for the year 1978 listed forty-two different occupations in the village. Significantly, only one old blacksmith remained and no brewers. A dentist, a doctor, a chiropractor, and two tax advisers were the most notable newcomers. Most people earn their living by working outside the village, the largest number in Offenburg, somewhat fewer in Lahr, and others in other towns or on the railroad.

Though the unemployment rate was about 7 percent in Baden-Wuerttemberg in 1988, it seemed close to zero in Oberschopfheim. Estimating the number of unemployed is difficult in any case, for several reasons. To be jobless still causes one to bear a stigma in the eyes of both adults and young people. Given this widespread public sentiment, families with one or more unemployed are not inclined to say much about it. This, of course, pleases politicians, who have a vested interest in the country seeming busy and prosperous. Oberschopfheimers say in 1988 that there are only two or three unemployed people in the village and that these are the sort of persons who don't look for work. They add that it is difficult to find people capable of doing truly skilled work, such as cement masonry, even though such jobs often command a princely forty *DM* per hour.[23]

For individuals, especially younger people from farms, the "economic miracle" was quite simple: it meant trading rural drudgery for a well paid job in the city. As side benefits there were paid vacations, medical insurance, pensions, and a more varied and interesting everyday life. The combination was irresistible for young Oberschopfheimers, especially when jobs at home dried up with the long decline of the tobacco industry. In 1949 some 117 villagers, most of them men, commuted to work elsewhere, but by 1973 the number was over a thousand, both men and women. Moreover, some 100 to 150 outsiders, most of them women, now worked *in* Oberschopfheim, primarily in the featherbed cover factory. To the delighted amazement of all those employed, real wages doubled, tripled, quadrupled, and more. Millions of women streamed into the work force alongside the men, partly to share in the bonanza, partly from need to replace the six million men who had been killed, wounded, or were still prisoners in the immediate postwar years.

Some of the social repercussions of these momentous changes were wryly humorous. As postwar prosperity spread all over West Germany the *Deutschmark* climbed steadily in value relative to the dollar, and living standards rose visibly in Oberschopfheim. Old ladies who had formerly grumbled about the laziness and irresponsibility of youth now spoke admiringly of their sons and sons-in-law who were earning high salaries at their good jobs in the city. Such remarks indicated a social change in progress, one that frequently follows in the wake of expanding American influence—a tendency to categorize people less by land ownership or traditional class, more by their jobs and salaries—though, in fact, the growing differences in types of employment and income did not produce any perceptible class polarization in Oberschopfheim. What it did produce was an occupational revolution and a more subtle, only half-admitted, psychological reorientation. From being primarily farmers with side jobs of some other sort most Oberschopfheimers had become office or factory workers who might or might not do a bit of farming in their spare time.[24]

# 12

# A NEW AGE EMERGES

THE "ECONOMIC MIRACLE" transformed everyday life for the people of Oberschopfheim, as indeed it did for most people everywhere in Germany. The vast improvement in village housing, for instance, had many desirable side effects apart from the mere pleasure most people derive from residing in attractive and convenient quarters. One tangible change was the installation of central heating between 1965 and 1973, even though the global oil crisis and the subsequent upsurge of oil prices in the latter year caused some people to return to their traditional wood stoves. Even when central heating was retained, as it was by most who had installed it, a wood stove was still commonly employed for cooking by older people though not by the younger. Thus most houses still had woodpiles outside and in many the kitchen, as of old, remained the only truly warm room in the house. Even so, the introduction of central heating represented a signal advance in human comfort. No longer did villagers have to spring heroically out of bed in the dark on midwinter mornings and shiver while they lit a wood fire to lift the chill.

Another significant triumph for greater human happiness was less tangible but no less real. Though most of the new houses were big enough to hold several families, more than half of them were inhabited by only one, thus giving everyone more room, more privacy, and a heightened sense of individuality. Even when two or more families occupied the same abode, life was much more pleasant for a new wife who could now live with her husband in a separate apartment in the building without having to share either the housework or the kitchen with her mother-in-law.

Other changes in village life also eased some of the burdens traditionally borne by women. With the general decline of agriculture women had less and less farm work to do. Most also stopped baking bread since "store bread" was cheap and of good quality. Few any longer smoked meat. It was easier to put it in a home freezer or communal locker. Few bothered anymore to mend old clothes or old furniture since everyone saw marvels of luxurious living on television and so wanted new furniture and new clothing. Above all, TV provided women with a continuous vision of shining urban homes embellished with so many "conveniences" that a degree in electrical engineering often seemed a prerequisite for inhabiting them. Thus in Oberschopfheim and neighboring villages housekeeping began to seem more important to many women just when, at last, they had the time necessary to undertake it seriously. One predictable result was a marked hankering for washing machines (though not for clothes driers) and a consequent rise in personal cleanliness. This was accompanied by an increase in feminine *pride* in cleanliness. Where flies, mosquitoes, and general dirt had been deplorably common in the village in times past, it gradually became a point of honor to keep a sparkling house—especially at Easter and Christmas. By 1988 even window screens were beginning to appear in a few domiciles.

Changes in public, even "official," attitudes contributed to rising standards of sanitation and cleanliness too. Interest in village beautification has grown rapidly in recent years. Countywide competitions are now held regularly to see which village can restore old homes most impressively, devise the most beautiful floral displays, boast the cleanest streets, plant the most trees, or provide similar evidence of community concern to improve appearances. Oberschopfheim won third prize for such endeavors in Ortenau county in 1987.

Specific actions of the village government helped notably too. Before World War II few villagers had indoor plumbing, and those who did had septic tanks. By 1970, not merely in Oberschopfheim but in other villages in Lahr county as well, sewer systems had been installed and most families had acquired modern plumbing. This was supplemented by a garbage pickup service in the 1970s.

Perhaps most important, as more people abandoned farming for city jobs, the number of farm animals declined. Consequently many adjoining rooms once used for housing malodorous pigs or cows were now torn down or refurbished for human habitation. Only in a few backwaters in the Black Forest or in isolated hamlets elsewhere did such innovations still lay mostly in the future.[1]

The remarkable upsurge in wages for every sort of work was soon reflected in vastly increased consumption of various foods, some of which had formerly been luxuries. Sales of wine, chocolate, cigarettes, coffee, beef, pork, eggs, milk, poultry, and fresh fruit soared. Most villagers undoubtedly benefited from more and better food both in improved health and in personal pleasure. For some, however, particularly the elderly, eating better while doing less physical labor than formerly merely made them fat. Some such obese oldsters would then try to persuade a compliant doctor that they needed to take a "cure" at some hot spring. If such treatment was prescribed the patient would go to a resort to spend a pleasant fortnight attending concerts, dancing, or otherwise enjoying life, all paid for by state medical insurance. To be sure, such patients were also put on strict diets, which occasionally caused the fattest of them to lose as much as fifty pounds in two weeks. Soon after returning home from such restorations, however, the erstwhile dieters often ate as heartily as ever and joked about their brief sojourns on short rations.

Of the melange of interrelated developments that changed the face (and soul) of Oberschopfheim after the 1950s, the two most important were the advent of television and the proliferation of automobiles. Nationally, the latter phenomenon can only be called incredible. The number of private automobiles skyrocketed from 500,000 in 1950 to 4,500,000 in 1960 to 22,000,000 in 1980, and German road traffic became the densest in Europe.[2] The contrast this struck with Oberschopfheimers' traditional modes of travel was the sharpest possible.

Before the 1930s if a peasant had to make a long trip he took the train. Anywhere else, he walked. During the 1930s a handful of Oberschopfheimers acquired trucks and cars, and a larger number began to ride bicycles. Most bought bicycles between 1945 and 1960. It was not that in 1960 everyone suddenly *needed* an automobile, in an economic sense. Bus service to the cities, where so many Oberschopfheimers worked, was quite good. What was ardently desired was something else: the status that comes with ownership of a car and the mobility and freedom one gains. If one had an auto he could go away on weekends, sightsee far and near, and take the old folks to visit relatives in neighboring towns. Youthful sports could drive from village to village at night seeking adventure or girls, or both. A minor social revolution followed. Business fell off in *Gasthaeuser.* Interest in clubs declined. Organized singing became rarer, save in the church choir. Young people increasingly "paired off" rather than meeting and socializing in groups. Tradition-minded elders, like their sort everywhere, railed at the youthful spendthrift lunatics who roared about heedlessly in their expensive cars, listened avidly to ghastly noisemakers from the nether regions of rock and roll music, affected long hair and jeans, adulated scandalous creatures from the theatrical world, and habitually sought their amusement away from their home villages.

For a short time in 1973 the Jeremiahs seemed vindicated. In that year of the great oil crisis the price of petroleum products shot upward by some 400 percent. Suddenly gasoline was both scarce and painfully expensive, and Sunday driving was prohibited. Walking regained its old popularity, people began to visit their neighbors again, the *Gasthaeuser* filled up, and the village experienced a major renaissance of sociability. But it did not last. Within a year the crisis had passed, and driving resumed its former popularity.

The coming of television was comparably revolutionary. Radios had been common in Oberschopfheim since Nazi times. Adults had long since grown accustomed to listening to weather forecasts, farm reports, and general news; though the spectacle and sound of children listening to rock music was abhorrent to many. Far more shocking was the advent of TV. In Germany, to be sure, as in Britain and France, television was controlled by public authorities. German television came on for only a few hours in the evenings, and its commercials were bunched at the beginning of the evening. Though it did present many American movies and popular television programs such as *Kojak* and *Dallas*, the emphasis was on "educational" programs. Thus it was far from being the "vast wasteland" of American TV. Nonetheless, TV jarred viewers in myriad ways, and it "broadened the horizons" of the tens of millions who viewed it every day. In particular it widened the "generation gap," for what young people saw on TV was stridently secular and obviously based on different assumptions about the nature and purpose of life than those enjoined by their elders.

In the short run, television increased sociability in the village since those who first bought sets invited neighbors to watch with them. This phase was brief, for within a few years most of the homes in Oberschopfheim had televisions. In the long run, sociability declined as people increasingly stayed home to watch TV instead of visiting neighbors. This reduced personal contacts and friendship in the village, but it also greatly reduced the petty rancor and quarrels of times past.

Most marked were changes in the attitudes of the young. Most of them began to accept divorce without qualms, to strive at almost any cost to ascend the social ladder, to care little for family honor (at least in the view of their elders), and to dress with studied casualness. The last was of greater significance than most Americans might suppose since, in German villages, certain clothes had always been associated with certain occasions. To skimp on food was regarded as a lesser evil than skimping on clothing since everyone could see the latter.[3] As for school children, ever since the early 1950s they had emulated their American peers in wanting to wear Sunday clothes to school, in disdaining old styles, and in wishing to look like "everyone else." This propensity was much reinforced among village teenagers when they began to attend the gymnasium in Lahr and were teased about their rustic appearance by the sophisticates of that metropolis.

Even older people began to make concessions to changing times. Men still wore white shirts with ties to church on Sundays in the 1960s, but espoused shirts of many hues in the 1970s. Women, especially old women, continued to wear black, though a trend toward brighter colors grew discernible among them too.

Anyone familiar with Oberschopfheim in decades past is immediately struck, in 1991, by how much more cosmopolitan everything seems to be and how mobile people have become. It is not uncommon now for young people, the middle aged of some affluence, or even old people who have managed to save some money to take vacations in places as diverse as Greece, Spain, North Africa, Poland, Finland, South Africa, Australia, the United States, even Thailand. Even those who do not go abroad travel a good deal at home on trains, in automobiles, or on motorcycles.

Reflecting both the influence of television and the new penchant for travel, village stores that carry groceries, hardware, clothing, or household goods increasingly resemble such stores anywhere in the Western world. Foreign foods have become common in the diets of many Oberschopf-heimers, some of the latest fashions can be found in village and small town shops, and wristwatches have become close to universal. Many younger women and girls wear slacks (and a few even shorts) in public, and for people of both sexes under forty blue jeans have become close to a national uniform. In the late 1980s many men no longer wear neckties on what were traditionally regarded as "dress up" occasions. Hikers have long abounded in Germany, but they have now been joined by occasional joggers who in the past, in Oberschopfheim anyway, would have been too tired from the day's farm work to have contemplated further *voluntary* exercise. Social relations within families have eased visibly. Patresfamilias treat their wives and children with greater indulgence and more outward affection, while the children stand much less in awe of their fathers and now speak freely to anyone. At the same time, family bonds have loosened appreciably be-cause young people now travel about, night and day, much more than formerly. Externally, fear and suspicion of strangers and the outside world has lessened. The tastes of younger Germans grow less like those of their parents, more like those of young people in other countries.

All these changes, of which the advent of automobiles and television have been the most important, have produced several *qualitative* changes. Perhaps the most notable has come in the popular attitude toward work. According to both formal studies and visual evidence, more and more of the young think about their jobs primarily in terms of shorter hours, higher pay, longer lunch breaks, and more vacations. To say that Germans once lived to work but now work to live, would be an exaggeration, but the drift is unmistakably in that direction.

One of the most evident effects of modernization in Oberschopfheim has been a heightened interest in education. During the year she spent in Burkhards, Ethel Nurge said she never saw an illiterate German.[4] She must have lived in a favored locale, for illiterates had not been uncommon in Oberschopfheim or other villages in Baden at any time before World War

II. In the postwar years this condition, and attitudes behind it, began to change. City work and higher incomes caused many to aspire to higher living standards and social status for themselves and their children. With the decline of agriculture and the steady increase in labor saving machinery, moreover, children's labor was needed less than formerly. Hence there was now more time for play and for school. Yet both in West Germany generally and in Oberschopfheim particularly the status of education and thought about it has been ambivalent, equivocal. Various studies have indicated that respect for the teaching profession has long been in decline. Adults grumble that teachers don't work hard enough and are less devoted to their tasks than formerly. Children, especially older ones, complain that school is boring, that what is taught has no relationship to what they want to do in life or what they will need in later years, that there should be more elective courses, and that the educational malaise is all the fault of their teachers.[5]

Since responsibility for education lies with individual German states, attempts to deal with such criticisms, and educational practices generally, differ somewhat from one *Land* to another. Some Germans, chiefly Social Democrats from urban areas, have called for federal control over education in order to bring to it greater liberal, democratic, "enlightened" uniformity. They have also opposed physical punishment of children and claimed that a majority of West German parents share their own desire to instill democratic attitudes in their children.[6] These contentions seem overblown. No German state has shown any inclination to surrender its control over education, and the objectives of aspiring educational "reformers" are decidedly not shared by many dwellers in Oberschopfheim.

What became quite clear in Oberschopfheim was that parents began to appreciate the practical advantages of education, particularly higher education. A few children, then more, began to think of themselves as eventual candidates for universities. By 1972 some 13 percent of those between ten and eighteen years of age were in fact enrolled in the Gymnasium in Lahr. Here nearly half of them studied English, French, Latin and other subjects in the pre-university curriculum. About two-thirds of them eventually passed the *Abitur* (an examination in their final year) which conveys eligibility to attend a university, technical school, or teachers' college. How much such progression is esteemed by students' families is indicated by the willingness of several members of many families to contribute to the support of one child, often the youngest, who would undertake such study. Even more impressive is the number of parents who spend large sums for "extras": music, books, special tutors, and trips that they hope will help their children get into a university and thus eventually into some secure, remunerative job. As in the United

States, far fewer Oberschopfheimers treasure learning for its own sake than as a presumed prelude to a good job and an impressive bank balance.

The coming of foreign armies of occupation in 1945 and after and especially the advent of television in the 1960s, markedly increased villagers' knowledge of the outside world and interest in it, though it cannot be said that most people's political convictions changed appreciably on that account. Domestically, the West German Republic was accepted, as were regimes before it, though without notable enthusiasm. The Bonn regime was luckier than the Weimar Republic in that it was not formed until four years after the war and so was not associated in the public mind with defeat, disasters, and dishonor but rather with national recovery. Even so, many found it strange and foreign. Accustomed to respect authority and to expect direction from above, people grumbled that politicians spent too much time in sterile argument and did too little, that there was little point in voting since one voice in millions was meaningless, that Germany was not yet ready for democracy, that the whole society was too materialistic, or that youth needed discipline rather than the ballot.[7] Yet a much higher percentage of eligible voters habitually vote in German elections than do in the United States. Incongruous though this may seem, there are reasons for it. Quite likely, many German complaints about the deficiencies of democracy do not indicate real hatred of it or even principled opposition: rather, mere fatigue with politics of any sort. As for heavy turnouts at the polls, they owe something to the German practice of allowing political parties, especially in cities, to administer the money appropriated to finance housing projects. Party leaders are usually able to "find accommodations" only for loyal party members who attend political meetings regularly, support party programs, and turn out faithfully to vote for party candidates.

Political habits, whether in the Ortenau or in various of its constituent parts, have changed but little since World War II save for a slow, steady leftward drift. In most elections, whether state or county, the Christian Democrats poll a bit less than half the vote. The SPD usually gets about 25 to 30 percent; the Free Democrats around 14 percent; the Greens, a radical anti-American party of the Left in foreign affairs that espouses conservation and environmentalism domestically, about 7 to 9 percent; and the Right wing FPD about 5 to 6 percent. In Oberschopfheim support for the CDU has eroded steadily, though slowly, because of the influx of outsiders. This has been supplemented by a steady trickle of young people from the CDU to the SPD, a trend that disgusts their elders.

In politics one of the products of modernization and affluence has been the rise of "social awareness." When jobs are plentiful, pay is good, and the welfare state appears to take care of everyone, it seems safe to assert that justice and equality are synonymous, to prate about soulless work, and to decry the horrors of consumerism.[8] Older citizens of Oberschopfheim have no sympathy for this inchoate, self-conscious high-mindedness. To those who can remember the 1920s, the Great Depression, the Second World War, or the dreary postwar decade, anyone young enough to have escaped any part of this dismal past ought to be grateful to have enough to eat, a room of his own, and free education. Alas! "Gratitude is seldom an outstanding virtue of young people."[9]

One contemporary current that *has* caught the imagination of many people of all ages in Oberschopfheim and neighboring villages is the conservation of natural resources. This owes much to a succession of disasters, near disasters, and ominous revelations tumbling rapidly over one another in the 1980s. Spillage from a Swiss chemical factory polluting the Rhine, emanations from French nuclear reactors across the Rhine damaging vineyards in Ortenau county, the larger and more general damage already done to German forests by industrial pollution, all capped by the Chernobyl nuclear accident, have caused much unease all over West Germany. German plans for nuclear construction have been suspended, criticism of the use of chemical fertilizers has grown, and the Greens, who stress defense of the environment, have gained significant public support. Though Oberschopfheimers feel powerless to *do* anything about the nuclear power policies of foreign nations, they have grown quite concerned about conservation in their homeland. Householders, for instance, carefully separate all sorts of trash that can be recycled—newspapers, glass, aluminum, steel, and tin cans—and save it for biweekly collections.

In Oberschopfheim most people's tempers are aroused less in national elections than by Baden provincial contests, where animosity between Christian Democrats and Social Democrats sometimes blazes. What seems to upset villagers most, however, is not actual election contests but political commentary on TV. Many complain bitterly that the Social Democrats are given all the better of it, much as American conservatives grouse that major newspapers and the TV networks favor the liberals.

Ethel Nurge said the Lutheran minister in the village of Burkhards told her that most of his people were still attached to the mystical thinking of the Third Reich and that they appeared to assume that ultimate questions about the salvation of their souls might be safely left to him.[10] This was not the case in Oberschopfheim. Though younger people grew increasingly remiss in church attendance, neither they nor their elders appeared to have any attachment to bygone Nazi myths or symbols. Most of them understood by now that the Nazis had valued them far less for themselves than as workers for the state. This is not at all to say that Oberschopfheimers relished hearing continuous denunciations of Nazism. Like most Germans,[11] they were thoroughly tired of the whole subject, particularly of foreign sermons on it, which they regarded as hypocritical.

As for the Jewish victims of Nazism, few Oberschopfheimers would discuss the subject in public for fear that anything other than unreserved sympathy for Jewish requests and support of Jewish positions would be distorted and the speaker labeled anti-Semitic. Among themselves, there were occasional remarks that ordinary people did not know what went on in the concentration camps, that the Jews "still have too much power," or that Jews had misrepresented the dilemmas and actions of German bishops and Pope Pius XI during the Nazi era. The sorest point of all was unquestionably the continued payment of reparations to Jews out of tax money. It was not that reparations *as such* were regarded as unjust. What was resented was that such payments had gone on for so many years to both individuals and to the state of Israel without any end to them ever being established or, seemingly, even contemplated.[12] In the minds of oldsters the whole situation stirred dark memories of Allied demands for war reparations in the early 1920s. At that time, no total sum had yet been specified, no schedule of payments established, and no mode of payment indicated.

Before 1990 the same ambivalence existed about the possible re-unification of Germany. Some sentiment for it remained among the elderly, but regionalism seemed as strong as ever, and few people of any age wanted to discuss the subject. When reunification actually took place in 1990, however, nearly all villagers welcomed it and did not demur at the prospect of paying higher taxes for a time to bring the East German economy up to Western standards.

Members of veterans' organizations differed little from other villagers in their attitudes. When they attended reunions with war buddies from other places, they all drank and talked about their adventures and about the funny things that had happened long ago, but they were as tired as everyone else of hearing about the Nazi era. In schools new books no longer harped relentlessly on the "lost eastern provinces." On maps, sharply contrasting colors were no longer used to mark off portions of pre-1939 Germany that had since become parts of Poland and Czecho-slovakia.

Nonetheless, memories of World War II were still fresh enough in the late 1980s that Oberschopfheimers mistrusted the Russians and accepted NATO as a geopolitical necessity, though this was not a popular conversational topic either. There has never been any serious anti-Americanism in the village, though complaints have been common that one saw too much military equipment everywhere and that there were far too many solders, both German and foreign, in the country. Since German reunification more people want *all* foreign troops out.

The only foreigners older Oberschopfheimers continued to actively and vocally dislike were their ancient enemies, the French. This was ironic because Franco-German relations improved visibly in the 1950s. Diplomatic relations became normal, various old disputes were settled, western European integration made significant strides, and the relationship between West German chancellor Konrad Adenauer and French president Charles de Gaulle was not merely one of "correctness" but evidenced a real spirit of cooperation. Nevertheless, Oberschopfheimers remained resolutely unimpressed. They were still indignant and resentful at what they regarded as bad Gallic treatment of them after they had surrendered to the French without resistance in 1945. Some griped that, even though the German economy was more productive than the French and Germany closer to the menacing Soviets, the French would always veto any proposal to allow Germany to acquire missiles for its own defense. Typical of the visceral distaste of many villagers for their old adversaries across the Rhine were remarks made in an interview with one of these writers. The interviewee observed that Louis XIV had kept Europe embroiled in wars for half a century, that Napoleon had done so for twenty years and that both had been responsible for the deaths of millions. He added that he had no doubt that if either of these Gallic conquerors had possessed the weapons available to Hitler he would have used them quite as readily as Der Fuehrer. Yet many French people had always honored and respected Louis XIV and Napoleon as national heroes. Contrarily, everyone was expected to condemn Hitler for ravaging Europe for a mere six years and to forget entirely that he had also conquered the Depression, put everyone to work, built the *Autobahnen*, restored national morale, and prohibited mechanization of cigar making.[13] An outsider is put in mind of the Irishman who proposed to an English acquaintance that they discuss Anglo-Irish relations without reference to ancient grievances and then began, "Now when Cromwell devastated our country . . ."

The influence of the church, like that of the *Gemeinde*, declined appreciably from the 1960s onward, though the process was more gradual. Oberschopfheim today is still overwhelmingly Catholic, at least nominally, but where there were only twenty-four Lutherans in the village in 1945, three decades later there were 156 non-Catholics.[14] This change did not create any particular "problems," partly because most contemporary Germans are not strident sectarians and partly because the ecumenical spirit expanded somewhat following the Vatican Council of the early 1960s.

Estimating the depth of people's religious convictions is notoriously uncertain. If one chooses to credit the impressions of a liberal American newspaperman or to take at face value what some German students have said when interviewed, most Germans who have grown up since 1945 believe in nothing. They just go through the motions of religious observances if, indeed, they bother to do so at all, and they have an almost totally casual attitude toward sex.[15] Such judgments may be accurate, of course, but it is as likely that they reflect mostly the particular milieu in which the observers live or represent chiefly their wishes. Certainly such generalizations did not indicate either the views or the conduct of most of the adult population of Oberschopfheim. There attendance at Sunday Mass fell off perhaps 20 percent through the 1950s and 1960s and more rapidly in the 1970s, though the number who took Communion at Easter declined but little.[16] As for a casual approach to sex, in Oberschopfheim quite the opposite prevailed. Most World War I widows eventually remarried. Many from World War II did not. Of the latter, a few became permanent "housekeepers" for village men. They acted thus not because they wished to join a sexual revolution but for the decidedly practical reason that they could thereby continue to collect their war widow's pensions.

The changes in spirit and ritual that convulsed international Catholicism after 1960 created much less turmoil and dissatisfaction in Germany than in the United States. If one chose to focus on the building of a new church in Oberschopfheim in 1955-1956, he could maintain plausibly that the villagers were at least as religious as their ancestors had been. They had already raised the necessary money to build the church as long ago as 1937, only to have the project stalled by the Nazis and then to see the money vanish with the repudiation of the *Reichsmark* in 1948. Now, in a time of extreme hardship, the zealots among them managed to collect the money anew. This time not the Nazis but the mayor adamantly opposed construction because the *Gemeinde* would have to pay for the bell tower, and the mayor did not want to spend village money thus. Many supported him, and for a time it appeared that the proposal would provoke a local civil war. At the height of the tension someone blasted the tower of the old church. At once street fights erupted.[17] When actual construction began, however, the differences vanished miraculously. To build a huge new church complete with basement, theater, hall, and pastor's house and then to install a heating system was expected to cost about one million *Deutschmark*, part of which would be provided by the archdiocese of Freiburg. Oberschopfheimers minimized much of the remaining burden by doing most of the construction themselves. As in the Middle Ages, men of every profession and occupation brought wagons, buckets, shovels, and the tools of carpenters and masons. Despite having already put in a long day at their regular tasks, they worked enthusiastically until midnight two to four nights a week. Women and children helped where they could and brought food and wine to the men. In just a year the church was built. It was a remarkable accomplishment, whether viewed as an expression of the people's religious commitment or as one more demonstration that Oberschopfheimers were world champion workers. At least as important, the village was unified again. In the common effort old divisions between Nazis and non-Nazis died down, and the original bitter quarrel over whether to build a church at all was laid to rest.

Another indicator of undiminished religiosity was the continued popularity of trips and pilgrimages to monasteries and shrines. Before 1939 these had always been to places nearby. By the 1960s rapidly rising incomes made it possible for parish clubs and similar groups to take extended trips to such distant places as Rome and Lourdes.

Nonetheless, in the latter half of the twentieth century secularism did advance in Oberschopfheim, though generally at a slower pace than elsewhere in the Western world. Whereas fewer than 10 percent of the people in the predominantly Lutheran hamlet of Burkhards went to church on Sundays in the 1960s,[18] in 1972 about half of registered Catholics in Oberschopfheim still did so. Even so, this was a marked drop from the near 100 percent attendance of the immediate postwar years. Backsliding was especially apparent among young married people with families, many of whom made it only once a month at best. Village wits joked that whereas one once asked the pastor for permission to work on Sunday now young people gave themselves permission to miss church.

Even more ominous for the future in this sphere was the sharp and progressive decline in religious vocations for young men and women alike after World War II. Many villages no longer had pastors by the 1970s—only visitors from elsewhere. Oberschopfheim still had a pastor, but he was an old man who had lost most of his former influence. An incident that took place in 1964 illustrates the point. The Young Men's Club decided to take up table tennis and began to play regularly in the church basement. Soon the pastor was complaining that the picture of a saint had been damaged, and both the priest and his cook grumbled that the frequent play was ruining the floor. Before long the pastor ordered the table tennis aficionados out, following which he ceased to pay much attention to the Young Men's Club. For their part, the young men indicated both by attitude and by actions that neither pastor nor their village patron, St. Bernhard, meant much to them anymore. More and more the old pastor lived in the rectory, said Mass, and left the rest of the world to its own devices. He still taught in the school, but even there his influence shrank sharply because the shortage of clerics was so severe that laymen had to be hired even to teach religion.

Changes in the flavor of Catholicism and in the influence of the institutional church were also reflected in changing marriage patterns in the village. Only six mixed marriages were recorded for the decade from 1939 to 1949, with the non-Catholic party in all cases agreeing that any children should be raised Catholic.[19] By the early 1970s mixed marriages were becoming common. Also, before the 1950s people married chiefly within their own village, secondarily from neighboring villages. A generation later secondary schools had been consolidated, children were being bused from rural villages to the main school in Lahr, and automobiles abounded. Inevitably, young people began to choose marital partners from farther afield. Since the early 1970s fewer than 5 percent of Oberschopfheimers wed persons from their own village.[20]

For a time in the middle 1970s it appeared that the arrival of a vigorous new pastor, Father Berthold Schwab, would reverse the erosion of Catholicism locally. In 1980 he persuaded villagers to erect a new kindergarten to replace the old one that had become overcrowded instead of putting the money into a building to house corpses awaiting burial. His main motive was probably fear that if mourners got in the habit of formally viewing deceased relatives and friends in a place erected for that specific purpose, many of them would gradually get out of the habit of coming to church for the burial service. Be that as it may, he urged that it was more sensible to build for the living than the dead and eventually devised a compromise that was acceptable to all. At a cost of eight hundred thousand marks, raised partly from local parishioners, the church built the kindergarten and assumed its management while the *Gemeinde* used the money set aside for the funeral parlor to build the community social center. In addition to his contributions to village welfare and his routine duties, the energetic priest is the pastor of Oberweier and teaches a total of eight hours per week in the schools of Oberschopfheim, Oberweier, and Friesenheim.

Village parishioners still seem as ready as ever to support the church financially. In 1973 they built the pastor a new house and soon after replaced an old gravel path to the church with a new brick walkway. Stone crosses scattered about the streets and fields have been repaired at a cost of eighteen thousand marks. In 1988 another thirty thousand marks was being collected to continue the process while an extensive, and expensive, renovation of the exterior of the church was planned for the near future.[21]

Nonetheless, the erosion of religious observance and seemingly belief as well, seems inexorable. Only about a quarter of the village people now go to church regularly, fewer still in Lahr. Attendees are not all old ladies, as is the case in so many places in France, Spain, and Italy, but old ladies are the most numerous group. Among the young, the public heroes of ages past—the saints—seem forgotten, replaced by rock musicians, movie actors, and figures from the increasingly popular world of sports.

The bishop's office has a policy of keeping a pastor in any village with more than two thousand Catholics, but in the consortium of five villages that includes Oberschopfheim there are only two pastors, one of them ailing, aided by a chaplain and a deacon who spends most of his time visiting hospitals. When the present pastor arrived in Oberschopfheim in 1975 there were four priests still alive who had been born in the village. In 1988 there were none. The last nun in any of the five villages retired in 1983. Only one girl from Oberschopfheim has entered a convent in recent years. Most of those few in the archdiocese who still become nuns enter contemplative orders. The old Catholic newspaper, *Lahrer Anzeiger,* is still received by perhaps two-thirds of the families in Oberschopfheim, but its name has been changed to *Badische Zeitung,* and it no longer has religious sponsorship. In the Oberschopfheim church the simplicity of the new altar and plainness of wall paintings contrast sharply with the beautiful baroque altars and statues in the churches of Ettenheim and nearby villages.

About one-third of all German marriages now end in divorce, with no significant difference between Catholics and non-Catholics, though divorce is still rare in Oberschopfheim. Papal directives have little visible effect on the conduct of most people there. Many young people ignore centuries of church teaching and simply live together, though most of them do get around to marrying within two or three years.

When queried about responsibility for the generally melancholy state of their church, clergymen do not ascribe it to any settled public hostility to religion or to resentment of the church tax. Rather, they blame secularism, the spirit of the age and, more particularly, sexual freedom among the young, a general decline in old loyalties, the heedlessness that so often accompanies prosperity, and the general ease with which one can now go to other places and do other things. One remarked to these writers that young people now have a cafeteria view of religion: they accept whatever doctrines happen to please them and reject the rest. Another voiced the optimistic expectation that many would eventually tire of materialism, recognize its sterility, and return to traditional allegiances. [22]

On the diocesan level these problems have been attacked with vigor and imagination. Married men and laicized priests have been recruited and educated to become deacons. They, along with women, often teach religion. Delayed religious vocations are encouraged, seminary regulations have been relaxed to enable seminarians to take up to two semesters of courses at universities of their choice, and priests have been brought in from other countries to minister to foreign workers of their own nationality. [23] In a sense such efforts have been a notable success. Over a thousand people are currently engaged in theological studies in the archdiocese of Freiburg—but most of them are lay people, and a high proportion are women. Moreover, none of these endeavors has had any appreciable influence in Oberschopfheim.

In the village, the pastor's influence has declined steeply, though much of this does not reflect either personal incompetence or the decline of religion but merely changing times. In all the centuries when the pastor was the only well-educated man in the village it was natural that his counsel was sought on all sorts of matters by political leaders and that his influence was enormous. Now that many are educated, political authorities ask him only about narrowly religious matters, and he concerns himself mostly with them. Moreover, since the administrative reorganization of 1971-1973 far fewer public questions of any moment are decided by anyone in Oberschopfheim.

In church affairs, lay people are as ready as ever to help, but they still look to the pastor for leadership. Women now sometimes share in the conduct of religious services by doing such things as reading the Gospels, but there are no local feminists clamoring to become priests. Parishioners obviously prefer to receive Communion from the pastor rather than from laymen, even though two of the latter have been trained for the purpose. There is particular aversion to taking the Sacrament from a mere neighbor. Doubtless, people know too much about their neighbors to regard them as convincing religious functionaries.

One of the most evident indications of the decline of religion in Oberschopfheim has been the steadily dwindling proportion of children in the village, silent evidence of the spread of family planning. In centuries past eight or more children in a family had not been uncommon. A childless couple had been looked at askance, and a barren woman had been regarded as having failed in her most fundamental social duty. Yet by the 1970s the falling birthrate of the interwar years had accelerated until the usual number of children per family was zero, one, two, or three, of whom oldsters complained, predictably, that "they got everything" and were in consequence hopelessly spoiled. As late as 1967 the usual number of births per year in Oberschopfheim varied between fifty and seventy. Afterward the figure fell rapidly to forty, thirty, even to a mere ten in the early 1970s. In 1972, of the 559 village "families" of more than one person, only 120 had any children.[24]

To be sure the catastrophic demographic prospects implied by such a trend were masked somewhat by a general decline in infant mortality everywhere in the Western world in the twentieth century and in Oberschopfheim by a reversal of the trend itself. After about 1975 the number of births per annum in the village began to inch back upward to twenty, thirty, even to forty by 1988. Significantly, though, this pattern does not appear to indicate a general return to religion but merely the effect of government subsidies for childbearing.[25] Symptomatic of the demographic shift was the building of a new grade school in 1966 that would hold only 140 children, though it could be enlarged to contain 180 to 200.[26] All these figures merely reflected national tendencies.[27]

Accounting for the decline in the number of children is less easy than recording it. Of course, in a rural society where everyone does much manual labor children are an economic asset while in a society that is growing urbanized they become a luxury instead. Perhaps, too, subconsciously the whole society becomes less friendly to children. For instance, dogs go in and out of stores, restaurants, and banks in West Germany, with both dogs and people remaining resolutely unconcerned, yet children are widely regarded as "out of place" in similar locales. In Oberschopfheim after World War II it became common to pave paths in the fields, but no playground equipment was provided for children at the school built in 1966.

Despite the general fall in the birthrate the population of Oberschopfheim has continued to grow, though more slowly than the rate of building. A major reason for this was that in 1988 some three hundred Canadians helped swell the local population to a total of 2,550. The Canadians have been caught in two squeezes: financial and social. The former is more serious since most of them live in apartments in the newly built houses, locales where the rent has risen steadily as the Canadian dollar has declined in relation to the *Deutschmark*. Contacts between the Canadians and native Oberschopfheimers long remained peripheral, since few of the visitors are Catholic and none of them belong to village clubs. Where they *are* frequently found is in the *Gasthaeuser.* Here, natives complain, their rowdiness has caused the social atmosphere to deteriorate. Rowdy or no, such grumbling demonstrates once more that no people ever love a foreign army of occupation. Even so, the Canadians are not really disliked and are less isolated than formerly. Some of them have learned German and made local friends. About twenty have married girls from Oberschopfheim. Tragically, many such matches have ended in divorce as homesick girls have grown disenchanted with the mountains, vast, thinly populated plains, and cold forests of so much of Canada.

So many and so rapid have been the changes in Oberschopfheim since 1960, and especially in the 1980s, that one might think that the old order had been swept away entirely. Hardly. All sorts of ancient attitudes survive, related to inheritances, proper conduct, medical treatment, religious activities, local customs, and mere conventional beliefs. Many of them have become so mixed with half-desired change or diluted by actual change that it sometimes seems that villagers live in three or four generations simultaneously. The anthropologist Robert Redfield has remarked how readily peasants all over the world have flocked into cities to become factory laborers ever since World War II, in the process abandoning their peasant habits and outlook, seemingly with no regrets.[28] Such a change took place in Oberschopfheim only gradually. In the 1960s the new factory workers frequently expressed regret that they could no longer work together with their families. By the 1980s they took it for granted. In the village it is still deemed particularly important to avoid any action that might cause one to be "talked about" and, despite recent relaxation of formality in dress, the elderly are still easily chagrined by being caught inappropriately clad. In 1988 an old lady was plainly embarrassed because she was not dressed in her Sunday best when visitors appeared unexpectedly and unannounced at 8:00 A.M.[29]

Pranks of various sorts remain as popular as ever, most of them exemplifying nothing more than the perennial high spirits of youth. On the first day of May, maypoles are still erected, nominally to commemorate the arrival of spring and as an expression of hope that the coming season will be fruitful but increasingly as an excuse for young bucks from different villages to have a big party and to try to steal or cut down one another's maypoles. *Poltarabend* is still celebrated, now more boisterously than ever. Sometimes so many of the groom's friends take part that cars carry trunks full of dishes to be smashed on doorsteps. Providing food and drink for all these "guests" can be more expensive than the wedding itself. Baby clothes are still occasionally hung on the houses of pregnant girls or those of newlyweds, though in the latter case they are often intended to be "good luck" symbols rather than embarrassing jokes.

Old attitudes derived from agriculture also endure after the original practical reasons for them have disappeared. The few remaining horses and cows in Oberschopfheim are still confined to stalls, and owners still cut grass and hay and bring it to them. Because farm work was always physically arduous, the ideal farm wife of yore was large, heavy set, with strong, rough hands as well suited to a hoe handle as to a baby's diaper. Even yet, older Oberschophfheimers still believe chunky, brawny people are the healthiest and most useful. In this attitude they are sharply set off from most young people. The latter, influenced by television and the movies, wish to be svelte themselves and think women should look like movie actresses rather than linemen on American football teams.

Old customs connected with the church are maintained with special tenacity. While children no longer sit by themselves in the front pews in church, and a fair number of women now sit with husbands and children on the "men's side" of the church, it still takes a male social pioneer to risk loss of face by sitting on the "women's side." New Year's pretzels are still eaten on New Year's Eve to bring luck and blessings during the coming year. Chalk that has been blessed is still employed to write the initials of the Three Kings above one's doorway on January 6. On Palm Sunday each churchgoer strives to secure the largest palm branches in order to have his house protected from lightning and other unholy forces. On *Corpus Christi* the streets and crucifixes are beautified with elaborate floral designs.

George Spindler describes an attitude and set of practices in the Swabian village of Burgbach, to which he gives the name ritualization. Visitors there are often given leaflets that stress the past history of the village and everyone's faithfulness to its splendid traditions, but the pamphlets simultaneously boast about how "modern" and "progressive" the place is. In late October the community stages a four-day festival not unlike a medieval fair. A vast array of goods is offered for sale. Young people dress in traditional costumes, and everyone sings, dances, drinks wine, speaks the local dialect, and acts hospitably to visitors. Each portion of the whole affair once had a serious meaning, but now it has become mainly a pageant to attract tourists or an excuse to have a good time. Most people enjoy it thoroughly, though a few young people and some self-conscious sophisticates disdain it as nonsensical, noisy, or unduly "establishment." [30] The ostensible respect for old usages is quite as pronounced farther west in Baden where the annual Offenburg fair still drew crowds of two hundred thousand in the 1980s. [31] In Oberschopfheim it is manifested mainly by continuing attachment to the local dialect and the persistence of church festivals and religious observances.

The struggle between the old and the new is especially marked in the field of medicine. In centuries past all the ailing save those in desperate circumstances were treated at home by their womenfolk. The latter had assailed them with a virtually infinite assortment of teas, herbs, ointments, poultices, plasters, purges, baths, and special foods. Some of these nostrums were doubtless helpful; most probably affected the victims but little; and few did much damage. More important was the gesture itself: someone close to the patient was "doing all she could"; her endeavor "aided nature"; and the whole family was drawn closer together by the efforts of loved ones to help the sufferer. The appearance of a regular doctor and druggist in Oberschopfheim signaled a fundamental change in this whole approach to medicine. Most people now simply go to the doctor if they are sick and take pills for their troubles if he sends them to the pharmacist. Soon the ancient and honored home remedies will be forgotten. [32]

In the case of that quintessentially feminine endeavor, childbearing, tradition still largely carried the day. After 1960 an occasional woman from Oberschopfheim would adopt city ways, see a doctor regularly during pregnancy, and then deliver in a city hospital. The great majority, however, adopted a stance toward the whole matter that in a man would have been termed "macho." They ignored restrictions on eating, declined to waste good money on prenatal care, prided themselves on working right up to delivery, usually gave birth with only a midwife in attendance, and expected to resume work a few days later.[33] For healthy women, the great majority after all, this attitude toward maternity made little difference in their lives.

The persistence of old ways indisputably blighted the lives of some local widows, though. No matter that social relations have become notably less formal all over the Western world in the late twentieth century, no matter the religious changes, no matter the rise of feminist sentiment, a widow in Oberschopfheim still found it almost as difficult to remarry agreeably in 1950 as in 1910—or 1810. It was not merely that vigilant relatives scrutinized her personal conduct remorselessly. Any intimation that she might be contemplating remarriage at once raised serious questions. These were not about her "happiness" but about land inheritance and so elevated the antenna of anyone with a pecuniary interest in the widow's marital fate. To be sure, strictures relaxed somewhat after about 1960 as farming declined and concern with land eased. Even so, the children of a widow contemplating remarriage usually pressured her to insist that her prospective new husband sign a premarital agreement forswearing all claims to the property of his wife-to-be.

The plight of a war widow who did not especially want to remarry could be even more forlorn. She might have such a dire need for a man to help her farm her lands that she would undertake a loveless match with a husband who would, under ordinary circumstances, be regarded as unsuitable; or relatives with the usual concern for her property might press her into some unwanted match that promised to safeguard an inheritance. It had always been onerous for a bride to enter the family house of her husband, to accept the tutelage of a mother-in-law, to have to share a kitchen with her, and to assume the obligation of caring for one or several elderly in-laws who were often ailing and cantankerous in the bargain. Many a woman's spirit was broken by the ordeal and her life reduced to a mere endurance contest.[34] To have to undergo such an experience twice was a hard turn of fate indeed.

Perhaps the most incongruous example of the persistence of old habits in Oberschopfheim has been the continuing propensity of the old to sacrifice for the young. In 1969 the government raised pensions 16 to 25 percent for some 2,600,000 victims of the war, most of them widows. In Bismarckian times a national old age pension system had been established for industrial workers. More than eighty years later, in the 1960s, it was extended to cover farmers and casual laborers, the last sizable groups of aging Germans who had not heretofore shared in its benefits. As icing on the cake, pension payments were now linked by law to wage levels. Since the latter rose far more rapidly than the cost of living, elderly pensioners became, for the first time in history, free from dependence on their children. Some celebrated by moving away from their children, even away from the village. But such a life was usually lonely, especially for people who had seldom or ever before been away from home. Moreover, it ran against the grain of custom centuries old. Soon most of the self-exiled returned. More never left: they simply continued to live in a portion of the family house, usually fitted out as an apartment for them. Despite their oft-expressed view that all too many of the younger generation were shiftless spendthrifts, many oldsters gave much of their pension money to their children and grandchildren, sometimes even when the "youthful" recipients were past thirty.[35]

# RUMINATIONS

FEW HURRICANES ever raged so fiercely over the world's political landscape as did Nazism from 1933 to 1945. Yet when it had been blown out by World War II neither the innate attitudes nor the personal conduct of most Oberschopfheimers had been affected much. Overall, their insularity had stood them in good stead. But what of the future? It is an article of faith in democratic countries that an informed and vigilant citizenry whose members feel personal responsibility for the conduct of their government is essential if democracy is to endure. Would the self-centered localism displayed by most Oberschopfheimers during the Nazi era be a sufficient support for democracy in some future crisis? It is difficult to answer.

Historically, democracy has been a fragile and transitory form of government—and not merely in Germany. There is no reason in the nature of things to assume that democracy is destined to inherit the earth, informed citizenry or no. In crises people everywhere notoriously crave leadership and assurance, not endless political discussion. In democratic America, for example, George Bush, heretofore a moderately popular president, saw his "official approval" rating soar to 85 to 90 percent in public opinion polls and all his Congressional critics fall silent during the brief United Nations war against Iraq in 1991.

For forty years after 1949 West Germany was remarkably fortunate. The country suffered no wars, depressions, or currency repudiations. Protected by the NATO nuclear shield and spurred by the need to rebuild the nation from the rubble of World War II, Germans lived through a long generation of dramatically rising prosperity from which all classes benefited. It was ideal soil for democracy to take root and grow.[1] Changes in Oberschopfheim from 1945 to 1991 seem comparably promising. Aged villagers still remember an old lady half a century ago who could never understand how radios worked because she could not imagine how the manufacturers could develop human beings small enough to fit inside them. Few like her still remain in contemporary Oberschopfheim, which has become somewhat of a "bedroom community" inhabited by people of moderate to excellent education. They watch the nightly world news on television and are as well informed about national and global affairs as most people are anywhere.

But, of course, political *awareness* is not the same thing as love of democracy or willingness to make painful sacrifices to defend it. In this realm much about Germany still remains unclear. Western governments acted pleased in public when Germany was reunified, but it is hard to imagine a non-German European really welcoming this development. As Germany has become an economic giant once more, many young people, and some politicians,[2] contend that the country deserves greater political influence in the world and should assume a more active role in shaping global destinies. Will such feelings eventually be followed by a clamor for mass destruction weapons? What will happen the first time the nation is gripped by a major economic crisis? For those who remember the Reich of the 1930s and 1940s such thoughts are unsettling.

It appears at this writing that the first real test of German democracy, comparable in complexity and seriousness to the tests Weimar Germany failed to surmount, is impending because of the reunification of Germany and the earthquakes that have shattered the Soviet Empire. Reunification has already proved both unexpectedly vexatious and enormously expensive, and the process is just beginning. East Germany's infrastructure is largely worn out, which discourages both foreign and West German investment. Many middle-aged and old people there have lived all or most of their lives under communism and find it difficult to change their habits and their outlook. Younger people are impatient with the slow rate at which East moves toward West German levels of development and civilization. There are 750,000 unemployed in the east (and rising) and 1,900,000 only partially employed. Some 1,200,000 claims have been filed for return of property "aryanized" by the Nazis before 1945 or confiscated by the communists afterward. Much of it has passed through several hands by now. In many cases return to original owners is impossible. "Compensation" has been promised to heirs. But what kind? And how much? Authorities have been slow to stir such a hornet's nest. Meantime crime and public disorder increase, especially in areas bordering the old Iron Curtain. The police cope inadequately because their numbers are too few, because they are uncertain about their position, powers, and orders, and because efforts are being made to weed out former members of the Stasi (East German secret police). Thousands have abandoned police work in disgust.

Worst of all are the steadily increasing floods of refugees. It is not merely the fifteen thousand per month who go from east to west *inside* Germany. They have been supplemented by 377,000 ethnic Germans, most from the USSR and Rumania, who poured into Germany in 1989, followed by 397,000 more in 1990. Behind them are untold millions of Russians and other Slavs who may flood westward should the USSR dissolve in anarchy or in a welter of civil wars. Already an estimated $100 billion has been spent by Bonn grappling with these interlocking problems, and taxes have risen more rapidly than expected.[3]

People in Oberschopfheim acknowledge that it is necessary and just to resettle refugees from the east, to reeducate many of them, to teach some new trades and some even a new language. They know, and accept, that this will cost much in time, effort, patience, and money. What dismays them is something else: the precedents being set, the uncertainty of it all. They recall that it took ten years after World War I even to establish a definite total sum and schedule of payments for German war reparations and that scores of billions have been paid to Israel and to individual Jews since World War II but that no final figure has ever been set and no definite end to the payments ever promised. They remember the multitude of East German refugees imposed upon them at the end of World War II, people for whose support they were never thanked, much less compensated. They are not anxious to repeat any of these experiences.

An example of what many fear may be a foretaste of things to come began in Oberschopfheim in the late 1980s and has not yet worked itself out completely. A refugee family from Eritrea, fleeing from a civil war there, was settled in Oberschopfheim. These unfortunate expatriates, whose homeland is mostly a tropical desert, found themselves isolated in a cool northern village amid strangers of a completely different culture who spoke an incomprehensible language. The newcomers have been given free housing, free job training, and living expenses for five years, during which time the husband is supposed to learn the German language and to master a trade so he can support his family henceforth. The expense to the West German government has been considerable, especially since the guests disliked the apartment to which they were assigned and requested a "nicer" house—which they were given! Nevertheless some of them remain perpetually homesick. How the whole social experiment will turn out is, at this writing, anyone's guess, but native Oberschopfheimers are less than delighted to provide the stage for it. They regularly remind themselves, and each other, that "nobody ever gave us anything" and marvel at the "ingratitude" of people who, having been given much, then demand more. To them it is a bitter reminder of the troublesome "guests" they had to endure in the late 1940s, and it arouses fears that swarms of similar indigents from the East may inundate them again in years to come.

Overall, the political, educational, and cultural gulf that separated Oberschopfheimers and many other rural Germans from their urban countrymen and from the Nazis alike in the 1930s and 1940s has been largely bridged. In a general way most Oberschopfheimers are reasonably contented politically and contemplate the future with optimism. But have they thereby become staunch, principled defenders of democracy? Have the rest of Germans, for that matter? Current signs are favorable, but the jury is still out.

# NOTES

## Abbreviations

CA     Obershopfheim church archives
LCA   Lahr city archives
PA     Private archives
VA     Obershopfheim village archives
Note: For publication facts of works cited, see bibliography, 262-74.

## Introduction

1. Peterson, *Limits of Hitler's Power,* 404.
2. See, for example, Foster, "Introduction: What Is a Peasant?" 2-13; Fallers, "Are African Cultivators to Be Called 'Peasants'?" 35-40; Wolf, *Peasants,* 2-3, 10-11.
3. Spindler grumbled that the term "peasant" has been immersed in so many misconceptions that he intends to abandon the term and use only "farmer." *Burgbach,* 11.
4. Bessel, "Living with the Nazis," 211.
5. Holborn notes that Junker officers in World War I usually knew their men far better than bourgeois officers did because in peacetime Junkers and their laborers lived in close proximity and even had Bible sessions and prayer meetings in common. *Germany and Europe,* 18.
6. Though most historians are not Marxists, many nonetheless regard Marxism as an intellectually impressive system of thought. Phillips observes that, given historical events since 1917, it is hard to think of anything more stupid than to believe that public ownership of the means of production will cause everyone to become just, fair, generous, peaceful, and wise. *Tragedy of Nazi Germany,* 103.
7. Blackbourn, "Peasants and Politics in Germany," 47.
8. Ibid., 69.
9. Blackbourn, *Populists and Patricians,* 134.

## 1. The Legacy of Centuries

1. Hoferer et al., *Kennezeichen,* 158-59, 170.
2. Kohler, *Aus Vergangenen Tagen,* 6-11.
3. The appalling human and economic costs of the war are discussed variously by Sagarra, *Social History of Germany,* 6; Sabean, *Power in the Blood,* 9; and Sabean, "Aspects of Kinship Behavior," 102.

4. Pesez and Ladurie, "Deserted Villages of France," describe the devastation of large areas in wars from the fourteenth to the seventeenth centuries and the human dislocation that accompanied them. Dispossessed French peasants remind one irresistibly of their brethren in Oberschopfheim and environs; see 91-92, 95, 99-100.

5. Kohler, *Aus Vergangenen Tagen*, 13.

6. *Geroldseckerland* 29 (1987): 54, 60; Hoferer et al., *Kennezeichen*, 162.

7. CA, Baptismal Book. Estimates of the population of Oberschopfheim are from PA, Messerer, 240; Roederer, *Ortsgeschichte von Oberschopfheim*, 24; VA, Kulturbauamt, Offenburg, 22 Aug. 1929; Flaechennutzungsplan, Oberschopfheim, 1966.

8. Baas, 17; *Geroldseckerland* 29 (1987): 55-61.

9. Kohler, *Aus Vergangenen Tagen*, 38-39.

10. Ibid., 44-47.

11. Keyser, *Deutsches Staedtebuch*, 4:334.

12. Pfaff's career as a freelance soldier is described at some length by Meister in *Kuerzell Village Archives*, 78-109, and two booklets have been written about him. His picture and gravestone are still on display in Kuerzell.

13. PA, Messerer, 228-32.

14. *Geroldseckerland* 25 (1983): 146. See also 139-45.

15. Diary of Magdalena Kopf of Kuerzell, cited in Meister, *Kuerzell Village Archives*, 95-97.

16. Walker, *German Home Towns*, 358-59; Sagarra, *Social History of Germany*, 346-47.

17. Walker, *German Home Towns*, 398.

18. Blackburn, *Class, Religion and Local Politics*, 79; Spindler, *Burgbach*, 12.

19. One man in Kuerzell bartered or surrendered his plots for a mere loaf of bread and then did not go to America after all! Meister, *Kuerzell Village Archives*, 21. Those given financial encouragement to emigrate showed remarkably little gratitude toward their benefactors; they were supposed to repay the money they were given but, according to village folklore, not one of those from Oberschopfheim did so.

20. Nurge, *Blue Light in the Village*, 104-5.

21. For instance, in southern Indiana and around Fort Wayne. See Poinsatte, *Fort Wayne*, 55-65.

22. Kopf Diary in Meister, *Kuerzell Village Archives*, 97-99.

23. Meister, *Kuerzell Village Archives*, 21.

24. In late Roman times the Alemanni erected stone statues at road crossings. After their conversion to Christianity these ancestors of Oberschopfheimers replaced the statues with religious crosses. The oldest one still standing dates from 1423. An expensive statue of Mary dates from 1775. At that time Oberschopfheim had some eight or nine hundred people.

25. Meister, *Kuerzell Village Archives*, 99.

26. Ibid., 101; Baas, 27, 32.

27. PA, Messerer, 14; Meister, *Kuerzell Village Archives*, 61-62; Hoferer et al., *Kennezeichen*, 142-43.

28. Kohler, *Aus Vergangenen Tagen*, 77-95.

29. Ibid., 49; Hoferer et al., *Kennezeichen*, 116-17.

30. Meister, *Kuerzell Village Archives*, 13.

31. Klem, *Die Roemer in Friesenheim*, 28.

32. Badisches Statist., Landesamt, *Statistisches Jahrbuch fuer das Land Baden* (1930), 57-60; Heizmann, *Der Amtsbezirk Lahr*, 41; Appel, *Baden in Wort und Zahl*, 7-8; interviews, Aug.-Sept. 1973.

33. Bell, *Fate and Honor, Family and Village*, 1.

34. Pitt-Rivers, *People of the Sierra*, 133-34.

35. E. Friedl, *Vasilika*, 42, 75, 77, 83, 86-87.

36. As was the case in a German-speaking Catholic mountain community in Switzerland, in sharp contrast to the nominally Greek Orthodox community or the nominally Catholic Spanish community noted above. See J. Friedl, *Kippel*, 37.

37. CA, Kirchenvisitationen; VA 264; PA, Messerer, 2, 223 (U); interviews, Aug.-Sept. 1973.

38. Oberschopfheimers were quite unlike Spanish peasants on this score. See Pitt-Rivers, *People of the Sierra*, 60-63.

39. VA 141, 25 July 1938, and Minister d. Innern, Karlsruhe; Rechnungsjahr 1930-1933; VA 31, 11 Jan. 1930, 23 May 1935; interview, Sept. 1973.

40. See Wilke and Wagner, "Family and Household," for the similarity of feelings on these matters between the inhabitants of Oberschopfheim and those of the village of Korle in the Fulda valley in northern Hesse, 140, 183. Historically, illegitimacy was regarded as less opprobrious in south Germany than in the north. See Sagarra, *Social History of Germany*, 72.

41. In rural France, many priests, perhaps still influenced by the Jansenism of the seventeenth and eighteenth centuries, denounced cabarets as centers of iniquity where peasants were corrupted by strong drink and subversive ideas. See Silver, *French Rural Response*, 155. Few German priests were Jansenist in spirit.

42. In 1988 the pastor was still teaching religion in the Oberschopfheim public school, for which he was paid a salary by the state.

43. Blackbourn, *Populists and Patricians*, 153, 159, 161, discusses this point.

44. Interview, Aug.-Sept. 1973.

## 2. The People of Oberschopfheim

1. Badische Landwirtschaft, 219; Appel, *Baden in Wort und Zahl*, 95; Roederer, *Ortsgeschichte von Oberschopfheim*, 24.

2. A comparison of Oberschopfheim with the village of Sulzthal, in Main-franken, is instructive. The main difference was that in the latter village the population was declining and the village was visibly dying. See Mueller, *Ein Deutsches Bauerndorf*, especially 19-29, 112-13, which is an excellent portrayal of the influence of tradition on a farm village and of the social and economic changes wrought within it in modern times, especially in the 1930s. See also LCA 41, 32-33; PA, Messerer, 240; Roederer, *Ortsgeschichte von Oberschopfheim*, 24; Geburtsregister.

3. *Geroldseckerland* 28 (1986): 48-53, quotation from p. 53.

4. Walker, *German Home Towns*, 187-88, describes these developments briefly.

5. A study of Komarov in southern Bohemia depicts in detail the lifestyle of peasants there that was still typical of European villages in the nineteenth century. It resembled that of Oberschopfheim, though the history of the two places became quite different after 1945. See Salzmann and Scheufler, *Komarov*, 15, 37.

6. The urbanization of Germany came late in history. In 1900, twice as many Germans still lived in villages with populations smaller than one thousand people as lived in cities with populations larger than one hundred thousand. This condition was more pronounced in Baden than anywhere else because of its historical division into a myriad of ecclesiastical properties, estates of Imperial Knights, and other minute divisions. For a detailed description of this phenomenon see the varied contributions of Hans Jurgen Puhle, Ian Farr, and Johnathan Osmond in Moeller, *Peasants and Lords in Modern Germany*, 5-20, 110, 171.

7. This example is taken from Mendras, *Vanishing Peasant*, 84-86.

8. This whole question has been examined exhaustively by many writers. See

Mendras, *Vanishing Peasant*, 1, 3, 12, 32-33, 75, 82-87, 92, 107-13, 117, 123-26, 131-32, 150-51, 170-75; Diaz, "Introduction: Economic Relations in Peasant Society," 50-54; Foster, "Peasant Society," 304-05, 313-15, 317, 319; Wolf, *Peasants*, 7-8, 14-17, 29; Silver, *French Rural Response*, 30-38, 63-68, 83. See J. Friedl, *Kippel*, 43-46, 53-59, 62, for an extreme case that nevertheless illustrates why consolidation of scattered farm plots was not always desirable or even possible.

9. This point is repeatedly emphasized by Silver, *French Rural Response*, 7-9, 11, 66-68, 86, 109-11. See also Foster, "Peasant Society," 320. Oberschopfheimers changed grape types several times when this appeared to be financially advantageous, but they were quite as suspicious as French peasants about "expert" advice on such matters.

10. Dovring, *Land and Labor*, 11, 40, 48, 113, 178, 202-4, 388-94, stresses the difficulty of agricultural experimentation on huge "factory farms" serviced by machines, 149-50.

11. Silver, *French Rural Response*, 19, claims that in the nineteenth century in the Loire valley, a hundred miles southwest of Paris, peasants raised livestock *primarily* for their manure, the best all-purpose fertilizer.

12. This aspect of Teutonic psychology has been the subject of much comment. See, for example, Nurge, *Blue Light in the Village*, 74, 78-79, 85-86, 99-100; Lowie, *Toward Understanding Germany*, 205-206; Wilke, "Sins of the Fathers," 178; and Mendras, *Vanishing Peasant*, 69, 164.

13. Wolf, *Peasants*, 14-15, 29.

14. In nineteenth century Russia, members of peasant families often had to hold more than one job to keep from starving. Koslow, *Despised and the Damned*, 40, 44. The choice was less stark and brutal for Oberschopfheimers, then or a generation or two later, but the plain need for extra income was the same.

15. See Morel, "Power and Ideology in Picardy," for the similarity of these attitudes to those of the French peasants of Picardy, 113-15.

16. PA, Messerer, 169; Roederer, *Ortsgeschichte von Oberschopfheim*, 62; *Badische Landwirtschaft*, 226-27.

17. One of the reasons state farms in the USSR never prospered was that caring for cows was long treated as merely a "job," for which one worked for wages just as he would on an assembly line in a factory. Lazy or irresponsible cow tenders were paid the same flat sums as their more conscientious peers, even though they might milk their charges irregularly or carelessly. Consequently, the cows often "dried up" months earlier than they should have and Soviet milk production consistently remained far below government projections or the innate capacity of the cows.

18. Dunn and Dunn, *Peasants of Central Russia*, 45.

19. In the Ukraine, a father's authority over his family was still absolute, even in the early twentieth century. A peasant who drowned his disobedient son was sentenced to three months in jail, not for murder but for "failure to bring the boy up in the sacred virtue of filial obedience." Koslow, *Despised and the Damned*, 50. Nothing comparable ever happened in Oberschopfheim.

20. Ember and Ember, *Cultural Anthropology*, 170.

21. E. Friedl, *Vasilika*, 18, 28, 48-53, 56, 65-68.

22. Such concerns were equally commonplace in other peasant communities. See Jolas and Zonabend, "Tillers of the Fields and Woodspeople," 134-35; Koslow, *Despised and the Damned*, 69-70; J. Friedl, *Kippel*, 62; and Pitt-Rivers, *People of the Sierra*, 152-53.

23. This whole subject is treated exhaustively by Goody, Ladurie, Berkner, Sabean, Howell, Thirsk, Cooper, and others in Goody, Thirsk, and Thompson, *Family and Inheritance*, especially 6-8, 10-12, 28, 44-46, 71-74, 89, 96-108, 113-14, 182-85, 190, 192-98. It is also discussed at length by Sabean, *Power in the Blood*, 137, 166-69, 202-4;

Mendras, *Vanishing Peasant*, 48-51; and Pitt-Rivers, *Mediterranean Countrymen*, 22-23, 211.

24. Berkner, "Inheritance, Land Tenure and Peasant Family Structure," 71-74.

25. For instance, in Burkhards. Nurge, *Blue Light in the Village*, 56-57.

26. For instance, in mid-twentieth century Andalusia. Pitt-Rivers, *People of the Sierra*, 46.

27. For example, in the Swiss mountains. J. Friedl, *Kippel*, 29, 60-61.

28. J. Friedl, *Kippel*, 29; Sabean, *Power in the Blood*, 166-69, 202-4. Even in Lebanon public attitudes about such matters were not notably different from those in German or other European villages. Peters, "Aspects of Rank and Status," 188-90.

29. Weber, *Peasants into Frenchmen*, 36-37, notes that such was the general opinion of peasants by others in France.

30. See Sagarra, *Social History of Germany*, 340-41, for a brief consideration of rural alcoholism.

31. In England in 1680 coffee was denounced in the House of Commons on the grounds that it "was useful for neither nourishment nor debauchery," though this draconian judgment did not prevent coffee houses from becoming popular meeting places a generation afterward. So it was with tobacco in Oberschopfheim.

32. This practice puts one in mind of those whimsical souls who frequent the public latrines of twentieth-century America and leave on the walls such messages as "Please do not throw cigarette butts in the urinals. It makes them soggy and hard to light." For more details about the introduction of tobacco see Boese, *Im Blauen Dunst*.

33. PA, Messerer, 244; Appel, *Baden in Wort und Zahl* (1928), 33.

34. The situation was much the same in the wine regions of France. Silver, *French Rural Response*, 21.

35. Sabean describes how villages specialized in certain products, *Power in the Blood*, 10-11. Sagarra reminds us that early modern Germans were unusually insular, lagging behind not merely Britain, France, Sweden, Spain, and the Netherlands, but even Russia, in overseas trade and colonization. She notes that in 1778 Saxon peasants refused to grow beets instead of cabbages even when it was demonstrated to them that the beets were both easier to cultivate and more nutritious. *Social History of Germany*, 11, 13-14.

36. Wilke, "Sins of the Fathers," emphasizes that in the Hessian village of Korle everyone knew who was "entitled" to free meat whenever any given villager butchered, 186.

37. Walker, *German Home Towns*, 410.

38. Sagarra, *Social History of Germany*, 333.

39. Between 1833 and 1871 in Kiebingen, a village located near Tubingen, which was, like Oberschopfheim, a heavily Catholic community, the village council vetoed almost 10 percent of all proposed local marriages on the grounds that the poor jobs, poor prospects, or spendthrift habits of the applicants made it likely that they would eventually become public charges. Kaschuba, "Peasants and Others," 254-55.

40. Walker, *German Home Towns*, 398-99, notes that in Baden illegitimate births were 17 percent of the total in the 1850s; in Bavaria 22.6 percent. These were the highest figures for any German states at that time.

41. VA, "Handswerkskammer in Allgemein," 1923; *Deutsches Reichsaddressbuch fuer Industrie, Gewerbe und Handel*, 247.

42. The barber of Oberschopfheim was a living latter-day reminder that in Old Europe there were many odd, marginal occupations that have long since vanished. There were men who supplemented their incomes by their expertise in inducing lactation in women who had recently given birth but for some reason were unable to nurse their babies. Other persons made a living or, more accurately, managed to keep

themselves alive, by picking wool or horsehair off hedges or bramble bushes where it had been left by passing animals. Sabean, *Power in the Blood*, 10.

43. The practice of indiscriminately forcing men into military service in the Old Regime is well known. Less well remembered, but far more common and comparably vexatious, was levying fines and other punishments for nonpayment of taxes or other misdeeds, not on individual offenders but on whole villages. See Higonnet, *Pont-de-Montvert*, 13.

44. This was roughly the same level of medical care experienced by people in similar villages in the USSR in the 1920s, save that in many of the latter there was not even a midwife. See Dunn and Dunn, *Peasants of Central Russia*, 20. For that matter, conditions differed but little in vast, thinly populated portions of the United States. When one of these writers was a child the nearest genuine doctor was forty miles away over unimproved dirt roads. Adults then told many stories about the local frontier "doctor," still alive, though senile, in the 1930s. Among his other medical exploits circa 1890-1905, he had pulled teeth with a pair of pliers.

45. VA 216; Zier, "Die Wirtschaftgeschichte der Ortenau," 226-27, 233-34; interviews, Sept.-Nov. 1973.

46. Zier, "Die Wirtschaftgeschichte der Ortenau," 292-93; interviews, Sept.-Nov. 1973. One of the few pieces of "machinery" in a typical cigar "factory" was a hand-operated device to chop off the ends of cigars. Many workers saved time by biting off the ends instead.

47. Sheppard, *Lourmarin in the Eighteenth Century*, 45-47.

48. Wilke, "Sins of the Fathers," 194.

49. Ibid., 191.

50. Kashuba, "Peasants and Others," 278.


## 3. Management of the Village


1. Before about 1850 what governments ruled France from Paris meant little to those who dwelt in rural French villages. Consciousness of being "Frenchmen" first and foremost gradually developed during the Second Empire (1852-1870) and after. See Higonnet, *Pont-de-Montvert*, 141-42. Greater general nationality consciousness gradually developed in the Soviet Union under Stalin and in places like Oberschopfheim chiefly after World War II with the multiplication of automobiles and the advent of television and consolidated schools. All over Mediterranean Europe peasants regarded government at all levels with mistrust and disdain. See Pitt-Rivers, *People of the Sierra*, 30, 144. Oberschopfheimers were more wary of remote authority than actively hostile.

2. So it had been in France too, traditionally. Sheppard, *Lourmarin in the Eighteenth Century*, 49-50, 82, 88.

3. For a discussion of German particularism, see Lowie, *Toward Understanding Germany*, 1-67.

4. Heizmann, *Der Amtsbezirk Lahr*, 62; PA, Messerer, 218; Badisches Statistische Landesamt, LCA, *Die Badische Landwirtschaft*, 200; VA 307.

5. *Anzeiger*, 30 Nov. 1933; interviews, Aug.-Dec. 1973.

6. Silver discusses this perennial problem in French villages. *French Rural Response*, 112, 124-25.

7. VA 40, VA 182; VA 31; PA, Messerer, 110; interviews, Sept.-Oct. 1973.

8. For instance, in Maudach, a small place in the Bavarian Palatinate, northwest of Baden. See Catt, "Farmers and Factory Workers," 150.

9. Sagarra, *Social History of Germany*, 351.

10. This condition is discussed more broadly by Hamilton, *Who Voted for Hitler?* 361. Spindler remarks that in Burgbach, a village near Stuttgart that was about the size of Oberschopfheim before 1939, the main differences among local inhabitants were the number of cows and farm implements owned, the size of the farms and houses, and the height of the manure piles in front of the latter. *Burgbach*, 17.

11. Interview, Sept. 1973.

12. For instance, in Andalusia, Pitt-Rivers, *People of the Sierra*, 70; and in rural Greece, E. Friedl, *Vasilika*, 32-39.

13. The same tacit arrangement existed in Burgbach. Spindler, *Burgbach*, 48. It also existed for centuries in Russia despite the consideration that at the same time husbands there might, with impunity, beat their wives without mercy. Koslow, *Despised and the Damned*, 51.

14. Kaschuba, "Peasants and Others," 259; Jeggle, "Rules of the Village," 278; Sagarra, *Social History of Germany*, 140-41. Oftentimes officeholders in Oberschopf-heim kept their positions a long time, but these never came to be regarded as family possessions. By contrast, in France under the Old Regime, differences in wealth and class within villages were marked, were keenly resented, and grew sharper in the years before the revolution of 1789. Higonnet, *Pont-de-Montvert*, 21-22, 27, 29, 39, 45, 58, 115.

15. Interviews, Aug.-Sept. 1973; VA 40; VA 160, 20 Apr. 1927; VA 31.

16. Alexander Solzhenitsyn, *August, 1914*, discusses this. Dunn and Dunn, *Peasants of Central Russia*, say this was still true in the early Bolshevik years, 39.

17. Many non-European peasant communities restricted the equivalent of local citizenship to people born and raised in the community. Wolf, "Closed Corporate Peasant Communities," 232. For Andalusian attitudes about citizenship, see Pitt-Rivers, *People of the Sierra*, 7-9, 77. The many nuances of citizenship in various German villages are discussed by Sabean, *Power in the Blood*, 13. Quite different from all these cases, the Greeks in Vasilika in the mid–twentieth century were far more proud of being heirs to the glories of ancient Greece than they were of anything connected with the home village. E. Friedl, *Vasilika*, 105-6.

18. VA 62, 8 June 1932; VA 100, VA 102, VA 103; PA, Messerer, 240; VA 31; interview, Sept. 1973.

19. PA, Messerer, 88; interview, Sept. 1973. Sicilian attitudes were similar on this point; they seemed to think that anyone born in a certain village would know all about it from that fact alone even though he might have lived most of his life elsewhere, whereas a "newcomer" who had resided in the place only thirty years could hardly be expected to understand anything important about it. Bell, *Fate and Honor, Family and Village*, 151-52.

20. In southern Spain this was so much the case that Andalusians would not form clubs or special interest groups lest these draw their basic loyalty away from their village as a whole. Pitt-Rivers, *People of the Sierra*, 77.

21. For instance Thalburg, the Westphalian town that was the subject of Allen's landmark study, *Nazi Seizure of Power.*

22. PA, Messerer, 246, 258, lists three veterans from 1866. Roederer, *Ortsgeschichte von Oberschopfheim*, 47-49, names four. See also VA 261, 28 Dec. 1928 and 15 July 1929; *Anzeiger*, 21 Mar. 1930 and 5 Mar. 1931; interviews, Aug.-Sept. 1973.

23. One of the meanest variations on this theme (vito) existed in Spain and consisted of composing and singing obscene songs about people marrying for the second time. The act did not indicate hatred of the newlyweds as individuals but of the idea of a second marriage, for this often involved stepchildren. Most people there took it for granted that stepparents would be cruel to stepchildren. Pitt-Rivers, *People of the Sierra*, 174-75.

24. This attitude seems close to universal among ordinary people. It is quite

typical of French peasants, for instance. See Weber, *Peasants into Frenchmen*, 67. American television personality Joe Garagiola, who began his life as a poor boy in an Italian district in St. Louis, has often remarked that when he returns to the environs of his boyhood old friends and acquaintances esteem him in direct proportion to how much he still seems to be one of them.

25. E. Friedl, *Vasilika*, 65.

26. The indifference of eighteenth-century French peasants to education with no "practical" dimension is discussed by Sheppard, *Lourmarin in the Eighteenth Century*, 69-71. After 1860 several different kinds of schools were established in Bochum, a factory town in the Ruhr, in an effort to help the sons of industrial workers rise in the world, but few parents believed that such a transformation was possible and so did not send their children. Crew, *Town in the Ruhr*, 91-93.

27. Blackbourn, *Populists and Patricians*, 153.

28. VA 147, Bd. Bezirksamt Lahr, 3 Nov. 1930 and Oberschopfheim, 14 and 27 Apr. 1931; VA 148 Bd. Bezirksamt Lahr, Nov. 1926 and 10 Dec. 1927; VA 50 Gesundheitsamt Lahr, 19 Nov. 1936.

29. Nurge, *Blue Light in the Village*, 159, notes that in Burkhards, a Hessian village north of Frankfurt, where most popular attitudes were similar to those in Oberschopfheim, in the 1960s only one villager would say openly that his neighbors valued education insufficiently. The man had a son in an American Ph.D. program. About 145 young men left Oberschopfheim from 1870 to 1914 to seek higher education or otherwise elevate themselves in the world.

30. See Allen, *Nazi Seizure of Power*, 30, 79, 92, 193.

31. Silver, *French Rural Response*, 163, 173.

32. In France the old pre-1789 system of weights and measures was still in common use in many isolated farm areas well into the twentieth century. Weber, *Peasants into Frenchmen*, 30-31.

33. Interviews, Aug.-Dec. 1973. E. Friedl, *Vasilika*, 14, remarks that Greek peasants tried to keep all their own family affairs secret, but were delighted to ferret out and exchange as much information as possible about their neighbors. The same proclivity was evident in Oberschopfheim.

34. Sabean, *Power in the Blood*, 148.

35. VA 386, 30 Aug. 1929; interviews, Sept.-Nov. 1973.

36. PA, DJK, Protokolbuch, 3-8 (Mussler family archives).

37. Campbell, "Kindred in a Greek Mountain Community," 77, 80, 95.

38. Pitt-Rivers, *People of the Sierra*, 27-30, 60-61.

39. Bell, *Fate and Honor, Family and Village*, 2-3, 11, 151.

40. Koslow, *Despised and the Damned*, thinks long victimization by despotic rulers was the cause of most of the disagreeable qualities in the Russian peasant character, 71, 83.

41. For example, among French peasants nothing aroused their hostility and mistrust as quickly as an indication that some stranger was connected with the law or some claim by him that he represented justice, a poignant commentary on the manner in which French governments at all levels had treated ordinary people for centuries. See Weber, *Peasants into Frenchmen*, 50.

42. This subject is well covered by Diaz, "Introduction: Economic Relations in Peasant Society," 162-63. See also Sagarra, *Social History of Germany*, 344.

43. In Andalusia everyone in the village formed a solid front behind those who milled black market grain because the conviction was unanimous that the government had no moral right to set artificial grain prices and that those set were so unrealistic that neither grain growers nor millers could live without violating them. Pitt-Rivers, *People of the Sierra*, 206-7. Oberschopfheimers particularly esteemed Mayor Adolf Holzenthaler, who skillfully defended village interests against the Nazis at great cost to himself before and during World War II.

44. Gypsies were romanticized mostly in Spain, the only country where anarchism has ever been a mass movement. Not merely various Spanish aristocrats but no less a personage than Primo de Rivera, the dictator of the 1920s, went to live with the gypsies for extended periods. Pitt-Rivers, *People of the Sierra*, 188.

45. Blackbourn, *Populists and Patricians*, 121-22, 170, 177, describes this overall attitude very well. So does J. Friedl, *Kippel*, 75.

46. See Hundsnurseher and Toddey, *Die Judischen Gemeinden in Baden*, 10-250, for a description of the Jews in Baden. See also *Juergen Stude, Die Juedischen Gemeinde Friesenheim.*

47. In the Anglo-Saxon world this view was presented most cogently and forcefully by the permanent head of the British Foreign Office in the 1930s. Vansittart, *Lessons of My Life*, was an unrelenting critic of the appeasers of Hitler in that decade. Taylor's much better known *Course of German History* expounded the same view, a bit more moderately.

48. For instance, Zweig, *World of Yesterday*, 10-25, 139ff, describes vividly the intense interest he and his Viennese friends had in literature and the arts in the 1880s and 1890s and their lack of concern with politics.

49. A matter elaborated pointedly by Lowie, *Toward Understanding Germany*, 106.

## 4. World War I and Its Aftermath

1. In the English civil war of the 1640s, supposedly crucial for the salvation and preservation of representative government in the world, ordinary soldiers on both sides cared so little for the principles involved that they fought willingly only when defending their immediate localities. When the time came to bring in the harvest they simply abandoned their arms and went home. For the dutiful resignation with which Russian peasants accepted the war, see Solzhenitsyn, *August, 1914*, 6, 10-11, 13, 64, 360, 375, 380ff; and for the French perspective, Weber, *Peasants into Frenchmen*, 43, 98-99, 110.

2. Moeller, *Peasants and Lords in Modern Germany*, 150-51, gives production statistics for grain and fodder and for numbers of farm animals in Westphalia and the Rhineland from 1913 to 1924. The overall picture is not notably different from that in Oberschopfheim.

3. The classic exposition of this all-but-universally shared grand strategic misapprehension is Farrar, *Short War Illusion*.

4. Wunderlich, *Farm Labor in Germany*, 29-30.

5. PA, Messerer, 60.

6. Farquharson, *Plow and the Swastika*, 222.

7. Walker, *German Home Towns*, 138.

8. Foster, "Introduction: What Is a Peasant?" 10. For a discussion of these conflicting attitudes, see Walker, *German Home Towns*, 113-14, 119; Mendras, *Vanishing Peasant*, 170-75; and Redfield, *Peasant Society and Culture*, 17, 27-29, 47, 64-65, 106-116.

9. Moeller, *German Peasants*, 51, 98.

10. Ibid., 147-53, describes the sharp practices of the peasants, the lamentations of urbanites, the fumbling efforts of the government, and the ruinous aftermath of it all.

11. Estimates of influenza casualties depend on how many are assumed to have died in India, where the epidemic was worst and where no statistics are reliable. See Crosby, *Epidemic and Peace*, for a good survey of the subject.

12. Roth, *Die Stadt Lahr,* 29; LCA 209, 151-53.

13. Moeller, *German Peasants*, 102.

14. Interview, May 1988.

15. PA, Messerer, 245; Roederer, *Ortsgeschichte von Oberschopfheim*, 22, 45-49;

Kraemer, "130 Jahre Zigarrenfabrikation," in *Geroldseckerland* 15 (1973): 185-87; *Freiburger Zeitung*, "Die Industrie in Oberbaden," Sonderheft, 30-48.

16. LCA 41:117; Heizmann, *Der Amtsbezirk Lahr*, 63; *Badische Landwirtschaft*, 197; interviews, Sept.-Oct. 1973.

17. Dunn and Dunn, *Peasants of Central Russia*, 10, describe the migrations of the Russian men—and often women as well—in the first half of this century. The father of one of these writers used to routinely "go harvesting" in his youth (1910-1920) in the American West.

18. So many left Oberschopfheim for the United States from 1845 to 1865 that nearly a century and a half later hardly anyone in the village did not have at least one relative in America. Some 3.6 percent of the population of Baden emigrated to America from 1852 to 1854 alone. Eighty years later, from 1919 to 1931, 860,000 left Baden for destinations elsewhere, a remarkably high exodus.


## 5. The Great Depression

1. VA 31; VA 91; VA, *Gemeinderechnung*, 1930, 1931, 1932.

2. "City" means a place with a population of more than nine thousand; a "small village" is one with fewer than three thousand people. VA 62; VA 298; VA 308.

3. But one duplicated by the government of Marburg county, albeit with considerable fiscal sleight-of-hand there. See Willertz, *National Socialism*, 215-17.

4. Dovring, *Land and Labor*, 377-78.

5. This point is emphasized by Farquharson, *Plow and the Swastika*, 26, 28, 30, 38-40.

6. The farm crisis was worse in northwestern Germany but existed to a considerable degree everywhere. See Noakes, *Nazi Party in Lower Saxony*, 109-110, 114-15.

7. Noakes and Pridham, *Documents on Nazism*, 89. The German rural malaise of that era is described by: Osmond, "Second Agrarian Mobilization?" 168-69, 175, 187; Jones, "Crisis and Realignment," 198-205; and Moeller, *Peasants and Lords in Modern Germany*, 14, 153, 161-62. Moeller, *German Peasants*, describes the vicissitudes of German agriculture both during World War I and afterward, contending that continuation of wartime controls into the Weimar years caused peasants to hate the Republic and turn Nazi.

8. VA, Haupzollamt Lahr, 22 July 1931, 27 Feb. 1932, and Oberschopfheim, 20 May 1932; *Anzeiger*, 12 Nov. 1930, 7; *Zeitung*, 12 Jan. 1932, 5; Appel, *Baden in Wort und Zahl*, 43; interviews, Sept. 1973.

9. *Anzeiger*, 31 Mar. 1933, 6.

10. VA 121, Minister d. Innern, Karlsruhe, 10 June 1930; Handwerkskammer Freiburg, 16 Aug. 1932; VA 111, *Anzeiger*, 9 Aug. 1932, 6.

11. *Anzeiger*, 5 Oct. 1932, 11; 7 Oct. 1932, 4; 13 Dec. 1932, 6.

12. VA 121, 28 Sept. 1932, 11 Nov. 1932; interviews, Sept. 1973.

13. VA 76 Freiburg, 16 June 1928, 29 Jan. 1929; VA 78 Oberschopfheim, 2 Jan. 1933; VA 77; VA 31, 15 Nov. 1931, 30 Nov. 1931; 3 Feb. 1932, and 6 Nov. 1932.

14. *Anzeiger*, 3 Dec. 1930, 7; 19 Dec. 1930, 7; 24 Jan. 1931, 5; 13 Feb. 1931, 7; and 18 June 1931, 5; *Freiburger Tagespost*, 21 Jan. 1931, quoted in PA, Schleicher, 263, with comments; LCA, Mitteilungen der Handelskammer Lahr, Oct. 1930, 91; interviews, Aug.-Sept. 1973.

15. *Anzeiger*, 4 Feb., 1931, 9; 28 Mar. 1931, 11; 17 Apr. 1931, 5; 5 May 1931, 7; 19 May 1931, 7; 13 Dec. 1932, 7; 24 Jan. 1931, 5; 28 Jan. 1931, 5; and 13 Feb. 1931, 7; VA 303, Geta Aktiengesellschaft, Bremen, 1 Dec. 1932; VA 302, Oberschopfheim, 6 June 1935; interviews, Sept.-Oct. 1973.

16. *Anzeiger,* 15 Oct. 1930, 5; VA 96; VA 357, Bezirkfuersorgeverband Lahr, 25 Mar. 1930 and 9 Aug. 1932.

17. LCA 104/8; VA 125; interview, Sept. 1973.

18. *Anzeiger,* 24 Nov. 1932, 5; VA 125.

19. VA 125, Arbeitsamt Lahr, 18 Apr. 1932 and 14 July 1932; interviews, Aug.-Nov. 1973.

20. VA 125 Arbeitsamt Lahr, 2 Sept. 1932, 12 Oct. 1932; interviews, Aug.-Nov. 1973.

21. *Anzeiger,* 22 Oct. 1930, 5, 30 Nov. 1930, 7; 17 Dec. 1931, 6, and 19 July 1932, 7; *Zeitung,* 9 Mar. 1932, 4; and 11 May 1932, 4; LCA 209, Wehrle, 160-62.

22. *Anzeiger,* 8 Aug. 1931, 5; 11 July 1931, 4; VA 357.

23. *Zeitung,* 6 Jan. 1932, 3-4; VA 4 Lahr, 25 July 1930; 21 May 1931; and 19 Nov. 1932; VA 367; VA 358, Landratsamt Lahr, 15 Dec. 1931, 7 Jan. 1932, 14 Jan. 1932, 6 Feb. 1932, 7 Mar. 1932, 29 Mar. 1932, and 10 May 1932; *Staatsanzeiger,* Karlsruhe, 30 Dec. 1932; *Anzeiger,* 19 Dec. 1931, 3; and 15 Dec. 1932, 6.

24. VA 31, 3 Feb. 1932, 4 Nov. 1932, 15 July 1932, 12 Nov. 1930, and 23 May 1932; VA 17, Bezirksamt Lahr, 13 Mar. 1930.

25. VA 4, Oberschopfheim, 25 July 1932.

26. VA 358, Oberbuergermeister Lahr, 2 Dec. 1931; CA, Kirchenvisitationen; *Zeitung,* 27 Jan. 1932, 6; VA 367, Lahr, 19 Feb. 1931; *Anzeiger* 20 Aug. 1931, 5; 27 Nov. 1931, 7; 26 Sept. 1932, 1; 19 Jan. 1933, 6; and 5 Nov. 1933, 6; interviews, Sept. 1973.

27. VA 89, Oberschopfheim, 5 Sept. 1931;, 10 Oct. 1932; VA 31, 1 May 1930; 24 Sept. 1932; 11 Oct. 1932; 23 Nov. 1932; 28 Nov. 1932; 15 Dec. 1932; and 29 Dec. 1932.

28. VA 31, 31 Oct. 1931; 28 Nov. 1932; VA 89, Oberschopfheim, 5 Sept. 1931; 13 Apr. 1934; LCA 744, May 1930, 50; VA 299, Oberschopfheim, 27 May 1930; Polizei Friesenheim, 25 Mar. 1930 (four letters); VA 31, Rechnungsjahr, 1930, 1931, 1932.

29. Allen, *Nazi Seizure of Power,* 23-24, 69, 132, 227.

30. Ibid., 24, 37, 41, 57, 67-69, 132-33.

31. Interviews, Aug.-Sept. 1973; PA, Messerer, 72-89.

32. Interviews, Aug.-Sept. 1973.

33. VA 306, 13 Mar. 1939; LCA 41, 32-33; VA A32, Flaechennutzungsplan, 1966; Roederer, *Ortsgeschichte von Oberschopfheim,* 24.

34. Noakes and Pridham, *Documents on Nazism,* 19-20, 65, 80.

35. *Anzeiger* 20 Jan. 1930, 7; 10 Apr. 1931, 7; 17 Apr. 1930, 7; interviews, Aug.-Dec. 1973.

36. VA 389, Bd. Bezirksamt, 4 Sept. 1930; VA 48; VA 31, 20 Nov. 1930.

37. VA 373, 21 Aug. 1931; interviews, Aug.-Dec. 1973.

38. VA 90, 13 May 1931; VA 31, 8 Apr. 1930; VA 373; Gegenbach, 3 Jan. 1933.

39. VA 153, 16 Dec. 1931; VA 160, Bezirk Lahr, 15 Jan. 1930; interviews, Aug.-Sept. 1973.

40. VA 31, 5 Jan. 1931, 21 Apr. 1931, 12 May 1932, and 8 Apr., 1932.

41. VA 345, *Anzeiger,* 1 Apr. 1931, 8.

42. PA, KJK, Protokolbuch, 12-14.

43. Ibid., 18, 31-32, 36, 41.

## 6. The Rise of the Nazis

1. This process is described at some length in Childers, *Formation of the Nazi Constituency,* 7, 24, 29, 199; and in Noakes and Pridham, *Documents on Nazism,* 21, 65.

2. Hamilton, *Who Voted for Hitler?* 365; Muhlberger, "Central Control vs. Regional Autonomy," 71, 94.

3. Richter, "Resource Mobilization and Legal Revolution," 115-18; Hamilton, *Who Voted for Hitler?* 422.

4. Bessel, "Violence as Propaganda," 142-43.

5. Farquaharson, *Plow and the Swastika*, 26, 41-42; Grill, *Nazi Movement in Baden*, 168-69; Gies, "NSDAP and Agrarian Organizations," 46-75; Juncovy, *Bavarian Peasantry*, 13-16.

6. Walker, *German Home Towns*, 109-10, 142, argues that Germans did not lack political experience: they merely lacked the kind of experience common to Frenchmen, Englishmen, and Americans, and which is often regarded by political writers as a universal norm. German political experience was more local, less national, than that of most western peoples.

7. Broszat, *Hitler State*, 28-29. More trivial, but not less significant, many middle class people were attracted to the Nazis because they disliked the sight of the unemployed "hanging about" unkempt, often unclean, and sometimes involved in crime. That too was, to them, reminiscent of "Bolshevism."

8. Hamilton, *Who Voted for Hitler?* 245-54, 262-64.

9. Ibid., 254-58, 561 n 34; Blackbourn, *Class, Religion and Local Politics*, 135-36, 149-55, 183-92, 234.

10. Hamilton, *Who Voted for Hitler?* 266-307; Allen, *Nazi Seizure of Power*, 133.

11. Hamilton, *Who Voted for Hitler?* 265, 374-81; and Noakes, *Nazi Party in Lower Saxony*, 222ff., 246-49. See also Koshar, "Contentious Citadel," 13-14, 21-24; Zofka, "Between Bauernbund and National Socialism," 57, 60; and Richter, "Resource Mobilization and Legal Revolution," 112-14.

12. Merkl, "Introduction," 5; Noakes and Pridham, *Documents on Nazism*, 105, 108.

13. Noakes and Pridham, *Documents on Nazism*, 105; Hamilton, *Who Voted for Hitler?* 309-27, 352-59.

14. Hamilton, *Who Voted for Hitler?* 329-35, 441-47.

15. Bessel, "Violence as Propaganda," 5; and Richter, "Resource Mobilization and Legal Revolution," 119-20, 135-42.

16. Noakes, *Nazi Party in Lower Saxony*, 123-24, 186.

17. Ibid., 215-19.

18. Allen, *Nazi Seizure of Power*, thought the incessant activism of the Nazis, especially the zeal and organizational ability of their local functionaries, crucial for their success in Thalburg, 36, 88, 274. Willertz, *National Socialism*, 32, 35-38, 40-41, 68-75, 91, 101, concurs for that community. See also Koshar, "Contentious Citadel," 28, 45; Zofka, "Between Bauernbund and National Socialism," 77; Muhlberger, "Central Control vs. Regional Autonomy," 118; and Richter, "Resource Mobilization and Legal Revolution," 129; and Hamilton, *Who Voted for Hitler?* 7.

19. Noakes, *Nazi Party in Lower Saxony*, 98.

20. Hamilton, *Who Voted for Hitler?* 310, 318-39, 335-51, 370, 576 n 21; Noakes, ibid., 126-27; 196-97, 250; Noakes and Pridham, *Documents on Nazism*, 20, 80. Merkl, *Making of a Stormtrooper*, describes and analyzes the types who gravitated to the Nazi movement and assesses their relative degrees of enthusiasm for its program.

21. Koshar, *Social Life, Local Politics, and Nazism*, maintains that such was the case in the Hessian university town of Marburg and implies that it was true elsewhere, 277-85. It was so only marginally in Oberschopfheim; clubs there were nonpolitical, though bickering between pro-Nazi and non-Nazi members did sometimes occur. See also Childers, *Formation of the Nazi Constituency*, 3-4; 32, 60.

22. In Schleswig-Holstein radical agrarian agitators shouted to crowds such messages as "Never has a nation voted itself sound; it had only fought itself sound"; and "The powers that be are ordained by Satan; the knife should be put to the throat of the state." Wunderlich, *Farm Labor in Germany*, 40. See also Farquaharson, *Plow and the*

*Swastika,* 4-12, for a description of the grievances of the farmers and the rapid gains the Nazis made there.

23. Hamilton, *Who Voted for Hitler?* 364, 371, 602 n 24; Kater, *Nazi Party,* 39-41.

24. Hamilton, *Who Voted for Hitler?* 371-72, 604 n 33.

25. On the importance of individuals as shapers of human affairs there is no better place to start than with Hook, *Hero In History.* See also "Historians Discuss Personality in History at Loccum," in the *German Tribune,* 4 Apr. 1976, 10, from *Hannoversche Allgemeine,* 23 Mar. 1976; and see also Lukacs, *Last European War.* Bert Edward Park, both a neurosurgeon and a knowledgeable student of history (a rare combination indeed), describes the array of drugs and medicines inflicted on Adolf Hitler by Dr. Theodor Morell and their ruinous effects. *Impact of Illness on World Leaders,* 149-219.

26. One who does acknowledge these "cold, hard facts of life," however distasteful, is Broszat, *Hitler State,* 22-24, 28-29.

27. Grill, *Nazi Movement in Baden,* 71, 73, 79, 101, 111, 121, 128-30, 139-51, 165-69, 173-74, 189, 237.

28. Allen, *Nazi Seizure of Power,* 126, 133, 270-71, 275-76; Willertz, *National Socialism,* 219-21, 229-35, 275-79, 316-18.

29. Allen, *Nazi Seizure of Power,* 10-22.

30. Blackbourn, "Peasants and Politics in Germany," 67.

31. Zeitung, 31 May 1928, 5-6; LCA, *Statistisches Jahrbuch,* 67; LCA, *Badisches Gemeindestatistik,* 33; *Anzeiger,* 9 Jan. 1930, 3; VA 285; interviews, Aug.-Dec. 1973. Convinced, like most historians, that Nazism was a "lower middle class" movement, Kater, *Nazi Party,* 24, professes to be mystified why farmers, part of the middle class, did not support the Nazis sooner. In Catholic Oberschopfheim the answer was simply that the pastor told them not to.

32. Farquharson, "Agrarian Policy," 236-37.

33. CA, Hirt, 10.

34. See appendix.

35. Hamilton points out that, far from being unique in human annals, the pattern of Nazi growth from 1920 to 1940 was quite similar to that of fascism in Italy and many lesser places. In all cases the movements grew up in lands either defeated in World War I or emerging from that conflict with the psychology of losers. Everywhere war veterans were prominent in the movements. The army, the police, and the judiciary were either cooperative or compliant. Landowners and industrialists lent some support. Students eager for action and adventure joined in considerable numbers. Not least, parties of the Center and Left seemed incapable of effective counteraction. *Who Voted for Hitler?* 453-61.

36. *Badische Staatsanzeiger,* 3 Apr. 1929.

37. For a detailed description of how thoroughly the SPD was run by elderly, cautious, "career" trade unionists who espoused the principle of seniority and distrusted the young, see Hunt, *German Social Democracy,* especially 56-75, 90, 94, 96, 104-10, 143-48, 178, 241-56. After World War II the Social Democrats underwent a notable revival and for a time possessed considerable appeal to the young, particularly during the years when the party was led by Willy Brandt. In the 1970s and early 1980s, however, it settled back into something like its condition in the 1920s, a refuge of the elderly and the old-fashioned, sometimes referred to as "old auntie." Helmut Herles, "The Social Democrats," in *The German Tribune,* 31 July 1988, 4.

38. Much of the British press, long accustomed to domestic "wild men" being tamed by the responsibilities of office, seemed incapable of imagining that Hitler might be intoxicated by it instead. This misjudgment was shared in Germany by the Center and by several of the liberal parties. The latter imagined that, in power, the Nazis would grow unpopular and that liberal forces could then regroup and displace them. In practice, liberal parties never made the slightest attempt to do this. See

Hamilton, *Who Voted for Hitler?* 245, 261-62, 563 n 53. In 1931 such disparate figures as Albert Einstein, Benedetto Croce, and Thomas Mann thought Nazi prospects nil. Sontag, *Broken World*, 160-61. As late as 1937 the aged British Prime Minister of World War I, David Lloyd George, expressed admiration for Hitler. See also Broszat, *German National Socialism*, 12; Glum, *Der Nationalsozialismus*, 280; Jarman, *Rise and Fall of Nazi Germany*, 187-88.

39. Grill, *Nazi Movement in Baden*, 227. The principle that the larger the proportion of Catholics the smaller the Nazi vote in these years agrees with the findings of a sociological study undertaken shortly after World War II by Loomis and Beegle, "Spread of German Nazism," 724-34. Noakes, *Nazi Party in Lower Saxony*, 154-55, notes that the Nazis got little support from 1928 to 1930 from deeply conservative Catholic areas in Lower Saxony where people still regarded them with suspicion as "radicals." Greater support for Nazis in urban rather than rural areas was true in Lahr county but not everywhere.

40. *Anzeiger,* 20 Mar. 1930, 3; 10 Apr. 1930, 3; 4 June 1930, 6; 20 Aug. 1930, 6; 2 Sept. 1930, 4; 11 Sept. 1930, 7.

41. *Anzeiger,* 22 Apr. 1930, 3; 29 July 1930, 1; 8 Sept. 1930, 6.

42. *Anzeiger,* 30 Aug. 1930, 6; 3 Sept. 1930, 7; 11 Sept. 1930, 5; VA 278 Bezirksrat Lahr, 9 Sept. 1930; Allen, *Nazi Seizure of Power,* 31-33; interviews, Aug.-Sept. 1973.

43. Hamilton, *Who Voted for Hitler?* 61-62, 513 n 47. See also Kater, *Nazi Party,* 141, 150; and Childers, *Formation of the Nazi Constituency,* 7.

44. See, for instance, Kater, *Nazi Party,* 141-44; 150-52; Childers, *Formation of the Nazi Constituency,* 7; Noakes, *Nazi Party in Lower Saxony,* 25, 60, 153-54, 159; Broszat, *Hitler State,* 2. Falter, "National Socialist Mobilization," inclines to this general view, though with many qualifications. His views are encapsulated in some twenty pages of prose, of which the following is a sampling: "To construct the tree we divide the 831 county units of our diachronically stable data set in a first step into two subsets which represent different value ranges of the first independent variable . . . (207)" "Statistically the most convincing (but still dangerous) way of inferring individual level relationships from macro data is the computation of transition probabilities between parties by means of ecological regression analysis. (223)" "To control for multicolinearity, i.e. unacceptably high intercorrelations of the predictor variables, we have computed for each pair of elections two separate regression equations . . . (226)" Not surprisingly, Falter concludes that the whole question is quite complex.

45. Noakes and Pridham, *Documents on Nazism,* 114-15; Blackbourn, *Populists and Patricians,* 218.

46. Broszat, *Hitler State,* 2, 15. In Germany new voters have frequently stampeded to one party or to a certain part of the political spectrum. Thus after 1890 many socialist votes came from people who had previously not voted at all (Munholland, *Origins of Contemporary Europe,* 127), just as much Nazi support came from the same quarter from 1930 to 1933. For an analysis of voting patterns from an unconventional point of view see Loewenberg, "Psychohistorical Approach," 88-91. For Thalburg, see Allen, *Nazi Seizure of Power,* 33-34. For Oberschopfheim, see *Anzeiger,* 15 Sept. 1930; and *Zeitung,* 15 Sept. 1930. For the motivation behind village balloting, interviews, Aug.-Dec. 1973. See also Sante and Ploetz, *Geschichte der Deutschen Laender* 2:467; Bracher, *German Dictatorship,* 206-7.

47. Hamilton, *Who Voted for Hitler?* chapters 1-3 and pp. 229-31, 423-24, 462-72, 643 n 82, 646 n 88. For examples of the viewpoint Hamilton criticizes, see Kater, *Nazi Party,* 2, 9, 22-23, 44, 46, 203-39; and Walker, *German Home Towns,* 428-29. Walker says the political success of the Nazis came from "the conversion of small town bigotries into national virtues," which the Nazis then turned into a program for national action. See also Eley, *From Unification to Nazism,* 263-68; Broszat, *Hitler State,* 30-32; and Zofka, "Between Bauernbund and National Socialism," 37, 50ff.

48. Hamilton, *Who Voted for Hitler?* chapter 1 and 67-73, 161-68, 198.

49. Ibid., 21, 31, 57-58, 121-23.

50. Ibid., 357.

51. Ibid., 80-85, 110-12, 119, 175, 185, 189, 198, 223-26, 382-85.

52. Big businessmen gave considerable money to *all* the parties of the Right, but before Hitler became chancellor they obviously preferred Hindenburg, Papen, and other conventional conservatives to Der Fuehrer. If Hitler had been the agent of the tycoons why didn't they clamor to have him named chancellor in 1932 instead of remaining loyal to Papen? It was only in February 1933, *after* Hitler had become chancellor, that major German industrialists began to make large, direct, regular contributions to the Nazis. Even afterward, business support for the Nazis was not undiluted. German business throve under the Nazis, but only to a degree. Dividends were restricted, interest rates were controlled by the government, and corporate taxes were high. Most businessmen disliked government controls, were not enthusiastic about the attempt to achieve autarky, and never enjoyed any influence in shaping decisions about foreign policy. Hamilton, *Who Voted for Hitler?* 401, 409, 429-32. See also Noakes and Pridham, *Documents on Nazism*, 125.

53. Hamilton, *Who Voted for Hitler?* 98-100, 126-28, 141, 154, 195, 236-38, 422, 434-37.

54. Hamilton, *Who Voted for Hitler?* 89-91, 110-12, 120-23, 138, 391, 434.

55. Hamilton, *Who Voted for Hitler?* 5-6, 14, 29, 38-41, 43, 50, 62-63, 86, 427, 452, 503, 513. A lower percentage of Catholics voted in most elections because most Catholics were bunched in particular districts. Since the "Catholic" party (usually the Center) or candidate ordinarily won overwhelmingly in such areas, it seemed less important for all eligible voters to go to the polls than in more religiously mixed locales. See 528 n 10. Whatever voting "patterns" might have been, it is well to recall that in July 1932, when the Nazis made their best showing in a free election, five-eighths of all German voters still supported other parties.

56. Hamilton, *Who Voted for Hitler?* 433-34, 627 n 25.

57. *Anzeiger,* 19 Nov. 1930, 9; 9 Jan. 1931, 5; 12 Jan. 1931, 8; interview, Sept. 1973. For Thalburg, see Allen, *Nazi Seizure of Power,* 157-58.

58. Kater, *Nazi Party,* 49, 54-55; Broszat, *Hitler State,* 32, 193, 235. Hitler was always suspicious of any rapid growth in NSDAP numbers. He figured correctly that many such were bound to be mere fair weather disciples, "front runners" who would look to the Party not to serve it but to get themselves a position of some sort and who would thereby lower the tone of the whole movement. In practice, the Nazis handled their rapid corporate expansion better than most organizations do and were able to retain their original elan. Noakes, *Nazi Party in Lower Saxony,* 156.

59. For example, see *Anzeiger,* 18 Aug. 1930, 7; 23 Dec. 1930, 7; 5 Mar. 1931, 5; 17 Apr. 1931, 10; 9 May 1931, 5; 20 June 1931, 5; 13 July 1931, 6; 19 Sept. 1931, 1; *Zeitung,* 12 Jan. 1932, 4; interviews, Oct. 1973.

60. Interviews, Sept. 1973; Allen, *Nazi Seizure of Power,* 88-90.

61. Allen, *Nazi Seizure of Power,* 90-95; Bracher, *German Dictatorship,* 208; *Zeitung,* 11 Apr. 1932, 4; 14 Mar. 1932, 4-5; VA 281, Bezirksamt Lahr, 2 Mar. 1932.

62. Interviews, Sept.-Oct. 1973. Glum, *Der Nationalsozialismus,* says the Depression was decisive for Nazi success in the rest of Germany as well, 159.

63. *Zeitung,* 14 Mar. 1932; 12 Apr. 1932.

64. Allen, *Nazi Seizure of Power,* 94, 113.

65. *Anzeiger,* 19 July 1932, 6; 21 July 1932, 4; 23 July 1932, 5; 26 July 1932, 9; 27 July 1932, 7.

66. Interviews, Sept. 1973.

67. *Anzeiger,* 1 Aug. 1932, 6; 7 Nov. 1932, 9; Bracher, *German Dictatorship,* 206-207; interviews, Sept.-Dec. 1973.

68. *Anzeiger,* 1 Aug. 1932, 6.

69. *Anzeiger,* 29 Oct. 1932; and 5 Nov. 1932; interviews, Sept.-Dec. 1973. So did Thomas Childers in 1986. He argues that the Nazis had reached their natural limits as a protest party in July 1932. Now their contradictory promises had begun to catch up with them. Splits developed in their ranks over strategy and tactics and over whether Hitler had missed a great chance by refusing to seize power in July. The NSDAP could not turn leftward in search of new supporters without alienating its middle class core, Childers maintains, while those who had voted for the Nazis out of mere disgust with other parties were not ideologically committed to anyone or anything and would soon have drifted away. Hitler's policy of "legality" had reached a dead end. Hence the "monstrous historical irony" of Papen, Schleicher, and others intriguing to present Hitler with the chancellorship at precisely the time when his movement was most likely over the hill and in imminent danger of disintegration. Significantly, Childers does not say which of the many now-discredited rival parties would have ascended to the seats of power in place of the Nazis or how they would have maintained themselves there. *Formation of the Nazi Constituency,* 237-55.

## 7. The Nazi Era in Peacetime

1. *Anzeiger,* 1 Mar. 1933; 30 Sept. 1933.

2. *Anzeiger,* 6 Mar. 1933. The Nazis got 44 percent of the vote in the whole country: 63 percent in Thalburg. Allen, *Nazi Seizure of Power,* 157; Bracher, *German Dictatorship,* 206-207.

3. For a discussion of this point see Turner, *Reappraisals of Fascism,* 122-26.

4. This theme runs throughout Allen, *Nazi Seizure of Power.* See also Noakes and Pridham, *Documents on Nazism,* 444; and Kater, *Nazi Party,* 75, 83-84.

5. For instance, Lukacs, *Last European War,* 323-24, argues that, unlike Bolshevik Russia, Nazi Germany never became entirely a police state.

6. See articles by Geoffrey Barraclough in *New York Review of Books,* 19 Oct. 1972, 37-43; 2 Nov. 1972, 32-38, 16 Nov. 1972, 25-31; and Phillips, *Tragedy of Nazi Germany.*

7. A majority of liberal and Left scholars have long maintained that the primary supporters of the Nazis were the middle class. Kele, *Nazis and Workers,* 215-16, demurs, insisting that the NSDAP was primarily a party of workers, as its full name, National Socialist German Workers Party, implies. Barbu, "Democracy and Dictatorship," 261-71, holds that Nazism was not a class movement at all but was composed of all sorts of people who had failed to integrate themselves into existing society.

8. Mayer, *They Thought They Were Free,* lived in a German town in the 1950s, made many friends and acquaintances there, and questioned them extensively about the Nazi past. He became convinced that distinctions between Nazis and non-Nazis were of as little consequence as the French have always assumed.

9. Dahrendorf maintains that the genuine popularity of the Nazi regime was so widespread that resistance to it was always minuscule. *Society and Democracy In Germany,* 415-16. See also Paterna et al., *Deutschland,* 11-54.

10. Peterson, *Limits of Hitler's Power,* xvi, 66, 435-37; and Phillips, *Tragedy of Nazi Germany,* 158-59.

11. This process has been sketched in some detail by Glum, *Der Nationalsozialismus.*

12. Allen, *Nazi Seizure of Power,* 159-240.

13. Willertz, *National Socialism,* 213.

14. *Anzeiger,* 7 Mar. 1933, 1; 11 Mar. 1933, 1; 13 Mar. 1933, 1; 5 Apr. 1933, 5; 7 Apr.

1933, 6; 12 Apr. 1933, 8; 28 Apr. 1933, 8; 3 May 1933, 6; 14 Oc. 1935, 4; VA 292 Kreis Offenburg, Vorlagen von 30 May 1933 and Niederschrift von 18 July 1933. Gauleiter Wagner (n Backfisch) was a "comer" among the Nazis. A decorated veteran of World War I, he became one of Hitler's earliest followers and was incarcerated in Landsberg prison with Hitler after the abortive putsch of 1923. He was a fervent Nazi who almost certainly would have occupied a major position in the Thousand Year Reich had Germany won World War II. During the war he had ruled Alsace ruthlessly. At war's end he remained unrepentant, defiant, and bellicose—which provided the French with *additional* reasons to shoot him.

15. *Anzeiger,* 9 Mar. 1933, 6; interview, Nov. 1973; Allen, *Nazi Seizure of Power,* 180; and his speech before the American Historical Association, 30 Dec. 1974, entitled, "Voluntary Associations and Resistance Among the SPD In Hitler's Germany."

16. All the Nazi artifices employed for the acquisition, management, and manipulation of the press are discussed in detail in Hale, *Captive Press in the Third Reich.*

17. This condition, so obvious despite being so often denied or glossed over in democratic countries, is discussed with unusual frankness by Phillips, *Tragedy of Nazi Germany,* especially 56, 65, 81-83.

18. Interviews, Sept. 1973.

19. Gemeinderatprotokolbuch, 16 Dec. 1933; 22 May 1934; 31 July 1934; 20 Nov. 1934; 14 Jan. 1935; interviews, Aug.-Sept. 1973; see appendix for Butz and Mueller.

20. Peterson, *Limits of Hitler's Power,* 299-302, 401-402, 405, 417-19.

21. Allen, *Nazi Seizure of Power,* 233-34. .

22. Peterson, *Limits of Hitler's Power,* 410-12.

23. VA 243, 14 July 1946; 27 Dec. 1946; *NSDAP Reichsorganisationsleiter, NSDAP Partei Statistik* 1:16, 34-39. See appendix for a list of the thirty-four members as of Dec. 1933.

24. Glum, *Der Nationalsozialismus,* 227; interview, Nov. 1973. Maschmann, herself a onetime member of the Hitler Youth, argues convincingly that most Party members were not gangsters or thugs but normal, conventionally decent people, not unlike most other Germans. See *Account Rendered,* 220-21. Noakes and Pridham, *Documents on Nazism,* 574-79, agree, as does Kater, *Nazi Party,* 182, 185. Phillips contends that Hitler and the Nazis were not unique at all, but common human types whom the world will see far more frequently in the future. See *Tragedy of Nazi Germany,* 8, 29. Hannah Arendt's observations about the "banality of evil," in the Nazi context, have become famous and the source of much controversy.

25. VA 243, Oberschopfheim, 17 Aug. 1946; interviews, Aug.-Dec. 1973. Such attitudes were also general among Bavarian peasants, according to Peterson, *Limits of Hitler's Power,* 417, and in the nation as a whole, according to Glum, *Der Nationalsozialismus,* 226.

26. Sabean, *Power in the Blood,* 95, remarks that most people are better understood not by analyzing a set of ideas to which they officially subscribe but by considering how they endeavor to adapt themselves to circumstances. This would seem especially the case during a paralyzing depression. Willertz, *National Socialism,* 237-45, 261, notes that Nazi leaders grumbled about all the opportunists, many of them civil servants and businessmen, who had been allowed to join the NSDAP in Marburg. Smith, *Russians,* 372, 377, 391, emphasizes that most ordinary Soviet citizens (late 1970s) think and talk far more about the routine events of daily life than about politics and that when they do contemplate politics, they do so in the fashion of Tammany Hall: Who do you know? What can your friends do for you? How can I obtain this, or get around that?

27. Mosse, *Nazi Culture,* 271-72.

28. Maschmann, *Account Rendered,* says that was the reason she joined the Party, 24. In Oberschopfheim only three boys joined the Hitler Youth from 1935 to 1940, but pressure raised the number to sixty by 1945.

29. Allen, *Nazi Seizure of Power,* 176, 197-205, 235-37; Willertz, *National Socialism,* 162-86, 237-45, 250 ff.; Peterson, *Limits of Hitler's Power,* 411; interviews, Aug.-Sept. 1973; VA 63.

30. Interviews, Aug.-Dec. 1973. VA 243, Liste Der Parteicommisariat de Lahr.

31. Willertz, *National Socialism,* 298.

32. Phillips, *Tragedy of Nazi Germany,* 40, discusses these propensities. In the USSR (late 1970s) political meetings were so unpopular with rank-and-file workers that to guarantee attendance the party often resorted to such expedients as holding them on paydays or when employees had to show their timesheets to gatekeepers. Smith, *Russians,* 381. Unless a strike or some major issue is on the agenda, the regular meetings of American labor unions are usually attended mainly by leaders and leaders-aspirant, supplemented by a few bored followers.

33. Interview, Sept. 1973.

34. Both Willertz, *National Socialism,* 219-21, 229-35, and Phillips, *Tragedy of Nazi Germany,* 5-6, 65-66, attribute these immense majorities in Hitler's plebiscites to genuine enthusiasm for the Nazi program and to general German contempt for democracy and consequent unconcern for the importance or implications of voting.

35. For example, see Walker, *German Home Towns,* 426-30; Bessel, "Living with the Nazis," 216-29.

36. *Zeitung,* 26 Oct., 1933; Glum, *Der Nationalsozialismus,* 239-40.

37. Though Hitler was born into a Catholic family, his whole career indicated his boundless contempt for religion of any kind.

38. *Anzeiger,* 20 Aug. 1934, 4-5; 22 Aug. 1934, 4; Glum, *Der Nationalsozialismus,* 275; VA 280, Oberschopfheim, 13 Aug. 1934 and 19 Aug. 1934.

39. See Weiss, *Fascist Tradition,* 108, 117-27, for a discussion of this subject.

40. These attitudes, hopes, and maneuvers are described by Broszat, *Hitler State,* 82-83, 89-90; and Noakes and Pridham, *Documents on Nazism,* 372, 582.

41. Broszat, *Hitler State,* 89-90.

42. Though the Nazis regarded all religions with contempt, they never treated Lutheranism as a fundamental theological enemy in the same sense that they did Catholicism. (The famous anti-Nazi Lutheran pastor Martin Niemoller, for instance, was thrown into a concentration camp until the end of World War II, but he was given special quarters there and was protected by the SS.) Probably the reason was that the Catholic church seemed a more formidable foe. It was cosmopolitan in a way that Lutheranism was not; more united in Germany and with a higher average attendance at its services; more independent of the state and thus possessed of greater spiritual influence. Broszat, *Hitler State,* 222, 229; Noakes and Pridham, *Documents on Nazism,* 370, 587.

43. Grill, *Nazi Movement in Baden,* 333-39, 345, 362, 392-403; Juncovy, *Bavarian Peasantry,* 268-73; Broszat, *Hitler State,* 222.

44. Grill, *Nazi Movement in Baden,* 303, 338-45, 362, describes the mutual mistrust and measured struggles of Catholics and Nazis in Baden before and during the war. He is convinced that had the Nazis won the war they would have dealt with uncooperative Catholics much as the same as they did with the Jews. See also Broszat, *Hitler State,* 234; Noakes and Pridham, *Documents on Nazism,* 306-309.

45. Sontag, *Broken World,* 164.

46. CA, Hirt, 10; VA 31, 18 Apr. 1934; *Anzeiger,* 27 June 1933, 7.

47. Glum, *Der Nationalsozialismus,* 124. For a discussion of Bishop Groeber's views and activities, see Zahn, *German Catholics and Hitler's Wars,* 119-42; and Wheaton, *Prelude to Calamity: The Nazi Revolution, 1933-1935,* 357-59.

48. A north Bavarian police report of 29 June 1939 indicated that disaffected priests in that area followed the same tactics as Dr. Hirt. It also noted that local Catholic peasants were more loyal to their church than to the Reich and that their attitude toward

the Nazis depended directly on how the latter treated the church. Noakes and Pridham, *Documents on Nazism*, 589.

49. VA 41, 13 Apr. 1934; CA, Hirt, 7; interviews, Sept.-Dec. 1973.

50. CA, Hirt, 10-11.

51. *Anzeiger,* 12 Dec. 1934, 28 Feb. 1935; Glum, *Der Nationalsozialismus,* 282; VA 136, Bezirksamt Lahr, 9 Feb. 1935; interviews, Sept. 1973; PA, Schleicher, 329, 460.

52. Jaeger, one of the indefatigable notetakers, had joined the NSDAP in 1933 for the most elementary of reasons, to get enough food to eat. Too poor to marry until 1934, he received the munificent bequest of a copy of *Mein Kampf* from Party superiors when he wed. In 1973 he told one of these writers that he had never read it. Interview, Aug. 1973.

53. Interview, Aug. 1973; CA, Hirt, 11-12.

54. CA, Hirt, 11-12; Grunberger, *Social History of the Third Reich,* 449; Allen, *Nazi Seizure of Power,* 224; Peterson, *Limits of Hitler's Power,* 413.

55. CA, Hirt, 11-12; interviews, Aug.-Sept. 1973.

56. CA, Hirt, 12; interviews, Aug.-Sept. 1973; letter from Messerer, 20 Jan. 1975.

57. VA 289, 14 Nov. 1935; interview, Sept. 1973.

58. Pitt-Rivers, *People of the Sierra,* 189-200.

59. Sabean, *Power in the Blood,* 33, 101, 174-98, 220.

60. Michael Baeuerle, "Geiste im Pfarrhof, *Pfarrfuehrer,* part 2, 9-12; PA, Messerer, 205; interviews, Sept. 1973.

61. CA, Hirt, 10-12.

62. Interviews, Sept.-Oct. 1973; Peterson, *Limits of Hitler's Power,* 317, 409, 413-14.

63. CA, Hirt, 13, taken from "Protokolbuch der Volksschule Oberschopfheim," unpublished record book, 7 Sept. 1936.

64. VA 256, 10 May 1935; VA 136, 15 Feb. 1935; VA 268; interviews, Aug.-Oct. 1973.

65. For observations about this *general* problem see Broszat, *Hitler State;* Broszat, *German National Socialism,* 19, 88; Noakes and Pridham, *Nazism, 1919-1945,* 238; Noakes and Pridham, *Documents on Nazism,* 22, 25-26.

66. This side of Nazism is explored thoroughly by Broszat, *German National Socialism,* 6, 11-16, 51, 72, and *Hitler State,* 133, 354-55.

67. Broszat, *German National Socialism,* 26, and *Hitler State,* xi, 29-30, 339-40; Noakes and Pridham, *Documents on Nazism,* 227, 266-67.

68. These proclivities of the Fuehrer are discussed at some length by Broszat, *Hitler State,* 34, 152-53, 254, 285-86. For instance, Rudolf Hess was appointed Deputy Fuehrer not because he had any special ability but because he was simultaneously loyal and not personally ambitious. Thus he could act as a buffer between Hitler and NSDAP party members. Thereby Hitler was spared many unwelcome confrontations during which he might have made enemies. See 202.

See also Noakes and Pridham, *Documents on Nazism,* 23, 241-42, 267; Noakes and Pridham, *Nazism, 1919-1945,* 205.

69. Broszat, *Hitler State,* 43, 282, 284; Broszat, *German National Socialism,* 21-25, 51-62.

70. Broszat, *Hitler State,* 319; Noakes and Pridham, *Nazism, 1919-1945,* 209.

71. In the interminable discussions among scholars about who are the primary beneficiaries of various twentieth century totalitarian systems it is often overlooked that the most obvious gainers are party members. Furthermore, to lapse into Muscovite parlance, it is not accidental that it is they who strive the hardest to perpetuate party rule; witness the domestic history of the USSR in the late twentieth century.

72. Broszat, *Hitler State,* 120-35, 201-202, 206-207, 213, 239, 242, 278-79, 286, 294-99; Noakes and Pridham, *Documents on Nazism,* 23, 25, 203ff.

73. Martin Bormann was especially likely to overrule directives issued by other top Nazis. Grill, *Nazi Movement in Baden,* 426. On one occasion Hitler's habit of issuing personal decrees that ignored administrative regulations as well as the formally unrepealed Weimar Constitution produced a situation in which Hitler himself was legally the subordinate of Minister of Interior Frick at the same time that Frick, like everyone else in Germany, was clearly subordinate to Der Fuehrer. Bavarian minister of the interior Wagner commented in a letter to Frick, "Admittedly I am no legal expert and historian but I doubt whether there has ever been a set-up like this before." From Broszat, *Hitler State,* 131 n 41; see also 236 n 20. Noakes and Pridham, *Nazism, 1919-1945,* 205, remark that "Hitler produced the biggest confusion in government that has ever existed in a civilized state."

74. Noakes and Pridham, *Documents on Nazism,* 25, 331, 375-76.

75. Broszat, *Hitler State,* 172-82.

76. Grill, *Nazi Movement in Baden,* 349-50.

77. Broszat, *Hitler State,* 159-61.

78. Grill, *Nazi Movement in Baden,* 311ff.

79. Farquharson, "Agrarian Policy," 245. Darré's policy usually prevailed. This is admitted even by philosophical Marxist Mason, "The Primacy of Politics," 175-97. See also Grill, *Nazi Movement in Baden,* 410-60.

80. Old fighters and ideologues like Hess and Bormann distrusted the civil service and longed to take it over while more conservative Nazis and career government officials delighted to see the ambitious Party parvenus balked. For instance, in 1933 the German ambassador in London, von Hoesch, could scarcely conceal his glee when Prime Minister Ramsay MacDonald declined to receive Alfred Rosenberg. Broszat, *Hitler State,* 239 n 49, 242; Kater, *Nazi Party,* 92; and Noakes and Pridham, *Nazism, 1919-1945,* 223.

81. Noakes and Pridham, *Nazism, 1919-1945,* 205.

82. See Phillips, *Tragedy of Nazi Germany,* 93, 112-14, 161ff; and Willertz, *National Socialism,* 195-210, 237-45. Bessel, *Life In the Third Reich,* xvii, calls the Nazi state a "chaotic and stunningly inefficient political system" crammed with competing people and organizations. For a description of the general indifference to duty and honesty in another totalitarian society, the USSR, see Smith, *Russians,* 69-70, 92, 102, 106-65.

83. Another such priest, knowledgeable enough to combat the Nazis on their own ground, and brave enough to try, was Andreas Rampp of Warmsried, in Bavaria. He sometimes routed Nazi speakers in open debate but, like Hirt, he was from an insignificant rural village and was careful to merely criticize, not to call for a rebellion. Peterson, *Limits of Hitler's Power,* 411.

84. *Anzeiger,* 16 Feb. 1935, 11; 1 Apr. 1935, 5; VA, Gemeinderechnung 1935; interview, Sept. 1973.

85. VA 31, *Gemeinderatprotokolbuch,* 14 Aug. 1935; *Anzeiger,* 26 Sept. 1935, 6; interviews, Sept.-Oct. 1973; Peterson, *Limits of Hitler's Power,* 419; Allen, *Nazi Seizure of Power,* 255, 259-60. In the Trier area some mayors never joined the Party. This shows how weak the NSDAP was in some parts of the country, and also that many Nazi officials were prudent men and not mindless fanatics. The NSDAP frequently refrained from appointing its own men as mayors if they or the Party were locally unpopular, because they did not want to make the office hated or hold it up to ridicule. Heyen, *Nationalsozialismus im Alltag,* 261-62. In Marburg the Kreisleiter once reported to his superior that men were turning down positions as Block and Cell leaders because they did not want to lose their friends. Willertz, *National Socialism,* 242-43.

86. *Gemeinderatprotokolbuch,* 14 Aug. 1935; VA 235, Oberschopfheim 1945; interviews, Sept.-Oct. 1973. Such "mistakes" were common among all the Western occupation authorities, usually from simple ignorance.

87. CA, Hirt, 12-13; Allen, *Nazi Seizure of Power,* 173-80; Peterson, *Limits of Hitler's Power,* 411-20; interviews, Sept.-Oct. 1973.

88. Noakes and Pridham, *Nazism, 1919-1945,* 255-56.

89. These aspects of life in the Third Reich are considered variously by Allen, *Nazi Seizure of Power,* 281; Mayer, *They Thought They Were Free;* Jarman, *Rise and Fall of Nazi Germany,* 184-90; and Goerlitz, *German General Staff,* 273.

90. For a comparison of national leadership and action to end the Depression in the United States and Germany, see Garraty, "New Deal, National Socialism," 908-44.

91. Phillips, *Tragedy of Nazi Germany,* is excellent on this subject, especially 62, 159. How deeply ingrained in the American soul is the faith that all right-thinking people yearn for democracy and abominate its alternatives is indicated amusingly by the very structure of intermediate level U.S. civics books a couple of generations ago. The text usually began with a few chapters on the British and American governmental systems, obviously the political modes best suited for people everywhere. Then followed a series of chapters with such titles as "The German Problem," "The Russian Problem," "The Spanish Problem," "The Italian Problem," etc.

92. See Noakes and Pridham, *Nazism, 1919-1945,* 574-81; and Kater, *Nazi Party,* 182-85.

93. Many "Aryan" doctors, for instance, were glad to be rid of their Jewish colleagues and competitors. Kater, *Nazi Party,* 113.

94. For examples, see Englemann, *In Hitler's Germany,* 71-86, 142-46. Englemann himself was active in hiding Jews and spiriting them across borders.

95. Noakes and Pridham, *Nazism 1919-1945,* 544-55, and *Documents on Nazism,* 467-68.

96. Engelmann, *In Hitler's Germany,* 124-39; and Bessel, "Living with the Nazis," 212.

97. The response of ordinary Germans to the Nazi campaign against the Jews has, of course, been dissected interminably. Two examples, from quite different points on the political spectrum, are Engelmann, *In Hitler's Germany,* 40-42, 47, 55-70, 126-29; and Laqueur, *Terrible Secret,* 55, 91, 100, 113, 133, 142-46, 151, 161, 169, 195, 201.

98. This compares with .76 percent of the population in the whole country. Jews were, in Germany, as elsewhere, mainly an urban people: 1.78 percent of the population of cities over one hundred thousand, 3.23 percent of the population of Breslau, 3.78 percent of that of Berlin, and 4.71 percent of the people of Frankfurt. Almost all were in trade, commerce, the professions, or some kind of self-employment. There were about five hundred thousand Jews in all Germany in 1933. Noakes and Pridham, *Nazism 1919-1945,* 522.

99. *Zeitung,* 17 Sept. 1933, 4; Allen, *Nazi Seizure of Power,* 167, 195, 209-213; interviews, Aug.-Oct. 1973.

100. Interviews, Aug.-Oct. 1973; Hundesnurseher, *Die Judischen Gemeinden,* 35-97, 154-250, 329.

101. Blackbourn, *Populists and Patricians,* 169-70; Blackbourn, *Class, Religion, and Local Politics,* 54-60, 106. For Bavaria, see Juncovy, *Bavarian Peasantry,* 276-81.

102. Blackbourn, *Populists and Patricians,* 172-75. In 1937 Gestapo officials in Munich specifically complained that peasants in heavily Catholic areas paid no attention to Nazi race teachings. Noakes and Pridham, *Nazism, 1919-1945,* 546.

103. The manner in which Oberschopfheim weathered the storm of the Nazi years was remarkably similar to the way many French villages endured and outlasted the gales of the French Revolutionary and Napoleonic years, 1789-1815. See Sheppard, *Lourmarin in the Eighteenth Century,* 208.

104. Interviews, Aug.-Dec. 1973. For a brief discussion of how one's place in history is often determined by when he happens to die, see Norling, *Timeless Problems in History,* 82.

105. Peterson, *Limits of Hitler's Power,* 427. NSDAP leaders also failed signally to

transform an entirely different sort of place, the international city of Danzig. For an analysis of what went on there see Levine, *Hitler's Free City.*

## 8. Offering the Nazi Carrot

1. Nazi economic planning and practice is discussed, from different ideological viewpoints, by Laqueur, *Russia and Germany,* 198-99, 245-48; Carr, *Arms, Autarky, and Aggression,* 61-64; Weiss, *Fascist Tradition,* 102; and Bracher, *German Dictatorship,* 330.

2. This subject is explored briefly by Phillips, *Tragedy of Nazi Germany,* 83, 96, 102, and elsewhere; and at greater length in Ortega y Gasset, *Revolt of the Masses.*

3. Allen, *Nazi Seizure of Power,* 267.

4. Weiss, *Fascist Tradition,* 102.

5. See Garraty, "New Deal, National Socialism," especially 934.

6. Interviews, Aug.-Nov. 1973; Allen, *Nazi Seizure of Power,* 262-63; Heiss, *Deutschland zwischen Nacht und Tag,* 186.

7. Edel, *German Labor Service,* 2.

8. Allen, *Nazi Seizure of Power,* 230-31, 264-65; Edel, *German Labor Service,* 21-23. Henning von Borcke-Stargordt, *Der Ostdeutsche Landbau zwischen Fortschritt Krise und Politik,* 63, cited in Schoenbaum, *Hitler's Social Revolution,* 161, says that only in 1934 did Nazi Germany's land reclamation figure exceed that of Weimar's bumper year, 1930. Once more, this "fact" was far less important than the *impression* that the Nazis were the first to attack national problems in earnest. Of course, some Nazi programs had already begun under the Weimar Republic. See Willertz, *National Socialism,* 116.

9. VA 351; VA 175; *Anzeiger,* 10 Jan. 1934, 7; 11 Jan. 1934, 6; *Zeitung,* 9 Dec. 1933, 3; 13 Dec. 1933, 4.

10. VA 331, Oberschopfheim, 21 Dec. 1934; VA 125, Arbeitsamt Lahr, 24 Feb. 1936; interview, Oct. 1973.

11. *Geroldseckerland* 29 (1987): 176-79.

12. Farquharson, *Plow and the Swastika,* 57.

13. This is the main theme of an excellent work by Barkin, *Controversy Over German Industrialization,* especially 5-6, 11-12, 58, 63, 71-84, 88-89, 161-83, 253-60, 273. See also Sagarra, *Social History of Germany,* 349, 354-55.

14. VA 174, Oberschopfheim, 1 Aug. 1934; VA 34; VA 63; VA 125; VA 246; interviews, Nov. 1973.

15. Guillebaud, *Economic Recovery of Germany,* 97.

16. Farquharson, "Agrarian Policy," 245, offers a vague estimate of 11 to 25 percent from 1932 to 1937.

17. Warriner, *Economics of Peasant Farming,* 30-31. Noakes and Pridham, *Nazism, 1919-1945,* say farm incomes rose 41 percent from 1932 to 1938, as compared to a 25 percent rise in incomes from labor. Where the Nazis made the biggest impact, though, was in trade and industry, where incomes soared 116 percent in the same years, 324.

18. See Noakes and Pridham, *Nazism, 1919-1945,* 279, 325; Kater, *Nazi Party,* 90-91; and Broszat, *Hitler State,* 180.

19. Juncovy, *Bavarian Peasantry,* vi-x, 43-47, 49-50, 263, 348-49, describes at length peasant attitudes and obstruction in Bavaria in the 1930s. Matters were little different in Oberschopfheim. See also Lichtenberger, *Third Reich,* 224-29; Mueller, *Ein Deutsches Bauerndorf,* 14-16; Schoenbaum, *Hitler's Social Revolution,* 162-63; *Anzeiger,* 18 May 1935; Willertz, *National Socialism,* 32-33, 283-87. In Marburg county farmers were so disgusted by mid-1937 that they no longer gave the Hitler salute. Willertz, *National Socialism,* 286.

20. VA 63; VA 178, Oberschopfheim, 20 Nov. 1933; VA 182; interview, Dec. 1973. The scale of these evasions is particularly interesting since the Nazis made much

of corruption in Weimar Germany. In Moscow the government press long dutifully ascribed irregularities in the USSR to the vestigial remnants of capitalism. Yet in both regimes every imaginable kind of corruption, political and personal, was and is as rife as in the most "decadent and contemptible" capitalist democracies. For many examples in the Third Reich see Phillips, *Tragedy of Nazi Germany*, 161ff. For the USSR the literature is enormous. Hedrick Smith, *Russians*, 10-65, 69-70, 92, 102, 264-319, provides a sampling.

21. Noakes and Pridham, *Nazism, 1919-1945*, 322-23.

22. Farquharson, *Plow and Swastika*, 113.

23. Noakes and Pridham, *Nazism, 1919-1945*, 279, 295.

24. Allen, *Nazi Seizure of Power,* 266-67.

25. *Anzeiger,* 5 Mar. 1934, 6; VA 345, Oct. 1936; VA 9; VA 13; VA 16; VA 24.

26. Schoenbaum, *Hitler's Social Revolution*, 130-32; VA 16 *Karlsruhe Staatsanzeiger,* Auszug ueber 4 Dec. 1935, Nr 113786. According to Schoenbaum, the number of craft apprentices in 1937 had dropped below that of 1931.

27. VA 122.

28. VA 28; VA 41; VA 125; VA 129 Oberschopfheim, 9 July 1934, 9 Oct. 1935; interview, Nov. 1973.

29. VA 32 Oberschopfheim, 2 Sept. 1935; VA 62, 16 Feb. 1935; VA 63, 1 Sept. 1935; interview, Nov. 1973.

30. Allen, *Nazi Seizure of Power,* 228-30, 264-65; Willertz, *National Socialism*, 214-17; *Anzeiger,* 23 Feb. 1933, 6; 24 Feb. 1933, 5-6; 22 Aug. 1935, 1; *Der Fuehrer,* 1 Oct. 1934, 3; 31 Aug. 1934; and Lahr courthouse plaque.

31. Stolper, *German Economy*, 123.

32. Garraty, "New Deal, National Socialism," 913-15, 921, 942; Lichtenberger, 232; Phillips, *Tragedy of Nazi Germany*, 146; and Neumann, *Behemoth*, 292.

33. VA 210, Oberschopfheim; VA 309, 24 Oct. 1935; interviews, Sept.-Dec. 1973.

34. VA 121; VA 122; VA 309, 24 Oct. 1935; interviews, Sept.-Dec. 1973.

35. Elsewhere in Germany, farmers, workers, and businessmen were watched even more closely than those in Oberschopfheim, though this was accompanied by the same confusion and vacillation when it came to the enforcement of controls. Like the villagers, some of them resented Nazi regulations while others did not. Those who objected were usually sufficiently prudent to keep their unwelcome sentiments to themselves. Neumann, *Behemoth*, 356; Garraty, "New Deal, National Socialism," 912, 916-17; and Trivanovich, *Economic Development of Germany*, 60.

36. *Anzeiger,* 11 May 1934; 1; 25 May 1934, 7; LCA 104, Aktenstueck 8, Stadt Lahr, Arbeitsamt; Allen, *Nazi Seizure of Power,* 229-31, 261-66; Trivanovich, *Economic Development of Germany*, 33-35, 56; and *Statistisches Jahrbuch fuer Baden 1938*, 218.

37. In Marburg the Nazis manipulated statistics in quite a different way to yield a desired political result. When Marburg's students were called up for military service their names were kept on the university's roster in order to obscure the decline in the number enrolled. Willertz, *National Socialism*, 290.

38. VA 222, Oberschopfheim, 23 Sept. 1936; VA 14; VA 89; VA 290; VA 380; VA 385; *Reichsaddressbuch 1934*, 253, and *Reichsaddressbuch 1936*, 264; VA 63; VA 32, Gemeinderatprotokolbuch.

39. Glum, *Der Nationalsozialismus*, 279; *Anzeiger,* 20 Apr. 1935, 12; Max Sering, "Die agrarischen Grundlagen der Sozialverfassung," in *Problem des deutschen Wirtschaftslebens*, 854, cited in Neumann, *Behemoth*, 512. Soon after, living standards leveled off and in some cases even declined, but it was the abrupt rise after 1933 that struck the public imagination.

40. Neumann, *Behemoth*, 510. Trivanovich gives slightly different figures, some of which are estimates. *Economic Development of Germany*, 61.

41. *Statistisches Jahrbuch fuer das Land Baden, 1938*, 218; LCA 104/8 Stadt Lahr, 30 June 1933, 1 June 1934, etc.; *Anzeiger,* 15 July 1935, 8.

42. VA, Arbeitsamt Lahr, 27 Nov. 1934, 11 Feb. 1935, 18 Oct. 1935; VA 62.

43. VA 5; VA 357; VA 358; VA 364; VA 367; interviews, Sept.-Dec. 1973.

44. Grill, *Nazi Movement in Baden*, 378-80.

45. *Zeitung*, 1 Nov. 1933, 5; VA 314, Bezirksamt Lahr, 21 Dec. 1936; VA 63; interview, Nov. 1973.

46. Grill, *Nazi Movement in Baden*, 381.

47. *Anzeiger,* 1 Feb. 1935, 4; 12 Mar. 1935, 7; 28 Mar. 1935, 7; *Zeitung*, 1 Nov. 1933, 5.

48. *Anzeiger,* 27 May 1935, 5; Allen, *Nazi Seizure of Power,* 231, 268-69; interviews, Oct.-Nov. 1973; Vogt, *Burden of Guilt*, 156-57. Engelmann, a half-Jewish German bitterly hostile to the Nazis, acknowledges that he thought the "Winter Aid" program a fine thing when it was introduced in 1933. *In Hitler's Germany*, 15.

49. Engelmann, *In Hitler's Germany*, 150-55.

50. Grill, *Nazi Movement in Baden*, 363-69, 382-83, 408-409.

51. Wunderlich, *Farm Labor In Germany*, 289-90; and Juncovy, *Bavarian Peasantry*, 286.

52. Noakes and Pridham, *Nazism, 1919-1945*, 413-15.

53. VA 32, *Gemeinderatprotokolbuch;* VA 302.

54. Noakes and Pridham, *Nazism, 1919-1945*, 444; Kater, *Nazi Party*, 75-84.

55. That what goes on in human imaginations is more important than objective historical "events" or "facts" is one of the main themes of an excellent historiographical work, Lukacs, *Historical Consciousness*. For a briefer treatment of the same theme, see Norling, *Timeless Problems In History*, chap. 1.

## 9. The Strength of Tradition

1. These endeavors are discussed by Grunberger, *Social History of the Third Reich*, 49-50; and Allen, *Nazi Seizure of Power,* 226.

2. Neumann, *Behemoth*, 366-67, emphasizes the importance of the old elites. Schoenbaum, *Hitler's Social Revolution*, 272-74, stresses the influence of the Nazi arrivistes. Other writers have claimed that the tendency toward greater equality in German society owed more to the Depression than to the Nazis.

3. VA, Gemeinderechnung 1934, 1935; VA 63, 21 July 1935; VA 32, 14 Aug. 1935, and following.

4. Four decades later Stefan Jaeger, who kept careful tabs on Pastor Hirt, acknowledged to one of these writers that Hitler, like everyone else, had made mistakes; but he added quickly that Der Fuehrer deserved praise for subsidizing child bearing and for ending the domination of German society by the "bluebloods." In Jaeger's view, the latter achievement had gone largely unrecognized because history was still written by the "bluebloods." Interview, Aug. 1973.

5. CA, Hirt, 8; VA 63; VA 48, Polizeistrafen; VA 386. The widespread propensity of Germans to see Hitler and the Nazis as bringers of domestic order, peace, and prosperity, and as champions of social and moral values against the rot of the Weimar era, is discussed variously by Ian Kershaw, Ulrich Herbert, and Bessel, who credits the Nazis with sharply curbing ordinary crimes in the Reich, in *Life in the Third Reich*, xiv-xv, 45-46, 97ff.

6. VA 182, Bad. Bezirksamt Lahr, 26 Apr. 1933, 29 July 1933; Bad. Bauernschaft Lahr, 14 Sept. 1933; Landesverband Bad. Tabakbauervereine, Karlsruhe, 8 Sept. 1933, and Oberschopfheim, 3 Apr. 1933; interviews, Nov.-Dec. 1973.

7. VA 48; VA 7; VA 146; VA 154.

8. Allen, *Nazi Seizure of Power,* 256-57.

9. *Anzeiger,* 9 Jan. 1934, 7; *Der Fuehrer,* 7 Oct. 1934, 9.

10. VA 110, Lahr Bad. Bezirksamt, 19 Oct. 1934 to 28 Mar. 1936; VA 258 Oberschopfheim, 18 Nov. 1935; VA 257; VA 389, Gendarmerie Friesenheim; VA 48, Polizeistrafen.

11. VA 289 Minister d. Innern, Karlsruhe, 13 July 1934; VA 63 Oberschopfheim, 17 Nov. 1935; interviews, Sept.-Dec. 1973.

12. Mayer, *They Thought They Were Free,* 52; interviews, Sept.-Dec. 1973.

13. In Korle, a village in Hesse about the size of Oberschopfheim, these conflicts were so intense that they broke down the traditional authority structure of most local families. Youthful enthusiasm for the Nazis began to wane there only when large numbers of men were drafted for military service. Kurt Wagner and Gerhard Wilke, "Dorfleben in Dritten Reich," in *Die Reihen fast Geschlossen,* Detlev Peukert, ed., 93, 98-99.

14. Noakes and Pridham, *Nazism, 1919-1945,* 355, 418; Allen, *Nazi Seizure of Power,* 249-51; Wagner and Wilke, "Dorfleben," 94; and interviews, Sept. 1973.

15. PA, Letter from William Kopf to Wilhelm Messerer, 15 Sept. 1933 in Messerer archives.

16. *Zeitung,* 16 Sept. 1933, 3; *Anzeiger,* 2 Oct. 1935, 6; interviews, Aug.-Sept. 1973. In most of Germany "youth" organizations appear to have borne greater resemblance to those of Oberschopfheim than to those of Thalburg or Lahr. In Marburg Hitler Youth were officially engaged in "fighting against hunger and cold," but in fact did little beyond tack up posters attesting to their "struggle." Willertz, *National Socialism,* 109.

17. Engelmann, *In Hitler's Germany,* 37-38; Lowie, *Toward Understanding Germany,* 332; Wagner and Wilke, "Dorfleben," 98.

18. Noakes and Pridham, *Nazism, 1919-1945,* 355, 429.

19. Grunberger, *Social History of the Third Reich,* 285; Allen, *Nazi Seizure of Power,* 249-50; Badisches Realienbuch; Buehl, Konkordia Verlag, vol. 23, 1927; *Deutsches Lesebuch fuer Volksschulen; Frisch Gesungen, Chorbuch C,* and *Frisch Gesungen, Sangbuch A.*

20. *Deutsches Lesebuch fuer Volksschulen,* 55, 93, 99-100 (textbook for the second class).

21. Noakes and Pridham, *Nazism, 1919-1945,* 433; Kater, *Nazi Party,* 91, 97, 100, 110, 126, 132-33.

22. *Anzeiger,* 11 Nov. 1935, 1.

23. VA 361, Minister d. Innern, Karlsruhe, 27 Dec. 1934, 1 Feb. 1934; Reischsgesetzblatt, 1 June 1933 and 20 June 1933; *Anzeiger,* 24 June 1933, 11.

24. VA, Heiratsregister; PA, Messerer, 252; LCA, Statistisches Jahrbuch (1938), 57; *Zeitung,* 18 May 1932, 5.

25. VA, Heiratsregister.

26. VA, Geburtsregister; *Zeitung,* 20 Apr. 1932, 12 Oct. 1933, 3; *Anzeiger,* 13 Jan. 1934, 3; LCA, Statistisches Jahrbuch (1938), 53.

27. Interestingly, the *native American* birthrate declined in the same years, yet the birth rate of *European immigrants to the United States* remained high. What this proves is uncertain. What it *suggests* is that people continue to have large families as long as they *anticipate* economic improvement.

28. VA 368; interviews, Oct.-Nov. 1973.

29. *Anzeiger,* 4 Oct. 1935, 7; VA 80, Berlin, 14 Dec., 1937. French governments in the 1930s undertook similar measures in an effort to raise the birth rate. They, too, enjoyed little success.

30. VA, Geburtsregister; *Zeitung,* 20 Apr. 1932, 4; LCA, Statisches Jahrbuch (1938), 53; Trivanovich, *Economic Development of Germany,* 53-55. The birth rate did not plummet in the rest of Germany as fast as it did in Oberschopfheim.

31. Wilke, "Village Life in Nazi Germany," 22.

32. *Frankfurter Zeitung*, 6 June 1939, cited in Schoenbaum, *Hitler's Social Revolution*, 184-85.


## 10. World War II and Its Aftermath


1. VA 243, Oberschopfheim, 27 July 1945; VA 346, Oberschopfheim, 15 July 1947; CA, Hirt, 14-15; Roederer, *Ortsgeschichte von Oberschopfheim*, 50. Slightly different numbers are given by different sources.

2. The matter is surveyed by Noakes and Pridham, *Documents on Nazism*, 654-55; and Noakes and Pridham, *Nazism*, 597-98.

3. Willertz, *National Socialism*, 320-21, 351-52, 385-86, 389-401.

4. Interview, May 1988.

5. CA, Hirt, 4, 14; interview, Sept., 1973.

6. *Zeitung*, 27 July 1933, 3.

7. Farquharson, *Plow and the Swastika*, 221-23.

8. This manufacture of red tape existed in other countries too, of course, but the Germans were undisputed world champions in its production. Interview, May 1988.

9. The minutiae of enforcement of these regulations is described in detail by Wunderlich, *Farm Labor in Germany*, 165-66, 196, 243.

10. All these efforts, before the war and during it, and the opposition they aroused among Bavarian peasants, are described at length by Juncovy, *Bavarian Peasantry*, 132-93, 236-55, 340-41. There was much less dairying in Oberschopfheim than in Bavaria, but Nazi efforts to force changes, and the Nazi inspection system, were the same in both places.

11. Juncovy, *Bavarian Peasantry*, 236-55, 348-49; and Wunderlich, *Farm Labor in Germany*, 196-97.

12. All these agricultural conundrums are discussed at some length by Kater, *Nazi Party*, 116-23, 135; and by Noakes and Pridham, *Documents on Nazism*, 648-50.

13. Wunderlich, *Farm Labor in Germany*, 200-202; and Farquharson, *Plow and Swastika*, 224-42.

14. Juncovy, *Bavarian Peasantry*, 50-59.

15. Interview, May 1988. Such subterfuges were too risky to attempt in larger towns and cities. There it was often unsafe to confide even in close friends during the war.

16. This condition was far more pronounced in the French village of Peyrane. As in Oberschopfheim, no fighting took place in the village itself; but six men of the village were killed elsewhere during the Fall of France, and some fifteen more were taken to Germany as prisoners of war for the next five years. At home wartime economic regulations forced everyone to break laws almost continuously in order to survive. This caused most people to feel like criminals. Worse, the sharp division between collaborators and resisters produced universal fear and suspicion of even old friends and neighbors. Community spirit was poisoned for many years afterward, and the native pessimism of the populace deepened. Wylie, *Village in the Vaucluse*, 27-30. Similar *tendencies* existed in Oberschopfheim, but were less severe.

17. Kater, *Nazi Party*, 116, 159, 225.

18. Noakes and Pridham, *Documents on Nazism*, 667-69.

19. Juncovy, *Bavarian Peasantry*, 317.

20. Lowie, *Toward Understanding Germany*, 176.

21. Grill, *Nazi Movement in Baden*, 458.

22. Lowie, *Toward Understanding Germany*, 53.

23. Noakes and Pridham, *Documents on Nazism*, 650.

24. Grill doubts that the Nazis could have succeeded. See *Nazi Movement In Baden*, 327-37, 459-60. Farquharson, *Plow and the Swastika*, 183-202, describes and comments on the general Nazi failure but is noncommittal about ultimate possibilities. Elsewhere, he agrees with Grill. See Farquharson, "Agrarian Policy," 254-55. Wunderlich, *Farm Labor in Germany*, 297-355, describes at length all the Nazi efforts to make Germany a pastoral land, and their ultimate failure. Even in the Soviet Union, one of the most regimented societies on earth, the same forces have been at work that are so evident elsewhere. Dunn and Dunn, *Peasants of Central Russia*, 87, 89.

25. Grill, *Nazi Movement in Baden*, 456.

26. In Marburg, the Kreisleiter and the mayor decided to surrender rather than undertake a hopeless resistance. Willertz, *National Socialism*, 499-501. In France in 1940 many mayors thought only of saving their towns and villages and so offered no resistance to the invading Germans, even though this hampered the feeble endeavors of their own armed forces. In the Philippines in December 1941, Gen. Douglas MacArthur attempted to save Manila from destruction by proclaiming it an open city and moving Allied troops away, but the Japanese invaders bombed and shelled it anyway.

27. Interview, May 1988.

28. Peterson, *Limits of Hitler's Power*, 403.

29. CA, Hirt, 15; *Geroldseckerland* 9, (1966-1967): 191.

30. VA 243.

31. VA 244.

32. For a description of the conduct of French soldiers in the spring of 1945, see Willis, *French Zone of Occupation in Germany*, 118-20.

33. Interview, May 1988. Willis, *French Zone of Occupation in Germany*, 115-17, points out that north African troops were used mostly in areas well north of Oberschopfheim and that most of the troops that invaded Lahr county came from the French Resistance. Nonetheless, there was a considerable sprinkling of Africans among the latter. Senegalese were not used in the invasion of Germany in 1945.

34. There are appalling descriptions of what took place in the east in Toland, *Last 100 Days*, 8-9, 22-23, 25, 30-31, 36-37, 48-50, 71-72, 128-29, 155-57, 186, 302-303, 354-55, 444, 544. In Vienna women fled to the roofs of churches and other tall buildings in the hope that Russian soldiers in the streets below would be too drunk or too lazy to come up after them.

35. Hoferer et al., *Kennzeichen*, 168-69.

36. VA 309.

37. Municipalities as well as private individuals often used the necessities of war to straighten their accounts. The Marburg city government, for instance, collected taxes routinely during the war, but since there was no new construction the money was used to retire the city debt. Willertz, *National Socialism*, 479. Many French peasants, who were able to accumulate some extra money during the war but unable to spend it on nonexistent or scarce consumer goods, used it to repair or improve their houses instead. Mendras, *Vanishing Peasant*, 207.

38. VA 53A; Industrie Betriebe, 16 June 1945.

39. Nurge, *Blue Light in the Village*, 132-33, notes that such was the case in the Hessian village of Burkhards. Of course this does not diminish the consideration that both Germans and Russians often treated each other's prisoners abominably in camps and elsewhere.

40. Interview, May 1988. See also Wimschneider, *Herbstmilch*, 105-12. This description of the refugee problem in and around Oberschopfheim could be applied, totally unchanged, to the village of Burgbach, near Stuttgart or to Korle in Hesse. Like Oberschopfheim, Burgbach was not bombed in the war, but nearby Stuttgart was, just as Lahr was near Oberschopfheim. The principal difference between the two places

was that Burgbach was in the American Occupation Zone. Spindler, *Burgbach*, 12, 18-21. In the case of Korle the only significant difference from Oberschopfheim was that most natives were Lutherans and most of the unwanted "guests" were Catholic. Wagner and Wilke, "Dorfleben," 103-4.

41. The state of German agriculture throughout the French zone of occupation, and the influence on it of French policy, is discussed by Willis, *French Zone of Occupation in Germany*, 177-80, 208-13.

42. Willis gives the higher figures. *French Zone of Occupation in Germany*, 208-209. *Bundesrepublik Deutschland*, 725-26, claims that throughout Baden the *average* caloric intake was below 1000.

43. Willis says the French cut less than 20 percent of the annual growth of German forests. He adds that the wood was badly needed in France. *French Zone of Occupation in Germany*, 223. Oberschopfheimers believed that the hated French cut far more than this.

44. Ortssippenbuch, Oberweier, 54.

45. Interview, July 1973.

46. Interview, May 1988.

47. Willis, *French Zone of Occupation in Germany*, 210.

48. For a lengthy discussion of French objectives, the many intramural disputes about them, and the subterfuges employed by the French to pursue them in the face of British and American disapproval, see Willis, *French Zone of Occupation in Germany*, especially 42-75, 101-102, 120-21, 134-37, 154-55, 179-80, 208-13.

49. Ibid., 247.

50. Ibid., 182-83.

51. *Geroldseckerland* 29 (1987): 184-86.

52. Willis, *French Zone of Occupation in Germany*, 233-37.

53. Grosser, *Germany In Our Time*, 50-52; and Willis, *French Zone of Occupation in Germany*, 124-30, 138-44, 211-12.

54. Willis, *French Zone of Occupation in Germany*, 248.

55. VA 149, 5 July 1945, 28 Aug. 1945.

56. Interview, May 1988. Interestingly, local people who spoke well of Holzenthaler when interrogated by the French refused to offer opinions of any kind about erstwhile Farm Leader Franz K. Roederer II. How much more concerned most ordinary people are with local affairs than with national or global ideologies was shown in a French village about the same size as Oberschopfheim, where a local maquis leader seized the village government at the end of the war. His superiors ordered him to arrest some local people as "collaborators." He tore the order to pieces and became thereby an instant village hero. Wylie, *Village in the Vaucluse*, 210.

57. Interview, May 1988.

58. VA 230, Oberschopfheim, 1946; VA 235, Oberschopfheim, 1945; VA 243, 25 Feb. 1946; VA 242, 17 May 1946; VA 245, 20 Mar. 1947ff; VA 242, 27 May 1946; VA 244, 7 June 1946; VA 246, 28 Sept. 1945; VA 286, Landratsamt Lahr, 21 Apr. 1947, 8 Nov., 1947.

59. *Bundesrepublik Deutschland*, 725-26.

60. Interview, Sept. 1973.

61. Grosser, *Germany In Our Time*, 53; Engelmann, *In Nazi Germany*, 331-33.

62. Kernan, *France on Berlin Time*, 115-16.

## 11. The Breakdown of the Old Order

1. Interview, May 1988.

2. This point is discussed by Blackbourn, "Peasants and Politics in Germany," 53. See also Weber, *Peasants into Frenchmen*.

3. Willis, *French Zone of Occupation in Germany,* 145-46, 223, 228-30; LCA, Wehrle, 149-50; interviews, Dec. 1973.

4. VA, Flachennutzungplan, 1966.

5. This whole problem is surveyed by Werner Berkenmaier in the *German Tribune* 15 May 1988, 4; by Jorg Bischoff, "Ethnic German Migrants," ibid., 13 June 1988, 4; and by Kusch, "Ethnic German Migrants from East," ibid., 31 July 1988, 5.

6. Grill, *Nazi Movement in Baden,* 291-92. After the revolutionary and Napoleonic eras in France comparable atrophy overtook village governments. They became mainly registrars of formalities and conveyers of orders from Paris, to the growing indifference of their inhabitants. Sheppard, *Lourmarin in the Eighteenth Century,* 217-18. As in so many such developments, rural and small town France anticipated Oberschopfheim by anywhere from two to five generations.

7. Nurge, *Blue Light in the Village,* 11. Of course the same is true in many other countries. Even in mid-century, in such a traditionally agricultural land as Poland, a survey of eighty villages in its southwestern sector, 1947-1957, showed that half the families there derived some of their income from industrial employment. Warriner, *Economics of Peasant Farming,* xxi.

8. For instance, Dovring, *Land and Labor,* 382-84.

9. Dovring notes that when the rulers of the USSR gave peasants on the collective farms their own family plots the peasants promptly reverted to traditional ways of farming on these plots while studiously neglecting the collectives that were farmed by machinery. *Land and Labor,* 383-84. Wylie, *Village in the Vaucluse,* emphasizes that its inhabitants so hate, despise, and mistrust all French government functionaries and all cooperative efforts that they ignore any advice tendered to them about how to increase yields or improve their lot in any way. See also Mendras, *Vanishing Peasant,* 177, 179-87; Spindler, *Burgbach,* 46, 78-80; J. Friedl, *Kippel,* 87, 108.

10. Nurge, *Blue Light in the Village,* 38.

11. For a discussion of these views among some French farmers, see Mendras, *Vanishing Peasant,* 187-88, 235.

12. Jeggle, "Rules of the Village," 283.

13. Nurge, *Blue Light in the Village,* 25. J. Friedl, *Kippel,* observed the same change in the Swiss mountain hamlet, 91-103. Such attitudes were common in the French countryside well before 1914. See Weber, *Peasants into Frenchmen,* 22, 174, 186-87, 246. Country girls talked openly of marrying someone from the city who could rescue them from bucolic drudgery and monotony. If they did marry a country man, they "looked at the gateway (indicating the size of the groom's farm) more than at the man," 246.

14. Spindler, *Burgbach,* notes that the same attitude existed in the somewhat larger village of Burgbach, near Stuttgart. Developments there after World War II, and the response of local people to them, were remarkably similar to what took place in Oberschopfheim in the same decades, 14-21, 70-84.

15. *Geroldseckerland* 15 (1973): 98-99.

16. This was also true in Burgbach. See Spindler, *Burgbach,* 81.

17. The basic optimism of Oberschopfheimers contrasts vividly with the pessimism of many French peasants in this respect. Despite the frequency of wars along the Rhine and French destruction of their fruit trees in 1945, Oberschopfheimers planted them anew. In Peyrane local farmers refused to plant apricot trees though both soil and climate are ideal for them, on the grounds that wars, natural disasters, or some stupid government policy would surely destroy the trees before they could bear fruit. Wylie, *Village in the Vaucluse,* 33.

18. Hoferer et al., *Kennezeichen,* 41.

19. Ibid., 180-81.

20. In Burkhards, where farms were larger, much new wealth was spent buying land and farm machinery rather than on house repairs and automobiles. Nurge, *Blue Light in the Village,* 108.

21. Interview, May 1988. The old gentleman who related this added that, as an adult, he had taken his first vacation in 1960. He had celebrated by going to a town five miles distant.

22. Hoferer et al., *Kennezeichen*, 51.

23. Interview, May 1988.

24. Spindler relates that he and his research aides gave an elaborate series of questionnaires and tests to schoolchildren in Burgbach. Most of them said that they thought those values and pursuits associated with tradition, the countryside, open air, and the simple life were superior to those associated with cities, factories, and offices. However, when they were asked what sort of houses they wanted to live in and what kinds of work they would prefer, most opted for what is modern, urban, and technical rather than simple or "natural." The reasons they cited were pragmatic: easier work, higher pay, cleaner surroundings, and more time off. *Burgbach*, 86-98, 118-32. J. Friedl's impression of the Swiss mountaineers of Kippel was much the same. *Kippel*, 6-7, 76-82, 112-14.

## 12. A New Age Emerges

1. Nurge, *Blue Light In the Village*, 28, 137, recorded with some dismay that in Burkhards manure piles were as prevalent as ever in the late 1960s, even in front of newly built houses. She ascribed it to the strength of tradition.

2. Many particulars and statistics about the "economic miracle" are given in Laqueur, *Germany Today*, 32, 176ff.; Grosser, *Germany in Our Time*, 176; and Dornberg, *New Germans*, 87.

3. Jeggle, "Rules of the Village," in Evans and Lee, *German Peasantry*, 275, notes that such was decidedly the case in the Bavarian Palatinate village of Kiebingen. It was in Oberschopfheim too.

4. Nurge, *Blue Light in the Village*, 123.

5. *German Tribune*, 18 Feb. 1988, 12.

6. These convictions and wishes are ascribed to West Germans by Dornberg, *New Germans*, 100, 117.

7. All these sentiments were expressed repeatedly by various of the fifty West Germans chosen at random in Heidelberg for interviews in the late 1960s. Neven-du Mont, *After Hitler*, 18, 68, 77-78, 89-90, 131, 181-84, 189, 193, 227-29, 239-40, 242, 249, 252, 265-66, 275, 286-87, 316.

8. Laqueur, *Germany Today*, 79-80, 188-89, 195-96.

9. Ibid., 49, also 50, 59.

10. Nurge, *Blue Light in the Village*, 96.

11. Neven-du Mont, 49, 101-102, 150, 192, 216, 220.

12. Since 1949 the German Federal Republic has paid about 80,000,000,000 marks to Jews at home and abroad in reparation for the crimes of the Nazis. Some 20,000,000,000 more will probably be paid in decades to come, though the well-publicized embezzlement of some 33 million DM in the 1980s by Werner Nachmann, chairman of the General Council of Jews in Berlin, is not apt to heighten a sense of obligation about the matter. See Gerda-Marie Schonfeld, "DM 33 Million Compensation Cash Swindle Revealed," in *German Tribune*, 5 June 1988, 4.

13. Interviews, Dec. 1973, May 1988.

14. PA, Kirchenvisitationen, book 17.

15. Dornberg, *New Germans*, 99-100, 102; Neven-du Mont, 189, 200, 317.

16. PA, Kirchenvisitationen, book 17.

17. In the French village of Peyrane it was political animosities that threatened to

produce fights and riots that would destroy town clubs. Wylie, *Village in the Vancluse*, 211. In Oberschopfheim only religious feeling could arouse the populace comparably. It is also noteworthy that in a community where it had always been close to impossible to guard any secret for long, nobody has ever discovered who bombed the church tower.

18. Nurge, *Blue Light in the Village*, 144, 150.

19. CA, Hirt, 8.

20. Interviews, Aug.-Dec. 1973; May 1988.

21. Interview, May 1988.

22. Interviews, May 1988.

23. Interview, May 1988.

24. VA, Allgemeine Verwaltung, no. 6.

25. This was candidly acknowledged by the pastor, who surely would have been pleased had he been able to claim the former. Interview, May 1988.

26. Flachennutzungsplan Oberschopfheim Kreis Lahr, 1966.

27. Eltern No. 10, Oct. 1973, 10-12; Laqueur, *Germany Today*, 23; *German Tribune*, 21 Feb., 1988, 5.

28. Redfield, *Peasant Society and Culture*, 137.

29. Interview, May 1988.

30. Spindler, *Burgbach*, 51-59, 84-85.

31. Hoferer et al., *Kennezeichen*, 93.

32. At least so it seems in Oberschopfheim. Spindler, *Burgbach*, 60-69, indicates that many of the people of Burgbach are still attached to the old home remedies and have not yet surrendered unconditionally to "medical science."

33. Nurge, *Blue Light in the Village*, notes, 74-75, that the same attitude prevailed among the women of Burkhards. See also Wylie, *Village in the Vaucluse*, 37.

34. This dolorous theme pervades the reminiscenes, published in 1987, of a peasant woman who had lived a long life of hard work and many cares. See Wimschneider, *Herbstmilch*.

35. Redfield holds that in societies where the future is expected to be like the past, changes, in fact, do take place slowly and that it is only where changes are desired and *expected* that they take place rapidly. See *Peasant Society and Culture*. Certainly this was true in the Swiss mountain village of Kippel, J. Friedl, *Kippel*, 110, 120-21. 123-27. The Russian countryside has been even more resistant to modernizing influences than has the German, Dunn and Dunn, *Peasants of Central Russia*, 61-62, 93.

## Ruminations

1. Walker, *German Home Towns*, 429-31, contends that the multitude of demographic, industrial, political, and social changes that have swept over Germany since 1945 have shattered "home town" (pro-Nazi) attitudes and influences in German society, though he does not speculate about what might replace them.

2. For instance, Hans Stercken, chairman of the Bundestag Foreign Affairs Committee. See *German Tribune*, Mar. 17, 1991, 2.

3. All these problems are discussed briefly in the *German Tribune*, Jan. 20, 1991, 6, 14, 15; Feb. 24, 1991, 3; Mar. 10, 1991, 4; Mar. 17, 1991, 4.

# BIBLIOGRAPHY

## Primary Sources

*Village archives, courthouse file folders*

2   Armenkinderpflege, 1917-1939

4   Unterstuetzungen einzelner Personen, 1929-1947

7   Unterstuetzungen einzelner Personen, 1933-1934

9   Landesbauordnung, 1869-1948

13   Baudarlehen, 1922-1928

14   Baudarlehen gesuche, 1929-1949

16   Foerderung des Wohnungsbaus durch Darlehen, Reichszuschuesse, 1925-1945

17   Massnahmen gegen Wohnungsmangel, Zwangswirtschaft, Darlehen, 1926-1931

24   Baugesuche und Genehmigungen, 1930-1938

26   Feuerschau und Schaden, 1856-1946

27   Brandfaelle, 1860-1950

28   Feuerwehr, 1920-1944

31   Gemeinderatprotokolbuch, 1929-1935

33   Verpachtung der Gemeindejagd, 1889-1938

34   Wildschadenschaetzer und Jagdaufseher, 1896-1949

40   Bad. Waldbesitzerverband, 1948-1949

41   Gemeindewald, 1876-1945

48   Ortsbereisungen, 1867-1936; Polizeistraftabellen

50   Ortsbereisungen, 1924-1929

62   Verband Badisches Gemeinden, 1930-1940

63   Oeffentliche Bekanntmachungen, 1934-1947

68   Steinsetzer, 1920-1932

71   Brunnenmeister, 1933-1940

76   Gemeindesatzung, Besoldung, 1922-1949

77   Fuersorgekasse, 1924-1949

78   Gemeinderat

89   Gemeinderueckstaende, 1926-1949

90   Gemeinderechnungswesen, 1916-1950

91 Kassenstuerze, 1928-1943
96 Ausgestellte Steuerkarten, 1925-1953
100 Verlosung der Allmend, 1904-1950
102 Holzkompetenzen, 1873-1920
103 Buergernutzen, 1930-1947
110 Ausgabe von Notgeld, Werbung fuer die Sparkassen, 1933-1945
111 Gewerbebetriebe, 1910-1949
121 Gewerbeanzeigen, 1920-1949
122 Sonntagsruhe, 1928-1949
125 Erwerbslosenfuersorge, 1923-1950
129 Arbeitsbeschaffungsprogramm, 1933-1944
136 Katholische Pfarrei, 1837-1950
141 Kirche und Pfarrhaus (Unterhaltung), 1923-1949
146 Schuldienst, 1930-1942
147 Schulkurse, 1841-1947
148 Schulpruefung, 1851-1929
149 (Denazification)
150 Schulreinigung, 1900-1949
153 Schularzt und Gesundheitspflege, 1924-1938
154 Lehrerbeitraege, 1931-1943
160 Kleinkinderschule, 1885-1948
162 Landwirtschaftliche Schulen, 1878-1950
174 Entwaesserung, 1919-1941
175 Entwaesserung, 1927-1949
178 Rebkrankheiten, 1926-1950
182 Tabakanbau, 1930-1949
202 Trinkwasserversorgung, 1872-1949
210 Schlachtvieh und Fleischbeschau, 1929-1950
216 Krankheiten, 1927-1948
217 Impfgesetz, 1929-1948
222 Friedhof und Friedhofordnung
224 Dienst des Leichenschauers, 1927-1940
230 Entmilitarisierung, 1945-1950
235 Anordnungen der Militaerregierungen, 1945-1950
242 Reinigung des Personals d. NSDAP, 1947-1949
243 Beschlagnahme u. Zaehlung, 1945-1948
245 Entnazifizierung, 1945-1950
246 Requisitionen, 1945-1947
256 Sammlungen, Lotterien, Lichtspielwesen, 1921-1950
257 Zigeunerplage, Bettler, 1926-1949
258 Meldewesen, Wanderbuecher, Fremdenverkehrsstatistik, 1926-1949
261 Gesetz ueber Schusswaffen, brennbare Fluessigkeiten, 1931-1946
264 Weltliche Sonn- und Feiertage, 1929-1949
268 Wegepolizeiordnung, 1935-1949
278 Reichstagswahlen, 1928-1930

281   Reichspraesidentenwahl, Volksabstimmung, 1925-1934
285   Landtagswahlen, 1929-1934
286   Landtagswahlen, 1946-1947
289   Beflaggung, Schmueckung, 1929-1949
290   Vertretung des Staates und Anfechtungsfristen, 1948
292   Kreisrat und Wahl der Bezirks-und Kreisabgeordneten, 1929-1939
298   Vollzug von Steuergesetzen, 1929-1949
299   Hunde- Wehr- und Schlachtsteuer, 1929-1939
302   Gebaeudesondersteuer, 1925-1942
303   Gebaeudesondersteuer, 1930-1942
306   Auswanderung, 1922-1949
307   Volkszaehlung, 1925-1946
308   Gemeindefinanzstatistik, 1925-1932
309   Verschiedene Statistische Nachweisungen, 1930-1950
314   Verwendung von Stiftungsmittel, 1856-1949
331   Strassenverbesserungen, 1935-1942
345   Gebaeudeversicherungsgesetz, 1924-1949
346   Feuerversicherung, 1927-1949
349   Sonstige Versicherungen
351   Hochwasser, 1906-1948
357   Fuersorge, 1929-1945
358   Nothilfe und Arbeitslosenhilfe, 1931-1942
364   Reichsfuersorgestatistik, 1926-1948
366   Fuersorge fuer Kinderreiche Familien, 1928-1938
367   Kinderfuersorge, 1929-1950
362   Darlehen
373   Streitigkeiten der Gemeinde, 1931-1948
380   Entschuldung und Zwangsversteigerungen, 1747-1949
385   Mahnregister, Prozesstabellen, Arresttabellen
386   Strafe
389   Buergermeisteramtlich erledigte Strafsachen und Beleidigungsklagen,
        1928-1950
A32   Buergerausschussprotokolbuch
        Flaechennutzungsplan Oberschopfheim, Kreis Lahr, 1966
        Geburtsregister
A31   Gemeinderatprotokolbuch
        Handwerkskammer im Allgemein, 1923
        Heiratsregister Rechnungsjahr, 1929-1938
        Kulturbauamt Offenburg
        Allgemeine Verwaltung, NR. 6
        Roederer, J. *Ortsgeschichte von Oberschopfheim*. Freiburg: author, 1956.
53A   (Statistics for French authorities)

*Church archives, rectory files*

Taufbuch (Baptismal Book)
Hirt, H. "Ortschronik: 1933-1949" (unpublished diary).
Kirchenvisitationen und Statistik (record book). Vol. 17., 1853-1948.


*Private archives, individually kept*

Deutsche Jugend Kraft (DJK). "Protokolbuch: 1927-1933." In Musser family
    archives.
Meister, Richard. Village History.
Messerer, Wilhelm. "Ortschronik von Oberschopfheim," 1938. Unpublished
    manuscript in two versions. Revised version quoted unless page number is
    followed by "U".
Ortssippenbuch Oberweier.
Schleicher, F. "Verkuendbuch" 1929-1931 and 1932-1936. Unpublished notes and
    diary.


*Lahr city archives, courthouse files*

36-38  Badisches Statistische. Landesamt, *Statistisches Jahrbuch fuer Baden*, Vol.
          42-44, 1925, 1930, and 1938. Karlsruhe.
   41   Badisches Statistische Landesamt. *Badische Gemeindestatistik*. Karsruhe:
          Bd. Kommunalverlag, 1927.
  579   Jahresbericht des Badischen. Weinbauinstitut. 1928.
  669   Die Wirtschaftswende, 1931.
  693   Verhaeltnisse der Zigarrenarbeiter.
  744   Mitteilungen der Handelskammer Lahr, 1930.
  749   Wirtschaftswirke, 1934-1935.
  800   Tabelle der Abgabe zur Arbeitslosenhilfe, 1932.
104/8  Stadt Lahr, Landesarbeitsamt
          S. W. Adressbuch von Lahr, 1931 and 1934.
          Stadt Lahr. *Statistische Zahlen ueber Lahr/Schwarzwald*, 1963 and 1965.
Wehrle, Winfried. "Die Industrie der Stadt Lahr, 1774-1960." Ph.D. diss.

## Secondary Sources

Abel, Theodore. *The Nazi Movement*. New York: Atherton, 1966.
Allen, William S. *The Nazi Seizure of Power: The Experience of a Single German Town,
    1930-1935*. Chicago: Quadrangle, 1965.
Anchor, Robert. *Germany Confronts Modernization: German Culture and Society,
    1790-1880*, Lexington, Mass.: Heath, 1972.
Appel, Richard. *Baden-Wuerttemberg, Land und Volk in Geschichte und Gegenwart*.
    Karlsruhe: Verlag G. Brown, 1961.

————. Badisches Statliche Landesamt. *Baden in Wort und Zahl.* Karlsruhe: Verlag C. Mueller, 1928.

————. *Badische Gemeindestatistik.* Karlsruhe: Bd. Kommunalverlag, 1927.

————. *Badische Landwirtschaft.* Vol. 3. Karlsruhe: Verlag Macklatsche, 1936.

Baas, K., ed. *Badisches Realienbuch.* Vol. 23. Konkordia: Buehl, 1927.

Baeuerle, P. Michael. "Geiste im Pfarrhof." In *Pfarrfuehrer.* Freiburg: Verlag Hombach, 1941.

Barbu, Zevedei. "Democracy and Dictatorship." In *An Age of Controversy,* ed. Gordon Wright and Arthur Mejia, Jr. New York: Dodd, Mead, 1971.

Barkin, Kenneth. *The Controversy Over German Industrialization, 1890-1902.* Chicago: Univ. of Chicago Press, 1970.

Barraclough, Geoffrey. *Medieval Germany, 911-1250.* Vol 2. Oxford: Basil Blackwell, 1938.

————. "Mandarins and Nazis: Part 1," *New York Review of Books,* 19 October 1972, 37-43.

————. "The Liberals and German History, Part 2," *New York Review of Books,* 2 November 1972, 32-38.

————. "A New View of German History, Part 3," *New York Review of Books.* 16 November 1972, 25-31.

Bell, Rudolph M. *Fate and Honor, Family and Village: Demographic and Cultural Change in Rural Italy Since 1800.* Chicago: Univ. Chicago Press, 1979.

Berkner, Lutz K. "Inheritance, Land Tenure and Peasant Family Structure: A German Regional Comparison." In *Family and Inheritance: Rural Society in Western Europe, 1200-1800,* ed. Jack Goody, Joan Thirsk, and E.P. Thompson. New York: Cambridge Univ. Press, 1976.

Bessel, Richard, ed. *Life In the Third Reich.* New York: Oxford Univ. Press, 1987.

————. "Living With the Nazis: Some Recent Writing on the Social History of the Third Reich," *European Historical Quarterly* 14 (1984): 211-20.

————. "Violence as Propaganda: The Role of the Storm Troopers in the Rise of National Socialism." In *The Formation of the Nazi Constituency, 1919-1933.* Towata, N.J.: Barnes and Noble, 1986.

Blackbourn, David. *Class, Religion and Local Politics in Wilhelmine Germany: The Centre Party in Wurttemberg before 1914.* New Haven: Yale Univ. Press, 1980.

Blackbourn, David, "Peasants and Politics in Germany, 1871-1914," *European History Quarterly* 14 (1984): 47-75.

Blackbourn, David. *Populists and Patricians: Essays in Modern German History.* London: Allen and Unwin, 1987.

Boese, Georg. *In Blauen Dienst.* Stuttgart: Deutsche Veriagsanstalt, 1957.

Bracher, Karl. *The German Dictatorship.* New York: Praeger, 1970.

Bridenthal, Renate. "Beyond Kinder, Kueche, Kirche: Weimar Women at Work," *Central European History* (June 1973): 148-66.

Brittain, Vera. *Testament of Youth.* London: Wideview, 1978.

Broszat, Martin. *German National Socialism, 1919-1945.* Santa Barbara, Calif.: Clio, 1966.

————. *The Hitler State.* New York: Longmans, 1981.

Carr, William. *Arms, Autarky and Aggression*. New York: Norton, 1972.

Catt, Cathleen S. "Farmers and Factory Workers." In *The German Peasantry*, ed. Richard J. Evans and W.R. Lee. New York: St. Martin's, 1986.

Childers, Thomas, ed. *The Formation of the Nazi Constituency, 1919-1933*. Towata, N.J.: Barnes and Noble, 1986.

Childs, David. *Germany Since 1918*. New York: Harper and Row, 1971.

Crew, Daniel F. *Town in the Ruhr: A Social History of Bochum, 1860-1914*. Ann Arbor, Mich.: University Microfilms, 1975.

Crosby, Alfred W. *Epidemic and Peace, 1918*. Westport, Conn.: Greenwood, 1976.

Dahrendorf, Ralf. *Society and Democracy in Germany*. Garden City, N.Y.: Doubleday, 1967.

*Deutsches Lesebuch fuer Volksschulen: 2. Schuljahr.* Lahr: Verlag von Moritz Schauenberg, 1937.

*Deutsches Reichsaddressbuch fuer Industrie, Gewerbe und Handel*. Berlin, 1930-1936.

Diaz, May N. "Introduction: Economic Relations in Peasant Society." In *Peasant Society: A Reader*, ed. Jack M. Potter, May N. Diaz, and George M. Foster. Boston: Little Brown, 1967.

Dornberg, John. *The New Germans: Thirty Years After.* New York: Macmillan, 1976.

Dorpalen, Andreas. *Hindenburg and the Weimar Republic*. Princeton, N.J.: Princeton Univ. Press, 1964.

Dovring, Folke. *Land and Labor in Europe in the Twentieth Century*. The Hague: Martinus Nijhof, 1965.

Dunn, Stephen P., and Ethel Dunn. *The Peasants of Central Russia*. New York: Holt, Rhinehart and Winston, 1967.

Durrenberger, E. Paul. *Chayanov, Peasants and Economic Anthropology*. New York: Academic, 1984.

Edel, Fritz. *German Labor Service*. 2d ed. Berlin: Terramara, 1938.

Eley, Geoff. *From Unification to Nazism: Reinterpreting the German Past*. Boston: Allen and Unwin, 1986.

Ember, Carol, and Melvin Ember. *Cultural Anthropology*. 5th ed. N.J.: Prentice-Hall, 1988.

Engelmann, Bernt. *In Hitler's Germany: Daily Life in the Third Reich*. New York: Pantheon, 1986.

Engelsing, R. *Kleine Wirtschafts und Sozialgeschichte Deutschlands*. Bremen: Schmalfelt, 1968.

Erbe, Rene. *Die National Sozialistiche Wirtschaftspolitik, 1933-1939, im Lichte der Modernen Theorie*. Zurich: Polygraphischer Verlag, 1958.

Evans, Richard J., and W.R. Lee, eds. *The German Family*. Towata, N.J.: Barnes and Noble, 1981.

———. *The German Peasantry*. New York: St. Martin's, 1986.

*Facts About Germany*. Bonn: Government Press and Information Office, 1972.

Fallers, L.A. "Are African Cultivators to Be Called 'Peasants'?" In *Peasant Society: A Reader*, ed. Jack M. Potter, May N. Diaz, and George M. Foster. Boston: Little Brown, 1967.

Falter, Jurgen W. "The National Socialist Mobilization of New Voters, 1928-1933."

In *The Formation of the Nazi Constituency, 1919-1933*. Towata, N.J.: Barnes and Noble, 1986.

Farquharson, J.E. "The Agrarian Policy of National Socialist Germany." In *Peasants and Lords in Modern Germany*, ed. Robert C. Moeller. Boston: Allen and Unwin, 1986.

Farquharson, J.E. *The Plow and the Swastika: The NSDAP and Agriculture in Germany, 1928-1945*. Beverly Hills, Calif.: Sage, 1976.

Farrar, L.L. *The Short War Illusion*. Santa Barbara, Calif.: Clio, 1973.

Fischer, Fritz. *Germany's Aims In the First World War: The Controversy over Germany's Aims in the First World War*. Trans. Lancelot L. Farras, Robert Kimber, and Rita Kimber. New York: Norton, 1974.

———. *World Power or Decline?* New York: Norton, 1974.

Flenly, Ralph. *Modern German History*. New York: Dutton, 1964.

Forster, Robert, and Orest Ranum, eds. *Rural Society in France*. Baltimore: Johns Hopkins Univ. Press, 1977.

*Foster, George M.* "Peasant Society and the Image of the Limited Good." In *Peasant Society: A Reader*, ed. Jack M. Potter, May N. Diaz, and George M. Foster. Boston: Little Brown, 1967.

Foster, George M. "Introduction: What Is a Peasant?" In *Peasant Society: A Reader*, ed. Jack M. Potter, May N. Diaz, and George M. Foster. Boston: Little Brown, 1967.

*Freiburger Zeitung*. "Die Industrie in Oberbaden 3." Sonderheft. Freiburg: Universitaetdruckerei Poppen und Ortmann, 1927.

Friedl, Ernestine. *Vasilika: A Village in Modern Greece*. New York: Holt, Rhinehart and Winston, 1962.

Friedl, John. *Kippel: A Changing Village in the Alps*. New York: Holt, Rhinehart and Winston, 1974.

*Der Fuehrer.*

Ganter, Horst, and Peter Daferner. *Ottenheim*. Selbsverlag, 1986.

Garraty, John. "New Deal, National Socialism, and the Great Depression," *American Historical Review* 78 (Oct. 1973): 908-44.

*German Tribune*. 1988-1991.

*Geroldseckerland*. Lahr, 1970-1991.

Geyl, Pieter. *Encounters In History*. New York: Meridian, 1961.

Gies, Horst. "The NSDAP and Agrarian Organizations in the Final Phase of the Weimar Republic." In *Nazism and the Third Reich*, ed. Henry A. Turner. New York: Quadrangle, 1972.

Glum, Friederich. *Der Nationalsozialismus, Werden und Vergehen*. Munich: Verlag Beck, 1962.

Goerlitz, Walter. *The German General Staff, 1657-1945*. New York: Praeger, 1955.

Goody, Jack, Joan Thirsk, and E.P. Thompson, eds. *Family and Inheritance: Rural Society in Western Europe, 1200-1800*. New York: Cambridge Univ. Press, 1976.

Grill, Jonpeter. *The Nazi Movement in Baden, 1920-1945*. Chapel Hill: Univ. North Carolina Press, 1983.

Grosser, Alfred. *Germany In Our Time: A Political History of the Postwar Years*. New York: Praeger, 1971.

Grunberger, Richard. *A Social History of the Third Reich*. London: Weidenfeld and Nicolson, 1971.

Guillebaud, C.W. *The Economic Recovery of Germany, from 1933 to the Incorporation of Austria in March 1938*. London: Macmillan, 1939.

———. *The Social Policy of Nazi Germany*. London: Cambridge Univ. Press, 1941.

Haffner, Sebastian. *The Meaning of Hitler.* Cambridge, Mass.: Harvard Univ. Press, 1979.

Hale, Oron J. *The Captive Press In the Third Reich*. Princeton, N.J.: Princeton Univ. Press, 1964.

Hales, E.E.Y. *The Catholic Church In the Modern World*. Garden City, N.Y.: Hanover, 1958.

Hamilton, Richard F. *Who Voted for Hitler?* Princeton, N.J.: Princeton Univ. Press, 1982.

Heberle, R. *From Democracy to Nazism*. Baton Rouge: Louisiana State Univ. Press, 1945.

Heinrichs, Pfusch, et al. *Frisch Gesungen. Chorbuch C.* 3 Auflage. Hanover: Verlag C. Mener, 1936.

———. *Frisch Gesungen, Singbuch A.* 78 Auflage. Hanover: Verlag C. Mener, 1937.

Heiss, Friederich. *Deutschland Zwischen Nacht und Tag*. Berlin: Volk und Reich Verlag, 1934.

Heizmann, Ludwig. *Der Amtsbezirk Lahr in Vergangenheit und Gegenwart*. Lahr: Anzeiger Verlag, 1929.

Heyen, Franz. *Nationalsozialismus im Alltag*. Boppard am Rhein: Boldt, 1967.

Higonnet, Patrice L-R. *Pont-de-Montvert: Social Structure and Politics in a French Village, 1700-1914*. Cambridge: Harvard Univ. Press, 1971.

Hildebrand, Klaus. *The Third Reich*. London: Allen and Unwin, 1984.

Hilfswerk of the Evangelical Churches in Germany. *Living Conditions in Germany, 1947*. Stuttgart, 1947.

Hoferer, Horst, et al. *Kennzeichen O.G.* Loerrach: Waldemar Lutz, 1987.

Holborn, Hajo. *Germany and Europe*. Garden City, N.Y.: Doubleday, 1970.

———. *A History of Modern Germany*. 3 vols. New York: Knopf, 1959.

———, ed. *Republic to Reich: The Making of the Nazi Revolution*. New York: Vintage, 1973.

Hook, Sidney. *The Hero In History*. New York: Humanities, 1950.

Hundesnurscher, Franz. *Die Judischen Gemeinden in Baden*. Stuttgart: W. Kohlhammer Verlag, 1968.

Hunt, Richard N. *German Social Democracy, 1918-1933*. New Haven: Yale Univ. Press, 1964.

Jarman, T.L. *The Rise and Fall of Nazi Germany*. New York: New York Univ. Press, 1956.

Jeggle, Utz. "The Rules of the Village." In *The German Peasantry*, ed. Richard J. Evans and W.R. Lee. New York: St. Martin's, 1986.

Jolas, Tina, and Francoise Zonabend. "Tillers of the Fields and Woodspeople." In *Rural Society in France*, ed. Robert Forster and Orest Ranum. Baltimore: Johns Hopkins, 1977.

Jones, Larry Eugene. "Crisis and Realignment: Agrarian Splinter Parties in the

Late Weimar Republic, 1928-1933." In *Peasants and Lords in Modern Germany*, ed. Robert C. Moeller. Boston: Allen and Unwin, 1986.

Juncovy, Jon. *The Bavarian Peasantry Under National Socialist Rule, 1933-1945*. Ann Arbor, Mich.: University Microfilms, 1987.

Kaschuba, Wolfgang. "Peasants and Others." In *The German Peasantry*, ed. Richard J. Evans and W.R. Lee. New York: St. Martin's, 1986.

Kater, Michael H. *The Nazi Party: A Social Profile of Members and Leaders, 1919-1945*. Cambridge: Harvard Univ. Press, 1983.

Kele, Max. *Nazis and Workers*. Chapel Hill: Univ. of North Carolina Press, 1972.

Kent, George O. *Bismarck and His Times*. Carbondale, Ill.: Southern Illinois Univ. Press, 1978.

Kernan, Thomas. *France on Berlin Time*. New York: Lippincott, 1941.

Keyser, Erich. *Deutsches Staedtebuch, Handbuch Staedtische Geschichte*. Vol. 4. Stuttgart" Kohlhammer, 1959.

Klem, Ekkehard. *Die Roemer in Friesenheim*. Heft 3. Friesenheim: Gemeinde of Friesenheim, 1986.

Kohler, Oskar. *Aus Vergangenen Tagen*. Karlsruhe: Samuel Degen, 1987.

Koshar, Rudy. "Contentious Citadel." In *The Formation of the Nazi Constituency, 1919-1933*. Towata, N.J.: Barnes and Noble, 1986.

Koshar, Rudy. *Social Life, Local Politics, and Nazism: Marburg, 1880-1935*. Chapel Hill, Univ. North Carolina Press, 1986.

Koslow, Jules. *The Despised and the Damned: The Russian Peasant Through the Ages*. New York: Macmillan, 1972.

Kraemer, Erich. "130 Jahre Zigarrenfabriken im Kreis Lahr," *Geroldseckerland* 15 (1973): 185-90.

*Lahrer Anzeiger*. 1927-1936.

*Lahrer Zeitung*. 1927-1936.

Laqueur, Walter. *Germany Today: A Personal Report*. Boston: Little, Brown, 1985.

———. *Russia and Germany: A Century of Conflict*. Boston: Little, Brown, 1965.

———. *The Terrible Secret: Suppression of the Truth about Hitler's 'Final Solution.'* Boston: Little, Brown, 1980.

Levine, Herbert. *Hitler's Free City*. Chicago: Univ. of Chicago Press, 1973.

Lichtenberger, Henri. *Germany and Its Evolution In Modern Times*. London: Constable, 1913.

———. *The Third Reich*. New York: Greystone, 1937.

Loewenberg, Peter. "A Psychohistorical Approach: The Nazi Generation," In *The Youth Revolution*, ed. Anthony Esler. Lexington, Mass.: Heath, 1974.

Loomis, Charles, "The Spread of German Nazism In Rural Areas, "*American Sociological Review* 11 (Dec. 1946): 724-34.

Lowie, Robert H. *Toward Understanding Germany*. Chicago: Univ. of Chicago Press, 1954.

Lukacs, John. *Historical Consciousness, or the Remembered Past*. New York: Harper and Row, 1968.

Lukacs, John. *The Last European War*. New York: Doubleday, Anchor, 1976.

Maschmann, Melita. *Account Rendered*. New York: Abelard-Schuman, 1965.

Mayer, Arno J. *The Persistence of the Old Regime.* New York: Pantheon, 1981.

Mayer, Milton. *They Thought They Were Free.* Chicago: Univ. Press, 1955.

Mendras, Henri, and Ioan Mihailescu, eds. *Theories and Methods in Rural Community Studies.* New York: Pergamon, 1982.

Mendras, Henri. *The Vanishing Peasant: Innovation and Change in French Agriculture.* Cambridge, Mass.: MIT Press, 1970.

Merkl, Peter H. "Introduction." In *German National Socialism, 1919-1945,* ed. Martin Broszat. Santa Barbara, Calif.: Clio, 1966.

Merkl, Peter. *The Making of a Stormtrooper.* Princeton, N.J.: Princeton Univ. Press, 1980.

Meyer, Henry Cord. *Five Images of Germany.* 2d ed. Baltimore: Waverly, 1960.

Meyerhoff, Hermann. *Herne 1933-45: Die Zeit des Nationalsozialismus.* Herne: C. Kartenberg, 1963.

Moeller, Robert C. *German Peasants and Agrarian Politics, 1914-1924: The Rhineland and Westphalia.* Chapel Hill: North Carolina Univ. Press, 1986.

Moeller, Robert C. ed. *Peasants and Lords in Modern Germany.* Boston: Allen and Unwin, 1986.

Morel, Alain. "Power and Ideology in Picardy." In *Rural Society in France,* ed. Robert Forster and Orest Ranum. Baltimore: Johns Hopkins, 1977.

Mosse, George L. *Nazi Culture.* New York: Grosset and Dunlap, 1966.

Mueller, Josef. *Ein Deutsches Bauerndorf im Umbruch der Zeit: Sulzthal in Mainfranken.* Wuerzburg: Verlag d. Universitaetsdruckerei H. Stuertz, 1939.

Muhlberger, Detlef. "Central Control vs. Regional Autonomy: A Case Study of Nazi Propaganda in Westphalia, 1925-1932." In *The Formation of the Nazi Constituency, 1919-1933.* Towata, N.J.: Barnes and Noble, 1986.

Munholland, J. Kim. *The Origins of Contemporary Europe, 1890-1914.* New York: Harcourt, Brace and World, 1970.

Neumann, Franz. *Behemoth: The Structure and Practice of National Socialism.* New York: Oxford Univ. Press, 1942.

Neven-du Mont, Jurgen. *After Hitler: A Report on Today's West Germans.* New York: Pantheon, 1970.

Noakes, Jeremy. *The Nazi Party in Lower Saxony, 1921-1933.* London: Oxford Univ. Press, 1971.

Noakes, Jeremy, and Geoffrey Pridham, eds. *Documents on Nazism, 1919-1945.* New York: Viking, 1975.

Noakes, Jeremy, and Geoffrey Pridham, eds. *Nazism, 1919-1945.* Vol. 2, *State, Economy, and Society, 1933-1939.* Exeter: Univ. of Exeter Press, 1984.

Norling, Bernard. *Timeless Problems In History.* Notre Dame, Ind.: University Press, 1970.

NSDAP Reichsorganizationsleiter. *Partei Statistik.* Vol. 1., 1935.

Nurge, Ethel. *Blue Light In the Village: Daily Life In a German Village in 1965-1966.* Ann Arbor, Mich.: University Microfilms, 1977.

O'Lessker, Karl. "Who Voted for Hitler in 1930 and 1932?" *American Journal of Sociology* 74 (July 1968): 63-69.

Ortega y Gasset, Jose. *The Revolt of the Masses.* New York: Norton, 1957.

Osmond, Jonathan. "Second Agrarian Mobilization?"." In *Peasants and Lords in Modern Germany*, ed. Robert C. Moeller. Boston: Allen and Unwin, 1986.

Park, Bert Edward. *The Impact of Illness on World Leaders*. Philadelphia: Univ. Pennsylvania Press, 1986.

Paterna, Erich, et al. *Deutschland von 1933 bis 1939*. A volume in *Lehrbuch der Deutschen Geschichte*, ed. J. Streisand. Berlin DDR: Deutscher Verlag, 1969.

Pesez, Jean Marie, and Emmanuel Le Roy Ladurie. "The Deserted Villages of France." In *Rural Society in France*, ed. Robert Forster and Orest Ranum. Baltimore: Johns Hopkins, 1977.

Peters, Emrys L. "Aspects of Rank and Status Among Muslims in a Lebanese Village." In *Mediterranean Countrymen: Essays in the Social Anthropology of the Mediterranean*, ed. Julian A. Pitt-Rivers. Paris: Mouton, 1963.

Peterson, Edward N. *The Limits of Hitler's Power*. Princeton: University Press, 1969.

Phillips, Peter. *The Tragedy of Nazi Germany*. New York: Pegasus, 1970.

Pitt-Rivers, Julian A., ed. *Mediterranean Countrymen: Essays in the Social Anthropology of the Mediterranean*. Paris: Mouton, 1963.

Pitt-Rivers, Julian A. *The People of the Sierra*. 2d ed. Chicago: Univ. of Chicago Press, 1971.

Poinsatte, Charles R. *Fort Wayne During the Canal Era, 1828-1855*. Indianapolis: Indiana Historical Bureau, 1969.

Potter, Jack M., May N. Diaz, and George M. Foster, eds. *Peasant Society: A Reader*. Boston: Little, Brown, 1967.

Redfield, Robert. *The Little Community: Viewpoints for the Study of a Human Whole*. Chicago: Univ. Chicago Press, 1955.

———. *Peasant Society and Culture*. Chicago: Univ. Chicago Press, 1956.

Reher, Werner. *Social Welfare in Germany*. Berlin: Terramare, 1938.

Richter, Michaela W. "Resource Mobilization and Legal Revolution: National Socialist Tactics in Franconia." In *The Formation of the Nazi Constituency, 1919-1933*. Towata, N.J.: Barnes and Noble, 1986.

Roth, Kaethe. *Die Stadt Lahr*. In *Forschungen zur Deutschen Landeskunde*. Bad Godesberg, 1961.

Sabean, David. "Aspects of Kinship Behavior." In *Family and Inheritance: Rural Society in Western Europe, 1200-1800*, ed. Jack Goody, Joan Thirsk, and E.P. Thompson. New York: Cambridge Univ. Press, 1976.

Sabean, David. *Power in the Blood*. New York: Cambridge Univ. Press, 1984.

Sagarra, Eda. *A Social History of Germany, 1648-1914*. New York: Holmes and Meier, 1977.

Salzmann, Zdenek, and Vladimir Scheufler. *Komarov: A Czech Farming Village*. New York: Holt, Rhinehart and Winston, 1974.

Sante, Georg, et al. *Die Deutschen Laender vom Wiener Kongress bis zur Gegenwart*. Vol. 2 of *Geschichte der Deutschen Laender*. Wuerzburg: Ploetz Verlag, 1971.

Schoenbaum, David. *Hitler's Social Revolution*. Garden City, N.Y.: Anchor, 1967.

Sheehan, James J. "Conflict and Cohesion Among German Elites in the Nineteenth Century." In *Modern European Social History*, ed. Robert Bezucha. Lexington, Mass.: Heath, 1972.

Sheppard, Thomas F. *Lourmarin in the Eighteenth Century: A Study of a French Village.* Baltimore: Johns Hopkins Univ. Press, 1971.

Shirer, William L. *The Rise and Fall of the Third Reich.* New York: Simon and Schuster, 1960.

Silver, Judith Ann. *French Rural Response to Modernization: The Vendomois, 1852-1885.* Ann Arbor, Mich.: University Microfilms, 1984.

Smith, Hedrick. *The Russians.* New York: Ballantine, 1976.

Solzhenitsyn, Alexander. *August 1914.* New York: Farrar, Straus and Giroux, 1972.

Sontag, Raymond. *A Broken World, 1919-1939.* New York: Harper Torchbook, 1971.

Spindler, George, and Student Collaboraters. *Burgbach: Urbanization and Identity in a German Village.* New York: Holt, Rhinehart and Winston, 1973.

*Staatsanzeiger.* Karlsruhe. 1929-1936.

Stern, Fritz. *The Failure of Illiberalism.* New York: Knopf, 1972.

Stolper, Gustav. *The German Economy: 1870 to the Present.* New York: Harcourt, Brace and World, 1967.

Strauss, Gerald, ed. *Pre-Reformation Germany.* London: Macmillan, 1972.

Stude, Juergen. *Die Juedischen Gemeinde Friesenheim.* Friesenheim: Gemeinde Friesenheim, Heft, 1988.

Taylor, A.J.P. *The Course of German History.* New York: Coward-McCann, 1946.

———. *From Napoleon to Lenin.* New York: Harper Torchbook, 1966.

———. *The Origins of the Second World War.* New York: Athaneum, 1962.

*TIME,* December 7, 1959.

Toland, John. *The Last 100 Days.* New York: Random, 1966.

Trivanovich, Vaso. *Economic Development of Germany Under National Socialism.* New York: National Industrial Conference Board, 1937.

Turner, Henry A., ed. *Nazism and the Third Reich.* New York: Quadrangle, 1972.

———, ed. *Reappraisals of Fascism.* New York: Watts, 1975.

Vansittart, Robert. *Lessons of My Life.* New York: Knopf, 1943.

Vogt, Hanna. *The Burden of Guilt.* New York: Oxford Univ. Press, 1964.

Wagner, Kurt, and Gerhard Wilke. "Dorfleben Im Dritten Reich: Koerle in Hessen." In *Die Reihen Fast Geschlossen,* ed. Detlev Peukert. Wuppertal: Hammer Verlag, 1981.

Walker, Mack. *German Home Towns: Community, State and General Estate, 1648-1874.* Ithaca: Cornell Univ. Press, 1971.

Warriner, Doreen. *Economics of Peasant Farming.* London: Frank Cass, 1964.

Weber, Eugen. *Peasants Into Frenchmen: The Modernization of Rural France, 1870-1914.* Stanford: Stanford Univ. Press, 1976.

Wedgwood, C. V. *The Thirty Years War.* Garden City, N.Y.: Doubleday Anchor, 1961.

Weiss, John. *The Fascist Tradition.* New York: Harper and Row, 1967.

Wheaton, Eliot. *Prelude to Calamity: The Nazi Revolution, 1933-1935.* New York: Doubleday, 1968.

Wilke, Gerhard. "Village Life in Nazi Germany." In *Life in the Third Reich,* ed. Richard Bessel. New York: Oxford Press, 1987.

Wilkie, Gerhard. "Sins of the Fathers." In *The German Peasantry,* ed. Richard J. Evans and W.R. Lee. New York: St. Martin's, 1986.

Wilkie, Gerhard, and Kurt Wagner. "Family and Household: Social Structures in a German Village Between the Two World Wars." In *The German Family*, ed. Richard J. Evans and W.R. Lee. Towata, N.J.: Barnes and Noble, 1981.

Willertz, John R. *National Socialism In a German City and County: Marburg 1933 to 1945*. Ann Arbor, Mich.: University Microfilms, 1970.

Willis, Frank R. *The French Zone of Occupation in Germany, 1946-1949*. Ann Arbor, Mich.: University Microfilms, 1987.

Wimschneider, Anna. *Herbstmilch*. Munich: Piper Verlag, 1987.

Wolf, Eric. "Closed Corporate Peasant Communities in Mesoamerica and Central Java." In *Peasant Society: A Reader*, ed. Jack M. Potter, May N. Diaz, and George M. Foster. Boston: Little Brown, 1967.

Wolf, Eric. *Peasants*. Edgewood Cliffs, N.J.: Prentice-Hall, 1966.

Wright, Gordon, and Arthur Mehia, eds. *An Age of Controversy*. New York: Dodd, Mead, 1971.

Wunderlich, Frieda. *Farm Labor In Germany 1810-1945*. Princeton: Princeton Univ. Press, 1961.

Wylie, Laurence. *Village in the Vaucluse*. Cambridge: Harvard Univ. Press, 1957.

Zahn, Gordon. *German Catholics and Hitler's Wars*. New York: Sheed and Ward, 1962.

Zier, H.. "Die Wirtschaftgeschichte der Ortenau im 19 und 20 Jahrhundert." *Die Ortenau* 40 (1960): 252-320.

Zofka, Zdenek. "Between Bauernbund and National Socialism." In *The Formation of the Nazi Constituency, 1919-1933*. Towata, N.J.: Barnes and Noble, 1986.

Zweig, Stefan. *The World of Yesterday*. Lincoln, Neb.: Univ. Nebraska Press, 1943.

Adenauer, Konrad, 185, 214
Adorno, Theodor, 5
African troops, 117-78
Albiker, Walter, 123-24, 131-32, 155, 157, 159-60, 163
alcohol, use of, 35, 40, 47, 51, 161
Allen, William S., 4, 157
Alsace, 15-16, 66-67, 97
*Annals of Kloster Schuttern*, 18
Anschluss, 117
*Anzeiger.* See *Lahrer Anzeiger*
Arbeitsbuch, 148
Arbeitsdienst, 140, 155
Autobahn, building of, 141, 214
automobile, advent and influence of, 207-209

Baden-Wuerttemberg, new state of, 193, 203
*Badische Zeitung*, 218
Beiser (mayor), 46
Berlin Blockade, 191
birth rate, 83, 162-63, 191, 219-20
Bismarck, Otto von, 44, 102, 133, 137, 193, 223
Black Death, 9
Black Market: during World War I, 63-66; in 1930s, 145; during World War II, 172, 183, 191
Bormann, Martin, 117
Bracher, Karl, 125
Broszat, Martin, 125
Brown Sisters, 41, 168
Bruening, Heinrich, 77, 82, 90, 104, 133
building boom in Oberschopfheim, 201-202
Burgbach, 222
Burkhards, 198, 209, 212, 216
Butz, Karl, 100

Canadian air force in Oberschopfheim, 192, 220
CARE packages, 182-83, 188
Caritas (Catholic relief organization), 151
Catholic: Church and religion, 2, 15, 19-22, 27, 50, 52, 58, 95, 108, 113, 179, 197; erosion of, 217-22; opposition to Nazis, 90-91, 99, 103-105, 110-11, 116-24, 132, 136-37, 144-45, 160, 163, 168-69; opposition wanes, 109-15
Center party, 50, 53, 79, 85, 90-91, 102-103, 107-109, 116, 194
Chamberlain, Houston Stewart, 135
Charles V, 10
children, 30-31, 61, 209
Christian Democrats, 211-12
cigarmaking. *See* tobacco
citizenship, village, 49-50, 196
cleanliness: increase in after 1950, 205-206
comfort: increase in after 1950, 205-206
communists and communism, 66, 72, 88, 90, 92-93, 96, 98, 102, 108, 155, 157
concordat, 106, 108, 116
conservation, 212
consolidation of lands, 143-44, 197, 200
courtship customs, 31
cows, raising and use of, 27, 29-30, 37, 45, 61, 169-70, 196, 198, 200

Darré, Walter, 88, 128, 142
De Gaulle, Charles, 185, 214
denazification, 183-85, 191
depression: of 1930s, 2, 70-84, 103, 106, 115, 139-40, 147, 150, 153, 190, 212-14; agricultural, 72, 74-75, 95
Deutschmark, introduction of, 191, 203, 215, 220

dialect, 51-52
Diersburg, 167, 194
*Drang nach Osten*, 174

"economic miracle," 2, 191, 200-205
education in Oberschopfheim, 21,
    52-53, 69, 84-85, 117, 159-61, 166-67,
    178, 184, 195, 208-11
Einsele, Wilhelm, 46, 84, 109-10, 118,
    186
emigration: of 1840s, 14-15, 82; of 1920s,
    69
Enabling Act, 116
Erbhof, 128, 144-45
Eritreans, 227
Ettenheim, 10, 218

Feldhueter, 83, 195
floods, 13, 16, 140, 175
France, Oberschopfheimers' dislike of,
    66-68, 184-87, 214
Franco-Prussian War, 51, 58
Frederick the Great, 137
Free Fire Fighters Club, 50
Freiburg, 3, 10, 17, 50, 98, 177, 179,
    215, 218; bishop of, 98, 103, 130
Freikorps, 91, 93
French occupation army, 12-13, 65,
    67-68, 71, 95, 97, 108, 177-87, 191
French Revolutionary and Napoleonic
    wars, 12-13
Friesenheim, 2, 9, 11, 15, 56, 194-95,
    217
fruit, cultivation and consumption of, 7,
    37, 44, 60, 73, 81, 199

Galen, Cardinal von, 117, 119
Gasthaeuser, 12, 21, 39, 51, 53-54, 81,
    86, 141, 146, 186, 207, 220
Gemeinde, 20-21, 24, 44, 49, 72, 77-85,
    124, 146-53, 156-57, 164, 179, 186,
    198, 214-17; post-World War II decline
    of, 193-95
Gemeinderat, 46, 48, 77, 81, 85, 110,
    194-95
German Girls' League, 113, 124, 159
Gestapo, 117, 121, 129, 135
ghosts, 1, 20, 122
Gissler, Rudolf, 183, 190
Goebbels, Josef, 115, 151
Goerdeler, Karl, 128
Goering, Hermann, 126

grapes, cultivation of, 7, 35, 44, 73-74,
    143-44, 199
Greens political party, 211-12
Groeber (bishop of Freiburg), 103, 118,
    120, 122, 136
*Gruesselhorn*, 98, 103, 109
"guest workers," 192
gypsies, 6, 56-57, 83, 115-16, 122, 158

Hamilton, Richard, 94, 99-120
harvests, bad, 10-11, 82
Heiligenzell, 11, 194-95
Heydrich, Reinhard, 117
Himmler, Heinrich, 126
Hindenburg, Paul van, 104, 115, 127
Hirt, Hermann, 96, 115-16, 118-24,
    130-32, 136, 156, 169, 176, 178
Hitler, Adolf: beliefs of, 125-26;
    building Nazi party, 88; character of,
    106, 115-16; political tactics of, 106,
    109, 117, 125-27, 147-48, 153;
    popularity of, 132-33, 137, 214; talents
    of, 94, 139
Hitler Youth, 112-13, 121-22, 124, 131,
    135, 157, 159-61, 171
Hofweier, 194
Holzenthaler, Adolf, 122-24, 130-32,
    175, 185-86
Horst Wessel Song, 159
Hugenberg (nationalist leader), 91, 101

illnesses, 40, 65, 106
industriousness of Oberschopheimers,
    28-29, 34
inflation of 1923, 14-15, 66-67, 71, 79,
    82, 95, 182, 190-91
inheritance customs, 32-34, 48
Isele, Pfarrer, 21, 99, 117-19

Jaeger, Stefan, 120
Jews, 63, 94, 103, 116, 155, 163, 165;
    Nazi hostility toward, 103, 125, 127,
    134-36; numbers of, 18, 56-57, 135;
    occupations and reputation of, 56, 88,
    91, 135; persecution of denounced,
    98, 121; postwar attitude of
    Oberschopfheimers toward, 213, 227
Johnson, Jack, 136
*Junge Fronte*, 120
Junkers, 4, 128, 154

Kaas (Center political leader), 90
Karlsruhe, 3, 56, 121, 141, 174

Kern, Eugen, 113
Kiebingen, 49
Kohler (Baden minister president), 140
Kohler, Franz, 84
*Konradsblatt*, 130
Korle, 159
Kuerzell, 2, 12, 15, 177-78
Kulturbampf, 52, 120, 135

*Lahrer Anzeiger,* 3, 53, 76, 80, 82, 96, 98,
    104-106, 109, 115, 130, 136, 139, 151,
    218
*Lahrer Zeitung,* 3, 53, 109, 115, 135, 139,
    151, 168, 218
Laimering, 110
Landesvolk, 120, 170
Landhilfe program, 142
Lebfromm, Franz, 113
Leutkirche, 19, 83, 175
Lutherans, 18, 53, 102, 115-17, 168, 181,
    212, 214, 216. *See also* Protestants

Magyars, 9
Mannheim, 56
Marburg, 95, 108, 110, 147, 158, 166
Marie Antoinette, 17-18
marriage customs, 31, 34, 42, 50, 218,
    223
Marshall Plan, 191
Marxists, 5, 9, 24, 27, 96, 100, 125-26,
    138. *See also* communists
medicine, 30, 35, 40-41, 171, 206-207,
    222-23
*Mein Kampf,* 97
Merkert, Karl, 113, 119-21, 131, 155
Merveldt, General, 12
Messerer, Bernhard, 14
Messerer, Herr, 157
migratory workers, 69
military club, 50-51
Mommsen, Hans, 125
Montecuccoli, 11
"Mother and Child" program, 163
Mothers' club, 21
Mueller, Angreas, 110, 150, 155
Mussler, Wilhelm, 121

NATO, 213, 225
NSLB (Nazi teachers' organization), 160
NSV (National Socialist
    Volkswohlfahrt), 151-52
Napoleon, 12-13, 23, 58, 117, 214
Nazi nurses. *See* Brown Sisters

Nazis: appeal to youth, 93, 97, 99, 113;
    attempt to assassinate Hermann Hirt,
    123-24; biological engineering, 116;
    economic program of, 138-53; energy
    and vigor, 97, 101; era, 2, 5, 106-89,
    212-13; general program of, 96-97,
    103, 127; local organization, 107-15,
    117-24, 130-32, 136, 154-55; political
    tactics, 91-93, 98, 102-103, 106,
    108-10; popularity of, 133-34; program
    for peasants, 142-45; program for
    women, 162-64; propaganda, 129, 159;
    social leveling, alleged, 154-55; radio,
    use of, 86, 98, 114; rise of, 70, 75, 77,
    86, 88-105; social program, 154-64;
    sources of support, 99-103, 110-13;
    ultimate failure of, 173-74, 176; voting
    strength, 94-96, 98-99, 114-16;
    wartime regulations, 169-71
Nazi farm system. *See* Erbhof
Niederschopfheim, 16, 194
Northeim. *See* Thalburg
Nuremberg, 160
Nurge, Ethel, 198, 209, 212

Oberweier, 11, 39, 168, 176-77, 194-95,
    217
Offenburg, 10, 16, 65-66, 186, 194, 203;
    fair, 222
Oldenburg, Karl, 142
Ortenau, Gau, 7, 30, 108; new county
    of, 193-94, 202, 206, 211-12
Ottenheim, 2, 200

peasants: animosity of, toward cities and
    outsiders, 21, 26, 44, 54-57, 62-64,
    66-67, 75, 78, 83, 150-51, 157; decline
    in numbers of, 196-200, 203-204;
    Enlightenment conception of, 5, 24;
    general characterization of, 4-6, 24-30,
    54-57; industriousness of, 28-30;
    liberal conception of, 4-6; Marxist
    conception of, 5-6, 24, 27; nationalist
    conception of, 6; Nazi conception of,
    5. *See also* Landesvolk
Peasants Revolt, 9
people's community. *See*
    Beolksgemeinschaft
Pfaff, George, 12
pigs, raising and consumption of, 38, 62,
    170-72, 176, 200
Poltarabend, 51, 221
potatoes, 10, 13, 37, 62, 176

primogeniture. *See* inheritance
prisoners of war: in World War I, 60-61; in World War II, 166, 171, 173, 178-80
Protestants, 2, 18-19, 58, 94, 99, 104, 152; relations with Nazis, 91, 102, 107, 117
Putsch of 1923, 92, 122, 161

radio, introduction of, 86-87, 208; Nazi use of, 98, 129, 158
Ranke, Leoppold von, 136
Redfield, Robert, 220
Reformation, 19
refugees, 166, 180-81, 192-93, 226-27
Reichsmark, 179, 182, 215
Reichstag, elections to, 99, 104, 106, 114
reunification of Germany, 213
revolution of 1848, 15
Rhineland, remilitarization of, 141
Ried (marshland), 16, 19, 44
Rinderle, August, 36, 60
Rinderle, Herman Joseph, 2, 69
Rinderle, Walter, 2
Roederer family, 48, 50
Roederer, Franz, 48, 50, 110, 113, 119, 122
Roederer, Franz K. II, 113, 131, 143, 145, 155
Roehm, purge of, 108
Roosevelt, Franklin, 133
Roosevelt, Theodore, 136
Rosenberg, Alfred, 115, 117, 119, 127

sanitation, improvements in, 40, 205-206
Schacht, Hjalmer, 128, 148
Schleicher, Pfarrer, 168
Schleswig-Holstein, 94-95
schools. *See* education
Schuttern, 2, 157, 168, 194-95; monastery of, 9-11, 17
Schwab, Berthold, 196, 217, 219
Schwendemann, Josef, 120
Sering, Max, 142
sexual mores in Oberschopfheim, 21-22, 215, 218
Social Democrats political party (SPD), 79, 85, 90-92, 96-97, 103, 106, 114, 138, 194, 210-12
socialists, German, 56-69, 63-66, 79, 85, 88, 90-93, 96-98, 103
Speer, Albert, 125
Spindler, George, 222
squabbles among villagers, 10, 27, 46-47, 53-54, 77, 81, 84, 86, 95, 110, 131, 156, 172, 187-88, 198, 208

Strasbourg, 7, 10, 15, 66; bombardment of, 175
Streicher, Julius, 117
style consciousness, advent of, 208

television, advent and impact of, 205, 207-12, 221
Thalburg, 4, 81, 84, 95, 98, 104-105, 108-11, 113, 117, 133, 135, 140, 145, 147, 157, 159-60
Thirty Years War, 10, 23
tobacco: cultivation of, 28-29, 35-36, 41, 44, 60, 67-68, 73, 76-79, 167, 198; factories, 28, 36, 41, 68-69, 77, 148-49, 167-68, 179, 203; use of, 35
tractors, 25-26, 297-98
Trajan (emperor), 9

unemployment in Oberschopfheim, 76-83

Versailles, Treaty of, 65, 72, 93
Volksgemeinschaft, 112, 155-56

Wagner, Adolf, 142
Wagner, Robert, 108
Warmsried, 110
weavers, 38-39, 49
Wehrmacht, 174
Weimar Republic, 65-66, 74, 83, 89, 91, 94, 96, 103, 106, 115-16, 125, 131, 142, 145, 157-61, 211, 226
Wenz, Lehrer, 113
West German Republic, 183, 191-93, 211, 225
West Wall: building of, 141; destruction of, 184
Wilhelm II (kaiser), 65, 160, 169
William of Organe, 9
wine, 36-37, 76, 143, 199
Winterhilfswerk (Winter Help), 151-52, 159
witches, 10, 123
World War I, 20, 51, 71, 79, 135, 165-66, 169, 171, 178, 227; hardships after, 177-89
World War II, 2, 13, 59, 61, 65, 71, 126, 132, 139, 164-76, 210-13; bombing during, 174-77, 182; hardships after, 14, 123, 168
Wuerttemberg, 65-66, 68-70

Young Men's Club, 21, 54, 85, 121-22, 216